J. Christopher Edwards

The Ransom Logion in Mark and Matthew

Its Reception and Its Significance for the Study of the Gospels

Mohr Siebeck

J. CHRISTOPHER EDWARDS, born 1982; 2011 PhD, University of St Andrews; since 2012 Lecturer in Religious Studies at St Francis College (Brooklyn Heights, NY).

ISBN 978-3-16-151780-8
ISSN 0340-9570 (Wissenschaftliche Untersuchungen zum Neuen Testament, 2. Reihe)

Die Deutsche Nationalbibliothek lists this publication in the Deutsche Nationalbibliographie; detailed bibliographic data are available on the Internet at *http://dnb.dnb.de*

© 2012 by Mohr Siebeck, Tübingen, Germany.

The book was printed by Laupp & Göbel in Nehren on non-aging paper and bound by Buchbinderei Nädele in Nehren.

Printed in Germany.

Preface

This monograph is a revised version of my doctoral thesis, which was submitted to the Faculty of Divinity at the University of St. Andrews in August 2011. I am supremely indebted to my supervisor, Dr. Grant MacAskill, without whose criticism and encouragement this thesis would not have been completed. I would like to thank my examiners, Dr. Kelly Iverson and Dr. John Dennis, for their many helpful suggestions that have improved the thesis considerably. I would also like to thank Prof. Dr. Jörg Frey, for accepting the thesis for publication, and to Dr. Henning Ziebritzki and his staff, especially Dominika Zgolik, for their assistance in formatting the manuscript for publication. Finally, I would like to thank Gloria Gianoulis for proofreading a draft of the manuscript. Of course, all remaining errors are my own.

This project has witnessed the strengthening of many old friendships as well as the creation of new ones. I am particularly grateful to Charles Huff, who has been my closest friend and confidant since undergraduate school. I am also thankful for the friendship of Justus and Ellen Hunter, Ryan Smith, and Jeff Webster. At St. Andrews, I developed close ties with many people, but especially dear to me are Shawn Bawulski, Sean Cook, Jeremy Gabrielson, Drew Lewis, Robert Joseph Matava, and Stephen Presley. I am deeply indebted to Dr. Jon Laansma, who introduced me to the critical study of the New Testament. I would like to thank Professor Darrell Bock, who helped me get started in the study of the canonical gospels. I am grateful to Professor Markus Bockmuehl for first suggesting that I investigate the reception of the ransom logion. Finally, I would like to thank Professor Jonathan Sassi, as well as my new colleagues at St. Francis College, especially Professors Sophie Berman, Priscilla Pedersen, and Alan Udoff.

I am most thankful to my family, who supported me unconditionally during the inevitable ups and downs of a doctoral thesis. First and foremost, I would like to thank my wife, Lucia, whose encouragement and companionship are the most valuable consistencies in my life. Our two sons, Vincent and Michael, made our time in Scotland a joy. I would also like to thank my parents, Darrell and Michelle Edwards, as well as my wife's parents, Anthony and Lucia Luciano.

New York, 1 June 2012   J. Christopher Edwards

Table of Contents

Chapter 1

Introduction and Methodology

1.1 Introduction

C. Evans states about Mark 10.45: "This is by far the most remarkable and probably most disputed saying in Mark."[1] It is certainly true that a lot of attention has been paid to Mark 10.45/Matthew 20.28.[2] This is not surprising since only here, and in the Last Supper, does Jesus give an interpretation of his pending death. However, no study to date has examined the early reception of the tradition that most famously manifests itself in Mark 10.45/Matthew 20.28. Throughout the study, I refer to this tradition, which is always comparable to Mark 10.45/Matthew 20.28, as the *ransom logion*.[3] Because no one has examined the early reception of the ransom logion, it follows that no one has explored the significance of that reception for the critical study of Mark 10.45/Matthew 20.28. The primary purposes of this study are to fill these lacunae in the literature. First, this study examines the reception of the ransom logion in the New Testament and in the following Early Christian periods through the third century. Second, this study explores the significance of the reception of the ransom logion for the critical study of Mark 10.45/Matthew 20.28.

Chapters Two through Four are devoted to examining the reception of the ransom logion from the New Testament through the third century. The methodology for this examination is given below in 1.3. Chapter Two surveys the reception of the ransom logion in the New Testament. Chapter Three surveys the reception of the ransom logion from the New Testament through 200 CE. Chapter Four surveys the reception of the ransom logion from 200 through 300 CE. Admittedly, the divisions of the survey are somewhat arbitrary. I chose these particular divisions because they divide the surveyed receptions into three manageable sections. I chose to stop the survey with Eusebius because his position as an historian and his interaction with earlier traditions

---

[1] C. Evans, *Mark 8:27–16:20* (WBC 34B; Nashville: Thomas Nelson Publishers, 2001), 119.

[2] Most of this attention concerns issues of background and authenticity.

[3] I chose the label *ransom logion* only because it is the common term for the tradition in Mark 10.45/Matthew 20.28. For a discussion of terminology, see 1.3.1 below.

make his work an appropriate capstone.[4] It is important to note that the examination in Chapters Two through Four can stand by itself and has value in its own right as part of historical theology.

Chapter Five is devoted to exploring the significance of the reception of the ransom logion for three issues in the study of Mark 10.45/Matthew 20.28. Section 5.3 explores the significance of the reception of the ransom logion for critical discussions regarding the development of the ransom logion in a Eucharistic setting, and the supposed connections between Mark 10.45/Matthew 20.28 and Mark 14.24/Matthew 26.28. Section 5.4 explores the significance of the reception of the ransom logion for critical discussions regarding a preexistent coming in Mark 10.45/Matthew 20.28. Section 5.5 explores the significance of the reception of the ransom logion for critical discussions regarding the scriptural background of Mark 10.45/Matthew 20.28. Much of the rationale for Chapter Five relies on the fact that there are observable patterns in the reception of the ransom logion from the New Testament through the third century. These patterns potentially reflect what is happening in Mark 10.45/Matthew 20.28. Or, Mark 10.45/Matthew 20.28, as receptions of the ransom logion, may themselves be participating in the patterns.

1.2 Three Issues in the Study of Mark 10.45/Matthew 20.28

The purpose of this section is to briefly introduce three issues in the study of Mark 10.45/Matthew 20.28 for which the reception of the ransom logion may be significant. The three issues are development in a Eucharistic setting (1.2.1), preexistent coming (1.2.2), and scriptural background (1.2.3).[5] The

---

[4] The survey in Chapter Four overflows into the fourth century because I include Eusebius, whose life is divided between the third and fourth centuries, but whose writings mostly come from the early fourth century.

[5] The major issue that this section does not discuss is authenticity – a topic for which the reception of the ransom logion is not relevant. For discussions about authenticity, see for example, A. Lee, *From Messiah to Preexistent Son: Jesus' Self-Consciousness and Early Christian Exegesis of Messianic Psalms* (WUNT 2/192; Tübingen: Mohr Siebeck, 2005), 189–93; S. McKnight, *Jesus and His Death* (Waco: Baylor University Press, 2005), 159–239; S. Page, "The Authenticity of the Ransom Logion (Mark 10:45b)," in *Gospel Perspectives: Studies of History and Tradition in the Four Gospels* (vol. 1; ed. R. France and D. Wenham; Sheffield: JSOT Press, 1980), 137–61; M. Wilcox, "On the Ransom-Saying in Mark 10:45c, Matt 20:28c," in *Geschichte–Tradition–Reflexion: Festschrift für Martin Hengel zum 70. Geburtstag*, vol 3: *Frühes Christentum* (ed. H. Cancik, H. Lichtenberger, and P. Schäfer; Tübingen: Mohr Siebeck, 1996), 173–86. My own opinion about the authenticity of the logion is very uncertain. Given the fate of the Baptist, I think that Jesus could have anticipated his own demise. Jesus is remembered as informing his disciples that they may die for his message, which presumably he thought he would die for (Mark 8.34–35). It would not be a huge step

purpose of Chapter Five is to explore the potential significance of the reception of the ransom logion for these three issues. The rationale for this exploration is discussed below in 1.5. Both the three issues and the rationale for the exploration in Chapter Five are introduced in Chapter One so that relevant phenomena can be noted throughout the survey of the ransom logion in Chapters Two through Four.

1.2.1 The (Dis)Association of the Ransom Logion with the Eucharist

It is common to assume that the ransom logion developed in a Eucharistic setting. For example, J. Roloff says about Mark 10.45 that the very firm and very early connection between the atoning death motif and the servant motif found its expression within the meal celebration.[6] Also, in his grand commentary on Mark, Pesch states: "it is unavoidable to accept the fact that the Eucharistic tradition and the Eucharistic service have impacted the formation of Mark 10.45."[7] These brief quotes from Roloff and Pesch demonstrate the assumption that there is a deep connection between the ransom logion and the Eucharist, and that the ransom logion probably developed in a Eucharistic setting.[8]

The assumption that the ransom logion developed in a Eucharistic setting is supported by the supposed connection between Mark 10.45/Matthew 20.28 and Mark 14.24/Matthew 26.28.[9] There are three factors that uphold this connection. First, both Mark 10.45/Matthew 20.28 and Mark 14.24/Matthew 26.28 share the concept of Jesus' beneficial death.[10] Second, Mark 10.45/

---

further to conjecture that Jesus conceived of his pending death as having some sort of larger meaning, but taking that step with any real certainty is, in my opinion, impossible.

[6] "Vieles spricht nämlich dafür, daß die hier vorliegende Verbindung des Sühntodmotivs mit dem Motiv des διακονεῖν Jesu sehr fest und alt ist, und daß in ihr ein sehr früh im Rahmen der Mahlfeier entwickeltes Verständnis des Todes Jesu seinen Niederschlag gefunden hat" (J. Roloff, "Anfänge der soteriologischen Deutung des Todes Jesu (Mk. X. 45 und Lk. XXII. 27)," *NTS* 19 [1972–73]: 50).

[7] "Daß Abendmahlstradition und Abendmahlsfeier auf die Bildung von V45 eingewirkt haben, ist hingegen eine unumgängliche Annahme" (R. Pesch, *Das Markusevangelium II. Teil: Kommentar zu Kap. 8,27–16,20* [HTKNT; Freiburg: Herder, 1977], 163).

[8] Also see M. Hengel, who states: "It was…the interpretative sayings of Jesus at the Last Supper which showed them [the disciples] how to understand his death properly…Mark 10.45 probably also belongs in the context of that last night; it will have been used by him to elucidate his mysterious symbolic action" (*The Atonement: The Origins of the Doctrine in the New Testament* [trans. J. Bowden; Philadelphia: Fortress Press, 1981], 73). Hengel's perspective is different than that of Roloff and Pesch in that he does not endorse the form-critical notion that Mark 10.45 developed in a Eucharistic *Sitz im Leben*, but that Mark 10.45 comes from Jesus at the Last Supper.

[9] Mark 14.24 and Matthew 26.28 are parts of the text on which the church's liturgical practice, known as "the Eucharist," is based.

[10] Mark 10.45/Matthew 20.28 and Mark 14.24/Matthew 26.28 (along with the Lucan parallel) are the only places in the synoptic gospels where Jesus gives a beneficial interpretation of his death.

Matthew 20.28 and Mark 14.24/Matthew 26.28 share the concept and vocabulary that Jesus' death is "for many" (preposition plus πολλῶν). Third, Mark 10.45/Matthew 20.28 and Mark 14.24/Matthew 26.28 supposedly share the same scriptural background of Isaiah 53.

The supposed connections between Mark 10.45/Matthew 20.28 and Mark 14.24/Matthew 26.28, which support the assumption that the ransom logion developed in a Eucharistic setting, have been questioned by Stuhlmacher, who states the following:

What is the source of this tradition [Mark 10:45]? The critical answer so common today, that it stems from the context of the early Christian theology of the Lord's Supper, stands on a very weak foundation. Neither *lytron*, the word so particularly characteristic of Mark 10:45 (Matt. 20:28), nor the concise formulation *anti pollon* is typical of the New Testament Lord's Supper texts. These speak of the covenantal blood of Jesus, poured out *hyper pollon* (also: *peri pollon*); they avoid the word *lytron* (or *antilytron*). Also missing in the Lord's Supper context are the title Son of Man and the saying about Jesus' "serving" (= *diakonein*). But one should expect a christological formulation alleged to have grown out of the early Christian Lord's Supper tradition to reflect clearly the language of this tradition! The Lord's Supper texts and Mark 10:45 (Matt. 20:28) overlap only in a single word, *pollon*, which in my view points to Isa. 53:10–12. There is really no compelling evidence for deriving Mark 10:45 from the Lord's Supper context; Mark 10:45 (Matt. 20:28) is related to the Lord's Supper tradition only with respect to subject matter.[11]

Stuhlmacher's criticism grants that Mark 10.45/Matthew 20.28 and Mark 14.24/Matthew 26.28 share in the same subject matter of Jesus' beneficial death. He is, however, unimpressed by the overlapping vocabulary of πολλῶν, which only indicates a mutual dependence on Isaiah 53.10–12 and not the dependence of the ransom logion on the Lord's Supper tradition. Stuhlmacher's most cutting criticism is his identification of the key items in Mark 10.45/Matthew 20.28 that are not mentioned in Mark 14.24/Matthew 26.28, such as the Son of Man, service, λύτρον, and the precise wording of ἀντὶ πολλῶν. In sum, Stuhlmacher believes there is no substantial evidence to associate Mark 10.45/Matthew 20.28 with Mark 14.24/Matthew 26.28 – the preposition plus πολλῶv and a shared subject matter are not enough. Given this lack of evidence, it follows that there is also no support for the assumption that the ransom logion developed in a Eucharistic setting.

There is evidence for and against a connection between Mark 10.45/Matthew 20.28 and Mark 14.24/Matthew 26.28. This connection is the primary support for the claim that the ransom logion developed in a Eucharistic setting. The purpose of Chapters Two through Four is to consider the association or disassociation between the ransom logion and the Eucharist from the standpoint of the reception history. The reception history will show whether the ransom logion and the Eucharist, or Last Supper traditions, are associated

---

[11] Stuhlmacher, *Reconciliation, Law, & Righteousness* (trans. E. Kalin; Philadelphia: Fortress, 1986), 18–19.

or disassociated throughout the New Testament and the Early Christian periods. This will enable us to form a better opinion on the supposed development of the ransom logion in a Eucharistic setting and the supposed connections between Mark 10.45/Matthew 20.28 and Mark 14.24/Matthew 26.28.

1.2.2 A Preexistent Coming in Mark 10.45/Matthew 20.28

Simon Gathercole's *The Preexistent Son* is a recent work that explores and defends the synoptic portrayal of Jesus' preexistence.[12] Although the back cover showcases several impressive reviews from leading scholars in the field, the work itself remains controversial. Such controversy is inevitable given that Gathercole's purpose is to overthrow the consensus that there is no preexistent christology in the synoptic gospels.[13] Gathercole's primary argument is that the ten sayings in the synoptic gospels where Jesus states: "I have come," followed by a purpose element, are meant to imply Jesus' coming to earth from his preexistent life with God.[14] According to Gathercole, the best parallel to Jesus' "I have come" sayings can be found in sayings of angelic figures who use a similar formula to describe their mission to earth from their preexistent life in heaven.[15] If Jesus' "I have come" sayings are parallel to the angelic sayings, then the synoptic writers are attempting to communicate Jesus' preexistence. Gathercole argues that this is not surprising given the established and widespread belief in Jesus' preexistence before the synoptic gospels were written,[16] as well as the lofty view of Jesus that is presented in the synoptic gospels themselves.[17]

Of the ten "I have come" sayings discussed by Gathercole, only Mark 10.45/Matthew 20.28 and Luke 19.10 have the Son of Man as the subject.[18] According to Gathercole, Mark 10.45/Matthew 20.28 offers a description of Jesus' ministry that covers the entirety of his first coming. The voluntary nature of that coming indicates a pre-incarnate consciousness, and therefore preexistence. In view of Gathercole's argument, Chapter Five explores the possibility of a preexistent coming in Mark 10.45/Matthew 20.28, not in light of

---

[12] S. Gathercole, *The Preexistent Son: Recovering the Christologies of Matthew, Mark, and Luke* (Grand Rapids: Eerdmans, 2006).

[13] For discussion of this consensus, see *The Preexistent Son*, 2–17. Gathercole's work conflicts with the widely held position that limits the New Testament confession of Jesus' preexistence to the Johannine corpus, or chronologically speaking, to the last decades of the first century.

[14] Ibid., 83–84.

[15] Ibid., 113–47.

[16] Ibid., 23–45.

[17] Ibid., 46–79.

[18] Gathercole excludes the saying in Matthew 11.19/Luke 7.34 because of the missing purpose element. He also excludes the additions to Luke 9.55 as not belonging to Luke's gospel (ibid., 88–91).

parallel angelic sayings, but in light of relevant patterns displayed in the reception of the ransom logion.

1.2.3 The Scriptural Background of Mark 10.45/Matthew 20.28

After authenticity, scriptural background is the most debated issue in the study of Mark 10.45/Matthew 20.28. Generally speaking, Isaiah 53, Daniel 7; 9, and Isaiah 43 are the three texts suggested as the background to Mark 10.45/Matthew 20.28.[19] Isaiah 53 is the traditional background; it has been

---

[19] The atoning deaths of the Maccabean martyrs are also frequently suggested to lie behind Mark 10.45/Matthew 20.28 (2Maccabees 7.37–38; 4Maccabees 6.28–29; 17.22) (E.g. C. Barrett, "The Background of Mark 10:45," in *New Testament Essays: Studies in Memory of T. W. Manson* [ed. A. J. B. Higgins; Manchester: Manchester University Press, 1959], 12). However, with regard to Mark 10.45, Watts asserts that πῶς γέγραπται in Mark 9.12 restricts the background to the canonical scriptures (*Isaiah's New Exodus and Mark* [WUNT 2/88; Tübingen: Mohr Siebeck, 1997], 259–60). Given the scriptural quotations that flow through Matthew, there is no difficulty assuming that Matthew would similarly want to construe Jesus' pending passion as according to the scriptures. Of course, it would be naïve to assert that we know the exact boundaries of the canonical scriptures for Mark's and Matthew's communities (M. Popović, ed., *Authoritative Scriptures in Ancient Judaism*. JSJSup 141. Leiden: Brill, 2010). However, it is instructive that there are no quotations from Maccabees in Mark or Matthew, or in any New Testament text. Besides, there is a strong possibility that the atoning deaths of the Maccabean martyrs are themselves dependent on the scriptures, specifically on Isaiah 53 (J. van Henten, *The Maccabean Martyrs as Saviours of the Jewish People: A Study of 2 and 4 Maccabees* [JSJSup 57; Leiden: Brill, 1997], 160). S. Williams is alone in denying that there is atonement present in 2Maccabees' presentation of the seventh son's request that the wrath of God end "in me" (ἐν ἐμοὶ [2Maccabees 7.38]) (*Jesus' Death as Saving Event: The Background and Origin of a Concept* [HDR 2; Missoula, MT: Scholars Press, 1975], 76–90). There are also potential Greek influences on Mark 10.45/Matthew 20.28 (J. Gibson, "Paul's 'Dying Formula': Prolegomena to an Understanding of Its Import and Significance," in *Celebrating Romans: Template for Pauline Theology* [ed. S. McGinn; Grand Rapids: Eerdmans, 2004], 20–41; Hengel, *The Atonement*, 1–32; H. Versnel, "Making Sense of Jesus' Death: The Pagan Contribution," in *Deutungen des Todes Jesu im Neuen Testament* [ed. J. Frey and J. Schröter; WUNT 181; Tübingen: Mohr Siebeck, 2005], 215–94). Again, however, Mark and Matthew want the reader to understand Jesus' atoning death as a fulfillment of the scriptures, though Greek ideas certainly influence any use of the scriptures to support Jesus' atoning death. Finally, some suggest that there is no direct scriptural background. U. Luz states about Matthew 20.28: "Matthew will hardly have been thinking here of an individual biblical text…Thus the precise meaning of the phrase remains relatively indefinite" (*Matthew 8–20* [Hermeneia; Minneapolis: Fortress Press, 1990], 546). Barrett essentially makes the same point when he states: "The question is not whether there may not be in our verse some distant echo of that passage, but whether the statement about the serving and dying of the Son of Man is directly based upon it" ("The Background of Mark 10:45," 2). This may be a fair point, but only if we assume that Mark and Matthew collected traditions without giving thought to their meaning or scriptural influences.

most recently defended by Rikki Watts.[20] The Isaiah 53 background was first questioned by Hooker[21] and Barrett.[22] Their criticism sparked a second position that takes its cue from the Son of Man and emphasizes Daniel 7; 9 as the background.[23] The third approach, which is supported mainly by German scholars, emphasizes Isaiah 43 as the background.[24] It is essential to recognize that proponents of each background build their case on one part of Mark 10.45/Matthew 20.28, which they feel is primary, and is neglected by the other positions – Thus, ὁ υἱὸς τοῦ ἀνθρώπου οὐκ ἦλθεν διακονηθῆναι (Daniel 7; 9) ἀλλὰ διακονῆσαι καὶ δοῦναι τὴν ψυχὴν αὐτοῦ (Isaiah 53) λύτρον ἀντὶ (Isaiah 43) πολλῶν (Isaiah 53). Since each group focuses on a part of Mark 10.45/Matthew 20.28, it follows that none of the positions are mutually exclusive. It would be possible to assert that all three suggested scriptural backgrounds are influencing Mark 10.45/Matthew 20.28. The next sections (1.2.1.1 through 1.2.1.3) offer brief arguments for each background.

1.2.3.1 Isaiah 53

Mark and Matthew use Isaiah to frame their picture of Jesus.[25] Whether or not this includes the use of Isaiah 53 in Mark 10.45/Matthew 20.28 is debatable.[26] The primary evidences for connecting Mark 10.45/Matthew 20.28 with Isaiah 53 are the linguistic and conceptual connections between the Son of Man's service unto death as a benefit to the many and the death of the Isaianic servant being a benefit to many. In Mark 10.45/Matthew 20.28, the Son of Man serves unto death (διακονῆσαι καὶ δοῦναι τὴν ψυχὴν αὐτοῦ). This is also true of the servant in 53.12 (παρεδόθη εἰς θάνατον ἡ ψυχὴ αὐτοῦ/נפשׁו הערה למות) and perhaps in 53.10 (אם־תשׂים אשׁם נפשׁו),[27] though in both cases there is no explicit self-giving aspect. Mark 10.45/Matthew 20.28 portrays the

---

[20] Watts, *Isaiah's New Exodus*, 270–84; "Jesus' Death, Isaiah 53, and Mark 10:45: A Crux Revisited," in *Jesus and the Suffering Servant* (ed. W. Bellinger, Jr. and W. Farmer; Harrisburg: Trinity Press International, 1998), 125–51.

[21] M. Hooker, *Jesus and the Servant: The Influence of the Servant Concept of Deutero-Isaiah in the New Testament* (London: S.P.C.K, 1959), 74–79.

[22] Barrett, "The Background of Mark 10:45," 1–18.

[23] McKnight, *Jesus and His Death*, 235–39; B. Pitre, *Jesus, the Tribulation, and the End of the Exile* (WUNT 2/204; Tübingen: Mohr Siebeck, 2005), 384–417; "The 'Ransom for Many,' the New Exodus, and the End of the Exile: Redemption as the Restoration of All Israel (Mark 10:35–45)," *LetSp* 1 (2005): 41–68.

[24] Initially by W. Grimm, *Weil ich dich liebe: Die Verkündigung Jesu und Deuterojesaja* (Frankfurt/M.: Peter Lang, 1976), 231–77; followed by Stuhlmacher, *Reconciliation*, 23–24.

[25] McKnight, *Jesus and His Death*, 207–24; Watts, "Jesus' Death," 125–51.

[26] Some of Mark's and Matthew's contemporaries use Isaiah 53 to interpret Jesus' death (Romans 4.25; Hebrews 9.28; 1Peter 2.21–25; Barnabas 5.2; 1Clement 16.3–14).

[27] It is difficult to tell whether תשׂים is 3fs ("If his person sets"), or 2ms ("If you set his person"). If 2ms, it is difficult to decide who is "you." Perhaps the LORD, but he is never addressed elsewhere in the song. Maybe it is the speaker of 53.1–6?

Son of Man's life-giving as a benefit to the many (ἀντὶ πολλῶν).[28] Similarly, the servant's loss of life is beneficial to the many (53.11 [πολλοῖς/לרבים]; 53.12 [πολλοὺς/ברבים, πολλῶν/רבים).[29] In Mark 10.45/Matthew 20.28, the Son of Man's death for the many is in the context of service (οὐκ ἦλθεν διακονηθῆναι ἀλλὰ διακονῆσαι), and so is the Isaianic servant's (53.11: εὖ δουλεύοντα πολλοῖς). Concerning the big picture, Watts makes a compelling statement when he says, "...where else, if not here, in the OT can we find any concept of a 'serving' figure who, in an eschatological context, gives his life for the 'many'?"[30]

Several objections have been brought against the parallel between Mark 10.45/Matthew 20.28 and Isaiah 53; the first two are the most serious. First, λύτρον is not in the LXX of Isaiah 53.[31] Second, the subject of Mark 10.45/Matthew 20.28 is not the Isaianic servant, but the Danielic Son of Man. This makes one wonder why one should even look in Isaiah 53 for the background to a statement that is clearly rooted in Daniel? Third, διακονεῖν is not in Isaiah 53 and עבד is never rendered as διακονεῖν in the LXX.[32] Finally, there is no parallel for ἀντί preceding πολλῶν in Isaiah 53.[33] Therefore, so the argument goes, although a reference to Isaiah 53 might initially seem apparent it is actually far from certain.

1.2.3.2 Daniel 7; 9

The strongest support for a Danielic background to Mark 10.45/Matthew 20.28 is the fact that Jesus is describing the mission of the Son of Man. The Son of Man in Mark 10.45/Matthew 20.28 is almost certainly a reference to Daniel 7.13–14.[34] Most supporters of an Isaiah 53 background acknowledge

---

[28] Πολύς is used throughout Mark and Matthew to describe those to whom Jesus ministers.

[29] The πολλοί/רבים are also mentioned in Isaiah 52.14, 15.

[30] Watts, "Jesus' Death," 143.

[31] According to Barrett and Hooker, if there were a connection between Mark 10.45/Matthew 20.28 and Isaiah 53, אשם (53.10) should be rendered as λύτρον, and not περὶ ἁμαρτίας. In the LXX, λύτρον only translates פדה, גאל, and כפר, and never אשם (Barrett, "The Background of Mark 10:45," 5–6; Hooker, *Jesus and the Servant*, 77).

[32] Barrett, "The Background of Mark 10:45," 4.

[33] Grimm notes that in Isaiah 53 ἀντί "überhaupt nicht als Präposition vor 'viele' verwendet" (*Weil ich dich liebe*, 236).

[34] Mark and Matthew are largely dependent on Daniel 7.13–14 for their Son of Man concept (Mark 8.38/Matthew 16.27; Mark 13.26/Matthew 24.30; Mark 14.62/Matthew 26.64). For an overview of the potential impact of Daniel 7–12 on the passion predictions, see J. Marcus, *Mark 8–16* (AYB 27A; New Haven: Yale University Press, 2009), 751–56; McKnight, *Jesus and His Death*, 233–39. It is important to note that authority is the issue in the early Son of Man sayings (Mark 2.10/Matthew 9.6; Mark 2.28/Matthew 12.8), as it is in Daniel 7.13–14 (S. Gathercole, "The Son of Man in Mark's Gospel," *ExpTim* 115 (2004): 366–72).

this reference. However, they then insist that the rest of Mark 10.45/Matthew 20.28 refers to the servant of Isaiah 53. Thus, Jesus is saying: "The Son of Man did not come to be served (as you were expecting from Daniel 7.13–14), but to serve...(as in Isaiah 53). Reaction against this tendency to acknowledge a brief dependence on the Danielic Son of Man and then hastily skip over him in a mad dash to Isaiah 53 has triggered a reexamination of how Mark 10.45/Matthew 20.28 can be explained from a complete dependence on Daniel 7; 9 without any recourse to Isaiah 53.[35]

The major points of contact between Mark 10.45/Matthew 20.28 and Daniel 7; 9 are as follows: (1) The Son of Man is the subject of interest in Daniel 7.13–14 and Mark 10.45/Matthew 20.28. (2) The messiah is killed in Daniel 9.26, though without the self-giving element, and the Son of Man/messiah is killed in Mark 10.45/Matthew 20.28.[36] (3) The messiah's death in Daniel 9.26 is discussed alongside the topic of atonement in Daniel 9.24, and Jesus' death is to be a ransom. (4) There is a linguistic connection between the "many" in Daniel 9.27 and Mark 10.45/Matthew 20.28.

There are two weaknesses of the Daniel 7; 9 background. First, the Danielic Son of Man never explicitly serves rather than being served (Daniel 7.14). Second, there is no explicit statement that the death of the messiah functions as a "*ransom* for many." Therefore, so the argument goes, although there is likely a Danielic background leading up to Mark 10.45/Matthew 20.28, it is not clear that the Danielic influence extends any further than the identification of Jesus as the Son of Man.

1.2.3.3 Isaiah 43

Following Hooker's criticisms of the traditional Isaiah 53 background, a new view arose that concentrates on two parts of that criticism: (1) the inability of אשם to correspond with λύτρον,[37] and (2) the absence of ἀντί in Isaiah 53.[38] This view finds both λύτρον and ἀντί to be conceptually present in MT Isaiah 43.3–4 where λύτρον ἀντί (Mark 10.45/Matthew 20.28[c]) corresponds to כפר...תחת. Among other correspondences are (1) λυτρόω in Isaiah 43.1, (2)

---

[35] Hooker states: "he [Jesus] would hardly have appealed to his hearers concerning the things which are written of the Son of Man if he were referring primarily to passages which they connected with a totally different concept [the Isaianic servant]" (*Jesus and the Servant*, 96).

[36] This would mean that Mark and Matthew understood the Son of Man from Daniel 7 and the messiah from Daniel 9 as the same person.

[37] Grimm says: "führt sprachlich kein Weg von אשם zu λύτρον" (*Weil ich dich liebe*, 235).

[38] Grimm points out that the prepositions ל and ב, which are attached to רבים, cannot correspond to ἀντί, which is the equivalent to תחת (ibid., 236).

the "Son of Man" paralleled by אדם in Isaiah 43.4,[39] (3) "giving his life" paralleled by אתן in Isaiah 43.4,[40] and (4) ψυχή paralleled by נפשך in Isaiah 43.4.

The most serious criticism of this view is that it requires Jesus to take the place of the nations as a ransom price for Israel. This is a difficult concept to relate to Jesus or the synoptics, unless a new synthesis is in view. Secondly, there are no motifs of service or death.[41] In sum, while Isaiah 43.3–4 has some linguistic parallels with Mark 10.45/Matthew 20.28, its required merger of Jesus and the nations casts doubts on its potential as a background to Mark 10.45/Matthew 20.28.

In conclusion, none of the above three scriptural backgrounds can easily claim the entirety of Mark 10.45/Matthew 20.28. Yet, all three have legitimate linguistic and conceptual connections with part of Mark 10.45/Matthew 20.28. Given all the ink that has gone into establishing these three positions, it might seem that the topic has been exhausted. However, no one has yet examined the scriptural background of Mark 10.45/Matthew 20.28 in light of the reception of the ransom logion.

1.3 Methodology for Examining the Reception of the Ransom Logion

Chapters Two through Four examine the reception of the ransom logion from the New Testament through the third century. There are three issues that must be discussed in order to develop a consistent methodology for this examination. First, there must be a standard terminology (1.3.1). Second, there must be tools for gathering the receptions of the ransom logion from the New Testament and the Early Christian periods (1.3.2). Third, there must be a standard for classifying receptions according to their similarity to a textual exemplar (1.3.3).

1.3.1 Standard Terminology

Concerning terminology, there are three important points. First, throughout the entire survey from the New Testament through the Early Christian periods, I identify the primary reception under examination as the *ransom logion*. I chose the label *ransom logion* because it is the common term for the tradition found preeminently in Mark 10.45/Matthew 20.28. It is important to note that by calling this tradition *ransom logion* I do not wish to affirm that -λυτ

---

[39] Grimm, *Weil ich dich liebe*, 253–54.
[40] Grimm believes that "δοῦναι τὴν ψυχὴν αὐτου...ist sachgemäße Deutung des אתן von Jes. 43,4" (ibid., 253).
[41] Watts, "Jesus' Death," 145.

vocabulary should be translated as *ransom*.[42] By using the term *logion*, I do not wish to affirm that all those who receive the tradition necessarily think they are using a saying of Jesus.

Second, by *ransom logion*, I mean *the tradition that is sufficiently similar to Mark 10.45/Matthew 20.28*. The concept of tradition, as I define it, allows for, but does not assume that there is textual dependence. Tradition includes the possibility of direct or indirect dependence on a textual source (both extant and not extant), but it also includes the possibility of dependence (both conscious and unconscious) on oral communications that do not result from contact with a text.[43] Therefore, the ransom logion – the tradition that is sufficiently similar to Mark 10.45/Matthew 20.28 – could result from direct or indirect dependence on the text of Mark 10.45/Matthew 20.28, or it could result from dependence on an oral tradition that is in no way dependent on the text of Mark 10.45/Matthew 20.28, but is, nevertheless, sufficiently similar to Mark 10.45/Matthew 20.28. In the New Testament period, all receptions of the ransom logion likely result from oral sources. In the Early Christian periods, the possibility of textual dependency increases as the Gospels of Mark and Matthew become increasingly widespread, though the possibility of oral dependence remains high.[44]

Third, whenever I speak of Mark 10.45 or Matthew 20.28, I am specifically referring to the verse in one of those gospels. If I do not wish to distinguish between the two, I may write: Mark 10.45/Matthew 20.28. If I wish to specify a part of the verse, then I will write, for example, Mark 10.45^c, or Mark 10.45/Matthew 20.28^{a-b}. Similarly, if I wish to specify that the ransom logion is sufficiently similar to a part of Mark 10.45/Matthew 20.28, then I will write, for example, the ransom logion^c.

---

[42] There are a few places in the New Testament where I believe the ransom logion is received, but -λυτ vocabulary is absent (e.g. Galatians 1.4; John 10.11). I still identify these as receptions of the ransom logion because, despite the absence of -λυτ vocabulary, I judge them to be sufficiently similar to Mark 10.45/Matthew 20.28.

[43] Of course, the question of textual dependency is much more open for Christian traditions in the early centuries CE than for Jewish traditions, which more assuredly come from textual sources.

[44] It is important to remember that the Early Christian use of a tradition, which is similar to a New Testament text, may result from dependence on an oral tradition that was at some point taken up into the New Testament, but the use of that tradition in the early centuries CE does not necessitate dependence on a New Testament text. In the two Early Christian periods, there are only four instances where the high degree of similarity between the ransom logion and Mark 10.45/Matthew 20.28 means that there is almost assuredly a textual dependence (Clement of Alexandria, *Paedagogus* 1.9.85.1–2; Origen, *Commentary on Matthew* 20.28; *Fragment on Luke* 14.16; Didascalia Apostolorum 16). For a helpful discussion of direct/indirect textual, or oral, dependency in Early Christian literature, see P. Foster, *The Gospel of Peter: Introduction, Critical Edition and Commentary* (TENTS 4; Leiden: Brill, 2010), 115–17.

Mark 10.45/Matthew 20.28^a = (καὶ γὰρ/ὥσπερ) ὁ υἱὸς τοῦ ἀνθρώπου οὐκ ἦλθεν
διακονηθῆναι
Mark 10.45/Matthew 20.28^b = ἀλλὰ διακονῆσαι
Mark 10.45/Matthew 20.28^c = καὶ δοῦναι τὴν ψυχὴν αὐτοῦ λύτρον ἀντὶ πολλῶν

1.3.2 Tools for Gathering Receptions of the Ransom Logion

Concerning tools for gathering receptions of the ransom logion, there are two
standards: one for the New Testament and one for the Early Christian periods
through the third century. For the New Testament (Chapter Two), I consult
several important works on traditions in the New Testament in order to select
texts that are sufficiently similar to Mark 10.45/Matthew 20.28.[45] The selected receptions of the ransom logion in the New Testament are limited to
the ransom logion^c – 1Timothy 2.6; Titus 2.14; Galatians 1.4; 2.20; Ephesians
5.2, 25; John 10.11, 15; 15.13; 1John 3.16. The standards I use to judge sufficient similarity to Mark 10.45/Matthew 20.28^c are sentence structure, -λυτ
language and/or the idea of self-giving. While none of these texts result from
contact with Mark 10.45/Matthew 20.28, I judge that they are part of a tradition that, depending on dating, either already exists in, or will be taken up
into, Mark 10.45/Matthew 20.28.

For the Early Christian periods through the third century (Chapters Three
and Four), I mostly depend on the first four volumes of *Biblia Patristica*.[46] In
order to be consistent, I examine every text that *Biblia Patristica* lists as sufficiently similar to Mark 10.45/Matthew 20.28 through the third century. In addition to *Biblia Patristica*, I consult Massaux,[47] Köhler,[48] and Evans, Webb

---

[45] R. Deichgräber, *Gotteshymnus und Christushymnus in der frühen Christenheit: Unter-*
suchungen zu Form, Sprache und Stil der frühchristlichen Hymnen (SUNT 5; Göttingen:
Vandenhoeck & Ruprecht, 1967), 112–113; Hengel, *The Atonement*, 35; W. Kramer, *Christ,*
Lord, Son of God (trans. B. Hardy; SBT 50; London: S. C. M. Press, 1966), 115–19; W. Popkes, *Christus Traditus: Eine Untersuchung zum Begriff der Dahingabe im Neuen Testament*
(Zurich: Zwingli Verlag, 1967), 196–201; K. Wengst, "Christologische Formeln und Lieder
des Urchristentums" (Ph.D. diss., Universität Bonn, 1967), 50–72.

[46] Biblia Patristica: Index des citations et allusions bibliques dans la littérature patristique,
vol. 1, *Des origines à Clément d'Alexandrie et Tertullian*; vol. 2, *Le troisième siècle (Origène*
excepté); vol. 3, *Origène*; vol. 4, *Eusèbe de Césarée, Cyrille de Jérusalem, Épiphane de*
Salamine (ed. J. Allenbach, *et al*; Paris: Éditions du Centre National de la Recherche Scientifique, 1975, 1977, 1980, 1987).

[47] E. Massaux, *The Influence of the Gospel of Saint Matthew on Christian Literature be-*
fore Saint Irenaeus (3 vols.; Macon, GA: Mercer University Press, 1990, 1992, 1993).

[48] W. Köhler, *Die Rezeption des Matthäusevangeliums in der Zeit vor Irenäus* (WUNT
2/24; Tübingen: Mohr Siebeck, 1987). I am aware of the criticisms laid at the maximalist
conclusions reached by Massaux and Köhler (A. Gregory, *The Reception of Luke and Acts in*
the Period before Irenaeus [WUNT 2/169; Tübingen: Mohr Siebeck, 2003], 7–15; A. Gregory and C. Tuckett, "Reflections on Method: What Constitutes the Use of the Writings that
Later Formed the New Testament in the Apostolic Fathers," in *The Reception of the New Tes-*
tament in the Apostolic Fathers [ed. A. Gregory and C. Tuckett; Oxford: Oxford University

and Wiebe,[49] all of whom list Early Christian receptions of the tradition that they judge to be sufficiently similar to Mark 10.45/Matthew 20.28. These authors are mostly in agreement with *Biblia Patristica*. I gleaned from Evans, Webb and Wiebe an additional reception from The Gospel of Philip. I also gathered additional receptions from Origen and Eusebius through a word search for λύτρον in the online version of *Thesaurus Linguae Graecae*.[50] I did not find additional receptions in the indices of the relevant volumes from the Griechischen Christlichen Schriftsteller or the Sources Chrétiennes series, which suggests that I have gathered a nearly complete listing of the tradition that others have judged to be sufficiently similar to Mark 10.45/Matthew 20.28 in the Early Christian periods.

It may be important to note that the texts that *Biblia Patristica* lists as receptions of Mark 10.45/Matthew 20.28 overlap with the texts that *Biblia Patristica* lists as receptions of the other appearances of the ransom logion in the New Testament. For example, *Biblia Patristica* lists Diognetus 9.2 as a reception of both Mark 10.45/Matthew 20.28 and 1Timothy 2.6, which is a text I identify as a reception of the ransom logion in the New Testament. 1Timothy 2.6 is particularly important because it is by far the closest parallel to Mark 10.45/Matthew 20.28[c] in the New Testament. In the Early Christian periods, the receptions that *Biblia Patristica* lists of the relevant part of 1Timothy 2.6 are also listed by *Biblia Patristica* as receptions of Mark 10.45/Matthew 20.28.[51] Or, the receptions that *Biblia Patristica* lists of the relevant part of 1Timothy 2.6 occur in very close proximity to receptions that *Biblia Patristica* lists for Mark 10.45/Matthew 20.28. The result is that in the course of examining all the receptions that *Biblia Patristica* lists for Mark 10.45/Matthew 20.28, I also discuss all the receptions that *Biblia Patristica* lists of the relevant part of 1Timothy 2.6, except one. The only reception that *Biblia Patristica* lists of the relevant part of 1Timothy 2.6 that does not in some way overlap with the receptions of Mark 10.45/Matthew 20.28 occurs in Origen's *Commentary on Romans* 3.7; 3.8. The text reads as follows: "He gave himself as the redemption price, that is to say, he handed himself over to the enemies and…just as Peter also writes in his epistle when he says, 'You were redeemed not with perishable silver or gold, but with the precious blood

---

Press, 2005], 61–82). However, my work is not affected by these criticisms since I am looking for a tradition that is similar to Mark 10.45/Matthew 20.28, rather than a distinct appeal to the literary text of Mark or Matthew.

[49] C. Evans, R. Webb, and R. Wiebe, *Nag Hammadi Texts and the Bible: A Synopsis and Index* (NTTS 18; Leiden: Brill, 1993).

[50] Origen, *Fragment on Ephesians* 1.7; *Fragment on 1Corinthians* 6.19–20; Eusebius, *De Theophania* 9 (*Thesaurus Linguae Graecae: A Digital Library of Greek Literature*. Accessed 29 July 2008. Online: http://www.tlg.uci.edu/).

[51] Of course, the relevant part of 1 Timothy 2.6 is limited to the first clause (ὁ δοὺς ἑαυτὸν ἀντίλυτρον ὑπὲρ πάντων, τὸ μαρτύριον καιροῖς ἰδίοις).

of the only begotten Son of God.'"[52] I decided not to give this text a separate examination in Chapter Four because it overlaps so nicely with the themes that are already strongly attested in Origen's other receptions of Mark 10.45/Matthew 20.28. Those themes are the ransom to Satan motif, and the 1 Peter 1.18–19 co-tradition.

Besides 1 Timothy 2.6, the other New Testament texts that are discussed in Chapter Two are Titus 2.14; Galatians 1.4; 2.20; Ephesians 5.2, 25; John 10.11, 15; 15.13; 1 John 3.16.[53] For the sake of completeness, I include below all of the receptions that *Biblia Patristica* lists for these New Testament texts through 300 CE (Most are from one writer – Origen, who is followed closely by Eusebius).[54] As discussed in the previous paragraph, some of these are included in the examination in Chapters Three and Four, but many are not. There are two reasons for this. First, and most commonly, they are not receptions of the specific part of the New Testament verse potentially containing the ransom logion. For example, Titus 2.14 states: "He gave himself for us to ransom us from all lawlessness and to purify for himself a special people, who are eager to do good." If an Early Christian writer says that Christians are a "special people" then *Biblia Patristica* will list this as a reception of Titus 2.14 (e.g. Clement of Alexandria, *Stromata* 1.89). Second, they simply no longer represent the New Testament text in a way that makes them sufficiently similar to Mark 10.45/Matthew 20.28, especially in a time when the Gospels of Mark and Matthew are widely known.

1 Timothy 2.6 (Diognetus 9.2; Clement of Alexandria, *Hypotyposes* 200,13; Irenaeus, *Against Heresies* 5.1.1; The Teachings of Silvanus 104.12–13; Origen, *Commentary on Romans* 3.7; 3.8; *Matthew Fragment* 242; *Luke Fragment* 164; Eusebius, *Demonstratio Evangelica*, 10.8.35; *Commentary on Isaiah* 2.42)

Titus 2.14 (Barnabas 14.5 [6]; Clement of Alexandria, *Stromata* 1.89; 6.106; 6. 159; The Acts of Paul 58,24; The Acts of Phileas 4.4)

Galatians 1.4 (Tertullian, *On the Apparel of Women* 2.6; The Acts of Paul 58,24; Geneva Papyrus 253; The Freer Logion; Gregory Thaumaturgus, *Fragments* (A) 590,5; Origen, *Against Celsus* 2.42; 5.32; 6.54; *Fragments on 1 Corinthians* (A) 87; *Fragments on Ephesians* 9, 27, 34; *Homily on Jeremiah* 17.3; *Commentary on John* 19.87; *Homily on Judges* 1.1; *Homily on Leviticus* 7.1; *Homily on Luke* 3; *On Prayer* 25.1; *On Passover* 1.34; *Fragments on Psalms* (C) 11,5; Eusebius, *Commentary on Isaiah* 1.54)

Galatians 2.20 (Clement of Alexandria, *Stromata* 4.12.6; Passion of Perpetua and Felicity 4.5; Hippolytus, *Benedictions of Isaac, Jacob and Moses* 2; De recta in Deum fide 222, 13; The Acts of Thomas 19; Origen, *Fragments on 1 Corinthians* 16; 30; *Commentary on the Song of Songs* 2; *Fragments on Ephesians* 19; 36; *Commentary on John* 1.23; 10.45; 13.351; 20.93; 28.39; *Homily on Judges* 2.1; *Homily on Leviticus* 7.2; *Homily on Luke* 12; 15; 22;

---

[52] T. Scheck, trans., *Origen, Commentary on the Epistle to the Romans: Books 1–5* (TFC 103; Washington: The Catholic University of America Press, 2001), 215.

[53] These are listed here in descending order of similarity to Mark 10.45/Matthew 20.28.

[54] For more complete bibliographic information for each of the primary texts listed below, one should consult the relevant volume of *Biblia Patristica*.

Exhortation to Martyrdom 12; *Fragments on Matthew* 218; 350; 487; *Commentary on Matthew* 12.25; *Commentary on Matthew* (A) 33; 97; *Homily on Numbers* 24.2; *On Passover* 1.6; *De Principiis* 4.4.2; *Fragments on Psalms* (E) 118.25; *Fragments on Romans* (B) 41; *Commentary on Romans* (A) 4.12; 5.8; 6.9; *Commentary on 1Thessalonians* 112,2; Eusebius, *Fragments* 676; *Commentary on Psalms* 297; 576; 604; 637)

Ephesians 5.2 (Clement of Alexandria, *Paedagogus* 2.67; Barnabas 2.10; Passion of Perpetua and Felicity 4.5; Ignatius of Antioch, *Epistle to the Ephesians* 1.3; Tertullian, *To the Martyrs* 2.4; *Answer to the Jews* 14.8; Methodius, *Conuiuium* 5.6, 8; Origen, *Commentary on Matthew* (A) 11; 102; *Commentary on the Song of Songs* 1; *Homily on Genesis* 13.2; *Commentary on John* 19.119; *Homily on Leviticus* 3.1; 5.4; 7.1; 10.1; *Homily on Numbers* 11.4; *On Passover* 1.18; *Commentary on Romans* (A) 7.10; Eusebius, *Demonstratio Evangelica* 8.2.118)

Ephesians 5.25 (Ignatius of Antioch, *Epistle to Polycarp* 5.1; Irenaeus, *Against Heresies* 4.20.12; 5.9.4; Tertullian, *On Modesty* 18.11; Clement of Alexandria, *Paedagogus* 3.94.5; *Stromata* 3.49.3; Passion of Perpetua and Felicity 4.5; Pseudo Clement of Rome, *Homilies* 7.5; Cyprian, *Epistles* 59.1; 69.2; 74.6; Hippolytus, *On Daniel* 1.16.2; Methodius, *Conuiuium* 3.10; *On Leprosy* 15.6; Novatian, *De bono pudicitiae* 2.2; 5.6; Peter of Alexandria, *Ad Alexandrinos* 80,5; Origen, *Homily on Genesis* 3.4; 3.6; *Commentary on the Song of Songs* 1, 2, 3; *Homily on the Song of Songs* 2.1; *Commentary on Matthew* 14.16)

John 10.11 (Clement of Alexandria, *Stromata* 1.169.1; 6.158.1; *Excerpta* 73.2; *Paedagogus* 1.37.3; 1.53.2; 1.84.1; 1.85.2; 1.97.3; 3; Irenaeus, *Fragments* 59,44; Melito of Sardis, *De fide* 244,43; Tertullian, *De anima* 13.3; *Flight in Persecution* 11.1; *On Modesty* 7.4); Cyprian, *Epistles* 8.1; 43.6; The Acts of Thomas 25; 39; The Teachings of Silvanus 18,56; Pseudo-Cyprian, *Ad Novatianum* 6.5; Hippolytus, *On David and Goliath* 11.5; *Apostolic Tradition* 41; Pseudo-Hippolytus, *Homily on Passover* 2.2; *In Sanctas Theophanias* 3; Methodius, *Conuiuium* 3.6; 4.6; Peter of Alexandria, *Ad Alexandrinos* 80,5; *Fragments* 11.14; Origen, *Commentary on John* 1.22; 1.122; 1.124; 1.126; 1.190; 1.198; 1.267; 2.125; 19.39; 32.117; *Fragments on Matthew* 187.2; 188; *Fragments on 1Corinthians* 40; *Fragments on Song of Songs* 145,24; *Commentary on Song of Songs* 2; *Homily on Song of Songs* 1.9; *Homily on Genesis* 9.3; *Homily on Jeremiah* 5.6; 18.3; *Homily on Jeremiah* (A) 3.4; *Fragments on Job* 73; *Fragments on Luke* 58; *Homily on Luke* 12; *Commentary on Matthew* (A) 137; *Homily on Numbers* 19.4; *Fragments on Psalms* (A) 120; *Commentary on Romans* (A) 3.3; 7.19; 8.6; Eusebius, *Demonstratio Evangelica* 7.2.17; 10.8.38; *De ecclesiastica theologia* 2.10; *Commentary on Isaiah* 1.90; 2.9; *Ecclesiastical History* 10.4.23; 10.4.28; 10.4.34; *General Elementary Intro* 3.40; 3.41; 4.34; *Oratio de Laudibus Constantini* 2.3; 2.5; 7.9; *Commentary on the Psalms* 249; 325; 428; 432; 541; 776; 960; *Theophania* (A) 120,24; 125,4; *Life of Constantine* 3.49)

John 10.15 (Justin Martyr, *Apology* 1.63.3; 1.63.13; Tertullian, *De anima* 13.3; *Against Praxeas* 8.3; 22.8; Origen, *Commentary on the Song of Songs* 2; *Commentary on John* 32.345; *De Principiis* 4.4.8; *De Principiis* (A) 359,31; 360, 31; *Fragments on Romans* (A) 30; *Commentary on Romans* (A) 1.18; Eusebius, *Commentary on Psalms* 725; *Theophania* 5.7; *Theophania* (A) 148,18; 203,13; *General Elementary Intro* 3.40)

John 15.13 (Clement of Alexandria, *Quis Dives Salvetur* 37.5; Passio Agapes et Eirenes et Chiones 5.3; Origen, *Homily on Genesis* 4.2; *Homily on Leviticus* 2.4; 5.11; *Fragments on Romans* (A) 30)

1John 3.16 (Clement of Alexandria, *Hypotyposes*, 214,10; Tertullian, *Flight in Persecution* 9.3; 12.7; *Scorpiace* 12.4; Epistula ecclesiarum Lugdunensis et Viennensis 406,4; The Acts of Thomas 72; Origen, *Homily on Genesis* 4.2; *Homily on Leviticus* 9.9; 10.2; *Exhortation to Martyrdom* 41; Eusebius, *Ecclesiastical History* 5.1.10)

1.3.3 Classification of Receptions

Chapters Two through Four of this study examine receptions of the ransom logion, as well as other traditions occurring alongside the ransom logion, from the New Testament through the third century. Part of this examination is to classify receptions according to how similar they are to a textual exemplar. To do this, I developed five "similarity categories," which are abbreviated as S1 through S5.[55]

S1 – Very Strong Similarity	The reception matches the exemplar verbatim or nearly verbatim.
S2 – Strong Similarity	The reception may have some different vocabulary than the exemplar, but has the same ideas and overall structure.
S3 – Significant Similarity	The reception shares key words with the exemplar and/or has a similar structure.
S4 – Limited Similarity	There are various reasons to think that the reception might be similar to the exemplar, but they are not explicit.
S5 – No Demonstrable Similarity	It is almost unrecognizable how the reception is similar to the exemplar.

These categories are different than the standard categories of quotation, allusion, and echo. I elected not to use the standard categories for two reasons. First, the standard categories tend to assume textual, rather than oral, sources.[56] Second, the standard categories may presume to know an author's intention.[57] The similarity categories are meant to avoid these problems by not assuming textual sources and not presuming to know an author's intention. Similarity categories are strictly limited to describing the minimal amount that a modern researcher can possibly describe, which is the degree of similarity

---

[55] It would be insufficient only to identify receptions without further classification, as if they were all the same. Obviously, any decision for a particular similarity classification is based on my own judgment, which I hold open to correction.

[56] When people talk about quotations, allusions, and echoes, they typically mean quotations of, allusions to, and echoes of a text. However, for those interested in the use of Christian traditions in the early centuries CE, it is not possible always to assume textual sources. Many Christian traditions are oral from the beginning, and there is no reason why they do not continue to be oral for some time. The use of a Christian tradition that is similar to a New Testament text may result from dependency on an oral tradition that was at some point taken up into the New Testament, but the use of that tradition in the early centuries CE does not necessitate dependence on a New Testament text.

[57] By claiming that a text is a quotation, allusion, or echo, one is also subtly claiming to know the author's intentions (e.g. "The author alludes to..."). It is impossible to know this information, unless perhaps the author tells you that he/she is quoting from a text – e.g. γέγραπται.

that a researcher perceives a tradition bears to a textual exemplar on which the tradition itself may or may not be dependent.[58]

The similarity categories are used for classifying receptions of the ransom logion, as well as other Jewish and Christian traditions that are received alongside the ransom logion for which there are textual exemplars in the LXX or the New Testament. There are some traditions that are received alongside the ransom logion that do not have a corresponding textual exemplar, such as the ransom to Satan motif. These traditions are not given a similarity classification.

I organize all the received traditions in charts at the conclusion of each section in Chapters Two through Four. The charts have five categories: source of the reception, supposed tradition, exemplar, similarity classification, and further comments. The function of the charts is not only to show the similarity classifications, but also to organize and summarize the traditions that are received in each source. It is important to note that the charts do not address the interrelatedness of traditions. It is assumed that the traditions within a particular text are somehow interrelated given their proximity to one another. When appropriate, detailed comments concerning how the traditions are interrelated are reserved for the main text. Below is an example of a chart from Origen, *Fragment on Ephesians* 1.7.[59]

Source	Supposed Tradition	Exemplar	Similarity	Further Comments
Origen, *Fragment on Ephesians* 1.7	Ransom Logion[c]	Mark 10.45[c]	S3	Blood replaces soul as ransom price
	Ephesians 1.7	Ephesians 1.7	S1	
	Ransom to Satan	N/A	N/A	

1.4 Social Memory

Perhaps the most interesting phenomenon in the reception of the ransom logion is the appearance of interpretive patterns, both expected and unexpected.[60] One of the challenges confronting the observer of these patterns is to find a way to describe the phenomenon of their existence, or non-existence.[61]

---

[58] For my definition of "tradition," see 1.3.1 above.

[59] Also see the chart below in 5.2, which focuses on the patterns in the reception of the ransom logion.

[60] See the chart in 5.2 for a list of these patterns. Also striking are the patterns that do not appear, but which were expected to appear, such as a Danielic motif.

[61] Certainly, there is some type of dependency involved, but dependency is very difficult to trace in early Christianity, and ancient history in general.

The purpose of this brief section is to introduce the concept of social memory as potentially providing a way to address this phenomenon.[62]

Social memory can be defined as the sociology of knowledge. It focuses on the idea that knowledge is gained and shaped by society, rather than by the individual.[63] When people become members of a society, through birth or life circumstances, they naturally take up that society's knowledge – its memory – and make it their own. The society continues to function as a confirmer and shaper of the member's knowledge. E. Zerubavel uses the phrase "mnemonic socialization" to describe this process by which individuals both gain and re-fine knowledge in order to reflect more closely the collective knowledge of a particular society.[64]

The scope of collective knowledge within a particular society consists of what that society determines should be known by its members. During the process of mnemonic socialization, a society passively dictates to its members

---

[62] Social memory can also be framed as collective or cultural memory. The contemporary notion of social memory is typically traced to M. Halbwachs, *Les Cadres sociaux de la mémoire* (Paris: F. Alcan, 1925). For a discussion of past research using social memory, see J. Olick and J. Robbins, "Social Memory Studies: From 'Collective Memory' to the Historical Sociology of Mnemonic Practices," *ARS* 24 (1998): 105–40. For an excellent discussion of social memory in an African context, see J. Vansina, *Oral Tradition as History* (Madison: The University of Wisconsin Press), 94–123. For a self-attested "comprehensive" look at social memory in a single article, see E. Zerubavel, "Social Memories: Steps to a Sociology of the Past," *QS* 19 (1996): 283–99. In recent years, social memory theory has made its way into early Christian studies, and especially Jesus/Gospel studies. See, for example, S. Byrsog, "A New Quest for the *Sitz im Leben*: Social Memory, the Jesus Tradition and the Gospel of Matthew," *NTS* 52 (2006): 319–36; D. Duling, "Social Memory and Biblical Studies: Theory, Method, and Application," *BTB* 36 (2006): 2–4; J. Dunn, "Social Memory and the Oral Jesus Tradition," in *Memory in the Bible and Antiquity: The Fifth Durham-Tübingen Research Symposium (Durham, September 2004)* (ed. S. Barton, L. Stuckenbruck, and B. G. Wold; WUNT 212; Tübingen: Mohr Siebeck, 2007), 179–94; A. Kirk and T. Thatcher, eds., *Memory, Tradition, and Text: Uses of the Past in Early Christianity* (Semeia 52; Leiden: Brill, 2005); A. Le Donne, *The Historiographical Jesus: Memory, Typology, and the Son of David* (Waco, TX: Baylor University Press, 2009), 41–92; R. Rodriguez, *Structuring Early Christian Memory: Jesus in Tradition, Performance and Text* (LNTS 407; London: T&T Clark International, 2010).

[63] In this way, social memory is similar to what Gadamer calls interpretive prejudice, inso-far as interpretive prejudice is conditioned by current society (H. Gadamer, *Truth and Method* ([2d rev. ed.; trans. J. Weinsheimer and D. Marshall; London: Continuum, 2004], 278–306; G. Warnke, *Gadamer: Hermeneutics, Tradition and Reason* [Stanford: Stanford University Press, 1987], 75–82).

[64] "Social Memories," 286. It is important to note that while all members of a particular society undergo the process of mnemonic socialization, not all the members have the same knowledge. This is because individuals are often members of many different societies. People who are part of religious movement share a collective knowledge, but they can also have a collective knowledge with those in their professions that does not overlap with the knowledge shared within their religious group.

what information is relevant and what is irrelevant, what to remember and what to forget, what interpretation is correct and what is incorrect. This dictation is known as distortion.[65] The knowledge distortion process occurs naturally as a society develops a core set of knowledge that is collective and serves the needs of the society in the present. This collective knowledge, which is dictated to a society's members, is itself always evolving as the society reacts to various external factors. Societies sometimes attempt to freeze their ever-evolving collective knowledge in writing, creed, art, etc.

The interpretive patterns in the reception of the ransom logion must at some level be the result of mnemonic socialization and distortion.[66] Throughout the remainder of this study, I will periodically refer back to these processes in order to provide a potential explanation for the appearance and disappearance of patterns in the receptions of the ransom logion.

1.5 Rationale for Exploring the Reception's Significance for the Study of Mark 10.45/Matthew 20.28

1.5.1 The Pre-Markan Connectedness of the Ransom Logion

The question about the pre-Markan connectedness of the ransom logion is partially linked to the rationale for exploring the significance of the reception of the ransom logion for the study of Mark 10.45/Matthew 20.28. Therefore, before discussing the rationale for the exploration to be conducted in Chapter Five, we must first address the debate about the pre-Markan connectedness of the ransom logion.[67]

---

[65] Le Donne prefers the term "refraction" because "distortion carries too many negative associations" (*The Historiographical Jesus*, 51).

[66] The appearance of these patterns cuts against the emphasis in the current "social memory" school, which according to Dunn "is characterized by an emphasis on the *creative*, rather than the *retentive* function of memory" ("Social Memory," 180).

[67] A separate issue concerns how the ransom logion came into Mark's Gospel. The typical assumption is that at sometime in the pre-Markan history, Mark 10.45 was separate from what precedes it. Mark 9.35 supports the notion of a tradition ending in Mark 10.44 to which all or part of Mark 10.45 was eventually attached (R. Bultmann, *The History of the Synoptic Tradition* [trans. J. Marsh; New York: Harper and Row, 1963], 143). The attachment was supposedly made on the basis of shared service themes with 10.43–44 and/or shared notions of voluntary suffering with 10.37–38. The final connection to Mark 10.35–44 (or 10.41–44) was made by means of the connective particle καὶ γὰρ (Pesch, *Das Markusevangelium*, 162; Stuhlmacher, *Reconciliation*, 17–18, 26 n. 8–9). While I am uncertain about how the ransom logion came into Mark's Gospel, I remain confident that all of Mark 10.45 is original to Mark's gospel. There is no textual evidence to show that Mark 10.45 was ever not part of Mark's Gospel, and the entirety of Mark 10.45 is incorporated into Matthew 20.28.

Two positions are typically put forward concerning the pre-Markan connectedness of the ransom logion. The first position emphasizes that the ransom logion[a–b] was separate from the ransom logion[c] in the pre-Markan history. The second position emphasizes that the ransom logion[a–c] was together in the pre-Markan history.[68] These two positions are discussed below, followed by my own position.

Bultmann is primarily responsible for popularizing the position that the ransom logion[a–b] was separate from the ransom logion[c] in the pre-Markan history. He argues that Luke 22.24–27, which famously omits the ransom logion[c], is more original than Mark 10.41–45.[69] The assumed originality of Luke 22.24–27 prompts the conclusion that there was a time when the ransom logion[a–b] was not attached to the ransom logion[c].[70] Given the greatness of Bultmann, this conclusion has some appeal. However, it has often been effortlessly discarded by the majority, who point to the overwhelming consensus that Luke used Mark, including Mark 10.45[c]. Luke's possession of Mark 10.45[c] throws the originality of Luke's version into doubt. However, despite this overwhelming consensus that Luke's copy of Mark contains 10.45[c], Bultmann's conclusion about the originality of Luke 22.27 is sometimes still considered correct. This is due to the enduring conviction that Luke's omission of Mark 10.45[c] results from his dependence on a hypothetical source that predates Mark and does not include the ransom logion[c].[71] Of course, theories that envision a hypothetical source are never falsifiable and are also never completely convincing. My own view is that while Luke may have used various oral and textual sources that are no longer extant (Luke 1.1–2), his omission of Mark 10.45[c] does not primarily result from his dependence on these sources. Rather, Luke's omission of Mark 10.45[c] primarily results either from

---

[68] The issue is one of emphasis. It is possible that the ransom logion[a–b] and the ransom logion[c] could have been separate and then brought together all in the pre-Markan history. However, if it was brought together in the pre-Markan history, then it likely did not have a wide dissemination.

[69] Bultmann states: "Lk. 22[27] is doubtless original over against Mk. 10[45]" (*The History of the Synoptic Tradition*, 144).

[70] The assumption is that the ransom logion[c] was being developed in Pauline traditions, and was then attached to ransom logion[a–b] by Mark, or someone immediately prior to Mark (H. Branscomb, *The Gospel of Mark* [MNTC; London: Hodder and Stoughton Limited, 1937], 190–91; D. Nineham, *The Gospel of Saint Mark* [New York: Penguin, 1963], 280–81).

[71] H. Schürmann argues that Luke 22.24–27 is based partly on a non-Markan source that does not include a parallel to Mark 10.45[c] (*Jesu Abschiedsrede, Lk 22, 21–38. III Teil, Einer quellenkritischen Untersuchung des lukanischen Abendmahlsberichtes Lk 22, 7–38* [NA 20/5; Münster: Aschendorff, 1957], 64–92). J. Green makes the same point (*The Death of Jesus: Tradition and Interpretation in the Passion Narrative* [WUNT 2/33; Tübingen: Mohr Siebeck, 1988], 44–46). Against the argument of Schürmann and Green, C. Katter argues that Luke 22.24–27 is solely a redaction of Mark 10.41–45 ("Luke 22:14–38: A Farewell Address" [Ph.D. diss., University of Chicago, 1993], 193–204).

his desire to postpone mention of Jesus' atonement until Acts 20.28, or from his desire not to remove the narrative's climax from the Last Supper saying in Luke 22.19–20 (See 2.6.1). Therefore, I demur from the position that the ransom logion[a–b] was separate from the ransom logion[c] in the pre-Markan history on the grounds that Luke 22.27 is somehow more original than Mark 10.45.

The second position – that the ransom logion[a–c] was together in the pre-Markan history – may be the more widely-held of the two.[72] Some of the popularity for this position results from the desire to tie the entirety of Mark 10.45 back to the historical Jesus. Historical Jesus scholars tend to endorse the first part of Mark 10.45 as plausibly authentic. McKnight states: "Had the words of Jesus not moved into the realm of a ransom for many, few would have doubted these words as genuine."[73] Therefore, if Mark 10.45[c] can be inextricably attached to Mark 10.45[a–b] then it can absorb the same claims for authenticity. We see this reasoning by Gundry, who states: "But in the tradition v 45b[c] could hardly have existed by itself; so the chances of its authenticity are enhanced by the arguments already canvassed for the authenticity of v 45a[a–b], with which v 45b[c] was one in the tradition."[74]

A better argument for the pre-Markan connectedness of the ransom logion[a–c] might be found in 1 Timothy 2.5–6, which states ἄνθρωπος Χριστὸς Ἰησοῦς, (v.5) ὁ δοὺς ἑαυτὸν ἀντίλυτρον ὑπὲρ πάντων (v.6). It is sometimes argued that this text represents a full version of the ransom logion[a–c].[75] Given that the author of 1 Timothy is likely not dependent on Mark or Matthew, it follows that there must have been a pre-Markan oral existence of the full ransom logion that entailed a heavenly figure coming to serve and to give himself as a ransom for all.[76] This tradition was then used by the author of 1 Timothy and was not the result of Markan redaction. However, this argument is not probable. While it is widely recognized that 1 Timothy 2.6 closely parallels Mark 10.45[c], ἄνθρωπος in 1 Timothy 2.5 does not parallel a hypothetical oral tradition about the coming of a heavenly figure to serve. Also

---

[72] D. Hare notes: "a consensus in favor of attributing this saying in its entirety to pre-Markan tradition" (*The Son of Man Tradition* [Minneapolis: Fortress Press, 1990], 202). Roloff states: "Die Kombination von Mk 10,45a.b mit 10,45c ist sicher nicht erst ein Werk der markinischen Redaktion…" (*Der erste Brief an Timotheus* [EKKNT 15; Zürich: Benziger Verlag, 1988], 112). Cf. Stuhlmacher, *Reconciliation*, 18.

[73] McKnight, *Jesus and His Death*, 162.

[74] R. Gundry, *Mark: A Commentary on His Apology for the Cross* (Grand Rapids: Eerdmans, 1993), 588–89.

[75] E.g. J. Jeremias, *New Testament Theology: Part 1, The Proclamation of Jesus* (trans. J. Bowden; New York: Charles Scribner's Sons, 1971), 293.

[76] Tertullian, *De Carne Christi* 15.1, does read Daniel 7.13 next to 1 Timothy 2.5 – "'Upon the clouds (he came) as the Son of Man.' The Apostle Paul likewise says: 'The man Christ Jesus is the one Mediator between God and man.'" This may indicate that Tertullian knows a tradition that connects ἄνθρωπος Χριστὸς Ἰησοῦς (1 Timothy 2.5) with the heavenly υἱὸς ἀνθρώπου (Daniel 7.13).

given the service motifs in 1 Timothy 3.10, 13; 4.6; 6.2, it is unlikely that the author of 1 Timothy would omit the service element of this tradition. Therefore, it is best to conclude that the ransom logion in 1 Timothy is limited to the parallel with Mark 10.45^c in 1 Timothy 2.6. The parallel between ἄνθρωπος in 1 Timothy 2.5 and ὁ υἱὸς τοῦ ἀνθρώπου in Mark 10.45^a is coincidental rather than meaningful.[77]

My own position is that the ransom logion^c has an independent oral existence before its incorporation into Mark 10.45. This is closer to the first position discussed above, though the rationale is entirely different.[78] The evidence for my position is the early and independent receptions of the ransom logion^c that are examined below in Chapter Two (1 Timothy 2.6; Titus 2.14; Galatians 1.4; 2.20; Ephesians 5.2, 25; John 10.11, 15; 15.13; 1 John 3.16 [cf. Epistle to Diognetus 9.2 in Chapter Three]). These texts, which are all slightly different in wording, are evidence that the ransom logion^c likely had an independent oral existence before its incorporation into Mark 10.45, and before its attachment to a tradition about a heavenly (Son of Man) figure coming, not to be served, but to serve (the ransom logion^{a-b}).

The counter claim to my position, which is the same as the second position discussed above, is that the pre-Markan ransom logion did connect the tradition about a heavenly figure coming, not to be served, but to serve with the tradition about giving one's life as a ransom for many. The reception history of the ransom logion may provide some indirect evidence to support this counter claim. This evidence amounts to the following two interrelated points.

First, there is a strong pattern in the reception history to receive the ransom logion^c. Early Christian writers, who know the texts of Mark and/or Matthew, largely do not mention the ransom logion^{a-b}.[79] Likewise, New Testament writers only emphasize the ransom logion^c. This suggests the possibility that Early Christian and New Testament writers are actively omitting the ransom logion^{a-b} from their collective knowledge, perhaps in an effort to avoid the title, Son of Man.[80]

Second, among those patristic writers who do receive the ransom logion^{a-b}, there is a tendency to separate it from the ransom logion^c. Patristic writers who separate the ransom logion thus include Clement of Alexandria (Οὐκ ἦλθον, φησί, διακονηθῆναι, ἀλλὰ διακονῆσαι...καὶ δοῦναι τὴν ψυχὴν τὴν ἑαυτοῦ λύτρον ἀντὶ πολλῶν [*Paedagogus* 1.9.85.1–2]) and Origen

---

[77] For a further critique, see 2.2 below.

[78] My position is not influenced by Bultmann's theory about the originality of Luke 22.24–27, or the theory that envisions a hypothetical source behind Luke 22.24–27 that does not contain the ransom logion^c.

[79] Patristic receptions of the ransom logion^{a-b} with a good similarity classification include Clement of Alexandria, *Paedagogus* 1.9.85.1–2; Origen, *Commentary on Matthew* 20.28; *Fragment on Luke* 14.16; Didascalia Apostolorum 16.

[80] For more on the omission of the Son of Man, see 5.5.1.2 below.

(καὶ γὰρ ὁ υἱὸς τοῦ ἀνθρώπου οὐκ ἦλθεν διακονηθῆναι, ἀλλὰ διακονῆσαι...δοῦναι τὴν ἑαυτοῦ ψυχὴν λύτρον ἀντὶ πολλῶν [*Commentary
on Matthew* 20.28; cf. *Fragment on Luke* 14.16]). It is possible that this tendency to split the ransom logion[a–b] from the ransom logion[c] reflects a much
earlier practice wherein a tradition about a heavenly coming, not to be served,
is routinely separated from a tradition about self-giving as a ransom. If this
were true, then Mark 10.45 would represent the only New Testament use of
the unified ransom logion[a–c]. Other New Testament writers, like later patristic
writers, split the ransom logion between [a–b] and [c], and then drop [a–b], perhaps
because the coming of a mysterious figure (the Danielic Son of Man) or the
service theme, are seen to be irrelevant for the growing gentile mission.

In order for the above two points to have solid support, there needs to be
demonstrable evidence within the New Testament of the trends to split the
ransom logion between [a–b] and [c], and then drop [a–b]. This is where the counter
claim falls short. There is no good evidence within the New Testament that a
tradition connecting Jesus' service to ransom has been split, and then the service element dropped. None of the primary receptions of the ransom logion[c] in
the New Testament, which are discussed in Chapter Two (1Timothy 2.6; Titus 2.14; Galatians 1.4; 2.20; Ephesians 5.2, 25; John 10.11, 15; 15.13; 1John
3.16), show any evidence of splitting off or dropping the ransom logion[a–b]. As
discussed above, the possibility that the ransom logion[c] in 1Timothy 2.6 is
preceded by a remnant of the ransom logion[a–b] in 1 Timothy 2.5 is highly
doubtful since the single word, ἄνθρωπος, in 1Timothy 2.5 does not parallel a
hypothetical oral tradition about the coming of a heavenly figure to serve.
Also, the saying in 1Timothy 1.15 (Χριστὸς Ἰησοῦς ἦλθεν εἰς τὸν κόσμον
ἁμαρτωλοὺς σῶσαι) is not only too far removed from 1Timothy 2.6 to be
considered a split tradition, but it also lacks both an explicit service motif and
a contrastive element that are necessary for being considered a use of the ransom logion[a–b]. Concerning Luke 22.27, the author omits the ransom logion[c]
from his Markan source, probably because of his desire not to remove the narrative's climax from the Last Supper saying in Luke 22.19–20. However, the
author's removal of the ransom logion[c] is different than the removal of the
ransom logion[a–b], which is the evidence that the counter claim requires.

To conclude, there is no good evidence within the New Testament that a
tradition connecting the ransom logion[a–b] to the ransom logion[c] has been split,
and then the ransom logion[a–b] dropped. This means that all the receptions of
the ransom logion[c] in the New Testament, which are all slightly different in
wording, are evidence of an independent oral tradition that exists before its
incorporation into Mark 10.45, where it is attached to a tradition about a
heavenly figure coming, not to be served, but to serve (ransom logion[a–b]).[81] It

---

[81] It is likely that some of the Early Christian receptions of the ransom logion[c] also result
from independent oral sources.

is important to note that this tradition (ransom logion[a–b]) is not attested any-where in the New Testament outside of Mark 10.45, which further diminishes the possibility that it was ever connected to ransom logion[c] in the pre-Markan history. It may even be that the tradition about Jesus coming as the heavenly figure to serve originated in the mind of Mark. Whatever the case, there is no demonstrable evidence within the New Testament to support the pre-Markan connectedness of the ransom logion[a–c].[82] There is demonstrable evidence for the independent oral existence of the ransom logion[c] before its incorporation into Mark 10.45. Given this evidence, it is most probable that the connection of the ransom logion[c] with a tradition about the coming of a heavenly figure, not to be served, but to serve (ransom logion[a–b]) was first the work of Mark, which may have occurred under the influence of Pauline theology (Philippians 2.6–8), or Christian interpretations of Isaiah 53, but probably not Eucharist traditions (See Chapter Five).

The below diagram illustrates the significance of the independent pre-Markan ransom logion[c] for the examination of the reception of the ransom logion in Chapters Two through Four. Chapter Two examines the New Testament receptions of the ransom logion. These result from contact with an oral version of the ransom logion[c]. Chapters Three and Four examine the Early Christian receptions of the ransom logion. Early Christian receptions of the ransom logion[c] may result from (in)direct contact with Mark 10.45/Matthew 20.28[c], an oral version of the ransom logion[c], or other New Testament receptions of the ransom logion[c] (e.g. 1Timothy 2.6). Early Christian receptions of the ransom logion[a–b] very likely result from (in)direct contact with Mark 10.45/Matthew 20.28, because there is no evidence that the ransom logion[a–b] ever existed in the pre-Markan history.

All of the New Testament and Early Christian receptions of the ransom logion are examined based on their similarity to Mark 10.45/Matthew 20.28.

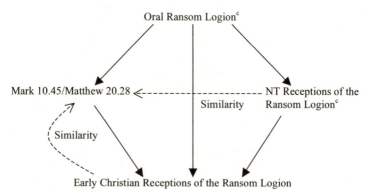

---

[82] If the ransom logion[a–c] did exist in the pre-Markan history then it did not have a wide enough dissemination to be taken up into other parts of the New Testament.

1.5.2 Rationale for Exploring the Reception's Significance for the Study of Mark 10.45/Matthew 20.28

The field of New Testament Studies is experiencing a growing interest in reception history. However, it is still unknown how large a voice reception history should have for historical-critical work on the New Testament.[83] It is also unknown what critical evaluation of reception history should involve. There is a degree of skepticism among exegetes and New Testament historians concerning the ability of reception studies to become anything more than an add-on activity to the gold standard of historical-critical research into the first-century world. Such skepticism is partially just, since it is not very compelling to allow unique receptions, which are often far removed from the text, to have any bearing on the historical-critical interpretive process.[84] I agree with this concern. In my opinion, late and/or unique receptions are of little value for first-century history or exegesis.[85] However, I would like to suggest that the situation is different when receptions are early and are guided by an interpretive pattern.[86] There are two ways of appropriating this suggestion.

First, patterned receptions of a particular tradition in the Early Christian periods have the potential to reflect meaningfully how that tradition is used in

---

[83] Despite the prodding of scholars who say it should have a significant voice: e.g. M. Bockmuehl, "A Commentator's Approach to the 'Effective History' of Philippians," *JSNT* 18 (1996): 57–88; *Seeing the Word: Refocusing New Testament Study* (STI 1; Grand Rapids: Baker Academic, 2006), 161–88; "New Testament Wirkungsgeschichte and the Early Christian Appeal to Living Memory," in *Memory in the Bible and Antiquity: The Fifth Durham-Tübingen Research Symposium (Durham, September 2004)* (ed. S. Barton, L. Stuckenbruck, and B. Wold; WUNT 212; Tübingen: Mohr Siebeck, 2007), 341–61; U. Luz, *Matthew 1–7* (trans. W. Linss; Hermeneia; Minneapolis: Augsburg Fortress, 1990), 95–99; *Matthew in History: Interpretation, Influence, and Effects* (Minneapolis: Fortress Press, 1994), 1–38; W. Lyons, "Hope for a Troubled Discipline? Contributions to New Testament Studies from Reception History," *JSNT* 33 (2010): 207–20; R. Nicholls, *Walking on the Water: Reading Mt. 14:22–33 in the Light of Its Wirkungsgeschichte* (BIS 90; Leiden: Brill, 2008), 1–27.

[84] For discussions of the historical-critical approach, see J. Barton, "Historical-Critical Approaches," in *The Cambridge Companion to Biblical Interpretation* (ed. J. Barton; Cambridge: Cambridge University Press, 1998), 9–20; J. Fitzmyer, *The Interpretation of Scripture: In Defense of the Historical-Critical Method* (New York: Paulist Press, 2008), 61–69.

[85] It is difficult to define what constitutes lateness. Certainly medieval receptions are too late to have value for first-century history or exegesis. I am inclined to think that the fourth and fifth centuries are also too late. This is partly why I have made the end of the third century (Eusebius) the cut-off date for this study. Concerning memory, Bockmuehl notes: "it is relatively easy to show that the reality of living memory opens up a uniquely privileged window of up to 150 years" (*Seeing the Word*, 169–70). Therefore, as far as communal memory is concerned, the end of the third century will be pushing the limits of what might be considered appropriate for maintaining traditions that potentially have meaningful contact with Mark, Matthew, and their communities.

[86] While emphasizing patterns, I do not want to exclude the possibility that singularly represented interpretations could be part of patterns that are not present in our extant sources.

earlier Christian communities, and perhaps in the New Testament itself. This is because interpretive patterns potentially witness to an interpretation that predates all known participants in the pattern. Patterned interpretations of the ransom logion in the Early Christian periods may attest to an even earlier interpretation which, because of its closer proximity to Mark 10.45/Matthew 20.28, may better reflect the earliest meaning given to those texts.[87] This first point, that patterned interpretations of a tradition in the Early Christian periods have the potential to reflect meaningfully how that tradition is used in the New Testament, is the most basic rationale for the exploration in Chapter Five. It can be diagramed as follows:

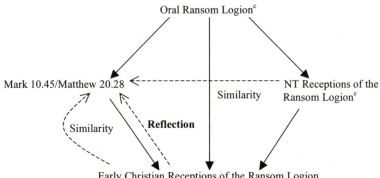

Second, when interpretive patterns in the reception of a tradition are so early that they potentially predate that tradition's incorporation into the New Testament, then there is the possibility that the New Testament reception of the tradition is itself participating in those patterns. Thus, when interpretive patterns in the reception of the ransom logion potentially predate Mark 10.45/Matthew 20.28, then there is the possibility that Mark 10.45/Matthew 20.28, as receptions of the ransom logion, may themselves participate in those patterns. This is where the pre-Markan connectedness of the ransom logion becomes important. The New Testament receptions of the ransom logion suggest that the ransom logion[c] has an independent oral existence before its incorporation into Mark 10.45/Matthew 20.28. Therefore, the interpretive patterns in the reception of the ransom logion[c] may predate the incorporation of the ransom logion[c] into Mark 10.45/Matthew 20.28. This means that we can consider the possibility that Mark 10.45/Matthew 20.28[c] is participating in those patterns. This second point is diagramed below.

---

[87] An analogy could be drawn with the quest for the historical Jesus where the multiply attested effects of the historical Jesus, as recorded in the earliest layers of the gospel tradition, are seen to reflect an even earlier tradition, which may be in contact with the actual person.

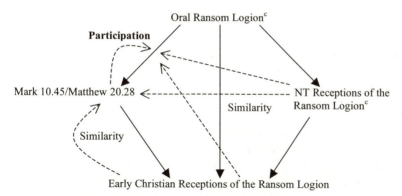

The above two points concern the potential for early interpretive patterns to reflect the earliest meaning given to New Testament texts, and the potential for New Testament texts to participate in early interpretive patterns. Both points represent an attempt to give a rationale for why early reception history has the potential to function as a valuable conversation partner and framer of questions for those doing historical-critical work on the New Testament. In Chapter Five of this study, I use this rationale to explore the potential significance of the reception of the ransom logion for the historical-critical study of the three issues discussed above in 1.2.1 through 1.2.3.

It is appropriate to conclude this section with a provocative query from Bockmuehl, who asks: "And most important of all…can the history *generated* by the text shed any light whatsoever on the history and world of meaning represented by the text itself?"[88] For this study, I would like to rephrase the question as: "Can the history generated by the ransom logion shed any light whatsoever on the history and world of meaning represented by the text of Mark 10.45/Matthew 20.28?" As will be seen in Chapter Five, the answer to this question is a very modest "yes." I hope that the notions of pattern, reflection, and/or participation help to answer the question of why the answer is yes.[89]

---

[88] Bockmuehl, "New Testament Wirkungsgeschichte," 344. Along similar lines, R. Nicholls states: "However for anyone concerned to produce a close reading of a biblical passage, it is necessary to turn back from the contemplation of the 'effects' to make a return journey to a *Wirkungsgeschichte*-enriched exegesis. Very little work has yet been done on making explicit what this return journey, integrating the 'history of effects' and exegesis, involves. Without this return journey, the study of the *Wirkungsgeschichte* of a text is simply an extra bolt-on procedure for exegetes: an interesting excursion, but no real help in reaching their higher destination" (*Walking on the Water*, 23–24).

[89] I did not begin this study attempting to show how early reception history might be relevant for New Testament exegesis. I began by investigating the reception of the ransom logion simply to see if there was anything interesting in the second and third centuries. It came as a surprise to me that there were interpretive patterns, and these patterns seemed relevant to his-

1.6 Conclusion

The purposes of this study are to examine the reception of the ransom logion from the New Testament through the third century, and then to explore the potential significance of that reception for the critical study of Mark 10.45/Matthew 20.28.

This chapter introduces three issues surrounding the critical study of Mark 10.45/Matthew 20.28 that are explored in Chapter Five in light of the reception history. These are development in a Eucharistic setting, preexistent coming, and scriptural background. These three issues are introduced in Chapter One in order to enable the observation of relevant phenomena throughout the examination in Chapters Two through Four. They are also introduced to show the stalemate that exists in some of the discussion, which highlights the need to add early reception history as another profitable tool to be used in historical-critical work on the New Testament.

Methodological consistency for the examination of the reception of the ransom logion necessitates the discussion of several issues. The primary results of that discussion are as follows. First, concerning terminology, the *ransom logion* is defined as the tradition (oral or textual) that is sufficiently similar to Mark 10.45/Matthew 20.28. Second, concerning tools, several important works on New Testament traditions guide the selection of receptions in the New Testament. *Biblia Patristica* is the primary source for obtaining receptions in the subsequent Early Christian periods. Third, concerning classification, five categories are used to classify traditions according to the similarity they bear to textual exemplars on which the traditions themselves may or may not be dependent.

The concept of social memory is briefly introduced as a way of explaining the interpretive patterns in the reception history of the ransom logion. Because social memory insists that knowledge is shaped and maintained by society, it is the ideal tool for thinking about the particular interpretations of the ransom logion that are patterned throughout the reception history.

The rationale for exploring the significance of the reception for Mark 10.45/Matthew 20.28 is augmented by a discussion of the pre-Markan connectedness of the ransom logion. It is concluded that the ransom logion[c] exists orally in the pre-Markan history, but there is no extant evidence for the oral existence of the ransom logion[a–b] in the same time period. This conclusion generates a diagram showing the formation and reception history of the ransom logion. The rationale for exploring the significance of this reception history for Mark 10.45/Matthew 20.28 is grounded in the potential for interpre-

---

torical-critical questions about Mark 10.45/Matthew 20.28. It was only then that I began to ask if something later could be relevant for something prior. The presence of interpretive patterns suggested that it could if I granted the possibility of reflection and/or participation.

tive patterns in the reception history to reflect the earliest meaning given to New Testament texts, and the potential for New Testament texts to participate in early interpretive patterns.

The remainder of this study is devoted to surveying the reception history of the ransom logion (Chapters Two through Four) and testing its significance for the historical study of Mark 10.45/Matthew 20.28 (Chapter Five). In the end, some conclusions will be drawn about the potential of early reception history to be a useful tool for the historical approach to the New Testament.

Chapter 2

The Reception of the Ransom Logion
in the New Testament

2.1 Introduction

Mark 10.45/Matthew 20.28 contains the most famous reception of the ransom logion in the New Testament.[1] The previous chapter introduced three issues surrounding the study of Mark 10.45/Matthew 20.28. Chapter Five is devoted to exploring the significance of the overall reception of the ransom logion for these three issues.

The primary purpose of the present chapter is to examine the other ten receptions of the ransom login in the New Testament. These are all limited to the reception of the ransom logion[c].[2] They are listed below in descending order, according to their similarity to Mark 10.45/Matthew 20.28[c].[3]

---

[1] Throughout Chapters Two through Four, I do not distinguish between Mark 10.45 and Matthew 20.28. In both Gospels, the ransom logion is part of the same larger context following the third passion prediction, and the saying itself is identical with the exception of the opening words of καὶ γὰρ in Mark 10.45 versus ὥσπερ in Matthew 20.28. Of course, there are some differences between Mark and Matthew that affect our understanding of the ransom logion in each Gospel. I will comment on these differences in Chapter Five.

[2] I have chosen not to include discussions of Luke 19.10 and 1Timothy 1.15 as receptions of the ransom logion[a–b] because they lack both an explicit service motif and a contrastive element; Luke is aware of the service motif and the contrastive element (Luke 22.27 [see 2.6.1 below]). Additionally, neither Luke 19.10 nor 1Timothy 1.15 showcase in the reception history of the ransom logion discussed in Chapters Two through Four.

[3] I selected these ten based upon similar sentence structure to Mark 10.45/Matthew 20.28[c], -λυτ language and/or the idea of self-giving. Guiding my selection were the following works: R. Deichgräber, *Gotteshymnus und Christushymnus in der frühen Christenheit: Untersuchungen zu Form, Sprache und Stil der frühchristlichen Hymnen* (SUNT 5; Göttingen: Vandenhoeck & Ruprecht, 1967), 112–113; M. Hengel, *The Atonement: The Origins of the Doctrine in the New Testament* (trans. J. Bowden; Philadelphia: Fortress Press, 1981), 35; W. Kramer, *Christ, Lord, Son of God* (trans. B. Hardy; SBT 50. London: S. C. M. Press, 1966), 115–19; W. Popkes, *Christus Traditus: Eine Untersuchung zum Begriff der Dahingabe im Neuen Testament* (Zurich: Zwingli Verlag, 1967), 196–201; and K. Wengst, "Christologische Formeln und Lieder des Urchristentums" (Ph.D. diss., Universität Bonn, 1967), 50–72. These works frequently mention Romans 4.25 and 8.32 as additional occurrences of the tradition I am surveying. I exclude them because they lack both -λυτ language and the idea of self-giving. I

Mark 10.45[c]	δοῦναι τὴν ψυχὴν αὐτοῦ	λύτρον	ἀντὶ πολλῶν
1 Timothy 2.6	ὁ δοὺς ἑαυτὸν	ἀντίλυτρον	ὑπὲρ πάντων
Titus 2.14	ἔδωκεν ἑαυτὸν	ὑπὲρ ἡμῶν, ἵνα λυτρώσηται ἡμᾶς	
Galatians 1.4	τοῦ δόντος ἑαυτὸν	ὑπὲρ τῶν ἁμαρτιῶν ἡμῶν	
Galatians 2.20	παραδόντος ἑαυτὸν	ὑπὲρ ἐμοῦ	
Ephesians 5.2	παρέδωκεν ἑαυτὸν	ὑπὲρ ἡμῶν	
Ephesians 5.25	ἑαυτὸν παρέδωκεν	ὑπὲρ αὐτῆς	
John 10.11	τὴν ψυχὴν αὐτοῦ τίθησιν	ὑπὲρ τῶν προβάτων	
John 10.15	καὶ τὴν ψυχήν μου τίθημι	ὑπὲρ τῶν προβάτων	
John 15.13	ἵνα τις τὴν ψυχὴν αὐτοῦ θῇ	ὑπὲρ τῶν φίλων αὐτοῦ	
1 John 3.16	ὅτι ἐκεῖνος ὑπὲρ ἡμῶν τὴν ψυχὴν αὐτοῦ ἔθηκεν		

In addition to these ten primary texts, this chapter discusses two other receptions that are classified as "ambiguous" due to the difficulty in satisfactorily determining whether they are sufficiently similar to Mark 10.45/Matthew 20.28.[4] These are Luke 22.27 and 1 Peter 1.18–19.

It is assumed that all ten primary texts discussed in this chapter are earlier than 130 CE. Providing more specific dates for these New Testament texts is a notoriously difficult task. Therefore, for the sake of argument, this thesis adopts consensus positions for dating the ten primary texts. Paul writes Galatians sometime between the late 40s and the late 50s CE.[5] Ephesians is pseudo-Pauline and written sometime between Paul's death and the end of the first century (i.e. 70–100 CE).[6] John and 1 John are written by the same author at the end of the first, or the beginning of the second century CE.[7] Finally, 1 Timothy and Titus are written by the same pseudo-Pauline author around the close of the first century or the beginning of the second century CE when Christian communities are becoming more institutionalized and their adversaries are advancing "myths and endless genealogies" (1 Timothy 1.4), as well as appealing to γνῶσις (1 Timothy 6.20).[8]

---

do, however, give Romans 4.25 and 8.32 attention in my comments on Galatians 1.4 and Diognetus 9.2.

[4] The present chapter is the only one containing "ambiguous" receptions. In subsequent chapters, I am almost completely dependent on *Biblia Patristica*, and so my own judgment, which causes the ambiguity, is removed from the equation.

[5] There is a longstanding, and ultimately irresolvable, debate about where Galatians should be more specifically dated within this period (J. Dunn, *Beginning from Jerusalem: Christianity in the Making, vol. 2* [Grand Rapids: Eerdmans, 2009], 720).

[6] For a discussion of Ephesians as pseudo-Pauline, see Dunn, ibid., 1106–09.

[7] Some of the best discussion of the date and development of the Johannine literature is still found in the classic works by R. Brown, *The Gospel According to John (i–xii)* (AB 29; New York: Doubleday, 1966), lxxx–lxxxvi; *The Epistles of John* (AB 30; New York: Doubleday, 1982), 100–101. If there are different authors for the Gospel of John and 1 John, then I assume that the author of 1 John knows the Gospel of John.

[8] For a discussion of the Pastorals as pseudo-Pauline, see B. Ehrman, *The New Testament: A Historical Introduction to the Early Christian Writings* (New York: Oxford University Press, 1997), 335–39. According to P. Towner, when the single authorship of the Pastorals is

While the above dates are assumed for the ten primary texts, this chapter does not discuss them in chronological order. Rather, they are discussed according to their similarity to Mark 10.45/Matthew 20.28, which means starting with the Pastorals, followed by Galatians, Ephesians, and the Johannine texts.[9] This may seem awkward since there is such a large time gap between Galatians and the Pastorals. However, the strong similarity classification of the ransom logion in the Pastorals, as well as the large scholarly discussion generated by that similarity, makes it more advantageous to ground the chapter there.

Finally, this chapter does not address literary dependency, other than to assume that Matthew is dependent on Mark.[10] It is possible that Mark and/or Matthew are dependent on Pauline literature (i.e. Galatians).[11] It is possible

---

challenged, it is normally only to exclude 2Timothy (*The Letters to Timothy and Titus* [NICNT; Grand Rapids: Eerdmans, 2006], 27). There are, however, some who are attempting to revive an older argument that 1Timothy and Titus have different authors. For example, J. Herzer argues that the author of 1Timothy is dependent on Titus and 2Timothy, which were written earlier by a different author, or different authors ("Rearranging the 'House of God': A New Perspective on the Pastoral Epistles," in *Empsychoi Logoi – Religious Innovations in Antiquity: Studies in Honour of Pieter Willem van der Horst* [ed. A. Houtman, A. de Jong, and M. Misset-van de Weg; AJEC 73; Leiden: Brill, 2008], 547–66).

[9] The ambiguous receptions, Luke 22.27 and 1Peter 1.18–19, are listed randomly, since it is not possible to judge adequately their similarity to Mark 10.45/Matthew 20.28.

[10] Markan priority is a firmly established position. The Griesbach hypothesis is untenable. The differences between the other two good solutions to the synoptic problem – the Two-Source hypothesis and the Farrer hypothesis – are irrelevant since they both assume that Matthew is dependent on Mark. The Farrer hypothesis is currently championed by M. Goodacre, *The Case Against Q: Studies in Markan Priority and the Synoptic Problem* (Harrisburg, PA: Trinity Press International, 2002).

[11] It is reasonable to assume Mark and Paul were in similar spheres of influence, which accounts for the similarities in their writings. However, the Gospel of Mark shows no direct knowledge of the Pauline epistles. For a discussion, see J. Fenton, "Paul and Mark," in *Studies in the Gospels: Essays in Memory of R. H. Lightfoot* (ed. D. Nineham; Oxford: Blackwell, 1955), 89–112; Hengel, *The Atonement*, 45–46; J. Marcus, *Mark 1–8* (ABC 27; New York: Doubleday, 1999), 73–75; "Mark – Interpreter of Paul," *NTS* 46 (2000): 473–87; W. Telford, *The Theology of the Gospel of Mark* (NTT; Cambridge: Cambridge University Press, 1999), 164–69; *Writing on the Gospel of Mark* (GABR; London: DEO Publishing, 2009), 147–49, 467–69. Marcus is probably correct when he states: "The most reasonable conclusion would seem to be that Mark writes in the Pauline sphere of activity and shows some sort of Pauline influence on his thought, although he is not a member of a Pauline 'school'…he has not studied, internalized, and imitated Paul's letters" (*Mark 1–8*, 75). The important point for this study is that Mark has not "studied, internalized, and imitated Paul's letters." So while it is reasonable to assume that both Mark and Paul use the ransom logion in their similar spheres of influence, Mark did not receive it from direct dependence on Paul's work. The same conclusions can be drawn between Matthew and Paul. They were in similar spheres of influence but are not in direct contact (P. Foster, "Paul and Matthew: Two Strands of the Early Jesus Movement with Little Sign of Connection," in *Paul and the Gospels: Christologies, Conflicts*

that Paul and/or pseudo-Paul are dependent on Markan literature.[12] It is possible that John is dependent on Pauline and/or Markan literature.[13] However, all of these options are too speculative. None of the New Testament authors directly cite one another, nor do they refer to one another's work. Further, no reception of the ransom logion examined in this chapter is exactly alike. The best explanation of the ransom logion in the New Testament is a common oral tradition rather than dependence on written sources.

2.2 1Timothy 2.6 and Titus 2.14

| Mark 10.45[a–b] | ὁ υἱὸς τοῦ ἀνθρώπου | οὐκ ἦλθεν διακονηθῆναι ἀλλὰ... |
| 1Timothy 2.5 | ἄνθρωπος Χριστὸς Ἰησοῦς, | |

Mark 10.45[c]	καὶ δοῦναι	τὴν ψυχὴν αὐτοῦ	λύτρον	ἀντὶ πολλῶν
1Timothy 2.6	ὁ δοὺς	ἑαυτὸν	ἀντίλυτρον	ὑπὲρ πάντων
Titus 2.14	ἔδωκεν	ἑαυτὸν	ὑπὲρ ἡμῶν, ἵνα λυτρώσηται ἡμᾶς

The above comparison demonstrates why there is little doubt among scholars that 1Timothy 2.6 and Titus 2.14 are influenced by a version of the ransom logion very similar to that found in Mark 10.45/Matthew 20.28[c].[14] The foll-

---

and Convergences [LNTS 411; ed. M. Bird and J. Willitts; London: T&T Clark International, 2011], 86–114); contra D. Sim, who argues that Matthew had Paul's letters ("Matthew and the Pauline Corpus: A Preliminary Intertextual Study," *JSNT* 31/4 [2009]: 401–22). Sim's criterion of availability is strong, but his single parade-evidence of Matthew 16.17–18[a]//Galatians 1.12, 16–17; 1Corinthians 10.4[c] does not demand that Matthew has direct access to Paul's letters.

[12] Any proposal that Paul is dependent on Mark requires the acceptance of J. Crossley's early dating of Mark (*The Date of Mark's Gospel: Insight from the Law in Earliest Christianity* [JSNTSup 266; London: T & T Clark, 2004]). As for the pseudo-Pauline epistles, the most tempting connection is between the Pastorals and Mark. The ransom logion in 1Timothy 2.6 is a very close parallel to Mark 10.45/Matthew 20.28[c]. However, this is likely not due to direct dependence on Mark (See 2.2 below).

[13] For the dependency of John on Mark, see R. Bauckham, "John for Readers of Mark," in *The Gospels for All Christians* (ed. R. Bauckham; Grand Rapids: Eerdmans, 1998), 147–71.

[14] F. Büchsel, "λύτρον, ἀντίλυτρον, λυτρόω, λύτρωσις, λυτρωτής, ἀπολύτρωσις," *TDNT* 4:349; M. Dibelius and H. Conzelmann, *The Pastoral Epistles* (trans. P. Buttolph and A. Yarbro; Hermeneia; Philadelphia: Fortress Press, 1972), 43; Hengel, *The Atonement*, 35; A. Lau, *Manifest in Flesh: The Epiphany Christology of the Pastoral Epistles* (WUNT 2/86; Tübingen: Mohr Siebeck, 1996), 82–83; I. Marshall, *The Pastoral Epistles* (ICC; Edinburgh: T & T Clark, 1999), 431; Popkes, *Christus Traditus*, 199; J. Roloff, *Der erste Brief an Timotheus* (EKKNT 15; Zürich: Benziger Verlag, 1988), 111–12; H. Stettler, *Die Christologie der Pastoralbriefe* (WUNT 2/103; Tübingen: Mohr Siebeck, 1998), 67; Towner, *The Letters to Timothy and Titus*, 183; P. Trummer, *Die Paulustradition Der Pastoralbriefe* (BET 8; Frankfurt am Main: Peter Lang, 1978), 197; K. Wengst, Christologische Formeln, 67; *et al.*

owing discussion in 2.2.1 and 2.2.2 demonstrates how these two occurrences of the ransom logion are read in light of Isaiah 42.6–7; 49.6–8.

Isaiah 42.6–7: I the Lord God called you in righteousness, and will hold your hand, and will strengthen you; and I gave you unto a covenant of a race, unto a light of the Gentiles, in order to open the eyes of the blind, to bring out the bound, and those who sit in darkness out of the prison-house.

Isaiah 49.6–8: And he said to me, it is a great thing for you to be called my servant, to establish the tribes of Jacob, and to recover the dispersion of Israel. Behold, I have set you unto a covenant of a race, unto a light of the Gentiles, in order that you might be unto salvation to the end of the earth. Thus says the Lord who delivers you...I gave you unto a covenant of the Gentiles in order to establish the earth...

However, before that discussion it is necessary to make two further points. First, it is highly unlikely that the author of 1Timothy and Titus is dependent on a text of Mark or Matthew since the Pastorals show no direct knowledge of the canonical gospels.[15] Second, there is a scholarly consensus that 1Timothy 2.6 closely parallels Mark 10.45/Matthew 20.28[c]. J. Jeremias supports an additional parallel between ἄνθρωπος Χριστὸς Ἰησοῦς in 1Timothy 2.5 and ὁ υἱὸς τοῦ ἀνθρώπου in Mark 10.45/Matthew 20.28[a].[16] Many scholars reject this additional parallel since it suggests that the author of 1Timothy 2.5–6 is dependent on a version of the ransom logion that is similar to Mark 10.45/Matthew 20.28[a–c]. This would mean that the author skipped over the service statement (οὐκ ἦλθεν διακονηθῆναι ἀλλὰ διακονῆσαι) in order to get to the atonement, which is difficult to accept in light of the service motifs in 1Timothy 3.10, 13; 4.6; 6.2.[17] Also, in Titus 2.14 when the same author uses the same parallel to Mark 10.45/Matthew 20.28[c], there is no accompanying parallel to Mark 10.45/Matthew 20.28[a].

2.2.1 Titus 2.14

The ransom logion[c] in Titus 2.14 is augmented by two ἵνα clauses that serve to expand its meaning. The two ἵνα clauses following the self-giving statement (ὃς ἔδωκεν ἑαυτὸν ὑπὲρ ἡμῶν) are (1) ἵνα λυτρώσηται ἡμᾶς ἀπὸ

---

[15] There is, however, an outside chance that J. Quinn is correct in his argument that the author of Luke/Acts, who has access to a text of Mark, is also the author of the Pastorals ("The Last Volume of Luke: The Relation of Luke–Acts to the Pastoral Epistles," in *Perspectives on Luke–Acts* [ed. C. Talbert; Edinburgh, 1978], 62–75). For a convincing criticism of Quinn's thesis, see L. T. Johnson, *The First and Second Letters to Timothy* (ABC 35A; New York: Doubleday, 2001), 88–89.

[16] J. Jeremias, *New Testament Theology: Part 1, The Proclamation of Jesus* (trans. J. Bowden; New York: Charles Scribner's Sons, 1971), 293.

[17] P. Towner, *The Goal of Our Instruction: The Structure of Theology and Ethics in the Pastoral Epistles* (JSNTSup 34; Sheffield: JSOT Press, 1989), 55. For more on this issue, see 1.5.1.

πάσης ἀνομίας, and (2) καὶ [ἵνα] καθαρίσῃ ἑαυτῷ λαὸν περιούσιον. The vast majority of secondary literature sees the same texts behind the first and second ἵνα clauses. The first ἵνα clause is said to be influenced by Psalm 130.8 [129.8 LXX], the second ἵνα clause is influenced by Exodus 19.5, and both clauses are influenced by Ezekiel 37.23.[18] I suggest instead that Isaiah 42.6–7 and 49.6–8 are behind the two ἵνα clauses. I suggest this in part because the two ἵνα clauses in Titus 2.14 are almost completely parallel to Barnabas 14.6, and Barnabas 14.6 is nothing more than the author's summary of Isaiah 42.6–7; 49.6–7, which is quoted in Barnabas 14.7–8. Below is a comparison of the three texts most often suggested as influencing the ἵνα clauses in Titus 2.14 (Psalms 130.8; Ezekiel 37.23; Exodus 19.5), as well as Barnabas 14.6.

Titus 2.14[a]	ἵνα λυτρώσηται	ἡμᾶς	ἀπὸ πάσης ἀνομίας
Barnabas 14.6[a]	λυτρωσάμενον	ἡμᾶς	ἐκ τοῦ σκότους,
Psalm 130.8	αὐτὸς λυτρώσεται	τὸν Ἰσραηλ	ἐκ πασῶν τῶν ἀνομιῶν αὐτοῦ
Ezekiel 37.23	ῥύσομαι	αὐτοὺς	ἀπὸ πασῶν τῶν ἀνομιῶν αὐτῶν

Titus 2.14[b]	καὶ καθαρίσῃ	ἑαυτῷ	λαὸν περιούσιον
Barnabas 14.6[b]	ἑτοιμάσαι	ἑαυτῷ	λαὸν ἅγιον
Ezekiel 37.23	...καθαριῶ...	μοι	εἰς λαὸς
Exodus 19.5		μοι	λαὸς περιούσιος

Barnabas 14.6 shares the same concepts and unbroken word order with both ἵνα clauses in Titus 2.14. Ezekiel 37.23, Psalm 130.8, and/or Exodus 19.5 are also very close. What is interesting is that Barnabas 14.6 is not an appeal to Ezekiel 37.23, Psalm 130.8, and/or Exodus 19.5, but is explicitly the author's summary of Isaiah 42.6–7; 49.6–7, which is quoted in Barnabas 14.7–8.

Barnabas 14.6: γέγραπται γὰρ πῶς αὐτῷ ὁ πατὴρ ἐντέλλεται, λυτρωσάμενον ἡμᾶς ἐκ τοῦ σκότους, ἑτοιμάσαι ἑαυτῷ λαὸν ἅγιον.

Barnabas 14.7: λέγει οὖν ὁ προφήτης· Ἐγὼ Κύριος ὁ Θεός σου ἐκάλεσά σε ἐν δικαιοσύνῃ, καὶ κρατήσω τῆς χειρός σου καὶ ἐνισχύσω σε, καὶ ἔδωκά σε εἰς διαθήκην γένους, εἰς φῶς ἐθνῶν, ἀνοῖξαι ὀφθαλμοὺς τυφλῶν, καὶ ἐξαγαγεῖν ἐκ δεσμῶν πεπεδημένους καὶ ἐξ οἴκου φυλακῆς καθημένους ἐν σκότει (Isaiah 42.6–7). γινώσκομεν οὖν πόθεν ἐλυτρώθημεν.

---

[18] Büchsel, "λύτρον," 4:351 n. 14; J. Kelly, *A Commentary on the Pastoral Epistles* (BNTC; London: Adam & Charles Black, 1963), 247; T. Knöppler, *Sühne im Neuen Testament: Studien zum urchristlichen Verständnis der Heilsbedeutung des Todes Jesu* (WMANT 88; Neukirchen-Vluyn: Neukirchener Verlag, 2001), 186; Lau, *Manifest in Flesh*, 151–52; Marshall, *The Pastoral Epistles*, 284–85; L. Oberlinner, *Die Pastoralbriefe. Dritte Folge, Kommentar zum Titusbrief* (HTKNT 11/2; Freiburg: Herder, 1996), 138; Stettler, *Die Christologie der Pastoralbriefe*, 260; Towner, *The Letters to Timothy and Titus*, 760–66; *et al.* Another minority option put forward by Lau and Oberlinner suggests 2Samuel 7.23 as a possible background (Lau, *Manifest in Flesh*, 152; Oberlinner, *Die Pastoralbriefe*, 138).

Barnabas 14.8: πάλιν ὁ προφήτης λέγει· Ἰδού, τέθεικά σε εἰς φῶς ἐθνῶν, τοῦ εἶναί σε εἰς σωτηρίαν ἕως ἐσχάτου τῆς γῆς· οὕτως λέγει Κύριος ὁ λυτρωσάμενός σε Θεός (Isaiah 49.6–7).

What initially makes the summarizing function of Barnabas 14.6 evident is the introductory language of γέγραπται. Also, the phrase in 14.6, αὐτῷ ὁ πατὴρ ἐντέλλεται, is a reference to God's (the Father's) call on the Isaianic servant (Jesus) in Isaiah 42.6/Barnabas 14.7. Further, Barnabas' language of ἐκ τοῦ σκότους in 14.6 comes from the quotation of Isaiah 42.6–7 in Barnabas 14.7. The -λυτ language in 14.6 could be influenced by Isaiah 49.6–7, which is quoted in Barnabas 14.8, though Barnabas is the only witness to -λυτ in the Greek text of Isaiah.[19] Given the strong parallel between Barnabas 14.6 and the two ἵνα clauses in Titus 2.14, one is justified to investigate whether the two ἵνα clauses in Titus 2.14 are not reflections on Ezekiel 37.23, Psalm 130.8, and/or Exodus 19.5, as is commonly assumed, but are summaries of Isaiah 42.6–7; 49.6–7.[20]

The influence of Isaiah 42.6–7; 49.6–7 on the two ἵνα clauses in Titus 2.14 makes sense of the emphasis on universal salvation in the greater context of Titus 2.11–14 (ἐπεφάνη γὰρ ἡ χάρις τοῦ θεοῦ σωτήριος πᾶσιν ἀνθρώποις [Titus 2.11]). It was common for early Christian writers to appeal to Isaiah 42.6 and/or 49.8 in order to justify the universal extension of salvation (Luke 2.32; Acts 13.47; 26.23; Barnabas 14.1–8; Justin, *Dialogue with Trypho* 26; 121–122; Tertullian, *An Answer to the Jews* 12.2; *Against Marcion* 3.20.4; 5.6.1.). The universal perspective is much stronger in 1Timothy 2.1–7, where it is combined with the idea of Jesus as a covenant mediator, which also matches the thought in Isaiah 42.6–7; 49.6–8. If one thinks of Titus 2.11–14 and 1Timothy 2.1–7 in the context of early Christian appeals to scripture supporting the extension of salvation to everyone, then it would hardly be a surprise if Isaiah 42.6; 49.8 are influencing Titus 2.11–14 and 1Timothy 2.1–7.

2.2.2 1Timothy 2.6

If the ransom logion[c] in Titus 2.14 is intertwined with a summary of Isaiah 42.6–7; 49.6–8, then one might question if the same author reads the ransom logion in 1Timothy 2.6 with the same texts from Isaiah. There are two reasons to think that the author does. First, in Isaiah 42.6; 49.8 and in 1Timothy 2.1–7

---

[19] It could also be that the -λυτ term in Barnabas 14.5–8 is due to influence from the ransom logion[c].

[20] The connection between Titus 2.14 and Isaiah 42.6–7; 49.6–7 is almost completely missed in modern scholarship because the connection between Titus 2.14 and Barnabas 14.6 is never appreciated. This connection between Titus 2.14 and Barnabas 14.6 is not a secret. It is listed in *Biblia Patristica* 1.518 and A Committee of the Oxford Society of Historical Theology, *The New Testament in the Apostolic Fathers* (Oxford: Clarendon Press, 1905), 14.

there is a shared emphasis on universal salvation. In 1Timothy the concern is explicitly for all people (πάντων ἀνθρώπων–2.1; πάντων τῶν ἐν ὑπεροχῇ ὄντων–2.2; πάντας ἀνθρώπους–2.4), even the gentiles (ἐθνῶν–2.7). As stated above, it was common for early Christian writers to allude to Isaiah 42.6 or 49.8 as proof that God's salvation extends to everyone. Second, the language of mediator (μεσίτης) in 1Timothy 2.5 likely implies a covenant (διαθήκη).[21] The vocabulary of ברית/διαθήκη occurs in Isaiah 42.6 and 49.8,[22] and it is probable that the peculiar phrase, ברית עם, in Isaiah 42.6 and 49.8 indicates a covenant mediator (μεσίτης).[23] In sum, it is easy to see how the thought in 1Timothy 2.5 immediately preceding the ransom logion that "there is one God and one [covenant] mediator between God and all human-ity" is perfectly parallel to Isaiah 42.6–7; 49.6–8.

Previous studies on the Pastorals have failed to observe how the author of 1Timothy and Titus reads the ransom logion in light of Isaiah 42.6–7; 49.6–8. The influence of Isaiah 42.6–7; 49.6–8 makes sense of the two ἵνα clauses and the universal perspective in Titus 2.11–14, as well as the idea of a cove-nant mediator, combined with a universal perspective, in 1Timothy 2.1–7. This does not mean that Ezekiel 37.23, Psalm 130.8, and/or Exodus 19.5 have no impact on the language in Titus 2.14, but it is best to consider Isaiah 42.6–7; 49.6–8 as primary.[24]

---

[21] In the New Testament, μεσίτης is almost always linked with the idea of covenant (Gala-tians 3.15–20; Hebrews 8.6; 9.15; 12.24).

[22] There is a variant of διαθήκη in Isaiah 49.6 LXX.

[23] Isaiah 42.6 and 49.8 are the only places where ברית עם occurs in the Hebrew Bible. The rarity and difficulty of this phrase has generated much debate. For a brief discussion see M. Smith, "Běrît 'am/Běrît 'ôlām: A New Proposal for the Crux of Isa 42:6," *JBL* 100/2 (1981): 241–43. If taken as an objective genitive then a mediator is implied, i.e. a covenant [media-tor] with the people. This appears correct, given that in Isaiah 42.6 ברית עם is parallel with לאור גוים, and the sense of לאור גוים is that the servant will mediate light to the nations (K. Baltzer, *Deutero-Isaiah: A Commentary on Isaiah 40–55* [trans. M. Kohl; Hermeneia; Min-neapolis: Fortress Press, 2001], 131–32).

[24] Two additional notes on Titus: First, a reading in the Hamburg Papyrus of the Acts of Paul states parenthetically about Jesus Christ that he gave himself for us (Ἰησοῦ Χριστοῦ τὸν ὑπὲρ ἡμῶν δόντα ἑαυτόν). This may be due to dependence on Titus 2.14 (C. Schmidt and W. Schubart, *ΠΡΑΞΕΙΣ ΠΑΥΛΟΥ: Acta Pauli: Nach dem Papyrus der Hamburger Staats- und Universitäts-Bibliothek* (Glückstadt and Hamburg: J. Augustin, 1936), 58 (line 24). It is unknown if this reading is original, and in any case it does not provide an insight to the discussion in this section. Second, because it has no direct bearing on the argument of this section, I made no mention of the great debate over whether ἐπιφάνειαν τῆς δόξης τοῦ μεγάλου θεοῦ καὶ σωτῆρος ἡμῶν Ἰησοῦ Χριστοῦ in Titus 2.13 refers to God and Christ, or to Christ alone. However, I think that my method of examining the occurrences of the ran-som logion[c] in 1Timothy 2.6 and Titus 2.14 together is applicable for what immediately pro-ceeds the ransom logion[c]. The ransom logion[c] in Titus 2.14 is immediately proceeded by the contentious text: τοῦ μεγάλου θεοῦ καὶ σωτῆρος ἡμῶν Ἰησοῦ Χριστοῦ (2.13). The ran-som logion[c] in 1Timothy 2.6 is proceeded by Εἷς γὰρ θεός, εἷς καὶ μεσίτης θεοῦ καὶ

Source	Supposed Tradition	Exemplar	Similarity	Further Comments
Titus 2.14;	Ransom Logion[c]	Mark 10.45[c]	S2	
1Timothy 2.6	Isaiah 42.6–7; 49.6–8	Isaiah 42.6–7; 49.6–8	S4	Secured by parallel text in Barnabas 14

2.3 Galatians 1.4

Mark 10.45[c]	καὶ δοῦναι	τὴν ψυχὴν αὐτοῦ	λύτρον ἀντὶ πολλῶν	
Galatians 1.4	τοῦ δόντος	ἑαυτὸν	ὑπέρ[25] τῶν ἁμαρτιῶν ἡμῶν	

There are several small discussions revolving around Galatians 1.4. First, there is a discussion about whether 1.4 is polemical. Jesus' death becomes polemical after 2.15, and the ransom logion[c] is used in a polemical context in 2.20. However, such explicit polemic appears absent in 1.4.[26] Second, there is a discussion concerning how much the traditional material in 1.4 is preceded by traditional material in 1.3 and followed by traditional material through the rest of 1.4 and into 1.5.[27] I am inclined to limit the traditional material to the first part of 1.4 since the ransom logion[c] occurs independently elsewhere in the New Testament.[28]

ἀνθρώπων, ἄνθρωπος Χριστὸς Ἰησοῦς (2.5). In both cases, the ransom logion[c] is proceeded by mention of θεός, plus Χριστὸς Ἰησοῦς/Ἰησοῦς Χριστός. It is clear in 1Timothy 2.5 that the author portrays θεός and Χριστὸς Ἰησοῦς as separate persons. Therefore, we should consider the same to be true in Titus 2.13. For a fuller discussion, see J. Edwards "The Christology of Titus 2.13 and 1 Tim 2.5," *TynB* 62/1 (2011): 141–47.

[25] $\mathfrak{p}^{51}$ $\aleph^1$ B H 0278. 6. 33. 81. 326. 365. 1175 read ὑπέρ. $\mathfrak{p}^{46}$ $\aleph$ A D F G Ψ 1739. 1881 $\mathfrak{m}$ read περί. The external evidence is evenly divided. The internal evidence supports ὑπέρ (Galatians 2.20; cf. Galatians 3.13; 1Corinthians 15.3; Ephesians 5.2, 25; 1Timothy 2.6; Titus 2.14). Περί may have been introduced into the text because of the similarity in letters between ὑπέρ and περί. However, περί may also be original and part of an allusion to the work of the servant in Isaiah 53. Περί better matches the language of Isaiah 53.4, 10 – οὗτος τὰς ἁμαρτίας ἡμῶν φέρει καὶ περὶ ἡμῶν ὀδυνᾶται…ἐὰν δῶτε περὶ ἁμαρτίας.

[26] See S. Shauf, "Galatians 2.20 in Context," *NTS* 52 (2006): 98; F. Trolmie, *Persuading the Galatians: A Text-Centered Rhetorical Analysis of a Pauline Letter* (WUNT 2/190; Tübingen: Mohr Siebeck, 2005), 36; J. Vos, "Die Argumentation des Paulus in Galater 1,1–2,10," in *The Truth of the Gospel: Galatians 1:1–4:11* (ed. J. Lambrecht; MSB; BEC 12; Rome: Benedictina Publishing, 1993), 15.

[27] Some limit the traditional material to 1.4[a] (J. Martyn, *Galatians: A New Translation with Introduction and Commentary* [ABC 33A; New York: Doubleday, 1997], 90). Others include all of 1.4 (Deichgräber, *Gotteshymnus und Christushymnus*, 113 n. 2). Still others include 1.4–5 (F. Bovon, "Une Formule Prepaulinienne dans L'Epitre aux Galates (Ga 1,4–5)," in *Paganisme, Judaïsme, Christianisme: Influences et affrontements dans le monde antique: Mélanges offert à Marcel Simon* [ed. A. Benoit; Paris: Boccard, 1978], 91–107).

[28] See the discussion on the pre-Markan connectedness of the ransom logion above in 1.5.1.

The purpose of this section is to focus on a third discussion, which concerns the composition of Galatians 1.4. It appears that Galatians 1.4 is a conflation of the ransom logion[c] and Isaiah 53. The primary difficulty in demonstrating the use of the ransom logion[c] and Isaiah 53 in Galatians 1.4 is the overlap in their language and concepts. It is uncertain if the notions of giving (δίδωμι) and "for us" (ὑπὲρ ἡμῶν) are dependent on the ransom logion[c], Isaiah 53, or (likely) both. Therefore, it is helpful to separate out those elements that are specific to the ransom logion[c], and those elements that are specific to Isaiah 53.

Specific to the ransom logion[c] is the concept of Jesus' self-sacrifice.[29] This concept is rare in Paul, which suggests the use of traditional material (Galatians 1.4; 2.20; pseudo-Paul [Ephesians 5.2, 25–27; 1Timothy 2.6; Titus 2.14]). Of course, aside from the absence of -λυτ, the ideas and structure of Galatians 1.4 are entirely similar to Mark 10.45/Matthew 20.28[c] (See the above comparison).[30] Therefore, the concept of self-sacrifice in Galatians 1.4 is considered part of a reception of the ransom logion[c].[31]

Specific to Isaiah 53 is the phrase: ὑπὲρ τῶν ἁμαρτιῶν ἡμῶν. This phrase has substantial similarities with Isaiah 53.4, 5, 6, 10, 11, 12 LXX.[32] Also, the

---

[29] Concerning origins, it is frequently suggested that the Pauline version of Jesus' self-sacrifice is a result of modification to the very old tradition in which Jesus is passively handed over (1Corinthians 11.23; by God – Romans 4.25; 8.32) (Deichgräber, *Gotteshymnus und Christushymnus*, 112; V. Furnish, "'He Gave Himself (Was Given) Up...': Paul's Use of a Christological Assertion," in *The Future of Christology: Essays in Honor of Leander E. Keck* [ed. A. Malherbe and W. Meeks; Minneapolis: Fortress Press, 1993], 111; Kramer, *Christ*, 116; Wengst, "Christologische Formeln," 50–53). I am not convinced that this is the case. In order to be convinced, one would have to know that the tradition in which Jesus is passively handed over is earlier than the tradition in Galatians 1.4. I see no way of validating this since they both occur in Paul, and are both in places where we are certain (1Corinthians 11.23), and fairly confident (Galatians 1.4), that Paul is relying on traditional material.

[30] Concerning the absence of -λυτ, Galatians 1.4 interprets Jesus' self-sacrifice as being ὑπὲρ τῶν ἁμαρτιῶν ἡμῶν. Dutero-Paul elsewhere equates the forgiveness of sins with ἀπολύτρωσιν (Colossians 1.14; Ephesians 1.7). Thus, perhaps Paul could have said in Galatians 1.4: "τοῦ δόντος ἑαυτὸν ἀπολύτρωσιν ὑπὲρ ἡμῶν."

[31] It should also be noted that the pseudo-Pauline letters of 1Timothy (2.6) and Titus (2.14) are dependent on a version of the ransom logion[c] that is very similar to Mark 10.45/Matthew 20.28[c]. If later letters written in the Pauline-school make such clear use of the ransom logion[c] then we might suspect the same of earlier letters written by Paul (In contrast to the other instances of the ransom logion[c] in the Pauline and pseudo-Pauline corpuses that use παραδίδωμι [Galatians 2.20; Ephesians 5.2, 25], Galatians 1.4 shares δίδωμι with 1Timothy 2.6 and Titus 2.14, and with Mark 10.45/Matthew 20.28).

[32] These are the verses in Isaiah 53 that speak of the servant's work to remove sin. See H. Hübner, *Vestus Testamentum in Novo* (vol. 2; Göttingen: Vandenhoeck & Ruprecht, 1997), 398. In addition to Isaiah 53, one is obligated to mention the Maccabean martyrs as a possible influence on Paul in Galatians (S. Cummins, *Paul and the Crucified Christ in Antioch: Maccabean Martyrdom and Galatians 1 and 2* [SNTSMS 114; Cambridge: Cambridge University

phrase is part of the tradition that Paul says he received in 1Corinthians 15.3.[33] Galatians 1.4 and 1Corinthians 15.3 are the only places in the Pauline corpus where the phrase, ὑπὲρ τῶν ἁμαρτιῶν ἡμῶν, occurs. 1Corinthians 15.3 asserts that Christ's death for our sins is according to the scriptures. While Paul may have had several scriptures in mind, one of them was almost certainly Isaiah 53.[34] We can assert this confidently because of the dependence Paul shows on Isaiah 53 in the parallel statement from Romans 4.25[a], which is the only Pauline text that is conceptually similar to 1Corinthians 15.3 and Galatians 1.4.

Romans 4.25[a]	ὃς παρεδόθη διὰ τὰ παραπτώματα ἡμῶν
Isaiah 53.6	κύριος παρέδωκεν αὐτὸν ταῖς ἁμαρτίαις ἡμῶν
Isaiah 53.12	διὰ τὰς ἁμαρτίας αὐτῶν παρεδόθη
Romans 4.25[b]	καὶ ἠγέρθη διὰ τὴν δικαίωσιν ἡμῶν[35]
Isaiah 53.11	יצדיק צדיק עבדי לרבים
	δικαιῶσαι δίκαιον εὖ δουλεύοντα πολλοῖς[36]

Press, 2001]), and more specifically on the view that Jesus' self-sacrifice is instrumental in atoning for sin. In my opinion, the primary support for the martyrs' influence on Paul is his use of καταλλάσσω and καταλλαγή (Romans 5.10–11; 11.15; 1Corinthians 7.11; 2Corinthians 5.18–20). These are the only places that these words occur in the New Testament or the Apostolic Fathers. Other than 1Corinthians 7.11, the use of these words always concerns the reconciliation brought about by Christ's death. The only places these words occur in the LXX are Isaiah 9.4; Jeremiah 31.39; 2Maccabees 1.5; 5.20; 7.33; 8.29. It is only the usages in Maccabees that parallel Paul's, especially when καταλλάσσω is the hopeful result of the martyrs' sacrifice (7.33). Having said this, it remains true that Paul is more demonstrably dependent on Second Isaiah (Romans 2.24; 3.15–17; 10.15, 16; 11.34; 14.11; 15.21; 2Corinthians 6.2; 6.17; Galatians 4.27; See especially Romans 4.25). In my view, this makes the Isaiah 53 allusion more probable in Galatians 1.4.

[33] On the traditional nature and structure of 1Corinthians 15.3–5 see A. Eriksson, *Traditions as Rhetorical Proof: Pauline Argumentation in 1 Corinthians* (CB – NTS; Stockholm: Almqvist & Wiksell International, 1998), 86–97. For a detailed analysis on the similarities between Galatians 1.4 and 1Corinthians 15.3, see L. De Saeger, "'Für unsere Sünden': 1 Kor 15,3b und Gal 1,4a im exegetischen Vergleich," *ETL* 1 (2001): 170–80.

[34] For a discussion of the Isaiah 53 background of 1Corinthians 15.3, see O. Hofius, "The Fourth Servant Song in the New Testament Letters" in *The Suffering Servant: Isaiah 53 in Jewish and Christian Sources* (ed. B. Janowski and P. Stuhlmacher; Grand Rapids: Eerdmans, 2004), 177–80.

[35] I agree with D. Moo, who believes that the second διά in Romans 4.25 is prospective, rather than retrospective (*The Epistle to the Romans* [NICNT; Grand Rapids: Eerdmans, 1996], 289).

[36] In the LXX of Isaiah 53.11, it is most natural to read δίκαιον as the object of δικαιῶσαι since the previous string of infinitives all have κύριος as the subject. On the other hand, the Hebrew text, without any emendations, and taking the preposition ל as an object-marker, understands צדיק עבדי to be the subject of יצדיק (S. Shum, *Paul's Use of Isaiah in Romans: A Comparative Study of Paul's Letter to the Romans and the Sibyline and Qumran Sectarian Texts* [WUNT 2/156; Tübingen: Mohr Siebeck, 2002], 197–198). The Hebrew text, or a lost

Scholars are as close as scholars come to being unanimous that Romans 4.25 echoes Isaiah 53,[37] though it remains puzzling why Paul is not elsewhere more explicit about his dependence on Isaiah 53 for his understanding of the salvific effects of Jesus' death.[38] The influence of Isaiah 53 on Romans 4.25 is significant because other than the self-sacrifice motif, the structural and conceptual parallels between Romans 4.25 and Galatians 1.4 are almost exact.

Romans 4.25   ὃς παρεδόθη   διὰ τὰ παραπτώματα ἡμῶν
Galatians 1.4   τοῦ δόντος ἑαυτὸν   ὑπὲρ τῶν ἁμαρτιῶν ἡμῶν

If Paul is almost certainly dependent on Isaiah 53 in Romans 4.25, then there is little reason to doubt a similar dependence in Galatians 1.4.

In my opinion, the capstone on the discussion of the influence of Isaiah 53 on Galatians 1.4 is Clement's citation of Isaiah 53.6 in 1Clement 16. 1Clement 16.3–14 quotes from a text of Isaiah 53.1–12, and it quotes Isaiah 53.6 as reading "καὶ κύριος παρέδωκεν αὐτὸν ὑπὲρ τῶν ἁμαρτιῶν ἡμῶν."[39] Although Clement is writing later than Paul, this is hard evidence

---

Greek version that is closer to the Hebrew, provides a better match to the thought in Romans 4.25[b].

[37] C. Cranfield, *A Critical and Exegetical Commentary on the Epistle to the Romans* (2 vols.; ICC; Edinburgh: T & T Clark, 1975, 1979), 1.251; J. Dunn, *Romans* (2 vols.; WBC 38A, 38B; Dallas: Word Books, 1988), 1.241; J. Fitzmyer, *Romans* (ABC 33; Garden City: Doubleday, 1993), 389; Hengel, *The Atonement*, 35; Hofius, "The Fourth Servant Song," 180–81; M. Hooker, "Did the Use of Isaiah 53 to Interpret His Mission Begin with Jesus?," in *Jesus and the Suffering Servant* (ed. W. Bellinger, Jr. and W. Farmer; Harrisburg: Trinity Press International, 1998), 101; R. Jewett, *Romans* (Hermeneia; Philadelphia: Fortress Press, 2007), 342–43; Moo, *The Epistle to the Romans*, 288; N. Perrin, "The Use of (para)didonai in Connection with the Passion of Jesus in the New Testament," in *Der Ruf Jesu und die Antwort der Gemeinde* (Göttingen: Vandenhoeck und Ruprecht, 1970), 211; Popkes, *Christus Traditus*, 221; Shum, *Paul's Use of Isaiah in Romans*, 189–93; J. Wagner, *Heralds of the Good News: Isaiah and Paul 'In Concert' in the Letter to the Romans* (NovTSup 101; Leiden: Brill, 2003), 342; *et al.* Shum's discussion is the most helpful.

[38] An explanation of this phenomenon is offered by A. Collins, who lists the uses of the fourth servant song in Romans 10.16, 15.21, and Luke 22.37, and then states: "...the identification of Jesus with the Servant, and his passion with the Servant's suffering, was primary. Thus the other uses are best seen as elaborations or extensions of that early interpretation" ("The Suffering Servant: Isaiah Chapter 53 as a Christian Text," in *Hebrew Bible or Old Testament?* [ed. R. Brooks and J. Collins; Notre Dame: University of Notre Dame Press, 1990], 204). Therefore, Paul assumed a connection between Isaiah 53 and a salvific understanding of the effects of Jesus' death. This comes out in Romans 4.25. Other, more explicit, uses of the fourth servant song in Paul are simply elaborations on that assumption. For a similar perspective see R. Hays, who suggests that "there is a metaleptic suppression of Isa 53 in Paul and that has worked effectively as a trope to highlight the uncited material" ("'Who Has Believed Our Message?' Paul's Reading of Isaiah," in *The Conversion of the Imagination: Paul as Interpreter of Israel's Scripture* [Grand Rapids: Eerdmans, 2005], 43–44).

[39] For a discussion see C. Markschies, "Jesus Christ as a Man before God: Two Interpretive Models for Isaiah 53 in the Patristic Literature and Their Development," in *The Suffering*

that the precise phrase, ὑπὲρ τῶν ἁμαρτιῶν ἡμῶν, could be extracted directly from a text of Isaiah 53.6.

In conclusion, Galatians 1.4 represents a combination of influences from the ransom logion[c] and from Isaiah 53. The recognition of this combination solves the uncertainty raised by Betz about an allusion to Isaiah 53 in Galatians 1.4. Betz states: "Uncertain is also the question of the possible influence of Isa 53, because that passage does not have the concept of self-sacrifice (cf. Isa 53.6, 12)."[40] The simple solution is that the self-sacrifice motif comes from the ransom logion[c]. Galatians 1.4 is the first occurrence of what becomes a pattern in the reception of the ransom logion, which is to read the ransom logion alongside influence from Isaiah 53.

Source	Supposed Tradition	Exemplar	Similarity	Further Comments
Galatians 1.4	Ransom Logion[c]	Mark 10.45[c]	S3	
	Isaiah 53.4, 5, 6, 10, 11, 12 LXX	Isaiah 53.4, 5, 6, 10, 11, 12 LXX	S3	Confirmed by parallel in Romans 4.25, and 1Clement 16.7

2.4 Galatians 2.20; Ephesians 5.2, 25

Mark 10.45[c]	καὶ δοῦναι	τὴν ψυχὴν αὐτοῦ	λύτρον ἀντὶ πολλῶν
Galatians 2.20	παραδόντος	ἑαυτὸν	ὑπὲρ ἐμοῦ
Ephesians 5.2	παρέδωκεν	ἑαυτὸν	ὑπὲρ ἡμῶν[41]
Ephesians 5.25		ἑαυτὸν παρέδωκεν	ὑπὲρ αὐτῆς

In Galatians 1.4 the ransom logion[c] is intertwined with influence from Isaiah 53. However, in the remainder of Galatians, and Ephesians, the ransom logion[c] is not united with Isaiah 53, but with a love motif. The ransom logion[c] is preceded by mention of Christ's love, either for "me" (Galatians 2.20), for "us" (Ephesians 5.2),[42] or for the church (Ephesians 5.25).[43] This tendency to

---

Servant: Isaiah 53 in Jewish and Christian Sources (ed. B. Janowski and P. Stuhlmacher; trans. D. Bailey; Grand Rapids: Eerdmans, 2004), 237–39; D. Bailey, "Appendix: Isaiah 53 in the Codex A Text of 1 Clement 16:3–14," in *The Suffering Servant: Isaiah 53 in Jewish and Christian Sources* (ed. B. Janowski and P. Stuhlmacher; trans. D. Bailey; Grand Rapids: Eerdmans, 2004); 237–39.

[40] H. Betz, *Galatians* (Hermeneia; Philadelphia: Fortress Press, 1979), 42 n. 55.

[41] Several witnesses read ὑμῶν, but external evidence overwhelmingly favors ἡμῶν. Perhaps the traditional nature of ἡμῶν caused less variation than in the preceding clause where there is a difficult decision between ἡμᾶς and ὑμᾶς (B. Metzger, *A Textual Commentary on the Greek New Testament* [2d ed.; Stuttgart: Deutsche Bibelgesellschaft, 2002], 538–539).

[42] Ephesians 5.2 also combines the ransom logion[c] with a phrase alluding to cultic sacrifice (προσφορὰν καὶ θυσίαν τῷ θεῷ εἰς ὀσμὴν εὐωδίας).

[43] Ephesians 5.25 is unique in that Christ gives himself for the church. Attached to this tradition are three ἵνα clauses indicating the purification that takes place preceding the

combine the ransom logion[c] with a love motif in the Pauline and pseudo-Pauline literature has encouraged several scholars to group the occurrences of this phenomenon together as I have also done.[44]

The personal nature of Galatians 2.20 suggests that the combination of the ransom logion[c] with a love motif may have begun with Paul,[45] who does have a preoccupation with love throughout his letters.[46] However, it is also possible that the combination of the ransom logion[c] with a love motif began with the tradition behind the Johannine corpus, which is discussed next.

Source	Supposed Tradition	Exemplar	Similarity	Further Comments
Galatians 2.20; Ephesians 5.2, 25	Ransom Logion[c]	Mark 10.45[c]	S3	
	Love motif	N/A	N/A	Sacrifice motivated by love for "me," "us," and the "church"

2.5 John 10.11, 15; 15.13; 1John 3.16[47]

Mark 10.45[c]	καὶ δοῦναι τὴν ψυχὴν αὐτοῦ	λύτρον	ἀντὶ πολλῶν
John 10.11	τὴν ψυχὴν αὐτοῦ τίθησιν		ὑπὲρ τῶν προβάτων
John 10.15	καὶ τὴν ψυχήν μου τίθημι		ὑπὲρ τῶν προβάτων
John 15.13	ἵνα τις τὴν ψυχὴν αὐτοῦ θῇ		ὑπὲρ τῶν φίλων αὐτοῦ
1John 3.16	ὅτι ἐκεῖνος ὑπὲρ ἡμῶν τὴν ψυχὴν αὐτοῦ ἔθηκεν		

There are several receptions of the ransom logion[c] in the Johannine literature. It is unknown if this is because the author of the Johannine corpus knows Mark's Gospel, or is simply influenced by similar oral traditions.[48] Whatever the case, early copyists of John's Gospel recognized the connection with

---

church's glorious presentation. Concerning purification compare with Titus 2.14 (ἵνα...καθ-αρίσῃ).

[44] Furnish, "He Gave Himself," 111; M. Gese, *Das Vermächtnis des Apostels: Die Rezeption der paulinischen Theologie im Epheserbrief* (WUNT 2/99; Tübingen: Mohr Siebeck, 1997), 208 n. 360; Popkes, *Christus Traditus*, 248.

[45] G. Berényi states: "...there is no [clear] pre-Pauline text in the NT which speaks of Christ's love; all the texts alluding to it are posterior to Gal" ("Gal 2:20: a pre-Pauline or a Pauline text?," *Biblica* 65/4 [1984]: 506). An exception to this might be Romans 8.32, which contains elements of traditional material and links them with a love motif (8.35, 37).

[46] Regarding Paul and the love motif see V. Furnish, *The Love Command in the New Testament* (London: SCM Press, 1972), 91–131.

[47] Cf. John 10.17–18; 13.37–38.

[48] Bauckham, "John for Readers of Mark," 147–71. Though also see W. North, "John for Readers of Mark? A Response to Richard Bauckham's Proposal," *JSNT* 25/4 (2003): 449–68.

Mark 10.45/Matthew 20.28[c], and sought to match John's language accordingly.[49]

The Johannine receptions are parallel to the receptions of the ransom logion[c] in Galatians 2.20 and Ephesians 5.2, 25. Like them, John receives the ransom logion[c] alongside a love motif. The reception of the ransom logion[c] alongside a love motif is fairly clear in John 15.13 and 1John 3.16.[50] Although ἀγάπη vocabulary is not present in John 10.11, 15, if these verses are read in light of John 15.13, then it becomes clear that the shepherd lays down his life because he loves the sheep. This is opposed to the hired hand in John 10.13, who is not concerned about (i.e. does not love) the sheep.

While there are certainly other things happening within the Johannine reception of the ransom logion[c], the primary motif is love – Jesus' love for us and the love we ought to have for one another. The dominance of this motif is not surprising given the importance of love throughout the Johannine corpus (John 13.1, 23, 34; 14.21; 15.9, 12, 13; 19.26; 21.7, 20; 1John 3.16).

In conclusion, the Johannine reception of the ransom logion[c] with a love motif parallels the reception in Galatians 2.20 and Ephesians 5.2, 25. It also parallels a later reception in Clement of Alexandria, who reads the ransom logion[c] specifically through John's motif of Jesus' love for his followers.[51]

Source	Supposed Tradition	Exemplar	Similarity	Further Comments
John 10.11, 15; 15.13; 1John 3.16	Ransom Logion[c] Love motif	Mark 10.45[c] N/A	S3 N/A	

2.6 Ambiguous Texts (Luke 22.27; 1Peter 1.18–19)

2.6.1 Luke 22.27

Mark 10.45[a–b]   καὶ γὰρ ὁ υἱὸς τοῦ ἀνθρώπου οὐκ ἦλθεν διακονηθῆναι ἀλλὰ διακονῆσαι

Luke 22.27   τίς γὰρ μείζων, ὁ ἀνακείμενος ἢ ὁ διακονῶν; οὐχὶ ὁ ἀνακείμενος; ἐγὼ δὲ ἐν μέσῳ ὑμῶν εἰμι ὡς ὁ διακονῶν

---

[49] In John 10.11, 𝔭[45] ℵ D *et al* change τίθησιν to δίδωσιν. Similarly, in John 10.15, 𝔭[45, 66] ℵ D W *et al* change τίθημι to δίδωμι. See Metzger, *Textual Commentary*, 196. Clement of Alexandria, *Paedagogus* 1.9.85.1–2, conflates Mark 10.45/Matthew 20.28 with the shepherd from John 10 (See 3.2.1 below).

[50] John 15.13: μείζονα ταύτης ἀγάπην οὐδεὶς ἔχει, ἵνα τις τὴν ψυχὴν αὐτοῦ θῇ ὑπὲρ τῶν φίλων αὐτοῦ.

1John 3.16: ἐν τούτῳ ἐγνώκαμεν τὴν ἀγάπην, ὅτι ἐκεῖνος ὑπὲρ ἡμῶν τὴν ψυχὴν αὐτοῦ ἔθηκεν· καὶ ἡμεῖς ὀφείλομεν ὑπὲρ τῶν ἀδελφῶν τὰς ψυχὰς θεῖναι.

[51] Clement of Alexandria, *Quis Dives Salvetur* 37.3–4 (See 3.2.2 below).

Luke 22.27 represents the climax of Luke's version of the dispute over who is the greatest (Luke 22.24–27). It is clear that Luke 22.24–27 is the author's parallel to Mark 10.41–45$^{a–b}$. The content shared between Luke 22.24–27 and Mark 10.41–45$^{a–b}$ is identical. Both Mark and Luke begin with a dispute about greatness (Mark 10.35–41/Luke 22.24), followed by Jesus' comment on the abuse of power among gentile rulers (Mark 10.42/Luke 22.25), and the need for service to characterize his followers (Mark 10.43–44/Luke 22.26). Jesus then points to his own service as an example (Mark 10.45$^{a–b}$/Luke 22.27).[52]

Given the strong parallel between Luke 22.24–27 and Mark 10.41–45$^{a–b}$, what remains striking is the drastically different wording between the two texts, and specifically between Luke 22.27 and Mark 10.45.[53] This verbal discrepancy has generated a host of difficult questions concerning the origins, reception, and redaction of the tradition shared between Luke 22.24–27 and Mark 10.41–45.[54] However, there are two items about which scholars are fairly confident: (1) Luke uses Mark (and Matthew for those who prefer the Farrer Hypothesis), and (2) Luke's version of Mark contains Mark 10.41–45.[55] Therefore, regardless of how Luke 22.24–27 results from the influence

---

[52] For a brief comparison of the presentations in Mark and Luke, see S. McKnight, *Jesus and His Death* (Waco: Baylor University Press, 2005), 164.

[53] V. Taylor, *The Passion Narrative of St Luke: A Critical and Historical Investigation* (SNTSMS 19; Cambridge: Cambridge University Press, 1972), 61–64.

[54] Among the speculative questions are the following: Has Luke completely rewritten Mark? Is Luke using a special source that contains an entirely different version of the Markan story (F. Bovon, *L'Évangile Selon Saint Luc 19,28–24,53* [CNT IIId; Genève: Labor et Fides, 2009], 213; J. Green, *The Death of Jesus: Tradition and Interpretation in the Passion Narrative* [WUNT 2/33; Tübingen: Mohr Siebeck, 1988], 44–46; H. Schürmann, *Jesu Abschiedsrede, Lk 22, 21–38. III Teil, Einer quellenkritischen Untersuchung des lukanischen Abendmahlsberichtes Lk 22, 7–38* [NA 20/5; Münster: Aschendorff, 1957], 63–92; Taylor, *Passion Narrative*, 61–64)? Is only Luke 22.25–26 a redaction of Mark, while 22.27 is from a special source (J. Fitzmyer, *The Gospel According to Luke (I–IX), (X–XXIV)* [2 vols.; ABC 28, 28A; Garden City: Doubleday, 1981, 1985], 2.1413; M. Soards, *The Passion According to Luke: The Special Material of Luke 22* [JSNTSup 14; Sheffield: Sheffield Academic Press, 1987], 31)? Is Luke's version of the story more original than Mark's (R. Bultmann, *The History of the Synoptic Tradition* [trans. J. Marsh; New York: Harper and Row, 1963], 144)? Is Luke's placement of the story near the Eucharist more original than Mark's placement (J. Roloff, "Anfänge der soteriologischen Deutung des Todes Jesu (Mk. X. 45 und Lk. XXII. 27)," *NTS* 19 [1972–73]: 55)? Do Mark 10.45 and Luke 22.27 represent two parts of the same saying that is unified in their common source (I. Marshall, *The Gospel of Luke: A Commentary on the Greek Text* [NIGTC; Exeter: The Paternoster Press, 1978], 813–14)? See J. Harrington for an extended history of the debate surrounding many of these questions, though focused on a different part of Luke's Gospel (*The Lukan Passion Narrative The Markan Material in Luke 22,54–23,25: A Historical Survey: 1891–1997* [NTTS 30; Leiden: Brill, 2000]).

[55] Since Matthew's version certainly contains Mark 10.41–45 and since there are no extant manuscripts that do not contain Mark 10.41–45, there is no reason to believe that Luke's ver-

of Mark 10.41–45 or from a different form of the same tradition, the facts remain that Luke knows Mark 10.41–45 and largely leaves it out of his Gospel, especially Mark 10.45.

There is not much in Luke 22.27 that directly resembles Mark 10.45 besides the language of διακονέω. Comparison can be made between ἐγὼ (Luke 22.27) and ὁ υἱὸς τοῦ ἀνθρώπου (Mark 10.45) or between ἐν μέσῳ ὑμῶν εἰμι ὡς ὁ διακονῶν (Luke 22.27) and οὐκ ἦλθεν διακονηθῆναι ἀλλὰ διακονῆσαι (Mark 10.45).[56] However, what Luke 22.27 completely omits is the phrase δοῦναι τὴν ψυχὴν αὐτοῦ λύτρον ἀντὶ πολλῶν (Mark 10.45[c]).

It is not likely that Luke omits Mark 10.45[c] because he wants to diminish the idea of atonement as one of his central themes.[57] In Luke 22.19–20 and Acts 20.28, Luke demonstrates that he is not opposed to being explicit about the atoning power of Jesus' death.[58] There also may be an implicit notion that Jesus' death is atoning because of the citations from Isaiah 53 in Acts 8.32–33. Therefore, there is little reason to believe that Luke would not be willing to include Mark 10.45[c] in his narrative. So how does one account for Luke's omission of Mark 10.45[c] in Luke 22.27? In my view, there are two reasonable suggestions, though both suggestions have problems.

First, Dunn observes Luke's tendency to omit or downplay pieces of Mark's Gospel because he wants to delay their impact until Acts.[59] If this is true, then perhaps Luke omits Mark 10.45[c] because he wants to save its impact until Acts 20.28.[60] There are two difficulties with this solution. First, it requires Luke 20.19–20 not to be original to Luke's gospel because Luke 20.19–20 contains an atonement theme, which then nullifies Luke's need to

---

sion of Mark did not have these verses. This means that the debate over the secondary nature of Mark 10.45[c] is irrelevant insofar as it only concerns the pre-Markan development of the text. I should note that D. Burkett has developed a theory that would not require Luke to know Mark 10.45, or as Burkett conceives it: material from Proto-Mark A (*Rethinking the Gospel Sources: From Proto-Mark to Mark* [New York: T & T Clark International], 2004).

[56] It is also possible that Luke has moved the material from Mark 10.45/Matthew 20.28[a] to Luke 19.10, which states: ἦλθεν γὰρ ὁ υἱὸς τοῦ ἀνθρώπου ζητῆσαι καὶ σῶσαι τὸ ἀπολωλός.

[57] Fitzmyer well criticizes the idea that Luke wishes to diminish atonement (*The Gospel According to Luke*, 1.219–21).

[58] Cf. Luke 1.77; 3.3; 24.47; Acts 4.12; 5.31; 10.43; 13.38–39; 26.18.

[59] J. Dunn notes that Luke omits Jesus' words to destroy the temple (Mark 14.58) only to reserve it for Stephen (Acts 6.14). He also omits the clean and unclean discussion in Mark 7.1–23 in order to highlight Peter's experience in Acts 10. Luke may have also omitted the death of the Baptist (Mark 6.17–29) in order to save the themes of that story for Acts 24.24–26. All this means that Luke foresaw what he wanted to discuss in Acts while writing his Gospel (*The Acts of the Apostles* [EC; Peterborough, UK: Epworth Press, 1996], xv).

[60] Acts 20.28: τὴν ἐκκλησίαν τοῦ θεοῦ, ἣν περιεποιήσατο διὰ τοῦ αἵματος τοῦ ἰδίου.

save that theme until Acts 20.28. Second, the verbal parallels between Mark 10.45^c and Acts 20.28 are poor.

Second, Luke may omit Mark 10.45^c because he does not want to detract from the soteriological emphasis in Luke 22.19–20. Luke knows that if he keeps Mark 10.45^c in Luke 22.27, then the climax of the narrative would move away from Luke 22.19–20.[61] The major shortcoming of this view is that it requires the inclusion of Luke 22.19–20 into the original Gospel of Luke. However, there are good reasons for including it.[62] Further, if including Luke 22.19–20 explains what Luke has done with Mark 10.45^c, then that is all the more reason to support its inclusion.[63]

In conclusion, Luke is aware of Mark 10.41–45, and he places the same story in Luke 22.24–27. It is ultimately unknown why Luke omits the material parallel to Mark 10.45^c. The best suggestions are that he wants to postpone the impact of the atoning value of Jesus' death until Acts 20.28, or that he does not want to take the climax away from Luke 22.19–20.

Source	Supposed Tradition	Exemplar	Similarity	Further Comments
Luke 22.27	Ransom Logion^{a-b}	Mark 10.45^{a-b}	S4	

2.6.2 1Peter 1.18–19

Mark 10.45^c καὶ δοῦναι τὴν ψυχὴν αὐτοῦ λύτρον ἀντὶ πολλῶν

1Peter 1.18–19   εἰδότες ὅτι οὐ φθαρτοῖς, ἀργυρίῳ ἢ χρυσίῳ, ἐλυτρώθητε ἐκ τῆς ματαίας ὑμῶν ἀναστροφῆς πατροπαραδότου ἀλλὰ τιμίῳ αἵματι ὡς ἀμνοῦ ἀμώμου καὶ ἀσπίλου Χριστοῦ

---

[61] Supporting this view are Fitzmyer, *The Gospel According to Luke*, 2.1413–14, and A. Hentschel, *Diakonia im Neuen Testament* (WUNT 2/226; Tübingen: Mohr Siebeck, 2007), 288.

[62] There is a small textual tradition in the Western text (D it$^{a, d, ff2, i, l}$) that omits Luke 22.19^b–20. While the omission could be preferred as a Western non-interpolation, the overwhelming amount of external witnesses support the inclusion of 22.19^b–20 (Fitzmyer, *The Gospel According to Luke*, 2.1387–89; Metzger, *Textual Commentary*, 148–50). Also, the deviations from Lucan style in 22.19^b–20 are no greater than the deviations in the immediate context of 22.17–19^a, nor are they any greater than the deviations in other canonical Last Supper narratives (K. Petzer, "Style and Text in the Lucan Narrative of the Institution of the Lord's Supper," *NTS* 37 [1991]: 113–29).

[63] It may be significant that Luke is the only gospel to include the words, τὸ ὑπὲρ ὑμῶν διδόμενον, in the bread section of his Last Supper (Luke 22.19). Perhaps Luke has blended some of the language from Mark 10.45^c into Luke 22.19. However, this makes the absence of λύτρον a difficulty.

The influence of the ransom logion[c] on the traditional material in 1 Peter 1.18–19 is ambiguous.[64] -λυτ is the only shared vocabulary with the exemplar. There is evidence that -λυτ vocabulary is used elsewhere with reference to the effectiveness of Jesus' death without also being dependent on the ransom logion[c].[65] Further, it is likely that use of ἐλυτρώθητε in 1 Peter 1.18 is partially due to influence from Isaiah 52.3, where the Lord declares: οὐ μετὰ ἀργυρίου λυτρωθήσεσθε.

Having said this, I still include 1 Peter 1.18–19 as an ambiguous reception of the ransom logion[c]. It is possible that the ransom logion is influencing 1 Peter's use of λύτρόω in 1.18–19 in that the author may be interpreting Isaiah 52.3 through the lens of the ransom logion[c]. Several modern commentators consider this to be plausible.[66] The inclination of Early Christian writers, especially Origen and Eusebius, to use 1 Peter 1.18–19 in connection with the ransom logion[c] reinforces this plausibility.[67]

Assuming that the ransom logion[c] is influencing 1 Peter 1.18–19, then how is it being understood?[68] To answer this question, we will focus on the price given for the ransom, that is, οὐ φθαρτοῖς, ἀργυρίῳ ἢ χρυσίῳ...ἀλλὰ τιμίῳ αἵματι ὡς ἀμνοῦ ἀμώμου καὶ ἀσπίλου Χριστοῦ.[69] There could be several allusions here to the Jewish Scriptures.[70] Isaiah 52.3 has already been identified. It explains the negative aspect of the price (οὐ φθαρτοῖς, ἀργυρίῳ ἢ χρυσίῳ). The influence is more vague regarding the background to the positive aspect (ἀλλὰ τιμίῳ αἵματι ὡς ἀμνοῦ ἀμώμου καὶ ἀσπίλου Χρισ-

---

[64] The lead participle, εἰδότες, suggests known traditions (cf. Romans 5.3; 6.9; 1 Corinthians 15.58; 2 Corinthians 4.14; 5.6; Galatians 2.16; Ephesians 6.9; Colossians 3.24; 1 Thessalonians 1.4; etc).

[65] Hebrews 9.12; 1 Clement 12.7.

[66] J. Michaels states: "Peter's interest in the ransom price comes...from the interpretation of Jesus' death embodied in the Gospel tradition (specifically the λύτρον ἀντὶ πολλῶν of Mark 10.45 // Matthew 20.28)...so Peter draws his language from Isa 52.3 but his thought from Christian reflection on Jesus' death" (*1 Peter* [WBC 49; Waco: Word Books, 1988], 63). Also see P. Achtemeier, *1 Peter* (Hermeneia; Philadelphia: Fortress Press, 1996), 127; J. Elliott, *1 Peter: A New Translation with Introduction and Commentary* (ABC 37B; New York: Doubleday, 2000), 370.

[67] See Origen and Eusebius below (4.3 and 4.10).

[68] The main difficulty with this question is that the traditions in 1 Peter 1.18–21 are so subtle that it is hard to be confident about the presence of any particular one (including the ransom logion[c]).

[69] Simply because the dative is used rather than the genitive of price does not mean that the idea of ransom price is not involved (Contra Achtemeier, *1 Peter*, 128). If the thought is coming from Isaiah 52.3, where the idea of price is present, then there is no reason to think it is not also present here. Plus, in Revelation 5.9 the dative (with ἐν) is used where the blood of Christ is the price. Also, Origen, *Commentary on Matthew* 20.28, groups together 1 Peter 1.18 and 1 Corinthians 7.23 (genitive of price).

[70] The Roman practice of manumission of slaves is also a possible background (Achtemeier, *1 Peter*, 127; Michaels, *1 Peter*, 64).

τοῦ). The "unblemished and spotless lamb" is some kind of allusion to a Hebrew cultic practice or scripture. There are three more specific explanations of these words.[71]

(1) Ἀμνοῦ ἀμώμου καὶ ἀσπίλου is a reference to the Passover lamb.[72] There is early evidence that Christians thought of Jesus as the Passover lamb (1Corinthians 5.7; John 1.29; 19.36). We also know that the author of 1Peter has just made an allusion to Isaiah 52.3. Perhaps the author is now thinking of Isaiah 52.4, which mentions Israel's time in Egypt and sparks thoughts of deliverance from Egypt and of the Passover lamb.

(2) Ἀμνοῦ ἀμώμου καὶ ἀσπίλου is a general reference to the Hebrew sacrificial system.[73] This explanation relies on the conceptual and verbal inequities between the lamb in 1Peter 1.19 and the Passover lamb of the Exodus. Conceptually, the Exodus redemption happened, not because of the Passover lamb, but because of YHWH's powerful arm (λυτρώσομαι ὑμᾶς ἐν βραχίονι ὑψηλῷ [Exodus 6.6]). Verbally, the Passover lamb is expected to be τέλειον (Exodus 12.5), not ἀμώμου (1Peter 1.19).[74] These objections lead to the thesis that the lamb of 1Peter 1.19 should be thought of in general terms of the Hebrew sacrificial system, where the sacrifices function to remove sin and are required to be ἄμωμος (ἄσπιλος is not in the LXX).[75]

(3) Ἀμνοῦ ἀμώμου καὶ ἀσπίλου is a reference to Isaiah 53.7.[76] This is the most provable explanation, even though the only connective word is ἀμνός. The author of 1Peter believes that Isaiah 53 finds fulfillment in Jesus (1Peter 2.22–25). Specifically 1Peter 2.23, which reflects on Jesus' silence in the face of abuse, is influenced by Isaiah 53.7. Given that the author believes that Jesus is parallel to the silent lamb in Isaiah 53.7, then it is probable that the lamb in 1Peter 1.19 also alludes to Isaiah 53.7. The adjectives, ἀμώμου καὶ ἀσπίλου, can be explained as sacrificial language used to comment on Jesus' innocence as expressed in Isaiah 53.7, 9/1Peter 2.22–23. This explanation is congruent with all the other uses of ἀμνός in the New Testament and

---

[71] In addition to these three, W. van Unnik suggests that a Jewish proselyte ceremony best explains all the language in 1Peter 1.18–19 ("The Redemption in 1Peter 1:18–19 and the Problem of the First Epistle of Peter," in *Sparsa Collecta: The Collected Essays of W. C. van Unnik* [*NovTSup* 30; Leiden: Brill, 1980], 3–82). For a critique see Achtemeier, *1 Peter*, 130.

[72] F. Beare, *The First Epistle of Peter* (Oxford: The Alden Press, 1947), 80; E. Best, *1 Peter* (NCB; London: Oliphants, 1971), 90; P. Davids, *The First Epistle of Peter* (NICNT; Grand Rapids: Eerdmans, 1990), 72.

[73] Achtemeier, *1 Peter*, 128–29.

[74] In my opinion, it is not necessary to make a rigid distinction between τέλειον and ἀμώμου, especially since ἄμωμος is used elsewhere to translate the word in question from Exodus 12.5, תמים (Exodus 29.1; Leviticus 1.10; *et al*).

[75] The deliverance in 1Peter 1.18 is from a former way of life. However, the association between sin and the former way of life is surely present.

[76] Elliott, *1 Peter*, 373–74.

Apostolic Fathers, where it is used either in a quotation of Isaiah 53.7 (Acts 8.32; 1Clement 16.7; Barnabas 5.2) or in a combination of Isaiah 53.7 with the Passover lamb (John 1.29).[77] It may even be possible that Revelation 5.6, 9 represents a vague combination of Isaiah 53.7, the Passover lamb, and the ransom logion[c].[78]

In conclusion, the best explanation of the phrase, ἀμνοῦ ἀμώμου καὶ ἀσπίλου, is that it is drawing on Isaiah 53.7 or perhaps a confluence of Isaiah 53.7 and the Passover lamb. What remains uncertain is whether there is also influence from the ransom logion[c]. The thickly traditional nature of the material in 1Peter 1.18–19 makes it difficult to say with any confidence. On a separate note, if the ransom logion[c] is influencing 1Peter 1.18–19, then this is the first occurrence of what becomes a pattern, that is, identifying "blood," rather than "soul," as the ransom payment.

Source	Supposed Tradition	Exemplar	Similarity	Further Comments
1Peter 1.18–19	Ransom Logion[c]	Mark 10.45[c]	S4	ἐλυτρώθητε is the only connection; blood is the ransom price
	Isaiah 52.3	Isaiah 52.3	S3	
	Isaiah 53.7	Isaiah 53.7	S4	ἀμνοῦ is the only connection
	Passover lamb	N/A	N/A	

---

[77] The Passover is a very important concept for John, as is the concept of Jesus being the Passover lamb (John 19.36). In John 1.29, Jesus is presented as the lamb of God who takes away the sins of the world. This combination of atonement with the lamb may actually be the combination of the Passover lamb with influence from Isaiah 53 (specifically 53.7). For a similar combination see Melito's *Peri Pascha* 4; 12; 64; 67.

[78] In Revelation 5.6 the author sees a slain lamb (ἀρνίον...ἐσφαγμένον). Scholars typically understand this lamb as reflective of either Isaiah 53.7 or the Passover lamb (G. Beale, *The Book of Revelation* [NIGTC; Grand Rapids: Eerdmans, 1999], 51, though also see G. Schimanowski, *Die himmlische Liturgie in der Apokalypse des Johannes: Die frühjüdischen Traditionen in Offenbarung 4–5 unter Einschluß der Hekhalotliteratur* [WUNT 2/154; Tübingen: Mohr Siebeck, 2002], 222–23). In Revelation 5.9, the slain lamb is mentioned again, and in a context that is conceptually close to the ransom logion.

Mark 10.45[c]   δοῦναι τὴν ψυχὴν αὐτοῦ   λύτρον   ἀντὶ πολλῶν
Revelation 5.9   ἐσφάγης...   ἠγόρασας τῷ θεῷ... ἐκ πάσης φυλῆς...

See The Acts of Thomas 72 below for an example of reading Revelation 5.9 with the ransom logion. There is also a potential example in The Gospel of Truth (I,3 20.13–14), but there the presence of the ransom logion is in serious question.

2.7 Conclusion

There are two important motifs that accompany the ransom logion in the New Testament, both of which continue into the next two periods from the New Testament through 200 CE, and from 200 CE through 300 CE.

First, the ransom logion is accompanied by a love motif. This motif focuses primarily on Jesus' love for the community, and also on the love that the members of the community ought to have for one another (Galatians 2.20, Ephesians 5.2, 25, and the Johannine literature).[79] First-century Greco-Roman religion emphasized the distance, rather than the love, between the deity and the worshipper.[80] As Christianity moves into the Greco-Roman world, it appears to have taken advantage of this lacunae in pagan worship by emphasizing the love of God and of his Son for humanity.[81] The undoubted effectiveness of this motif explains its general inclusion in the social memory of early Christians, and specifically as a rationale for the self-giving element in the ransom logion[c] – Jesus gave himself *for us because he loves us.*[82]

Second, the ransom logion is accompanied by influence from Isaianic servant texts. 1Timothy 2.6 and Titus 2.14 read the ransom logion alongside influence from Isaiah 42.6–7; 49.6–8. The ransom logion is not accompanied by Isaiah 42.6–7; 49.6–8 elsewhere in the New Testament, nor in the Early Christian periods. However, Isaiah 42.6–7; 49.6–8 are similarly used elsewhere to promote gentile inclusion. Galatians 1.4 reads the ransom logion alongside influence from Isaiah 53. The traditional nature of Galatians 1.4 means that Isaiah 53 may be one of the earliest interpretive paradigms for

---

[79] Other passages that combine an emphasis on Jesus' love and sacrifice include 1Clement 49.1–6, Revelation 1.5, and Romans 8.32–37. Jesus' love for humanity may represent the ascription of an activity to Jesus that is typically reserved for YHWH, especially in Exodus 34.6–7. It could be explored whether other exalted figures, who were thought to have once dwelt on the earth (e.g. Moses, David, Enoch, etc.), are ever said to be agents of YHWH's love towards the covenant community.

[80] J. Bremmer, *The Rise of Christianity through the Eyes of Gibbon, Harnack and Rondey Stark* (Groningen: Barkhuis, 2010), 71–72.

[81] Christianity inherits the notion of divine love from Judaism (e.g. Exodus 34.6–7).

[82] W. Meeks states about the early Christian community: "The notions that the members are peculiarly 'loved' by God and that they are 'known' by him are also striking...Repetitive use of such special terms for the group and its members plays a role in the process of resocialization by which an individual's identity is revised and knit together with the identity of the group" (*The First Urban Christians* [New Haven: Yale University Press, 1983], 85–86).

reading the ransom logion[c].[83] However, it is not nearly as widespread among New Testament receptions of the ransom logion as is the love motif.[84]

Another observation is that within the New Testament, all the primary occurrences of the ransom logion are limited to the ransom logion[c], and none of these are exactly alike. This suggests that the ransom logion[c] has an independent oral existence apart from its incorporation into Mark 10.45/Matthew 20.28.[85] The ransom logion[a–b] occurs nowhere in the New Testament outside of Mark 10.45/Matthew 20.28, which means this tradition likely began with Mark or his immediate predecessors. It may be that Mark is the first to join the ransom logion[a–b] with the ransom logion[c].[86]

Finally, there are a few contributions that the New Testament receptions of the ransom logion make to the three debatable issues surrounding Mark 10.45/Matthew 20.28, which are introduced above in 1.2. First, concerning the (dis)association of the ransom logion with the Eucharist, Luke's placement of Mark 10.41–45[b] in Luke 22.24–27 is near the statements about the bread and the wine at the Last Supper (Luke 22.15–20). This could result from Luke's dependence on an early (hypothetical) non-Markan source, which may have the material parallel to Mark 10.41–45 next to these statements because the Mark 10.41–45 material originated in the context of the Eucharist. However, Luke's placement of Mark 10.41–45 probably has more to do with Jesus' condemnation of the one who would betray him (Luke 22.21–23) than with the development of the ransom logion in a Eucharistic setting.[87] Another notable item is 1Peter 1.18–19's identification of Jesus' blood as the ransom payment. If 1Peter 1.18–19 is aware of the ransom logion that includes soul as the ransom payment, then 1Peter is the first text to replace soul with blood. There is no indication that the author of 1Peter uses Last Supper traditions to guide this replacement.[88] The replacement of soul with blood later becomes a pattern, especially in Origen and Eusebius, both of whom are guided by 1Peter 1.18–19.

---

[83] It is an enduring mystery why Isaiah 53 appears to influence early traditional statements regarding the atoning value of Jesus' death (Romans 4.25; 1Corinthians 15.3; 1Peter 2.21–25), but is also spread so thinly across the New Testament (see n. 38 above).

[84] There may be additional influence from Isaiah 53 on the ransom logion in 1Peter 1.18–19. K. Romaniuk believes that all the above texts from the Pastorals, Galatians, and Ephesians originate from reflection on Isaiah 53 ("L'origine des formules pauliniennes 'Le Christ s'est livré pour nous', 'Le Christ nous a aimés et s'est livré pour nous'," *NovT* 5/1 [1962]: 55–76).

[85] A common oral tradition is the best explanation of the differences between receptions of the ransom logion[c] in the New Testament.

[86] See 1.5.1 for a more detailed discussion.

[87] See 5.3.1 below.

[88] By *Last Supper traditions*, I mean those that are in any way similar to the ones described in the Synoptics and Paul (Matthew 26.26–29; Mark 14.22–25; Luke 22.15–20; 1Corinthians 11.23–25).

Second, concerning a preexistent coming in Mark 10.45/Matthew 20.28, there is nothing in the New Testament receptions of the ransom logion that contributes to this issue.

Third, concerning the scriptural background of Mark 10.45/Matthew 20.28, Galatians 1.4 (Cf. 1Peter 1.18–19) combines the ransom logion[c] with influence from Isaiah 53. There are no uses of the ransom logion with Daniel 7; 9 or Isaiah 43 in the New Testament. The fact that the ransom logion is not received with Daniel 7 may be expected since Daniel 7 requires a connection with the Son of Man from the ransom logion[a], which is absent from New Testament outside of Mark 10.45/Matthew 20.28.

Chapter 3

The Reception of the Ransom Logion
from the New Testament through 200 CE

3.1 Introduction

There are six receptions of the ransom logion in the period from the New Testament through 200 CE. They are as follows: Clement of Alexandria, *Paedagogus* 1.9.85.1–2; *Quis Dives Salvetur* 37.4; Irenaeus, *Against Heresies* 5.1.1 (Cf. 1Clement 49.6); Epistle to Diognetus 9.2; The Gospel of Truth I,3 20.14; The Sentences of Sextus 336. These six are all the receptions of Mark 10.45/Matthew 20.28 that are listed in *Biblia Patristica* through 200 CE.[1]

This chapter gives some attention to the dates of the receptions. This is because they all must fit into the period from the New Testament through 200 CE. However, once it is determined that a reception likely fits into that period, there is not a further attempt to provide a more detailed chronological arrangement. The chapter begins with Clement of Alexandria.

3.2 Clement of Alexandria, *Paedagogus* 1.9.85.1–2; *Quis Dives Salvetur* 37.4[2]

Mark 10.45	ὁ υἱὸς τοῦ ἀνθρώπου οὐκ ἦλθεν διακονηθῆναι ἀλλὰ διακονῆσαι καὶ δοῦναι τὴν ψυχὴν αὐτοῦ λύτρον ἀντὶ πολλῶν
Paedagogus 1.9.85.1–2	Οὐκ ἦλθον...διακονηθῆναι, ἀλλὰ διακονῆσαι...δοῦναι τὴν ψυχὴν τὴν ἑαυτοῦ λύτρον ἀντὶ πολλῶν
Quis Dives Salvetur 37.4	λύτρον ἑαυτὸν ἐπιδιδούς

---

[1] *Biblia Patristica* 1.273–74. In order to be consistent, every text is examined that *Biblia Patristica* lists as sufficiently similar to Mark 10.45/Matthew 20.28. However, some texts, such as The Sentences of Sextus 336, lack a strong similarity to Mark 10.45/Matthew 20.28.

[2] The primary text for *Paedagogus* comes from M. Marcovich, *Clementis Alexandrini Paedagogus* (VCSup 61; Leiden: Brill, 2002). The primary text for *Quis Dives Salvetur* comes from O. Stählin, *Clemens Alexandrinus III. Stromata Buch VII und VIII, Excerpta Ex Theodoto – Eclogae Propheticae, Quis Dives Salvetur – Fragmente* (GCS; Berlin: Akademie-Verlag, 1970).

Clement of Alexandria's writings date from the latter part of the second century into the first decade of the third. There are two places where Clement receives the ransom logion: *Paedagogus* 1.9.85.1–2 and *Quis Dives Salvetur* 37.4. Both receptions contain themes from John's Gospel. Also, both receptions contain an incarnation motif, which probably results from the influence of Philippians 2.6–8. In what follows, we examine both receptions, starting with *Paedagogus* since it contains the fuller rendition of the ransom logion.[3]

3.2.1 Paedagogus 1.9.85.1–2

The reception of the ransom logion in *Paedagogus* 1.9.85.1–2 occurs within a chiasm, which I identified and reconstructed. The chiasm is immediately preceded by an allusion to Isaiah 43.2 (*Paedagogus* 1.9.84.4).[4] The chiasm itself is as follows:

(A) Τοιοῦτος ἡμῶν ὁ παιδαγωγός, ἀγαθὸς ἐνδίκως.
(B)   Οὐκ ἦλθον, φησί, διακονηθῆναι, ἀλλὰ διακονῆσαι. Διὰ τοῦτο εἰσάγεται ἐν τῷ εὐαγγελίῳ κεκμηκώς,
(C)   ὁ κάμνων ὑπὲρ ἡμῶν καὶ δοῦναι τὴν ψυχὴν τὴν ἑαυτοῦ λύτρον ἀντὶ πολλῶν ὑπισχνούμενος.
(D)   Τοῦτον γὰρ μόνον ὁμολογεῖ ἀγαθὸν εἶναι ποιμένα·
(C¹)   μεγαλόδωρος οὖν ὁ τὸ μέγιστον ὑπὲρ ἡμῶν, τὴν ψυχὴν αὐτοῦ, ἐπιδιδούς,
(B¹)   καὶ μεγαλωφελὴς καὶ φιλάνθρωπος, ὅτι καὶ ἀνθρώπων, ἐξὸν εἶναι κύριον, ἀδελφὸς εἶναι βεβούληται·
(A¹) ὃ δὲ καὶ εἰς τοσοῦτον ἀγαθός, ὥστε ἡμῶν καὶ ὑπεραποθανεῖν.[5]

---

[3] Clement likely receives the ransom logion from Matthew's Gospel, which he quotes from as much as the other three canonical gospels combined (C. Kannengiesser, *Handbook of Patristic Exegesis* [ed. D. Bingham; BAC 1; Leiden: Brill, 2004], 507). For discussion of Clement's use of the Gospels, see C. Cosaert, *The Text of the Gospels in Clement of Alexandria* (NTGF 9; Atlanta: Society of Biblical Literature, 2008). According to Cosaert, "Clement's Gospel citations focus almost exclusively around the words of Jesus. His tendency for the majority of these quotations is to cite the passage from memory. This can often result in a conflation of similar passages or even a very loose citation" (ibid., 30).

[4] The shared vocabulary between Clement's version of Isaiah 43.2 and the LXX consists only of ἐὰν διαβαίνω, followed by a negation. The brevity of the allusion is consistent with Van den Hoek's observation that Clement's "borrowings are heavily abbreviated and condensed" ("Techniques of Quotation in Clement of Alexandria: A View of Ancient Literary Wording Methods," *VC* 50 [1996]: 235). The allusion to Isaiah 43.2 may be significant since Isaiah 43.3–4 is one of the texts that are often considered to lie behind Mark 10.45/Matthew 20.28 (See 1.2.1.3 above). If Clement believes there is a connection between the first few verses of Isaiah 43 and the ransom logion, then it is possible that his allusion to Isaiah 43.2 functions as the catalyst for his use of the ransom logion. However, the separation of Isaiah 43.2 from the boundaries of the chiasm makes this difficult to determine.

[5] (A) Such is our instructor, righteously good
   (B) I came not, he says, to be served, but to serve. Therefore, he is introduced in the gospel as wearied,

The chiastic structure is not difficult to observe. A and A¹ emphasize goodness (ἀγαθός). Goodness is also the turning point in D. C includes the ransom logionᶜ. This is repeated in C¹ as ὑπέρ ἡμῶν, τὴν ψυχὴν αὐτοῦ, ἐπιδιδούς. Perhaps the most interesting part of the chiasm is B and B¹. B contains the ransom logionᵃ⁻ᵇ (Οὐκ ἦλθον, φησί, διακονηθῆναι, ἀλλὰ διακονῆσαι). This is mirrored in B¹ with a reference to the voluntary incarnation of the Lord as a human (ἐξὸν εἶναι κύριον, ἀδελφὸς εἶναι βεβούληται). Clement's contrast between the position that Jesus held in his (preexistent) Lordship with his voluntary desire to humble himself as a human may be influenced by Philippians 2.6–7, where the preexistent Jesus voluntarily undergoes his κένωσις and becomes a human. Therefore, at the very least, Clement gives an incarnational interpretation to the ransom logionᵃ⁻ᵇ, and this interpretation may be influenced by Philippians 2.6–7.

There are themes from John's Gospel throughout the chiasm. The ransom logionᵃ⁻ᵇ (B) is separated from the ransom logionᶜ (C) by a reference to the "gospel," presumably John 4.6, where Jesus is presented as "weary."[6] Thinking of the ransom logion alongside John's Gospel leads Clement to John's story of the good shepherd (D),[7] which Clement alluded to earlier in *Paedagogus* 1.9.84.2 amidst a reference to Ezekiel's shepherd (Ezekiel 34.14–16). Given Clement's transition from the ransom logion (B–C) to the good shepherd (D), we can suggest that in C¹ and A¹, when Clement states that Jesus gives his life/dies for us, he may be focusing on those aspects of the good shepherd story that mirror the ransom logion (John 10.11, 15).

In B¹ there is a love motif expressed by the word φιλάνθρωπος. Love is a major theme in Clement's next reception of ransom logionᶜ in *Quis Dives Salvetur*.

3.2.2 Quis Dives Salvetur 37.4

The reception of the ransom logionᶜ in *Quis Dives Salvetur* 37.4 is preceded by a discussion of what Clement perceives are the feminine characteristics involved when God expresses his love for us, the greatest proof of which is his begetting Jesus out of himself (αὐτὸς ἐγέννησεν ἐξ αὐτοῦ) (37.1–2).

(C) The one who toiled for us and promised to give his life as a ransom for many.
    (D) For this one alone is confessed to be the good shepherd.
    (C¹) Therefore, he is generous who gives the greatest thing for us: his life;
    (B¹) and exceedingly beneficent and loving to humankind, in that, while it was right for him to be Lord, he wished to be a human.
    (A¹) and he was so good that he died for us.
[6] The vocabulary is κάμνω in *Paedagogus*, and κοπιάω in John 4.6.
[7] The language of ἀγαθός dominates the chiasm though it does not occur regularly in John's Gospel (John 1.46; 5.29; 7.12), and specifically not in the story of the good (καλός) shepherd.

This notion of begetting gives way to the incarnation, in which God's preexistent begotten self comes down (κατῆλθε), clothes himself as a man (ἄνθρωπον ἐνέδυ), and voluntarily suffers human conditions (τὰ ἀνθρώπων ἑκὼν ἔπαθεν), in order that he might bring us to his strength (37.3).[8] This incarnation narrative immediately precedes the ransom logion[c] (37.4). It is possible that Clement substitutes this narrative for the ransom logion[a–b], just as he did in B and B[1] from the chiasm in *Paedagogus*.

In *Quis Dives Salvetur* 37.4 itself, Clement focuses on a particular moment in Jesus' life when Jesus was about to be offered up (σπένδεσθαι) and give himself as a ransom (λύτρον ἑαυτὸν ἐπιδιδούς). The moment Clement is thinking of is the Upper Room Discourse beginning in John 13.1, when John states that Jesus knew his time had come to depart from this world. Clement's next statements are a conglomeration of ideas from the Upper Room Discourse and other parts of the Johannine corpus that center on Jesus' love as expressed in his self-sacrifice. Clement relates the Johannine ideas as follows: καινὴν ἡμῖν διαθήκην καταλιμπάνει (John 13.34)·[9] ἀγάπην ὑμῖν δίδωμι τὴν ἐμήν (John 14.27)·[10] τίς δέ ἐστιν αὕτη καὶ πόση; ὑπὲρ ἡμῶν ἑκάστου κατέθηκε τὴν ψυχὴν τὴν ἀνταξίαν τῶν ὅλων· (John 10.11, 15, 17; 15.12–13; 1John 3.16)[11] ταύτην ἡμᾶς ὑπὲρ ἀλλήλων ἀνταπαιτεῖ (John 13.14, 34–35; 15.12, 17; 1John 3.11, 23; 4.7, 11–12; 2John 5).

In sum, in both *Paedagogus* 1.9.85.1–2 and *Quis Dives Salvetur* 37.4, Clement receives the ransom logion in a similar manner. In both texts, but especially in *Quis Dives Salvetur* 37.4, Clement receives the ransom logion alongside themes from John's Gospel, such as love and self-sacrifice. Also in both texts, but especially in *Paedagogus* 1.9.85.1–2, Clement demonstrates his understanding that the ransom logion[a–b] is interchangeable with an incarnational narrative. This interchange may result from the influence of the incarnational narrative in Philippians 2.6–8.

---

[8] As in *Paedagogus*, this incarnation narrative in *Quis Dives Salvetur* 37.1–3 may be influenced by Philippians 2.6–8, which follows the same pattern of the incarnation of the divine as a man, followed by voluntary human suffering.

[9] Clement substitutes διαθήκην for John's ἐντολήν. It is unlikely that Clement makes this substitution because he finds the vocabulary of ἐντολήν as the distasteful language of the Jewish scriptures (See *Stromata* 2.6.29.2 where Clement states...τὴν διαθήκην καὶ τὰς ἐντολάς...δυνάμει μία οὖσαι...διὰ υἱοῦ παρ' ἑνὸς θεοῦ χορηγοῦνται). Instead, Clement probably makes the substitution unintentionally in a manner similar to his substitution in John 14.27 (See n. 10).

[10] Clement substitutes ἀγάπην for John's εἰρήνη.

[11] Ψυχὴν may be a reference to Mark 10.45/Matthew 20.28[c], but it is more likely that Clement's thought remains in John, which means he must be drawing on John 10.11, 15, 17; 15.12–13; 1John 3.16. These are the only places that could match Clement's thought: ὑπὲρ ἡμῶν ἑκάστου κατέθηκε τὴν ψυχήν.

Source	Supposed Tradition	Exemplar	Similarity	Further Comments
Clement of Alexandria, *Paedagogus* 1.9.85.1–2	Ransom Logion	Mark 10.45	S1	
	Isaiah 43.2	Isaiah 43.2	S3	Outside the chiasm
	John 10.11, 15	John 10.11, 15	S3	
	Love motif	N/A	N/A	
	Incarnation (Philippians 2.6–7)	Philippians 2.6–7	S4	Mirrors the ransom logion[a–b]
Clement of Alexandria, *Quis Dives Salvetur* 37.4	Ransom Logion[c]	Mark 10.45[c]	S3	
	Various Johannine texts, but primarily 13.34; 14.27; 10.11, 15; 13.14	John 13.34; 14.27; 10.11, 15; 13.14	S2–3	Used to emphasize love and self-sacrifice
	Love motif	N/A	N/A	Intertwined with Johannine texts
	Incarnation (Philippians 2.6–8)	Philippians 2.6–8	S4	Precedes ransom logion[c]

3.3 Irenaeus, *Against Heresies* 5.1.1 (Cf. 1Clement 49.6)[12]

Mark 10.45[c]   καὶ δοῦναι τὴν ψυχὴν αὐτοῦ λύτρον ἀντὶ πολλῶν

Against Heresies 5.1.1 (21, 29–31)   Τῷ ἰδίῳ οὖν αἵματι λυτρωσαμένου ἡμᾶς τοῦ Κυρίου καὶ δόντος τὴν ψυχὴν αὐτοῦ ἀντὶ τῆς ἡμετέρας ψυχῆς καὶ τὴν σάρκα τὴν ἑαυτοῦ ἀντὶ τῶν ἡμετέρων σαρκῶν

1Clement 49.6   ἐν ἀγάπῃ προσελάβετο ἡμᾶς ὁ δεσπότης· διὰ τὴν ἀγάπην, ἣν ἔσχεν πρὸς ἡμᾶς, τὸ αἷμα αὐτοῦ ἔδωκεν ὑπὲρ ἡμῶν Ἰησοῦς Χριστὸς ὁ Κύριος ἡμῶν ἐν θελήματι Θεοῦ, καὶ τὴν σάρκα ὑπὲρ τῆς σαρκὸς ἡμῶν καὶ τὴν ψυχὴν ὑπὲρ τῶν ψυχῶν ἡμῶν[13]

---

[12] The primary text for Irenaeus is from A. Rousseau, *Irénée de Lyon, Contre les Hérésie Livre V* (vol. 2; SC 153; Paris: Éditions du Cerf, 1969). The text for 1Clement is from B. Ehrman, *The Apostolic Fathers* (2 vols.; LCL 24, 25; Cambridge: Harvard University Press, 2003), 1.34–151.

[13] Unlike Irenaeus, *Against Heresies* 5.1.1, 1Clement 49.6 is not listed in *Biblia Patristica* as a reception of Mark 10.45/Matthew 20.28. There are two differences between 1Clement 49.6 and *Against Heresies* 5.1.1 that may have prevented its inclusion. First, 1Clement 49.6 uses ὑπέρ instead of ἀντί. Second, and more importantly, 1Clement 49.6 does not have -λυτ language. If 1Clement 49.6 were listed in *Biblia Patristica*, then I would classify it as a reception of the ransom logion[c] alongside a love motif. Love is the dominant theme of 1Clement 49–50.3. H. Lona mentions Galatians 2.20 and Ephesians 5.2 as possible backgrounds to 1Clement 49.6 (*Der erste Clemensbrief* [KAV 2; Göttingen: Vandenhoeck & Ruprecht, 1998], 529). Both Galatians 2.20 and Ephesians 5.2 are discussed above in chapter two as receptions of the ransom logion[c] with a love motif.

Irenaeus' writings come from the last two decades of the second century. His major work, *Against Heresies*, survives mainly in a Latin translation. There are, however, many fragments of his original Greek that are preserved in works by later writers. One of those fragments from *Against Heresies* 5.1.1 contains a reception of the ransom logion[c].[14]

Upon initial examination, the similarity that the fragment bears to Mark 10.45/Matthew 20.28[c] appears promising. They share the concept of self-sacrifice. They also share the language of δίδωμι, λυτ-, ψυχή αὐτοῦ, and ἀντί.[15] In fact, if all Irenaeus said was "λυτρωσαμένου ἡμᾶς τοῦ Κυρίου καὶ δόντος τὴν ψυχὴν αὐτοῦ ἀντὶ [ἡμῶν]" then we could be confident that this is a very strong reception of the ransom logion[c].[16] However, these words are not isolated, but are part of a traditional statement that Irenaeus has drawn from 1Clement 49.6 or a similar tradition (see below).[17] Some of the ideas in the traditional statement – that Jesus gives his soul specifically for our souls, and the juxtaposition of soul and flesh – are foreign to Mark 10.45/Matthew 20.28.[18]

Against Heresies 5.1.1	δόντος τὴν ψυχὴν αὐτοῦ ἀντὶ τῆς ἡμετέρας ψυχῆς καὶ τὴν σάρκα τὴν ἑαυτοῦ ἀντὶ τῶν ἡμετέρων σαρκῶν
1Clement 49.6	ἔδωκεν...τὴν σάρκα ὑπὲρ τῆς σαρκὸς ἡμῶν καὶ τὴν ψυχὴν ὑπὲρ τῶν ψυχῶν ἡμῶν

Besides the traditional material, the other important similarity between 1Clement 49.6 and *Against Heresies* 5.1.1 is that both texts understand Jesus' blood as of primary importance over his soul and flesh.[19] There is some evi-

---

[14] The fragment is preserved in the writings of Theodoret.

[15] There are some Greek fragments that read ὑπέρ instead of ἀντί.

[16] Also providing strength is that just a few lines earlier, Irenaeus demonstrates dependence on 1Timothy 2.6 – redemptionem semetipsum dedit (5.1.1 [19, 10–11]); the retroverted Greek version reads ἀντίλυτρον ἑαυτὸν δοὺς (5.1.1 [2, 17–19]).

[17] Irenaeus is aware of 1Clement – he mentions the epistle in *Against Heresies* 3.3.3. I confirmed through a *Thesaurus Linguae Graecae* search of ψυχή, σάρξ, and δίδωμι that these are the only two places where this statement occurs that Jesus gives his soul and flesh for our soul and flesh. Therefore, it seems probable that Irenaeus is dependent on 1Clement for the statement. However, the fact that Irenaeus reverses the order of soul and flesh, and uses different possessive pronouns, means that he is likely either recalling the 1Clement text from memory, or is dependent on the same tradition as 1Clement while being independent of 1Clement itself.

[18] The presence of σάρξ in the traditional statement leads A. Lindemann to point out that ψυχή does not refer to the whole person, as in Mark 10.45, but only to his inner-self (*Die Clemensbriefe* [HNT 17; Tübingen: Mohr Siebeck, 1992], 145).

[19] Lindemann suggests that a trichotomist perspective is in play here (*Die Clemensbriefe*, 145). However, this is rejected by Lona (*Der erste Clemensbrief*, 530), and by A. Orbe, *Teología de San Ireneo I: Comentario al Libro V del «Adversus haereses»* (BAC 25; Madrid: La Editorial Catolica, 1985), 73.

dence that 1Clement 49.6 is dependent on 1Peter 1.18–19 for the blood motif.[20] However, the blood motif in *Against Heresies* 5.1.1 does not result from the influence of 1Peter 1.18–19, but from Ephesians 1.7. In *Against Heresies* 5.2.2 (33, 27–30), Irenaeus cites Ephesians 1.7 and so reveals the source of his understanding that Jesus has redeemed us by his blood.[21] So while both 1Clement 49.6 and *Against Heresies* 5.1.1 share traditional material that is similarly preceded by the primacy of Jesus' blood, they may draw the blood motif from different influences.

In conclusion, both *Against Heresies* 5.1.1 and 1Clement 49.6 contain similar traditional material. In both cases the traditional material is preceded by mention of Jesus' blood. In 1Clement 49.6, the mention of Jesus' blood may be influenced by 1Peter 1.18–19, whereas Irenaeus' mention of redemption by Jesus' blood is influenced, at least in part, by Ephesians 1.7. What remains uncertain is if *Against Heresies* 5.1.1 is additionally a strong reception of the ransom logion[c]. Certainly the wording of λυτρωσαμένου...καὶ δόντος τὴν ψυχὴν αὐτοῦ ἀντι is very similar to Mark 10.45/Matthew 20.28, but its placement within the traditional material makes it too difficult to decide.

Source	Supposed Tradition	Exemplar	Similarity	Further Comments
Irenaeus *Against Heresies* 5.1.1 (21, 29–31)	Ransom Logion[c]	Mark 10.45[c]	S2	Made ambiguous by traditional material
	Ephesians 1.7	Ephesians 1.7	S4	Confirmed through citation in 5.2.2 (33, 27–30); blood is part of the ransom payment

---

[20] There is a high probability that 1Clement is dependent on 1Peter (D. Hagner, *The Use of the Old and New Testaments in Clement of Rome* [NovTSup 34; Leiden: Brill, 1973], 239–46), and particularly on 1Peter 1.18–19 in 1Clement 7.4, where Clement describes Jesus' blood as τίμιον τῷ πατρὶ αὐτοῦ. Assuming that 1Clement 7.4 draws on 1Peter 1.18–19 when speaking of Jesus' precious blood, then we may suspect a similar dependence in 1Clement 49.6.

[21] The retroverted Greek reads: τῷ αἵματι αὐτοῦ ἐλυτρώσατο ἡμᾶς, καθὼς καὶ ὁ ἀπόστολος αὐτοῦ φησιν· Ἐν ᾧ ἔχομεν τὴν ἀπολύτρωσιν διὰ τοῦ αἵματος αὐτοῦ, τὴν ἄφεσιν τῶν ἁμαρτιῶν (*Against Heresies*, 5.2.2 [33, 27–30]). The Latin reads: sanguine suo redemit nos. Quemadmodum et Apostolus ejus ait: In quo habemus...(*Against Heresies*, 5.2.2 [32, 27–30]). Rousseau consistently makes the mistake of claiming that the citation is from Colossians 1.14 because of the failure to notice Irenaeus' dependence on the blood as the means of the redemption.

3.4 Epistle to Diognetus 9.2[22]

Mark 10.45^c　　καὶ δοῦναι τὴν ψυχὴν αὐτοῦ　　λύτρον　ἀντὶ πολλῶν
Diognetus 9.2　αὐτὸς [θεὸς] τὸν ἴδιον υἱὸν ἀπέδοτο　λύτρον　ὑπὲρ ἡμῶν

The Epistle to Diognetus is one of the most enigmatic writings in early Christianity. It is not mentioned in any ancient source. Our only knowledge of the text comes from a 13th–14th century manuscript that was burned in a fire in 1870, though not before being copied several times. The ambiguity as to the origin and text of Diognetus has produced an enormous amount of discussion regarding its unity,[23] authorship,[24] and date. In most cases, opinions regarding the date of Diognetus correspond to opinions about unity and authorship. However, since there is so much ambiguity surrounding the unity and authorship, scholars generally date Diognetus according to how it fits within the evolving Christian ethos of the second and third centuries. Since the purpose of the work is to defend and explain the Christian faith to one, Diognetus, the work can be widely categorized with the Apologists. More specifically, there is a growing consensus that Diognetus should be dated in the second half of the second century, with opinions tending towards one end or the other of that

---

[22] The primary text comes from Ehrman, *The Apostolic Fathers*, 2.130–59.

[23] The single manuscript of Diognetus mentions two breaks in the text – at 7.6, and at 10.8. It is clear that the line of thought before the break at 7.6 is the same thought that continues after the break (See παρουσία in 7.6 and 7.9). However, scholars feel less confident about the continuity of thought between what is before and after 10.8. Indeed, a clear majority of scholars think that chapters 11–12 are from a different author. Having said this, there are some scholars who have challenged the assumption that chapters 11–12 represent a work from a different author (C. Hill, *From the Lost Teaching of Polycarp: Identifying Irenaeus' Apostolic Presbyter and the Author of Ad Diognetum* [WUNT 186; Tübingen: Mohr Siebeck, 2006], 106–27; H. Lona, *An Diognet: Übersetzt und erklärt* [KFA 8; Freiburg: Herder, 2001], 43–47). Also see L. Barnard, who thinks the same author is combining two of his works ("The Epistle ad Diognetum. Two Units from One Author?," *ZNW* 56 [1965] 130–37).

[24] If one accepts the minority view that chapters 11–12 are original, then the author claims to be a "disciple of the apostles" and a "teacher of the gentiles" (11.1). More specific opinions regarding the authorship of chapters 1–10 and/or 11–12 have been wide-ranging. Some of the names suggested for 1–10 include Apollos, Clement of Rome, Quadratus, Justin Martyr, Marcion, Apelles, Aristides of Athens, Theophilus of Antioch, Hippolytus of Rome, Pantaenus, Lucian of Antioch, and Ambrosius. Suggestions for chapters 11–12 include Hippolytus of Rome, Pantaenus, and Melito of Sardis (Ehrman, *The Apostolic Fathers*, 124–26; R. Tanner, "The Epistle to Diognetus and Contemporary Greek Thought," in *Studia Patristica* 15 [ed. E. Livingstone; 1984], 497). Hill has recently put forward a case that Polycarp is behind the whole book (*From the Lost Teaching of Polycarp*, 128–70). Unfortunately, none of these suggestions are conclusive, and it is best to say that we do not know who wrote the book.

period.[25] Although the issues of unity, authorship, and date dominate much of the literature, another important issue concerns the Christian traditional material present in Diognetus.[26] The primary purpose of this section is to examine the use of the ransom logion[c] in Diognetus 9.2, and its connections with traditions gleaned from Isaiah 53.[27]

The reception of the ransom logion[c] in Diognetus 9.2 is acknowledged by most scholars who comment on that verse.[28] The primary similarity to Mark 10.45/Matthew 20.28[c] is the words, λύτρον ὑπὲρ ἡμῶν (within the Christian scriptures, λύτρον is a word peculiar to Mark 10.45/Matthew 20.28[c]).[29] The preceding phrase, αὐτὸς [θεὸς] τὸν ἴδιον υἱὸν ἀπέδοτο, could also parallel Mark 10.45/Matthew 20.28[c], but it is normally considered to be more reflective of a tradition similar to Romans 8.32.[30] Besides λύτρον ὑπὲρ ἡμῶν,

---

[25] Ehrman, *The Apostolic Fathers*, 127; P. Foster, "The Epistle to Diognetus," *ExpTim* 118/4 (2007): 164; Hill, *From the Lost Teaching of Polycarp*, 99–100; Tanner, "The Epistle to Diognetus," 495.

[26] Lona, *An Diognet*, 49–55; H. Marrou, *A Diognète: Introduction, édition critique, traduction et commentaire* (SC 29; Paris: Éditions du Cerf, 1951), 269–74; H. Meecham, *The Epistle to Diognetus: The Greek Text with Introduction, Translation, and Notes* (Manchester: Manchester University Press, 1949), 53–58. There is no hard evidence that the traditional material in Diognetus 1–10 comes from dependence on any early Christian writings known today, though this does not necessarily mean that these writings are unknown to the author of Diognetus.

[27] Preceding the ransom logion[c] in Diognetus 9.2 is a love motif (ὦ τῆς ὑπερβαλλούσης φιλανθρωπίας καὶ ἀγάπης τοῦ Θεοῦ), but its connection to the ransom logion[c] is insignificant.

[28] Lona, *An Diognet*, 53, 267; Marrou, *A Diognète*, 271; Meecham, *The Epistle to Diognetus*, 129.

[29] In my opinion, the author's use of the words, λύτρον ὑπὲρ ἡμῶν, is not due to dependence on Mark 10.45/Matthew 20.28[c], but rather is symptomatic of the author's deep dependency on early Christian traditions (Lona, *An Diognet*, 267; Marrou, *A Diognète*, 199–200). There is, however, some small evidence that the author is dependent on Matthew/Mark's sequence of events: Diognetus 8.8 parallels Matthew 19.17/Mark 10.18; Diognetus 9.1[c] parallels Matthew 19.24, 26/Mark 10.25, 27; Diogntus 9.2 parallels Mark 10.45/Matthew 20.28[c] (Lona, *An Diognet*, 52; Marrou, *A Diognète*, 271). The author does not mention to whom the ransom is paid. In fact, the mention of ransom is made almost in passing. There is, however, the mention of exchange (ἀνταλλαγῆς) in Diognetus 9.5. But as Meecham states: "The context suggests that the 'exchange' is one of *state* rather than of *person*, of wickedness for justification, not the substitution of Christ for men" (*The Epistle to Diognetus*, 130). I largely agree with Meecham's assessment. The author of Diognetus does not appear to have in mind a ransom to Satan, or to evil powers. The language of σατάν or διάβολος never occurs in Diognetus.

[30] Diognetus 9.2 αὐτὸς τὸν ἴδιον υἱὸν ἀπέδοτο λύτρον   ὑπὲρ ἡμῶν
Romans 8.32   ὅς γε τοῦ ἰδίου υἱοῦ οὐκ ἐφείσατο ἀλλὰ ὑπὲρ ἡμῶν
πάντων παρέδωκεν αὐτόν

there are two other minor similarities to Mark 10.45/Matthew 20.28[c]. First, the apposition between λύτρον and τὸν ἴδιον υἱὸν matches the apposition in Mark 10.45/Matthew 20.28[c] between λύτρον and ψυχὴν. Second, the use of πολύς in Diognetus 9.5 parallels πολλῶν in Mark 10.45/Matthew 20.28[c].[31]

Turning to the presence of Isaiah 53, there are three statements in Diognetus 9.2–5 that parallel Isaiah 53.4, 11, or Christian traditions that are dependent on Isaiah 53.11. The first statement is in Diognetus 9.2, the second stretches from Diognetus 9.2 through 9.4, and the third covers the last half of Diognetus 9.5.[32] In what follows, I discuss each of these three statements that suggest influence from Isaiah 53.

Diognetus 9.2	ἐλεῶν αὐτὸς [θεὸς]	τὰς ἡμετέρας ἁμαρτίας	ἀνεδέξατο
Isaiah 53.4	οὗτος	τὰς ἁμαρτίας ἡμῶν	φέρει
Isaiah 53.11	καὶ τὰς ἁμαρτίας αὐτῶν αὐτὸς		ἀνοίσει

This first statement represents the clause directly preceding the one containing the ransom logion[c]. It is very likely a gloss of Isaiah 53.4, 11.[33] There are two potential difficulties involved in affirming an Isaianic gloss. The first is that Diognetus uses ἀναδέχομαι whereas Isaiah uses φέρω. Other early Christian texts that are dependent on Isaiah also use φέρω (1Peter 2.24; 1Clement 16.4, 12, 14; Justin *Apology* 50.8; 51.4). However, there is some fluidity as demonstrated by Matthew, who uses λαμβάνω (8.17). In Justin's *Dialogue with Trypho* 95.2, the Father wishes Christ to take upon himself the curses of all (ὁ πατὴρ τῶν ὅλων τὰς πάντων κατάρας ἀναδέξασθαι ἐβουλήθη).[34] This can be seen as an application of Isaiah 53.4 using ἀναδέχομαι. We know this because at the beginning of the next verse, *Dialogue with Trypho* 95.3, Justin clearly alludes to Isaiah 53.5, saying that by his bruises humanity might be healed (ἵνα τῷ μώλωπι αὐτοῦ ἴασις γένηται τῷ γένει τῶν ἀνθρώπων). Therefore, Diognetus' use of ἀνεδέξατο instead of φέρει, or ἀνοίσει, is not a problem.

The second difficulty is that in Diognetus 9.2, God receives the sin rather than his Son. In Isaiah 53, it is the servant who bears the sin. This difficulty can be resolved if we understand the next clause Diognetus 9.2 (αὐτὸς τὸν ἴδιον υἱὸν ἀπέδοτο λύτρον ὑπὲρ ἡμῶν) as indicating the means by which God receives sin. God receives sin *by* handing over his son as a ransom. What

---

Lona (*An Diognet*, 53, 266) and Marrou (*A Diognète*, 272) note the parallel with Romans 8.32. Lona believes that if we were to expect an actual dependence on New Testament texts, then we would see a mixed citation of Romans 8.32 and Mark 10.45 (*An Diognet*, 267).

[31] Πολύς in Diognetus 9.5 could also point to Romans 5.19 or Isaiah 53.11–12.

[32] In addition to these statements, we might also note the author's use of παῖς in Diognetus 8.9, 11; 9.1, though the author switches to υἱός in 9.2, 4, perhaps due to dependence on the Romans 8.32 tradition in Diognetus 9.2.

[33] Marrou, *A Diognète*, 270; Meecham, *The Epistle to Diognetus*, 129.

[34] Κατάρας comes from a quotation of Deuteronomy 27.26 in *Dialogue* 95.1 (cf. 96.1).

confirms this is the similarity in sound between αὐτὸς τὰς ἡμετέρας ἁμαρτίας ἀνεδέξατο and αὐτὸς τὸν ἴδιον υἱὸν ἀπέδοτο. These clauses should be read together, which means that God's reception of sin cannot be understood independently of his handing over his own son as a ransom for us.

In sum, there is no difficulty in maintaining an Isaiah 53.4, 11 gloss to this first statement, and this first statement should be read together with the following clause, which includes the ransom logion[c].

Diognetus 9.2	τὸν ἅγιον ὑπὲρ ἀνόμων, τὸν ἄκακον ὑπὲρ τῶν κακῶν, τὸν δίκαιον ὑπὲρ τῶν ἀδίκων, τὸν ἄφθαρτον ὑπὲρ τῶν φθαρτῶν, τὸν ἀθάνατον ὑπὲρ τῶν θνητῶν.
9.3	τί γὰρ ἄλλο τὰς ἁμαρτίας ἡμῶν ἠδυνήθη καλύψαι ἢ ἐκείνου δικαιοσύνη;
9.4	ἐν τίνι δικαιωθῆναι δυνατὸν τοὺς ἀνόμους ἡμᾶς καὶ ἀσεβεῖς ἢ ἐν μόνῳ τῷ υἱῷ τοῦ Θεοῦ;
1Peter 3.18	ὅτι καὶ Χριστὸς ἅπαξ περὶ ἁμαρτιῶν ἔπαθεν, δίκαιος ὑπὲρ ἀδίκων,
Isaiah 53.11	δικαιῶσαι δίκαιον εὖ δουλεύοντα πολλοῖς καὶ τὰς ἁμαρτίας αὐτῶν αὐτὸς ἀνοίσει

The second statement begins with a set of contrasts in the latter part of Diognetus 9.2, directly following the ransom logion[c]. One of those contrasts, δίκαιον ὑπὲρ τῶν ἀδίκων, is typically thought to parallel 1Peter 3.18.[35] The traditional material in 1Peter 3.18 appears to be the result of Christian reflection on Isaiah 53. If the language of δίκαιον ὑπὲρ τῶν ἀδίκων in Diognetus 9.2 is part of the same interpretive stream as 1Peter 3.18, then we must consider the possibility that it also results from reflection on Isaiah 53, where the servant is defined by being righteous (δίκαιος [Isaiah 53.11]). Isaiah 53.11's emphasis on righteousness also explains the thought that flows through Diognetus 9.3–4. In Diognetus 9.3, it is the righteousness of the Son that covers (καλύψαι) sin. Similarly, in Diognetus 9.4, the Son is singled out for the ability of his righteousness to envelope (ἐν) the lawless and ungodly. In Isaiah 53.11 the dominant characteristic of the servant is righteousness, and this righteousness allows the servant to justify/serve the many and to bear their sin.[36]

---

[35] Lona, *An Diognet*, 53, 268; Meecham, *The Epistle to Diognetus*, 129; Marrou, *A Diognète*, 273.

[36] If we take ἐν τίνι...ἐν μόνῳ τῷ υἱῷ τοῦ Θεοῦ to mean "*in* whom...*in* the Son of God alone," rather than "*by* whom...*by* the Son of God alone," then the distinction between the Greek and Hebrew texts of Isaiah 53.11 is almost irrelevant for maintaining a parallel with Diognetus 9.3–4 (See 2.3, n. 36 above). Translating with "in" means that the Isaianic servant only needs to be just, which he is emphatically in both Hebrew and Greek texts of Isaiah 53.11, rather than do any justifying, which only happens in the Hebrew text. Supporting the translation with "in" is that in Diognetus 9.5 ἐν is used with κρυβῇ, which requires a translation with "in" (W. F. Bauer, *et al*, "κρύπτω," *BDAG* 571.2). Also, "in" makes better sense if the thought in Diognetus 9.4 is similar to Paul's ἐν Χριστῷ.

Diognetus 9.5 ἵνα[37] ἀνομία μὲν *πολλῶν ἐν δικαίῳ ἑνὶ* κρυβῇ, *δικαιοσύνη δὲ ἑνὸς πολλοὺς ἀνόμους δικαιώσῃ.*

Romans 5.18[b] οὕτως καὶ δι' *ἑνὸς δικαιώματος εἰς πάντας ἀνθρώπους εἰς δικαίωσιν ζωῆς·*

Romans 5.19 ὥσπερ γὰρ διὰ τῆς παρακοῆς τοῦ ἑνὸς ἀνθρώπου ἁμαρτωλοὶ κατεστάθησαν *οἱ πολλοί,* οὕτως καὶ διὰ τῆς ὑπακοῆς τοῦ ἑνὸς *δίκαιοι κατασταθήσονται οἱ πολλοί.*

Isaiah 53.11 *δικαιῶσαι δίκαιον εὖ δουλεύοντα πολλοῖς καὶ τὰς ἁμαρτίας αὐτῶν αὐτὸς ἀνοίσει*

The third statement is from Diognetus 9.5 and is reflective of the tradition found in Romans 5.12–19.[38] Diognetus 9.5 is also reflective of the tradition in Isaiah 53.11.[39] The last part of the parallel in Diognetus 9.5 is particularly close to the end of Romans 5.19 and the first part of Isaiah 53.11, both verbally and conceptually.[40] It would appear that both Romans 5.18[b]–19 and Diognetus 9.5 both result from early Christian reflection on Isaiah 53.11.

In conclusion, Diognetus 9.2–5 presents a version of the ransom logion[c] alongside three statements that are influenced by Isaiah 53.4, 11. Out of these three, the first statement is most clearly dependent on Isaiah 53.4, 11. It is also most closely tied to the following clause containing the ransom logion[c]. The other two statements maintain a more vague influence from Isaiah 53.11 and/or from other early Christian reflections on Isaiah 53.11 (1Peter 3.18; Romans 5.18[b]–19). Overall, there is little doubt that the author of Diognetus is reading the ransom logion[c] in close connection with Isaiah 53.4, 11.

---

[37] The ἵνα clause indicates content (Meecham, *The Epistle to Diognetus*, 130).

[38] Lona, *An Diognet*, 53, 273; Meecham, *The Epistle to Diognetus*, 130; Marrou, *A Diognète*, 272.

[39] Various parts of Romans 5.12–19 are suggested to have their roots in Isaiah 53 (J. Fitzmyer, *Romans* [ABC 33; Garden City: Doubleday, 1993], 421; R. Jewett, *Romans* [Hermeneia; Philadelphia: Fortress Press, 2007], 387; D. Moo, *The Epistle to the Romans* [NICNT; Grand Rapids: Eerdmans, 1996], 345 n. 143; S. Shum, *Paul's Use of Isaiah in Romans: A Comparative Study of Paul's Letter to the Romans and the Sibyline and Qumran Sectarian Texts* [WUNT 2/156; Tübingen: Mohr Siebeck, 2002], 198–99; J. Wagner, *Heralds of the Good News: Isaiah and Paul 'In Concert' in the Letter to the Romans* [NovTSup 101; Leiden: Brill, 2003], 334 n. 106). Shum notes that "here what Paul [and I would add, Diognetus] draws on from the Suffering Servant Song is not simply (Second) Isaiah's language, but the prophet's concept of a *one-many-solidarity-relationship*" (*Paul's Use of Isaiah in Romans*, 199).

[40] At first glance it appears that the concept of wickedness (ἀνομ-) is missing from the parallel in Isaiah 53.11. However, it is certainly implied from the fact that the righteous servant must bear the sins of the many.

Source	Supposed Tradition	Exemplar	Similarity	Further Comments
Epistle to Diognetus 9.2	Ransom Logion[c]	Mark 10.45[c]	S3	Λύτρον ὑπὲρ ἡμῶν is the main connection
	Romans 8.32	Romans 8.32	S3	τοῦ ἰδίου υἱοῦ is the main connection
	Isaiah 53.4, 11	Isaiah 53.4, 11	S3	The first statement is the closest
	1Peter 3.18	1Peter 3.18	S1	δίκαιον ὑπὲρ τῶν ἀδίκων is in a list of similar statements
	Romans 5.18[b]–19	Romans 5.18[b]–19	S3	
	Love motif	N/A	N/A	Not in close proximity to the ransom logion[c]

3.5 The Gospel of Truth I,3 20.13–14[41]

Matthew 20.28[c]	καὶ δοῦναι τὴν ψυχὴν αὐτοῦ	λύτρον	ἀντὶ πολλῶν
GTr 20.13–14	ϫⲉ ⲡⲓⲙⲟⲩ ⲛ̄ⲧⲟⲟⲧϥ̄ ⲟⲩⲱⲛϩ̄	ⲛ̄ϩⲁϩ ⲡⲉ

The Gospel of Truth (GTr) was originally written in Greek.[42] It is normally dated to the second half of the second century.[43] One of the most intriguing aspects of GTr is its general allusiveness, both in regards to its theological system and its use of scripture.[44] While the author does not use introductory

---

[41] The primary text comes from H. Attridge and G. MacRae, "NCH 1, 3: The Gospel of Truth," in *Nag Hammadi Codex I (The Jung Codex): Introductions, Texts, Translations, Indices* (ed. H. W. Attridge; NHS 22; Leiden: Brill, 1985a), 82–117.

[42] There is a consensus that the original language was Greek, though there have been a few dissenters (ibid., 63).

[43] Dates are suggested from the middle of the second century when Valentinius was in Rome to the latter part of the second century when Irenaeus mentions a "Veritatis Evangelium" (*Against Heresies* 3.11.9).

[44] The development of a Gnostic (Valentinian) system is frequently discussed in the secondary literature, especially as it relates to dating. It is difficult to tell whether the GTr's allusive character is symptomatic of an underdeveloped Valentinian thought or of restraint by the author in order to make GTr more accessible to those outside Gnostic (Valentinian) circles. For a discussion, see H. Attridge, "The Gospel of Truth as an Exoteric Text," in *Nag Hammadi, Gnosticism, & Early Christianity* (ed. C. Hedrick and R. Hodgson, Jr; Peabody, MA: Hendrickson Publishers, 1986), 239–55; E. Thomassen, *The Spiritual Seed: The Church of the 'Valentinians'* (NHMS 60; Leiden: Brill, 2006), 146–48; W. van Unnik, "The 'Gospel of Truth' and the New Testament," in *The Jung Codex: A Newly Recovered Gnostic Papyrus* (trans. and ed. F. Cross; London: A. Mowbray & Co. Limited, 1955), 81–104; R. McL. Wilson, "Valentinianism and the *Gospel of Truth*" in *The Rediscovery of Gnosticism* (ed. B. Layton; Leiden: Brill, 1980), 1.133–41.

formulae that might specify a particular citation, it is clear that the author is familiar with the majority of Christian scriptures.[45] It is almost certain that the author is influenced by parts of Matthew's Gospel.[46] Of particular importance is the statement in GTr 20.13–14, which reminisces upon Jesus' knowledge that his death is life for many. According to *Biblia Patristica*, this statement represents a reception of the ransom logion[c], presumably from Matthew 20.28. However, the statement has a much stronger similarity to the Last Supper saying from Matthew 26.28 (τοῦτο γάρ ἐστιν τὸ αἷμά μου τῆς δια-θήκης τὸ περὶ πολλῶν ἐκχυννόμενον εἰς ἄφεσιν ἁμαρτιῶν).

The statement in GTr 20.13–14 occurs at the end of a larger allusion to the scene in Revelation 5.1–9.[47] The allusion to Revelation 5.1–9 begins with the mention of the book (Revelation 5.1/GTr 19.35–36),[48] followed by the observation that no one was able to take it (Revelation 5.3/GTr 20.4), followed by the mention of the slain one, who will take the book (Revelation 5.6/GTr 20.5–6). Next, there is an interlude that references themes from Hebrews – "The merciful one, the faithful one" (Hebrews 2.17/GTr 20.10); "accepting sufferings" (Hebrews 12.2/GTr 20.11). Following the interlude, the thought of Jesus taking the book is resumed (Revelation 5.9/GTr 20.12). Finally, the author of GTr says that Jesus knows that his death is life for many – ϫⲉ ⲡⲓ-ⲙⲟⲩ ⲛ̄ⲧⲟⲟⲧϥ̄ ⲟⲩⲱⲛϩ̄ ⲛ̄ϩⲁϩ ⲡⲉ (GTr 20.13–14).[49] If the author is still following the Revelation sequence, then he has substituted the language of Revelation 5.9 with language from the ransom logion[c], probably from Matthew 20.28[c], or from the Last Supper saying in Matthew 26.28. In what follows, I

---

[45] The allusive character of the scriptural allusions makes sense if GTr is an exoteric work in which the author is speaking with familiar scriptural allusions as a means of conveying an unfamiliar theology (Attridge, "The Gospel of Truth as an Exoteric Text," 242).

[46] C. Tuckett demonstrates that the author of GTr is dependent on Matthean redaction (*Nag Hammadi and the Gospel Tradition* [Edinburgh: T & T Clark, 1986], 57–68). Further, he argues that all the synoptic allusions can be explained by a dependence on Matthew alone, though this does not preclude the possibility that the author is also aware of Mark and/or Luke (Cf. J. Williams, *Biblical Interpretation in the Gnostic Gospel of Truth from Nag Hammadi* [SBLDS 79; Atlanta: Scholars Press, 1988], 184–85).

[47] For good discussions of this entire scene in which Jesus must bring into the material world the book containing the salvific names of the many, see Attridge, "The Gospel of Truth as an Exoteric Text," 245–47; C. Story, *The Nature of Truth in "The Gospel of Truth" and in the Writings of Justin Martyr: A Study of the Pattern of Orthodoxy in the Middle of the Second Christian Century* (NovTSup 25; Leiden: Brill, 1970), 126–27; Thomassen, *The Spiritual Seed*, 151–55; Williams, *Biblical Interpretation*, 41–44.

[48] By referring to the book as the "living book of the living," the author of GTr indicates that he understands the book in Revelation 5.1–9 as the same one described in Revelation 13.8 (cf. 17.8; 20.12, 15; 21.27), which contains the names of those who do not worship the beast.

[49] The author understands the "many" (GTr 20.14) as those whose names, which represent their true selves, are written in the book (GTr 21.3–5; Thomassen, *The Spiritual Seed*, 150–53). See GTr 22.20 and 30.37 for similar uses of ϩⲁϩ.

examine the rationale for both of these options. I will conclude that a much stronger case can be made for the Last Supper saying in Matthew 26.28.

Rev. 5.9	ἐσφάγης ... ἠγόρασας... ἐν τῷ αἵματί σου ἐκ πάσης φυλῆς
GTr 20.13–15	ϫⲉ ⲡⲓⲙⲟⲩ ⲛ̅ⲧⲟⲟⲧϥ̅ ⲟⲩⲱⲛⲁ̅ ⲛ̅ⲅⲁⲅ ⲡⲉ...ⲇⲓⲁⲑⲏⲕⲏ
Matthew 26.28	τὸ αἷμά μου τῆς διαθήκης τὸ περὶ πολλῶν ἐκχυννόμενον
Matthew 20.28[c]	καὶ δοῦναι τὴν ψυχὴν αὐτοῦ λύτρον ἀντὶ πολλῶν

The majority of scholarship prefers to see GTr 20.13–14 as a reception of the ransom logion[c].[50] However, the reasoning for this preference normally remains unsaid. In my estimation, the only possible reason for seeing a distinctive use of the ransom logion[c] is the linguistic similarity between τὴν ψυχὴν (Matthew 20.28[c]) and ⲟⲩⲱⲛⲁ̅ (GTr 20.14).

There are three major difficulties for seeing GTr 20.13–14 as similar to Mark 10.45/Matthew 20.28[c]. First, there is no self-giving motif. Second, and more significant, is the absence of "ransom" (ⲥⲱⲧⲉ) language.[51] Third, in Mark 10.45/Matthew 20.28[c] Jesus gives his life, but in GTr 20.13–14 Jesus' death is life. This lessens the force of the point listed in the previous paragraph.

The minority position understands GTr 20.13–14 as a reception of the Last Supper saying in Matthew 26.28.[52] There are four strong reasons to support this view. First, it explains the absence of the "ransom" language, which does not occur in the Last Supper saying. Second, the language of τῆς διαθήκης τὸ περὶ πολλῶν ἐκχυννόμενον in Matthew 26.28 explains well the transition that the author of GTr makes when he takes up the same vocabulary of ⲇⲓⲁⲑⲏⲕⲏ in GTr 20.15.[53] Third, Revelation 5.9 states that Jesus purchased

---

[50] S. Arai, *Die Christologie des Evangelium Veritatis: Eine Religionsgeschichtliche Untersuchung* (Leiden: Brill, 1964), 102; H. Attridge and G. MacRae, "NCH 1, 3: The Gospel of Truth," in *Nag Hammadi Codex I (The Jung Codex): Notes* (ed. H. W. Attridge; NHS 23; Leiden: Brill, 1985b), 58; C. Evans, R. Webb, and R. Wiebe, *Nag Hammadi Texts and the Bible: A Synopsis and Index* (NTTS 18; Leiden: Brill, 1993), 27; K. Grobel, *The Gospel of Truth: A Valentinian Meditation on the Gospel* (London: Adam & Charles Black, 1960), 63; Köhler, *Die Rezeption des Matthäusevangeliums in der Zeit vor Irenäus* (WUNT 2/24; Tübingen: Mohr Siebeck, 1987), 561; J. Ménard, *L'Évangile de Vérité* (NHS 2; Leiden: Brill, 1972), 97; Story, *The Nature of Truth*, 6; Tuckett, *Nag Hammadi and the Gospel Tradition*, 63; Williams, *Biblical Interpretation*, 46–48.

[51] Williams notes the "problematic" nature of omitting ransom language (*Biblical Interpretation*, 47).

[52] Van Unnik thinks that the author of GTr knows Mark 14.24/Matthew 26.28 ("The 'Gospel of Truth' and the New Testament," 111–12). Several commentators potentially see Matthew 26.28 behind the "covenant" language in GTr 20.15, but they inexplicably still see Matthew 20.28 as the primary allusion in GTr 20.13–14 (Attridge and MacRae, "NCH 1, 3," [b] 58; Ménard, *L'Évangile de Vérité*, 97).

[53] It is irrelevant if in GTr 20.15 the author transitions to allusions from other texts that use the language of διαθήκη to speak of a will (e.g. Galatians 3.15; Hebrews 9.16–17). The important thing is that the transition begins with an allusion to Matthew 26.28.

people for God with his blood (ἐν τῷ αἵματί σου). Since the author of GTr uses the statement in 20.13–14 as a substitute for Revelation 5.9, it is easy to see why the author would prefer Matthew 26.28's emphasis on blood (ὁ αἷμά μου τῆς διαθήκης). Fourth, λαμβάνω is used in Revelation 5.7–9 to describe Jesus' taking the book. The same language is used in Matthew 26.27 when Jesus "takes" the cup. The author of GTr could have used this word to transition between Revelation 5.7–9 and Matthew 26.27 since the taking of the book and the cup are both closely linked with Jesus' death.[54]

In conclusion, the above evidence demonstrates that a much stronger case can be made for the Last Supper saying in Matthew 26.28 as the background to GTr 20.13–14. The parallels drawn between the covenant, the blood, the taking of the cup/book, and the absence of "ransom" make a Last Supper background the best choice. Of course, this does not completely remove the possibility that the ransom logion[c] is also in the author's mind, but I think it is very unlikely.

Source	Supposed Tradition	Exemplar	Similarity	Further Comments
The	Ransom Logion[c]	Matthew 20.28[c]	S4	
Gospel	Matthew 26.28	Matthew 26.28	S4	
of Truth	Hebrews 2.17; 12.2	Hebrews 2.17;	S3	
I,3		12.2		
20.13–14	Revelation 5.1–9	Revelation 5.1–9	S3	Provides the over-arching context

3.6 The Sentences of Sextus 336[55]

Mark 10.45[a–b]   ὁ υἱὸς τοῦ ἀνθρώπου οὐκ ἦλθεν διακονηθῆναι ἀλλὰ διακονῆσαι
Sentences 336   ὑπηρετεῖν κρεῖττον ἑτέροις ἢ πρὸς ἄλλων ὑπηρετεῖσθαι

The Sentences of Sextus is a late second-century Christian compilation and redaction of various maxims, most of which originate in pagan circles.[56] There is a longstanding debate about whether Sentences is a Christian or a pagan compilation. Origen was the first to identify the work as from a "wise

---

[54] This is contra Thomassen, who thinks that the "taking" of the book comes from a tradition about the reception of wisdom (*The Spiritual Seed*, 153 n. 16).

[55] The primary text comes from R. Edwards and R. Wild, *The Sentences of Sextus* (TT 22; Chico, CA: Scholars Press, 1981).

[56] The original text is Greek, but we possess only two late manuscripts from the 10th and 14th centuries. There are much earlier versions in Latin, Syriac, Coptic, Armenian, and Georgian. For a discussion of the manuscript tradition see Edwards and Wild, *The Sentences of Sextus*, 1–6.

and believing man."[57] Jerome and many after him felt the work to be of purely pagan origins. However, there is a consensus in current scholarship, which is best reflected in Chadwick's statement: "a Christian compiler has edited, carefully revised and modified a previous pagan collection (or perhaps collections)."[58]

It is probable that several of these maxims reflect sayings of Jesus.[59] Among these, Sentences 336 has been suggested to reflect all, or parts, of Matthew 20.26–28 (Mark 10.43–45).[60] However, Jesus is nowhere mentioned in Sentences, much less the Son of Man. Also, Sentences 336 uses ὑπηρετέω instead of διακονέω.[61] Therefore, any comparison between Sentences 336 and Matthew 20.26–28 must be made on conceptual grounds.

Certainly within the Jesus tradition, Matthew 20.26–28 is the first place one might consider as a background for Sentences 336. However, the lack of verbal parallels makes it impossible to say with any degree of certainty whether or not Matthew 20.26–28 has influenced Sentences 336. A contextual reading is also unhelpful for examining Matthew 20.26–28's influence since Sentences 336 is thematically disconnected from the surrounding maxims. In sum, although scholarship has suggested a connection between Sentences 336 and Matthew 20.26–28 such a connection cannot be sufficiently demonstrated. If, hypothetically speaking, it could be demonstrated that Mathew 20.26–28 is influencing Sentences 336, then it would inform us of how Matthew 20.26–28 is adopted into the Christian wisdom tradition, that is, by emphasizing Jesus' servant ethic, without the necessity also to reference his atoning death.

---

[57] H. Chadwick, *The Sentences of Sextus: A Contribution to the History of Early Christian Ethics* (Texts and Studies 5; Cambridge: Cambridge University Press, 1959), 114–15.

[58] Ibid., 138.

[59] G. Delling, "Zur Hellenisierung des Christentums in den 'Sprüchen des Sextus,'" in *Studien zum Neuen Testament und zur Patristik. Festschrift für Erich Klostermann* (TU 77; Berlin: Akademie-Verlag, 1961), 219–33; R. Wilken, "Wisdom and Philosophy in Early Christianity," in *Aspects of Wisdom in Judaism and Early Christianity* (ed. R. Wilken; Notre Dame: University of Notre Dame Press, 1975), 154–58.

[60] This suggestion was first made by Chadwick (*The Sentences of Sextus*, 178), followed by Delling ("Zur Hellenisierung des Christentums," 231–32), followed by *Biblia Patristica* (1.273), followed by Köhler (*Die Rezeption des Matthäusevangeliums*, 561).

[61] The Coptic version is the earliest witness to *Sentences* and more than 500 years older than the earliest extant Greek witness (F. Wisse, "NHC XII, *I*: The Sentences of Sextus," in *Nag Hammadi Codices XI, XII, XIII* [ed. C. W. Hedrick; NHS 28; Leiden: Brill, 1990], 295). The Coptic version of *Sentences* 336 maintains ὑπηρετέω as a loan-word. This supports the notion that the original Greek likely used the verb ὑπηρετέω instead of διακονέω. Delling has observed that the διακον- word group never occurs in *Sentences*, but there is a consistent use of ὑπηρετ- ("Zur Hellenisierung des Christentums," 231). Therefore, if the author/compiler is making an allusion to Matthew 20.26–28 in *Sentences* 336, then it is very implicit.

Source	Supposed Tradition	Exemplar	Similarity	Further Comments
Sentences 336	Ransom Logion[a–b]	Mark 10.45[a–b]	S4	

3.7 Conclusion

There are not many strong receptions of the ransom logion in the period from the New Testament through 200 CE. The receptions that *Biblia Patristica* lists for The Gospel of Truth 20.13–14 and The Sentences of Sextus 336 are very weak and thus insignificant. The reception listed for Irenaeus, *Against Heresies* 5.1.1, is highly similar to Mark 10.45/Matthew 20.28, but is complicated by its inclusion within traditional material. On the positive side, there are three receptions that elicit some confidence. These are Clement of Alexandria, *Paedagogus* 1.9.85.1–2; *Quis Dives Salvetur* 37.4, and Diognetus 9.2. Clement of Alexandria knows Mark and Matthew and likely derives his use of the ransom logion from one of those Gospels. The ransom logion in Diognetus 9.2 probably comes from oral tradition.

The three receptions of the ransom logion that elicit the most confidence are also those that perpetuate the two motifs that accompany the ransom logion in the New Testament, which are love and the Isaianic servant. Additionally, there is a new phenomenon, which is to interpret the ransom logion[a–b] as an incarnational narrative.

The love motif is limited to Clement of Alexandria, especially *Quis Dives Salvetur* 37.4, where it results from dependence on Johannine literature. Clement's use of the love motif is not wholly motivated by evangelistic purposes, as was conjectured about the use of the motif in the New Testament, but rather by connecting similar statements about Jesus' self-sacrifice in the Johannine literature. As it happens, the statements about Jesus' self-sacrifice in the Johannine literature, which Clement finds interpretive for Mark 10.45/Matthew 20.28, frequently include a love motif. Surprisingly, Clement is the last person to receive the ransom logion with a prominent love motif. For an unknown reason, later interpreters expunge it from the mnemonic socialization process in favor of new patterns.

One of those new patterns is the use of an incarnational motif to interpret the ransom logion[a–b]. This pattern is first attested in the writings of Clement of Alexandria, although the pattern itself may be much older.[62] The incarnational story in Philippians 2.6–8 may be the factor that influences Clement of

---

[62] As in the New Testament, the suggested receptions of the ransom logion in this period are largely limited to the ransom logion[c]. Clement of Alexandria's clear reception of the ransom logion[a–b] represents its first reception for at least a century after the writing of Mark and Matthew. Clement's interpretation of the ransom logion[a–b] with an incarnational motif may be only the first *extant* occurrence of this pattern.

Alexandria's incarnational reading of the ransom logion. To Clement of Alexandria, both the ransom logion and Philippians 2.6–8 would be telling the same story of an incarnation from preexistence, followed by service, followed by death. The connection between the ransom logion and Philippians 2.6–8 continues into the period from 200 through 300 CE.

In Diognetus 9.2–5, the ransom logion is closely intertwined with themes from Isaiah 53.4, 11. Especially important is the gloss of Isaiah 53.4, 11 that directly precedes the ransom logion[c]. Both phrases share a strong assonance. This suggests that the author believes the phrases are mutually interpretive. The author uses the gloss of Isaiah 53.4, 11 to highlight the removal of sin, and thus matches the combination of similar ideas in Galatians 1.4.

Finally, there are some contributions that the reception of the ransom logion in this period makes to the three debatable issues surrounding Mark 10.45/Matthew 20.28 (See 1.2 above). First, concerning the (dis)association of the ransom logion with the Eucharist, Irenaeus, *Against Heresies* 5.1.1, identifies blood as the ransom price. Ephesians 1.7 influences this identification, and not Last Supper traditions from the synoptics or Paul.

Second, concerning a preexistent coming in Mark 10.45/Matthew 20.28, Clement of Alexandria interprets the ransom logion[a–b] with an incarnational narrative in *Paedagogus* 1.9.85.1–2. Clement also places an incarnational narrative before the ransom logion[c] in *Quis Dives Salvetur* 37.1–4, perhaps to replace the ransom logion[a–b]. In both *Paedagogus* 1.9.85.1–2 and *Quis Dives Salvetur* 37.1–4, Clement's incarnational reading of the ransom logion[a–b] is likely guided by Philippians 2.6–8.

Third, concerning the scriptural background of Mark 10.45/Matthew 20.28, Diognetus closely links the ransom logion[c] with statements influenced by Isaiah 53.4, 11.[63] As in the New Testament period, Daniel 7; 9 are not used with the ransom logion. This is likely due to the fact that there is only one reception of the ransom logion[a] in *Paedagogus* 1.9.85.1–2, and that reception omits the Son of Man. There is an allusion to Isaiah 43.2 before the chiasm in *Paedagogus* 1.9.85.1–2, but its placement outside the chiasm makes it difficult to discern if it possesses a meaningful connection with the ransom logion.

---

[63] Additionally, although Melito of Sardis is not discussed in this chapter, it should be noted that Perler's edition of *Peri Pascha*, suggests that *Peri Pascha* 103 contains the ransom logion[c]. There also may be influence from Isaiah 53 (O. Perler, *Méliton de Sardes, Sur la Pâque et Fragments: Introduction, Texte Critique, Traduction et Notes* [SC 123; Paris: Éditions du Cerf, 1966]). In *Peri Pascha* 103, the risen Jesus states: ἐγὼ τὸ λ[ύτρον] ὑμῶν (line 792 [The Latin text reads *redemptio*, Papyrus Chester Beatty-Michigan only has a λ, and Papyrus Bodmer XIII reads λουτρόν]). In the preceding line (791), the risen Jesus makes a potential allusion to Isaiah 53.7 when he states: [ἐγὼ ὁ] ἀμνὸς ὁ ὑπὲρ ὑμῶν σφαγείς. However, this is also similar to other New Testament texts, such as Revelation 5.6, 9.

Chapter 4

The Reception of the Ransom Logion
from 200 through 300 CE

4.1 Introduction

There are twenty-three receptions of the ransom logion in the period from 200–300 CE. That is more than the previous two periods combined. Among these are all the receptions of Mark 10.45/Matthew 20.28 that are listed in *Biblia Patristica* from 200–300 CE.[1] Additionally, there is a reception from *The Gospel of Philip*, which is listed in Evans, Webb, and Wiebe.[2] There are also additional receptions in Origen and Eusebius, which were gleaned through a search for "λύτρον" in the online version of *Thesaurus Linguae Graecae*.[3]

As in the previous chapter, some attention is given to the dates of the receptions in order to maintain the window of 200–300 CE.[4] Once it is determined that a reception likely fits into that period, there is not a further attempt to provide a more detailed chronological arrangement. Hippolytus and Origen are, however, placed towards the front and Eusebius at the end. The three Coptic texts are also grouped together (4.7–4.9).

---

[1] This is all the receptions of Mark 10.45/Matthew 20.28 listed in *Biblia Patristica* volumes two and three, as well as Eusebius from volume four. Again, in order to be consistent, every text is examined that *Biblia Patristica* lists as sufficiently similar to Mark 10.45/Matthew 20.28. However, some of the texts lack strong similarity to Mark 10.45/Matthew 20.28.

[2] The Gospel of Philip II,3 52.35–53.3 (C. Evans, R. Webb, and R. Wiebe, *Nag Hammadi Texts and the Bible: A Synopsis and Index* [NTTS 18; Leiden: Brill, 1993], 146).

[3] Origen, *Fragment on Ephesians* 1.7; *Fragment on 1Corinthians* 6.19–20; Eusebius, *De Theophania* 9 (*Thesaurus Linguae Graecae: A Digital Library of Greek Literature*. Accessed 29 July 2008. Online: http://www.tlg.uci.edu/).

[4] The writings of Eusebius spill over into the fourth century.

4.2 Hippolytus, *On the Great Song* 1;[5] *On Proverbs* 75[6]

Mark 10.45[c]	καὶ δοῦναι	τὴν ψυχὴν αὐτοῦ	λύτρον ἀντὶ πολλῶν
On the Great Song 1 (83, 6)		τῶν ψυχῶν	λυτρωτής
On Proverbs 75 (94, 4)		ἀνθρώπων λύτρον	

There is a great deal of ambiguity surrounding the authorship and provenance of the writings accredited to Hippolytus.[7] However, there is a consensus in current scholarship that a certain Hippolytus is responsible for a large amount of exegetical writings.[8] Cerrato refers to these as "core documents."[9] Among these core exegetical documents are Hippolytus' comments *On the Great Song*, as well as his comments *On Proverbs*. According to *Biblia Patristica*, each of these works contains a reception of the ransom logion[c].

4.2.1 On the Great Song 1

The first reception of the ransom logion[c] is in Hippolytus' comments on The Great Song of Moses (Deuteronomy 32).[10] The title, τῶν ψυχῶν λυτρωτής, is one of several that Hippolytus places upon Jesus in light of his descent into Hades in order to rescue Adam, and likely others as well.[11] It is difficult to discern whether this title should actually be considered a reception of the ransom logion[c]. The self-giving element is absent. There also is a significant difference between the idea of Jesus being the ransomer of souls and the idea of his giving his soul as a ransom for many. Additionally, there is nothing in the immediate context that matches the patterns displayed in the other receptions of ransom logion.[12] Therefore, this potential reception contributes little.

---

[5] The primary text comes from H. Achelis, *Hippolytus Werke I. 2. Kleinere exegetische und homiletische Schriften* (GCS; Leipzig: J. C. Hinrichs, 1897).

[6] The primary text comes from M. Richard, "Les fragments du commentaire de S. Hippolyte sur les Proverbes de Salomon," *Mus* 79 (1966): 75–94. Richard, who set the extant text in a critical edition, states: "Les anciennes editions des fragments de ce commentaire, y compris celle d'Achelis (GCS 1, 2, p. 155–177), sont inutilisables" ("Hippolyte de Rome (saint)," *DS* 7:531–71).

[7] For a discussion, see J. Cerrato, *Hippolytus between East and West* (OTM; Oxford: Oxford University Press, 2002), 3–123.

[8] Ibid., 127–146.

[9] Cerrato states that "late second- or early third-century dates [198–235]...have been assigned to the core of texts by scholars who differ greatly on theories of authorship and provenance" (ibid., 6).

[10] The fragment containing these comments was preserved by Theodoret, who incidentally believed that Hippolytus was from the East (ibid., 69–71).

[11] For a discussion, see C. Hill, "Hades of Hippolytus or Tartarus of Tertullian? The Authorship of the Fragment *De Universo*," *VC* 43 (1989): 105–06.

[12] The immediate context is as follows: "He who drew out of the nethermost Hades the man first formed of the earth, lost and held by the bonds of death; he who came down from above and bore upward him who was below unto the things above; he who becomes the

4.2.2 On Proverbs 75

The second reception of the ransom logion[c] is in fragment 75 of Hippolytus' comments on the Proverbs.[13] Fragment 75 opens with a citation of Proverbs 30.31, followed by a string of six clauses containing periphrastic aorist-passive participles. The language of φησίν, which occurs between the citation of Proverbs 30.31 and the six participial clauses, indicates that the following participial clauses are Hippolytus' interpretation of certain scriptures. The entirety of fragment 75 reads as follows:

Καὶ τράγος ἡγούμενος αἰπολίου (Proverbs 30.31)
(1) Οὗτος γάρ, φησίν, ἐστὶν ὁ ὑπὲρ ἁμαρτίας κόσμου σφαγεὶς
(2) καὶ ὡς θῦμα προσαχθεὶς
(3) καὶ ὡς ἐρήμῳ εἰς ἔθνη πεμφθεὶς
(4) καὶ κόκκινον ἔριον ἐπὶ κεφαλὴν ὑπὸ τῶν ἀπίστων στεφανωθεὶς
(5) καὶ ἀνθρώπων λύτρον γεννηθεὶς
(6) καὶ ζωὴ πάντων δειχθείς.[14]

The reception of the ransom logion[c] is in the fifth participial clause. The use of λύτρον makes this reception closer to Mark 10.45/Matthew 20.28[c] than the previous reception in *On the Great Song*. While it is possible that ἀνθρώπων is Hippolytus' interpretation of ἀντὶ πολλῶν, it remains that λύτρον is the only solid connection. However, λύτρον may be sufficient since this form of the word is peculiar to Mark 10.45/Matthew 20.28[c].

Stökl Ben Ezra believes that fragment 75 is influenced by Yom Kippur typology in which the goat leading the flock (Jesus) is presented "simultaneously as sacrificial goat and as scapegoat."[15] The imagery of the sacrificial goat is present in clauses 1–2 and the scapegoat imagery in clauses 3–4.[16] While the Yom Kippur imagery is certainly present, at least in clauses 3–4, we should also take into consideration *Biblia Patristica*'s suggestion that the

---

evangelist of the dead and the redeemer of souls and the resurrection of the buried; he it was who had become the helper of the conquered man..." (Translation from Hill, ibid., 105–06).

[13] Richard states that fragments 75 and 21 are the only ones that have a singular witness, which is Vatican gr. 1802 ("Les fragments, 73"). According to Richard, Vatican gr. 1802 wrongly accredits both fragments to John Chrysostom – The text of fragment 75 is present in Patrologia Graeca 64 (737, 44–48), where it appears under Chrysostom's fragments on Proverbs.

[14] The shorter text of Pseudo-Anastasius, which Richard parallels to Hippolytus (ibid., 82–94), only contains the following for the parallel to fragment 75: Τράγος ἡγούμενος αἰπολίου. Ὁ ὑπὲρ τῶν ἁμαρτίων τοῦ κόσμου σφαγιασθείς.

[15] D. Stökl Ben Ezra (*The Impact of Yom Kippur on Early Christianity: The Day of Atonement from Second Temple Judaism to the Fifth Century* [WUNT 163; Tübingen: Mohr Siebeck, 2003], 158).

[16] The sacrificial goat was slaughtered, and the scapegoat was sent into the wilderness (Leviticus 16). The scarlet wool (κόκκινον ἔριον) terminology is associated with the scapegoat by other patristic writers (Ben Ezra, *The Impact of Yom Kippur*, 158).

sacrificial imagery in clauses 1–2 is an allusion to Isaiah 53.6–7.[17] The strong parallels between clauses 1–2 and Isaiah 53.6–7 are as follows:

Clause 1 Οὗτος γάρ, φησίν, ἐστὶν ὁ ὑπὲρ ἀμαρτίας κόσμου σφαγεὶς
Clause 2 καὶ ὡς θῦμα προσαχθείς

Isaiah 53.6 κύριος παρέδωκεν αὐτὸν ταῖς ἀμαρτίαις ἡμῶν [πάντων]
Isaiah 53.7 ὡς πρόβατον ἐπὶ σφαγὴν ἤχθη

These parallels suggest that clauses 1–2 exhibit some influence from Isaiah 53.6–7. This means that within fragment 75 we might have a combination of the goat from Proverbs 30.31, the slain sheep from Isaiah 53.6–7, the scape-goat from Yom Kippur, and the ransom logion[c]. There is a similar combination of items in an early Christian homily, *On the Passover* I.21–22.[18] The homily combines the concepts of the goat used as a sin offering in the cultic system and the sheep/lamb of Isaiah 53.6–7. The homily reads as follows:

It remains to understand the sign of the sheep and the goat. Therefore, on the one hand, the sheep is the sign of the gentleness of Christ according to Isaiah: "As a sheep" for "he was led unto slaughter (σφαγήν) and as a lamb before the shearer is dumb," on the other hand, according to the law, the goat is a sacrifice in behalf of sin (ὑπὲρ ἀμαρτίας θῦμα). For "a goat" it says "out of the flock for a sin offering." Therefore, the gentle one was led (προσαχθείς) as a sheep, having been sacrificed (τέθυται) in behalf of sin as a goat, through gentleness giving himself unto the salvation of humanity (δοὺς ἑαυτὸν εἰς τὴν τῶν ἀνθρώπων σωτηρίαν), of which we hope to attain through faith and love of the one who suffered in behalf of us, the Lord Jesus Christ, through whom and with whom be glory to the Father with the Holy Spirit forever and ever. Amen.[19]

If nothing else, this homily is a very interesting parallel to fragment 75. The homily demonstrates the existence of an interpretive tradition that mixes the goat from the sacrificial system of Israel with the lamb sacrificial imagery of Isaiah 53.[20] This means that the goat of Proverbs 30.31 should not be seen as

---

[17] *Biblia Patristica* 2.157

[18] *On the Passover* is a collection of six homilies that were originally accredited to Chrysostom, then to Hippolytus, and then were broken up into groups of unknown authors (P. Nautin, *Homélies Pascales* [vol. 2; SC 36; Paris: Éditions du Cerf, 1953], 26–27).

[19] Ὑπολείπεται τοῦ προβάτου τὸ σύμβολον καὶ τοῦ ἐρίφου κατανοῆσαι. Ἔστι τοίνυν τὸ μὲν πρόβατον κατὰ τὸν Ἡσαίαν ἠπιότητος τῆς Χριστοῦ σύμβολον· Ὡς πρόβατον γὰρ ἐπὶ σφαγὴν ἤχθη καὶ ὡς ἀμνὸς ἐναντίον τοῦ κείραντος αὐτὸν ἄφωνος, ἔριφος δὲ κατὰ τὸν νόμον ὑπὲρ ἀμαρτίας θῦμα. Χίμαρον γάρ φησι ἐξ αἰγῶν περὶ ἀμαρτίας. Προσαχθεὶς οὖν ἤπιος ὡς πρόβατον, ὑπὲρ ἀμαρτίας ὡς χίμαρος ὢν τέθυται, διὰ τῆς ἠπιότητος δοὺς ἑαυτὸν εἰς τὴν τῶν ἀνθρώπων σωτηρίαν, ἧς εὐξόμεθα τυχεῖν διὰ πίστεως καὶ ἀγάπης τοῦ παθόντος ὑπὲρ ἡμῶν κυρίου Ἰησοῦ Χριστοῦ, δι'οὗ καὶ μεθ'οὗ τῷ πατρὶ ἡ δόξα σὺν ἁγίῳ πνεύματι εἰς τοὺς αἰῶνας τῶν αἰώνων. Ἀμήν (ibid., 75).

[20] Although the reference, Χίμαρον γάρ φησι ἐξ αἰγῶν περὶ ἀμαρτίας, likely refers to Numbers 7.16, similar wording is present in the Yom Kippur context of Leviticus 16.5, though there the reference is to two goats instead of one.

an obstacle for the author of fragment 75 to transition to the slain lamb of Isaiah 53.7 in clauses 1–2. Whether or not the author continues transitioning to the ransom logion[c] in clause five is unknown.

In conclusion, the reception of the ransom logion[c] in *On the Great Song* is highly uncertain. The reception of the ransom logion[c] in *On Proverbs* 75 is more likely given the use of λύτρον. If the ransom logion[c] is present in fragment 75, then it is part of an interpretation of Proverbs 30.31. To restate: this interpretation is composed of six participial clauses. The ransom logion is in clause 5. Clauses 1–2 draw on Isaiah 53.6–7. Clauses 3–4 draw on the scapegoat tradition from Yom Kippur.

Source	Supposed Tradition	Exemplar	Simi-larity	Further Comments
Hippolytus, *On the Great Song* 1	Ransom Logion[c]	Mark 10.45[c]	S4	
Hippolytus, *On Proverbs* 75	Ransom Logion[c]	Mark 10.45[c]	S3	λύτρον is the only strong connection
	Isaiah 53.6–7	Isaiah 53.6–7	S3	Clauses 1–2
	Yom Kippur	N/A	N/A	Scapegoat themes in clauses 3–4
	Proverbs 30.31	Proverbs 30.31	S1	

4.3 Origen

Origen incorporates the ransom logion into his writings on Matthew, Luke, Psalms, 1Corinthians, and Ephesians.[21] I examine each of these below. I begin the examination with Origen's *Commentary on Matthew*, which contains his most explicit and expansive treatment of the ransom logion.[22]

---

[21] The receptions in Matthew, Luke, and Psalms are listed in *Biblia Patristica* 3.261. I discovered the receptions in 1Corinthians and Ephesians through a *Thesaurus Linguae Graecae* search of λύτρον (Accessed on 29 July 2008).

[22] For an excellent discussion of Origen's life and work, see L. Johnson and W. Kurz, *The Future of Catholic Biblical Scholarship: A Constuctive Conversation* (Grand Rapids: Eerdmans, 2002), 64–90.

4.3.1 Commentary on Matthew 20.28[23]

Mark 10.45   καὶ γὰρ ὁ υἱὸς τοῦ ἀνθρώπου οὐκ ἦλθεν διακονηθῆναι ἀλλὰ
                διακονῆσαι καὶ δοῦναι τὴν ψυχὴν αὐτοῦ λύτρον ἀντὶ πολλῶν

Commentary   καὶ γὰρ ὁ υἱὸς τοῦ ἀνθρώπου οὐκ ἦλθεν διακονηθῆναι,
(497, 33–498, 2; ἀλλὰ διακονῆσαι· ἐπεὶ...δοῦναι τὴν ἑαυτοῦ ψυχὴν
498, 12–13)   λύτρον ἀντὶ πολλῶν

Strikingly, Origen's *Commentary on Matthew* 20.28 uses the ransom logion as it appears in Mark 10.45.[24] Origen notes his awareness of Mark 10.45, and apparently it influences his discussion of Matthew 20.28.[25]

Origen's commentary moves quickly through the first two clauses of the ransom logion[a–b]. Origen says that although Jesus (the Son of Man) was, in fact, served by angels and by Martha, this is not the purpose for which he stayed as a "visitor in the generation of humans" (ἐπεδήμησε γὰρ τῷ γένει τῶν ἀνθρώπων [498, 8–9]). Here Origen hints at an incarnation motif, which is likely triggered by the mention of Jesus' "coming." Origen shows no interest in discussing the title, "the Son of Man," or its Danielic background.[26] For Origen, the idea that Jesus is the incarnate Son of God expands upon and overshadows the Danielic background. Origen even replaces "Son of Man" with "Son of God" (δέδοται δὲ λύτρον ὑπὲρ ἡμῶν ἡ ψυχὴ τοῦ υἱοῦ τοῦ θεοῦ [499, 21–22]). He does something similar in his final comments on the ransom logion where he focuses on Colossians 1.15–16: "...the divinity of the image of the invisible God...was given as a ransom for many" (...ἡ θειότης τῆς εἰκόνος τοῦ θεοῦ τοῦ ἀοράτου...λύτρον ἐδόθη ἀντὶ πολλῶν" [500, 11–12; 18]).

According to Origen, Jesus came to serve unto salvation. The ultimate expression of this service occurs when Jesus gives his life as a ransom for many (ransom logion[c]).[27] As might be expected, Origen states that the ransom was

---

[23] The primary text comes from E. Klostermann, *Origenes Werke X. 1. Matthäuserklärung* (GCS; Leipzig: J. C. Hinrichs'sche Buchhandlung, 1935), 497, 33 through 501, 4. Fortunately, Origen's commentary on Matthew 13.36–22.33 has been preserved in the original Greek. The Latin translation, which runs from Matthew 16.13 to 27.66, comes from the sixth century (H. Vogt, "Origen of Alexandria," in *Handbook of Patristic Exegesis* [ed. D. Bingham; BAC 1; Leiden: Brill, 2004], 543).

[24] Origen cites Mark's version of the ransom logion, which begins with καὶ γὰρ, instead of Matthew's version, which begins with ὥσπερ.

[25] Klostermann, *Origenes Werke X. 1*, 490, 13–14.

[26] However, Origen does identify Jesus with the figure in Daniel 7.13 elsewhere in his *Commentary on Matthew* (Fragment 362) (E. Klostermann, *Origenes Werke XII. 3. Matthäuserklärung* [GCS; Leipzig: J. C. Hinrichs Verlag, 1941], 154).

[27] Origen immediately qualifies the "many" by adding "of those who believe in him" (Klostermann, *Origenes Werke X. 1*, 498, 10–14). I think this qualification is intriguing given the typical understanding of Origen's universalist tendencies. Origen does go on to state:

paid to the "evil one," or the "warlike one," "who possessed us as prisoners until he received the ransom" (498, 20–27; 500, 19–21). Also, as might be expected in light of Origen's trichotomist anthropology, only the soul of Jesus was given over as a ransom.[28] Jesus' spirit was given into his Father's hands when he said: "into your hands I commit my spirit" (Luke 23.46); concerning Jesus' body, Origen says: "we find nothing where so much has been written concerning it" (499, 22–28). What is interesting is that Origen is compelled by 1Peter 1.18–19 to make Jesus' blood a further distinctive element of his composition.[29] Origen appears to make the connection between the ransom logion[c] and 1Peter 1.18–19 based on the language of ransom and the idea of payment. He then makes a further connection with 1Corinthians 7.23 by connecting the language of τιμίῳ (1Peter 1.19) with τιμῆς (1Corinthians 7.23).[30]

In sum, according to Origen's *Commentary on Matthew* 20.28, Jesus as the incarnate Son of God gave his soul (not his spirit or body) as he also gave his blood, as a ransom to the evil one to purchase the many who believe in him.

4.3.2 Fragment on Luke 14.16[31]

Mark 10.45[a–b]	οὐκ	ἦλθεν διακονηθῆναι ἀλλὰ διακονῆσαι
Luke Fragment 210 (318, 9)	οὐ γὰρ	ἦλθεν διακονηθῆναι ἀλλὰ διακονῆσαι

The relevant text begins with the statement: "Christ is the servant who was sent for this purpose: to call everyone to serve the Father." Origen expands on this statement by combining the ransom logion[a–b] with Luke 22.27 and Philippians 2.7.

"And if according to purpose everyone believed in him, [then] he has given his life as a ransom for everyone" (ibid., 498, 15–18).

[28] On Origen's anthropology, see H. Crouzel, *Origen* (trans. A. Worrall; Edinburgh: T & T Clark, 1989), 87–92; P. Tzamalikos, *Origen: Philosophy of History & Eschatology* (VCSup 85; Leiden: Brill, 2007), 55. Origen states: "And after his soul had been given as a ransom for many, he did not remain with that which he gave as a ransom for many. Because of this it is said in the fifteenth Psalm 'You did not leave my soul in Hades' (Psalm 15.10) (Klostermann, *Origenes Werke X. 1*, 499, 29–35).

[29] Origen states: "Therefore, on the one hand, to the ones who scrutinize the gospel with rhetoric it has been written [that] our savior has given his life as a ransom (λύτρον) for many. On the other hand, it has been said by Peter that not by perishable things, like silver or gold, were we ransomed out of our empty way of life, which we inherited from our ancestors, but by precious (τιμίῳ) blood (1Peter 1.18–19); and the apostle said: 'You were bought with a price (τιμῆς); do not become the slaves of men' (1Corinthians 7.23). Therefore, on the one hand, we were bought with the precious blood of Jesus, and on the other hand, the soul of the Son of God was given as a ransom in behalf of us..." (ibid., 499, 9–22).

[30] This connection is also present in Origen's comments on Psalm 129.3–5 and 29.10 LXX.

[31] The primary text comes from M. Rauer, *Origenes Werke IX. Die Homilien zu Lukas* (GCS; Berlin: Akademie-Verlag, 1959), 318, 7–10.

δοῦλος δὲ ἀποστελλόμενος ὁ Χριστὸς διὰ τὸ εἰς πάντων κλῆσιν δουλεῦσαι τῷ πατρί· οὐ γὰρ ἦλθεν διακονηθῆναι ἀλλὰ διακονῆσαι (ransom logion[a–b]) καί· ἐγὼ ἐν μέσῳ ὑμῶν ὡς ὁ διακονῶν (Luke 22.27), μορφὴν δούλου λαβών (Philippians 2.7).

Origen states that Christ was sent (ἀποστελλόμενος), presumably from his preexistent life with the Father. The goal of the sending is service. Both the sending and the service are supported by the addition of the ransom logion[a–b], Luke 22.27, and Philippians 2.7. These three traditions have in common the notion of Jesus' service.[32] They also can be understood to share the notion of Jesus' incarnational coming from preexistence.[33] Therefore, Origen appears to believe that the same story of Jesus' preexistent coming as a servant is being told in the ransom logion[a–b], Luke 22.27, and Philippians 2.7, and these three together explain what it means for Christ to be sent.

4.3.3 Commentary on Psalm 29.10; 43.27; 115.3; 129.3–5 (Questionable Authenticity)

While it is certain that Origen wrote extensively on the Psalms, there is a great deal of uncertainty regarding the authenticity of the texts previously suggested as his.[34] There have been attempts to validate Origen's authorship of commentaries on the Psalms by using the criteria of agreement with Origen's known writings, and by making better use of the catenae of early writings for locating authentic material.[35] However, despite these efforts, there

---

[32] Romans 15.8, Mark 10.45/Matthew 20.28, Luke 22.27, and Philippians 2.7 are the only places in the New Testament where διακον- or δουλ- are connected with Jesus' service. The New Testament never connects Jesus with ὑπηρετ-.

[33] Concerning Philippians 2.7, Origen understands the phrase, μορφὴν δούλου λαβών, as a reference to the incarnation (G. Bostock, "Origen's Exegesis of the Kenosis Hymn (Philippians 2:5–11)," in *Origeniana Sexta: Origène et la Bible / Origen and the Bible* [ed. G. Dorival and A. le Boulluec; BETL 118; Leuven: Peeters/Leuven University Press, 1995], 531–47). Clement of Alexandria also understands the phrase as a reference to the incarnation (See discussion of *Paedagogus* 3.2.2 below in 5.4.1.3). Concerning the ransom logion[a–b], in Origen's *Commentary on Matthew* 20.28 he interprets the "coming" described in the ransom logion[a–b] as a "visitor in the generation of humans" (ἐπεδήμησε γὰρ τῷ γένει τῶν ἀνθρώπων) (See 4.3.1 above).

[34] The texts in question are primarily located in the editions of J. Pitra (*Analecta Sacra Spicilegio Solesmensi Parata* [vol. 3; Parisiis: Jonby et Roger, 1883]) and C. De La Rue (*Origenes II* [ed. J. Migne; PG 12; Paris, 1862). See E. Mühlenberg for a concise summary of the situation, which he rightly says: "liegt noch im Dunkeln" ("Zur Überlieferung des Psalmenkommentars von Origenes," in *Texte und Textkritik: Eine Aufsatzsammlung* [ed. J. Dummer; TU 133; Berlin: Akademie-Verlag, 1987], 441–42).

[35] The forthcoming volumes in the series entitled *Origenes Psalmenkommentierung* should bring some finality to the discussion of the cantenae tradition (Teil 1: Prologe [Franz Xaver Risch, Berlin]; Teil 2: Kommentar zu Psalm 1–50 [Barbara Hanus, Berlin]; Teil 3: Kommentar zu Psalm 51–100 [Cordula Bandt, Berlin]; Teil 4: Kommentar zu Psalm 101–151 [Franz Xaver Risch, Berlin]).

still remains much irresolution regarding Origen's supposed authorship of extant comments on the Psalms. Despite this uncertainty, all four of the questionable receptions listed in *Biblia Patristica* are still discussed (Psalm 29.10; 43.27; 115.3; 129.3–5 LXX).[36] Out of these, the comments on Psalm 43.27 and 115.3 are rather insignificant. Alternatively, the comments on Psalm 29.10 and 129.3–5 are important in that they both showcase themes that are recurrent in the reception of the ransom logion. For this reason Psalm 29.10 and 129.3–5 are given some brief discussion concerning their potential origin with Origen.[37]

4.3.3.1 Commentary on Psalm 29.10[38]

Mark 10.45[c]   καὶ δοῦναι τὴν ψυχὴν αὐτοῦ λύτρον ἀντὶ πολλῶν
Psalm 29.10 (393, 1–2)   δόντος τὴν ψυχὴν   λύτρον ἀντὶ πολλῶν

The greater context of this reception is as follows: "There has been much improvement and profit because the savior gave his soul as a ransom for many, as each person has been ransomed by his blood out of the empty life handed down from their ancestors. For it is the Father's good pleasure that the sin of the world might be taken away by the overflowing blood of his lamb."[39]

Concerning authenticity, there is uncertainty within the text itself about whether the comments come from Origen or Didymus.[40] Regardless of whether the comments are from Origen, the fact remains that they bear witness to co-traditional receptions with 1Peter 1.18–19 and John 1.29. 1Peter 1.18–19 influences the following statement: "each person has been ransomed by his blood out of the empty life handed down from their ancestors" (ὡς καὶ τῷ αἵματι αὐτοῦ ἕκαστον λελυτρῶσθαι ἐκ τῆς ματαίας ἀναστροφῆς πατροπαραδότου//ἐλυτρώθητε ἐκ τῆς ματαίας ὑμῶν ἀναστροφῆς πατ-

---

[36] *Biblia Patristica* 3.261.

[37] The only reason for devoting space to the discussion of authenticity is to show that the questionable texts may still be inside the third century. I am aware that this date is a bit arbitrary, but I wanted to try my best to keep the receptions as close to the end of the third century as possible. However, even if the comments on Psalm 29.10 and 129.3–5 are outside the third century, the fact remains that they represent witnesses to several recurrent themes in the reception of the ransom logion, even if they are a bit later than Origen himself.

[38] The primary text comes from M.-J. Rondeau, "A propos d'une édition de Didyme l'Aveugle," *RevG* 81 (1968): 385–400.

[39] Πολλὴ μὲν βελτίωσις καὶ ὠφέλεια γεγένηται τοῦ Σωτῆρος δόντος τὴν ψυχὴν λύτρον ἀντὶ πολλῶν, ὡς καὶ τῷ αἵματι αὐτοῦ ἕκαστον λελυτρῶσθαι ἐκ τῆς ματαίας ἀναστροφῆς πατροπαραδότου. Καὶ γὰρ τοῦ Πατρὸς ἡ εὐδοκία τῇ ἐκύσει τοῦ αἵματος τοῦ ἀμνοῦ ἀρθῆναι τοῦ κόσμου τὴν ἁμαρτίαν (ibid., 392, 19 through 393, 5).

[40] "Ὠρ(ιγένους) Δ(ιδύμου)" (ibid., 392, 19). For a discussion, see Rondeau (ibid., 392–93 n. 15). The lines immediately following the above text appear in the comments on Psalms credited to Origen by De La Rue. Compare Rondeau (ibid., 393, 5–9) with De La Rue (*Origenes II*, 1296, 50 through 1297, 3).

ροπαραδότου...τιμίῳ αἵματι [1Peter 1.18–19]). Origen previously referred to 1Peter 1.18–19 in his *Commentary on Matthew* 20.28 in a similar manner – making blood a further ransom payment in addition to Jesus' soul. John 1.29 influences the statement: "the sin of the world might be taken away by the overflowing blood of his lamb" (τῇ ἐκύσει τοῦ αἵματος τοῦ ἀμνοῦ ἀρθῆναι τοῦ κόσμου τὴν ἁμαρτίαν//ὁ ἀμνὸς τοῦ θεοῦ ὁ αἴρων τὴν ἁμαρτίαν τοῦ κόσμου [John 1.29]). The move from 1Peter 1.18–19 to John 1.29 is probably made based on the shared language of ἀμνός.

4.3.3.2 Commentary on Psalm 43.27[41]

Mark 10.45ᶜ   καὶ δοῦναι τὴν ψυχὴν αὐτοῦ λύτρον ἀντὶ πολλῶν
Psalm 43.27 (1428, 31–32)   τὴν ψυχὴν αὐτοῦ λύτρον διδοὺς ἀντὶ πολλῶν

In Origen's comments on Psalm 43.27, he states: "These things were spoken concerning the Savior when he was staying in the heart of the land at the time of [his] suffering in which, by giving his life as a ransom for many, he accomplished these things in behalf of the glory of his name."[42] Origen's use of the ransom logion does not appear to bear on his other comments. It is simply a parenthetical insertion that arose through connecting the word λύτρον from the ransom logionᶜ with the word λυτρόω from the Psalm.[43]

4.3.3.3 Commentary on Psalm 115.3[44]

Mark 10.45ᶜ   καὶ δοῦναι τὴν ψυχὴν αὐτοῦ λύτρον ἀντὶ πολλῶν
Psalm 115.3 (1577, 7–8)   ὅτι ἑαυτὸν ὁ Κύριος ἔδωκε λύτρον ἀντὶ πολλῶν ἡμῶν

As was the case with Psalm 43.27, Origen's comments on Psalm 115.3 are not elaborate. His reflection on the verse focuses, not on the question of what one can give the Lord but on all that the Lord has given. After a brief discussion of the Lord's incarnation (1577, 2–6), Origen reveals the content of "the plan in behalf of humanity" (τὴν ὑπὲρ τοῦ γένους τῶν ἀνθρώπων οἰκονομίαν), which is the ransom logionᶜ. Following this, Origen gives the ransom logionᶜ no further discussion.

---

[41] The primary text comes from De La Rue (*Origenes II*).

[42] Λέγοιεν τοιαῦτα πρὸς τὸν Σωτῆρα ἐν τῇ καρδίᾳ τῆς γῆς διατρίθοντα κατὰ τὸν τοῦ πάθους καιρόν· ὅς, τὴν ψυχὴν αὐτοῦ λύτρον διδοὺς ἀντὶ πολλῶν, ποιεῖ ταῦτα ὑπὲρ τῆς δόξης τοῦ ὀνόματος αὐτοῦ (ibid., 1428, 29–33).

[43] Psalm 43.27 LXX states: "Rise up, Lord, help us, and redeem (λύτρωσαι) us for your name's sake."

[44] The primary text comes from De La Rue, ibid.

4.3.3.4 Commentary on Psalm 129.3–5[45]

Mark 10.45ᶜ   καὶ δοῦναι τὴν ψυχὴν αὐτοῦ λύτρον ἀντὶ πολλῶν
Psalm 129.3–5 (327, 23–24)   Τὸ γὰρ τίμιον αὐτοῦ λύτρον ὑπὲρ ἡμῶν δέδωκεν αἷμα

Within the commentary on Psalm 129.3–5, the author states the following: Τὸ γὰρ τίμιον αὐτοῦ λύτρον ὑπὲρ ἡμῶν δέδωκεν αἷμα, γενόμενος ἀμνὸς τοῦ Θεοῦ· οὗτος γὰρ τὰς ἁμαρτίας ἡμῶν φέρει, καὶ περὶ ἡμῶν ὀδυνᾶται. Ἐποίησε δὲ καὶ λύτρωσιν τῷ λαῷ αὐτοῦ, κατὰ τὸν Ζαχαρίαν, καὶ κατὰ τὴν ἁγίαν Παρθένον· Ἀντελάβετο Ἰσραήλ (327, 23–29).

These words also appear in writings credited to Eusebius by Mai. Eusebius is said to have stated the following concerning Psalm 129.7 LXX: Τὸ γὰρ τίμιον αὐτοῦ αἷμα ὑπὲρ ἡμῶν δέδωκεν λύτρον, γενόμενος ἀμνὸς τοῦ Θεοῦ· οὗτος γὰρ τὰς ἁμαρτίας ἡμῶν φέρει, καὶ περὶ ἡμῶν ὀδυνᾶται. Ἐποίησε δὲ καὶ λύτρωσιν τῷ λαῷ αὐτοῦ, κατὰ τὸν Ζαχαρίαν, καὶ κατὰ τὴν ἁγίαν Παρθενον· Ἀντελάβετο Ἰσραήλ.[46] This text is exactly the same as the one accredited to Origen, except αἷμα and λύτρον are reversed in the Eusebius text. Of course, Eusebius' version is also questionable in terms of authenticity.[47] However, if the text is authentic, then perhaps Eusebius is showing his dependence on Origen. Or, if the comments on Psalm 129.3–5 are not from Origen, then perhaps they originated in the writings of Eusebius. We simply do not know.

The most intriguing part of the comments credited to Origen is the following: Τὸ γὰρ τίμιον αὐτοῦ λύτρον ὑπὲρ ἡμῶν δέδωκεν αἷμα, γενόμενος ἀμνὸς τοῦ Θεοῦ· οὗτος γὰρ τὰς ἁμαρτίας ἡμῶν φέρει, καὶ περὶ ἡμῶν ὀδυνᾶται (327, 23–26). There are three items of significance in this statement. First, the idea of τίμιον...αἷμα represents a connection with 1Peter 1.19. This connection leads the author to replace Jesus' soul with his blood as the ransom price. Although such a replacement does not happen in Origen's *Commentary on Matthew* 20.28, it is easy to see how his thought is going in that direction – "Therefore, on the one hand, we were bought with the precious blood of Jesus, and on the other hand, the soul of the Son of God was given as a ransom in behalf of us..."[48]

---

[45] The primary text comes from Pitra, *Analecta Sacra*.

[46] A. Mai, *Eusebii Pamphili: Commentaria in Psalmos* (ed. J. -P. Migne; PG 24; Paris, 1857), 24, 48–53. I located this parallel in Eusebius through a *Thesaurus Linguae Graecae* search of λύτρον (Accessed on 29 July 2008).

[47] According to M. -J. Rondeau and J. Kirchmeyer the comments on Psalm 95.3–150, in which this text falls, are of mixed authentic and inauthentic Eusebian material ("Eusèbe de Césarée," *DS* 4:1690).

[48] Klostermann, *Origenes Werke X. 1*, 499, 19–22. Cf. the above comments on Psalm 29.10 (4.3.3.1).

Second, the author makes a reference to Jesus as the ἀμνὸς τοῦ Θεου. This identification comes from John 1.29, and the move to John 1.29 could have been prompted by the ἀμνός language shared between 1Peter 1.19 and John 1.29.

Third, the author's statement, οὗτος γὰρ τὰς ἁμαρτίας ἡμῶν φέρει, καὶ περὶ ἡμῶν ὀδυνᾶται, is clearly a citation of Isaiah 53.4. It is difficult to determine whether the author understood οὗτος to be linked with the immediately preceding ἀμνός, or with the subject of δέδωκεν, or both. It is possible that the author only linked Isaiah 53.4 with ἀμνός, in which case Isaiah 53.4 would be connected with John 1.29, but not the ransom logion[c].[49] However, favoring a connection between the ransom logion[c] and Isaiah 53.4 is that in both cases the concern is for ἡμῶν. Such a concern is not present in John 1.29, nor within the psalm. Whatever the case, the author's citation of Isaiah 53.4 is in harmony with the psalmist's desire to obtain forgiveness from sin.

4.3.4 Fragments on Ephesians 1.7; 1Corinthians 6.19–20

4.3.4.1 Fragment on Ephesians 1.7[50]

| Mark 10.45[c] | καὶ δοῦναι τὴν ψυχὴν αὐτοῦ λύτρον ἀντὶ πολλῶν |
| *Eph.* 1.7 (238, 18) | ἔδωκεν οὖν ὁ σωτὴρ τὸ ὑπὲρ ἡμῶν λύτρον τὸ ἑαυτοῦ αἷμα |

The greater context of the fragment is as follows: ἐν ᾧ ἔχομεν τὴν ἀπολύτρωσιν διὰ τοῦ αἵματος αὐτοῦ, τὴν ἄφεσιν τῶν παραπτωμάτων (Ephesians 1.7). ἀπολύτρωσις [ἢ] λύτρωσις γίνεται τῶν αἰχμαλώτων καὶ γενομένων ὑπὸ τοῖς πολεμίοις· γεγόναμεν δὲ ὑπὸ τοῖς πολεμίοις τῷ ἄρχοντι τοῦ αἰῶνος τούτου καὶ ταῖς ὑπ᾽ αὐτὸν πονηραῖς δυνάμεσι, καὶ διὰ τοῦτο ἐδεήθημεν ἀπολυτρώσεως καὶ τοῦ ἐξαγοράζοντος ἡμᾶς ἵνα ἡμᾶς ἀπαλλοτριωθέντας αὐτοῦ ἀπολάβῃ· ἔδωκεν οὖν ὁ σωτὴρ τὸ ὑπὲρ ἡμῶν λύτρον τὸ ἑαυτοῦ αἷμα· διόπερ ἔχομεν τὴν ἀπολύτρωσιν διὰ τοῦ αἵματος αὐτοῦ, τὴν ἄφεσιν τῶν παραπτωμάτων (238, 9–16).

Within the fragment, it is easy to observe influence from the ransom logion[c] (ἔδωκεν οὖν ὁ σωτὴρ τὸ ὑπὲρ ἡμῶν λύτρον τὸ ἑαυτοῦ αἷμα). The substitution of blood for soul as the ransom price has become a frequent occurrence in Origen's receptions of the ransom logion[c]. Here the replacement is likely motivated by influence from Ephesians 1.7, where blood is the price of the redemption.[51] Preceding the ransom logion is a ransom to Satan

---

[49] This would make sense if the author is using Isaiah 53.4 to expand on the statement in John 1.29 that Jesus is the lamb of God *who takes away the sin of the world*.

[50] The primary text comes from J. Gregg, "The Commentary of Origen upon the Epistle to the Ephesians," *JTS* 10 (1902): 233–44.

[51] However, Origen does not allow ἀπολύτρωσιν from Ephesians 1.7 to replace λύτρον from the ransom logion[c].

motif. Satan appears to be described by the phrase, τῷ ἄρχοντι τοῦ αἰῶνος τούτου, which may be a reference to Ephesians 2.2 or 2Corinthians 4.4.

4.3.4.2 Fragment on 1Corinthians 6.19–20[52]

| Mark 10.45[c] | καὶ δοῦναι τὴν ψυχὴν αὐτοῦ λύτρον ἀντὶ πολλῶν |
| *1Cor. 6.19–20* (372, 9–10) | ἐδόθη λύτρον ὑπὲρ ὑμῶν τὸ αἷμα τοῦ χριστοῦ |

The greater context of this reception is as follows: πᾶν ἁμάρτημα ὃ ἐὰν ποιήσῃ ἄνθρωπος ἐκτὸς τοῦ σώματός ἐστιν (1Corinthians 6.18). ἐπειδὴ οὖν ἐδόθη λύτρον ὑπὲρ ὑμῶν τὸ αἷμα τοῦ χριστοῦ καὶ ἔλαβεν ὑμᾶς ἀπὸ τῆς ἐξουσίας τοῦ διαβόλου, δοξάσατε τὸν θεὸν ἐν τῷ σώματι ὑμῶν (1Corinthians 6.20) (372, 8–11).

Origen uses the ransom logion[c] to lead into the imperative, δοξάσατε τὸν θεὸν ἐν τῷ σώματι ὑμῶν (1Corinthians 6.20). 1Corinthians 6.20 reads in its entirety as: ἠγοράσθητε γὰρ τιμῆς· δοξάσατε δὴ τὸν θεὸν ἐν τῷ σώματι ὑμῶν. Therefore, it is likely that Origen has inserted the ransom logion[c] as an interpretation of 1Corinthians 6.20[a]: ἠγοράσθητε γὰρ τιμῆς.

Blood is the ransom price, and the Satan (διαβόλου) motif is explicit.

4.3.5 Conclusion

The high level of similarity Origen demonstrates in his reception of the ransom logion, as well as of other texts, is striking compared to other writers examined thus far. Origen makes thorough use of the ransom logion, although some of these uses might be questionable in terms of authenticity. There are five items that surface in Origen's use of the ransom logion.

First, Origen interprets the ransom logion[a–b] as an incarnational statement. This is clear in his *Commentary on Matthew* 20.28, and in the *Fragment on Luke* 14.16, where he uses Philippians 2.7 as a co-tradition.

Second, Origen consistently appeals to 1Peter 1.18–19 as an elaboration on the ransom logion[c]. There are allusions to 1Peter 1.18–19 in Origen's *Commentary on Matthew* 20.28, *on Psalm* 29.10, and *on Psalm* 129.3–5. Influence from 1Peter 1.18–19 is likely one of the main reasons that Origen begins to replace soul with blood as the ransom payment.

Third, the Ransom to Satan motif is present in Origen's *Commentary on Matthew* 20.28, *Ephesians* 1.7, and *1Corinthians* 6.19–20.

Fourth, Origen uses John 1.29 as a co-tradition to the ransom logion[c] in his *Commentary on Psalm* 29.10 and *Psalm* 129.3–5. In both of these places Origen also uses 1Peter 1.18–19. Therefore, the move to John 1.29 could be prompted by the ἀμνός language shared between 1Peter 1.19 and John 1.29.

---

[52] The primary text comes from C. Jenkins, "Origen on I Corinthians," *JTS* 35 (1908): 353–72.

Fifth, there is a clear use of Isaiah 53.4 in Origen's comments on Psalm 129.3–5, but it is difficult to tell if it is connected to the ransom logion[c].

Source	Supposed Tradition	Exemplar	Similarity	Further Comments
Origen, *Commentary on Matthew* 20.28	Ransom Logion	Mark 10.45	S1	
	Incarnation	N/A	N/A	
	Colossians 1.15–16	Colossians 1.15–16	S1	
	1Peter 1.18–19	1Peter 1.18–19	S1	Blood is an additional ransom payment
	1Corinthians 7.23	1Corinthians 7.23	S1	Linked with 1Peter 1.19
	Luke 23.46	Luke 23.46	S1	
	Psalm 15.10	Psalm 15.10	S1	
	Ransom to Satan	N/A	N/A	
Origen, *Fragment on Luke* 14.16	Ransom Logion[a–b]	Mark 10.45[a–b]	S1	
	Incarnation	N/A	N/A	ἀποστελλόμενος
	Philippians 2.7	Philippians 2.7	S1	
	Luke 22.27	Luke 22.27	S1	
Origen, *Commentary on Psalm* 29.10	Ransom Logion[c]	Mark 10.45[c]	S2	
	1Peter 1.18–19	1Peter 1.18–19	S1	Blood is an additional ransom payment.
	John 1.29	John 1.29	S2	
Origen, *Commentary on Psalm* 43.27	Ransom Logion[c]	Mark 10.45[c]	S1	
Origen, *Commentary on Psalm* 115.3	Ransom Logion[c]	Mark 10.45[c]	S2	
Origen, *Commentary on Psalm* 129.3–5	Ransom Logion[c]	Mark 10.45[c]	S3	
	1Peter 1.19	1Peter 1.19	S3	Blood replaces soul
	John 1.29	John 1.29	S3	
	Isaiah 53.4	Isaiah 53.4	S1	
Origen, *Fragment on Ephesians* 1.7	Ransom Logion[c]	Mark 10.45[c]	S3	Blood replaces soul
	Ephesians 1.7	Ephesians 1.7	S1	
	Ransom to Satan	N/A	N/A	
Origen, *Fragment on 1Corinthians* 6.19–20	Ransom Logion[c]	Mark 10.45[c]	S3	Blood replaces soul
	1Corinthians 6.18, 20	1Corinthians 6.18, 20	S1	
	Ransom to Satan	N/A	N/A	

4.4 The Acts of Thomas 39; 72[53]

Mark 10.45[c]   καὶ δοῦναι τὴν ψυχὴν αὐτοῦ λύτρον ἀντὶ πολλῶν
Acts of Thomas 39 (156, 18)   τοὺς ἰδίους λυτρωσαμένου
Acts of Thomas 72 (188, 7)   σῆς ψυχῆς ἧς ἔδωκας [ἀντικατάλλαγμα] ὑπὲρ ἡμῶν

The Acts of Thomas (Acts Thom.) dates to the first half of the third century. While there are many versions of Acts Thom., the principal ones are Syriac and Greek. The current scholarly consensus is that Acts Thom. was originally written in Syriac, and shortly thereafter translated into Greek. However, while acknowledging this consensus, Klijn states that it is "too easy to assume an original Syriac text which has been translated into Greek. We suppose that the Acts were written in a bilingual environment in which both the Syriac and Greek versions originated simultaneously."[54] In this study, I am dependent on the Greek version.[55]

4.4.1 The Acts of Thomas 39

Biblia Patristica says that the following text from Acts Thom. 39 contains a reception of the ransom logion: Ὁ δίδυμος τοῦ Χριστοῦ...ὃς ἐλεύθερος ὢν γέγονας δοῦλος καὶ πραθεὶς πολλοὺς εἰς ἐλευθερίαν εἰσήγαγες· ὁ συγγενὴς τοῦ μεγάλου γένους τοῦ τὸν ἐχθρὸν καταδικάσαντος καὶ τοὺς ἰδίους [αὐτοῦ][56] λυτρωσαμένου.[57] The primary evidences for the presence of the ransom logion are the similarities to Mark 10.45/Matthew 20.28 in-

---

[53] The primary text comes from Lipsius and Bonnet, *Acta Apostolorum Apocrypha* (Lipsiae: Apud Hermannum Mendelssohn), 1891–1903. *Biblia Patristica* (2.277) lists three receptions of Matthew 20.28 in *The Acts of Thomas*. Two are in the Greek version edited by Lipsius and Bonnet, and one is in the Syriac version edited by W. Wright (*Apocryphal Acts of the Apostles* [London: Williams & Norgate, 1871]). I am not discussing the reception in the volume edited by Wright because it is the same as the reception from *Acts Thom.* 72 in the volume edited by Lipsius and Bonnet.

[54] A. Klijn, *The Acts of Thomas: Introduction, Text, and Commentary* (NovTSup 108; Leiden: Brill, 2003), 3.

[55] It is standard practice to rely on the Greek version. The Syriac has been heavily edited, while the Greek better maintains the original (J. Elliott, *The Apocryphal New Testament: A Collection of Apocryphal Christian Literature in an English Translation based on M. R. James* [Oxford: Oxford University Press, 1993], 439–40).

[56] There is a textual problem concerning the sense of τοῦ μεγάλου γένους τοῦ...τοὺς ἰδίους [αὐτοῦ] λυτρωσαμένου. It appears that the μεγάλου γένους should be identified with the person of Jesus since it is clear in the second part of *Acts Thom.* 39 that it is Jesus who "ransoms his own sheep" (λυτρωσάμενος τοὺς ἰδίους ἄρας [Lipsius and Bonnet, *Acta Apostolorum*, 157, 15]). In order to clarify that μεγάλου γένους does refer to Jesus, a variant reading of αὐτοῦ has been inserted before λυτρωσαμένου. I have placed this variant in the text for the purposes of clarification.

[57] Lipsius and Bonnet, *Acta Apostolorum*, 156, 13, 15–18. *Biblia Patristica* (2.277) only lists the line containing τοὺς ἰδίους λυτρωσαμένου as the reception of Matthew 20.28.

volved in becoming a servant (δοῦλος), leading the many (πολλούς), and ransoming (λυτρωσαμένου).[58]

In my opinion, these evidences are not overly strong. However, they can be strengthened if the above text is read in light of its parallel at the end of Acts Thom. 39, where Thomas states the following about Jesus: ὁ ἀγαθὸς ποιμὴν ὁ ἑαυτὸν ἐκδοὺς ὑπὲρ τῶν ἰδίων προβάτων καὶ τὸν λύκον νικήσας καὶ λυτρωσάμενος τοὺς ἰδίους ἄρας.[59] This text uses the same expression as the above text from the first part of Acts Thom. 39, that is, λυτρωσ- τοὺς ἰδίους. This suggests that the text from the first part of Acts Thom. 39, and the one from the latter part of Acts Thom. 39, can be read together.

The text in the latter part of Acts Thom. 39 is certainly an allusion to John 10.11, 15.[60] However, there are clues that within the allusion to John 10.11, 15 the author is blending John's language with language from Mark 10.45/Matthew 20.28. These clues consist of the words ἐκδοὺς and λυτρωσάμενος, which are not paralleled in John 10.11, 15, but which resemble Mark 10.45/Matthew 20.28[c]. Given the linguistic similarities between the first part of Acts Thom. 39 and Mark 10.45/Matthew 20.28 (δοῦλος, πολλοὺς, and λυτρωσ-), and the additional language of λυτρωσ- and ἐκδοὺς within the allusion to John 10.11, 15 in the latter part of Acts Thom. 39, I think it is reasonable to suggest that there is sufficient similarity to Mark 10.45/Matthew 20.28 in Acts Thom. 39 to regard this as a reception of the ransom logion.

The ransom logion in Acts Thom. 39 is certainly linked with John 10.11, 15. There are two other motifs that also deserve mention. First, the statement about Thomas from the first part of Acts Thom. 39, ὃς ἐλεύθερος ὢν γέγονας δοῦλος, probably refers to the events in Acts Thom. 2. However, the language also appears to reflect what is said about Jesus in Philippians 2.6–7. Just as Jesus existed in the form of God and took on the form of a slave, so Thomas was free and also became a slave. Second, in both parts of Acts Thom. 39 there is a reference to the defeat of the ἐχθρὸν/λύκον directly preceding the mention of λυτρωσ-. This is probably a reference to a ransom to Satan motif, though "Satan" is not explicit.

---

[58] The functions of becoming a servant, and leading many into freedom, are attributed to Thomas. This is no doubt because of Thomas' close association with Christ.

[59] Lipsius and Bonnet, *Acta Apostolorum*, 157, 13–15. *Biblia Patristica* does not list this statement as a reception of Matthew 20.28. This is likely due to the fact that it is an obvious allusion to John 10.11, 15.

[60] ὁ ἀγαθὸς ποιμὴν ὁ ἑαυτὸν ἐκδοὺς ὑπὲρ τῶν ἰδίων προβάτων (Acts Thom. 39). Ἐγώ εἰμι ὁ ποιμὴν ὁ καλός. ὁ ποιμὴν ὁ καλὸς τὴν ψυχὴν αὐτοῦ τίθησιν ὑπὲρ τῶν προβάτων·...καὶ τὴν ψυχήν μου τίθημι ὑπὲρ τῶν προβάτων (John 10.11, 15).

4.4.2 The Acts of Thomas 72

The reception of the ransom logion[c] in Acts Thom. 72 encompasses more than the single line of text highlighted in the initial comparison. The larger context is as follows: Ἰησοῦ ὁ τύπον λαβὼν καὶ γενόμενος ὡς ἄνθρωπος καὶ πᾶσιν ἡμῖν φανεὶς ἵνα μὴ ἡμᾶς ἀποχωρίσῃς τῆς ἰδίας ἀγάπης· σὺ εἶ κύριε ὁ ἑαυτὸν δοὺς ὑπὲρ ἡμῶν καὶ τῷ αἵματί σου ἡμᾶς ἐξαγοράσας καὶ κτησάμενος ἡμᾶς κτῆμα πολυτίμητον· τί δὲ ἔχομέν σοι δοῦναι κύρ-ιε ἀντικατάλλαγμα τῆς σῆς ψυχῆς ἧς ἔδωκας ὑπὲρ ἡμῶν...[61]

The reception of the ransom logion[c] is first reflected in the words ὁ ἑαυτὸν δοὺς ὑπὲρ ἡμῶν. This is then repeated as: τῆς σῆς ψυχῆς ἧς ἔδωκας [ἀν-τικατάλλαγμα] ὑπὲρ ἡμῶν. Overall, τῆς σῆς ψυχῆς ἧς ἔδωκας [ἀντικα-τάλλαγμα] ὑπὲρ ἡμῶν, is conceptually indistinguishable from Mark 10.45/Matthew 20.28[c].[62]

There are two notable motifs in the immediate vicinity. First, it is highly probable that the statement, Ἰησοῦ ὁ τύπον λαβὼν καὶ γενόμενος ὡς ἄνθρωπος, is reflective of Philippians 2.7 (...μορφὴν δούλου λαβών, ἐν ὁμοιώματι ἀνθρώπων γενόμενος...). Second, the clause, καὶ τῷ αἵματί σου ἡμᾶς ἐξαγοράσας, may be an allusion to Revelation 5.9 (αἱ ἠγόρασας τῷ θεῷ ἐν τῷ αἵματί σου).

In conclusion, the author of Acts Thom. is someone who knows the scrip-tures and alludes to them frequently. None of the allusions discussed above are explicit, though several are certainly present. There is good evidence to suggest a reception of the ransom logion, and particularly the ransom logion[c] in Acts Thom. 72. Alongside the ransom logion are strong allusions to John 10.11, 15 (Acts Thom. 39) and Revelation 5.9 (Acts Thom. 72), as well as Philippians 2.6–7 (mostly in Acts Thom. 72). It is also probable that a form of the ransom to Satan motif is present (ἐχθρὸν/λύκον...λυτρωσ- [Acts Thom. 39]). It is significant that most of these allusions and motifs are linked with the ransom logion elsewhere. Such consistency validates the likely presence of the ransom logion in Acts Thom. 39 and 72, as well as demonstrates the strong traditions that existed for reading the ransom logion.

---

[61] Lipsius and Bonnet, *Acta Apostolorum*, 188, 2–7.

[62] Ἀντικατάλλαγμα has an overlapping semantic range with λύτρον, and it does not oc-cur in any form anywhere else in *Acts Thom.* The more basic form, ἄλλαγμα, appears near receptions of the ransom logion in Diongetus 9.2–5; Eusebius, *Commentary on Isaiah* 43.1; *Commentary on Psalm* 54.20 LXX.

Source	Supposed Tradition	Exemplar	Simi-larity	Further Comments
The Acts of Tho-mas 39	Ransom Logion	Mark 10.45	S3	First and second part of Acts Thom. 39
	John 10.11, 15	John 10.11, 15	S2	Second part of Acts Thom. 39
	Philippians 2.6–7	Philippians 2.6–7	S4	First part of Acts Thom. 39; precedes ransom logion
	Ransom to Satan	Ransom to Satan	N/A	ἐχθρὸν/λύκον; first and sec-ond part of Acts Thom. 39
The Acts of Tho-mas 72	Ransom Logion[c]	Mark 10.45[c]	S2	
	Philippians 2.7	Philippians 2.7	S2	Precedes ransom logion
	Revelation 5.9	Revelation 5.9	S3	

4.5 Pseudo Clement of Rome, *Homilies* 12.7.5[63]

Mark 10.45[a–b]   ὁ υἱὸς τοῦ ἀνθρώπου οὐκ ἦλθεν διακονηθῆναι ἀλλὰ διακονῆσαι

Homilies 12.7.5   δουλείαν ὑπέμεινεν, ἵνα ἡμᾶς πείσῃ μὴ αἰδεῖσθαι τοῖς ἀδελφοῖς
(177, 17–18)   ἡμῶν τὰς δούλων ποιεῖν ὑπηρεσίας

The Pseudo Clementines, *Homilies* and *Recognitions*, are two fourth-century redactions of an earlier third-century Greek work, often called the *Grund-schrift*.[64] Unfortunately, the *Grundschrift* is no longer extant, and only the two redactions survive. One of the redactions, *Homilies*, is preserved in its original Greek by two manuscripts from the 11th/12th and 14th centuries.[65] The other redaction, *Recognitions*, is extant mainly in Latin and Syriac versions. Since both *Homilies* and *Recognitions* are redactions of the same earlier work, we are able to have contact with that earlier work when *Homilies* and *Recognitions* are in agreement with one another.[66] Fortunately, *Homilies* and *Recogni-*

---

[63] The primary text for *Homilies* comes from B. Rehm, *Die Pseudoklementinen I. Homilien* (GCS; Berlin: Akademie-Verlag, 1953). The parallel text from *Recognitions* is in B. Rehm, *Die Pseudoklementinen II. Rekognitionen in Rufins Übersetzung* (GCS; Berlin: Akademie-Verlag, 1965).

[64] The *Grundschrift* is normally dated around 220 CE (F. Jones, "The Pseudo-Clementines," in *Jewish Christianity Reconsidered* [ed. M. Jackson-McCabe; Minneapolis: Fortress Press, 2007], 285), who follows C. Schmidt (*Studien zu den Pseudo-Clementinen* [TU 46.1; Leipzig: J. C. Hinrichs, 1929], 313).

[65] Rehm, *Die Pseudoklementinen I*, ix.

[66] According to Jones, "Those ideas and phrases that are found in both the *Homilies* and the *Recognitions* are the ones that can be assuredly ascribed to the underlying *Circuits of Pe-ter* [*Grundschrift*]" ("The Pseudo-Clementines," 290). While it is a standard view that *Homi-lies* and *Recognitions* are dependent on the same earlier work (*Grundschrift*), their depend-

tions are in agreement on the text in question. Therefore, I will limit my examination to the Greek text of *Homilies*.[67]

The greater context of *Homilies* 12.7.5 is a narration in which Clement asks Peter if he can be his servant (*Homilies* 12.5). Peter replies by pointing to his own humble lifestyle, and then suggests that it would be better that he serve Clement (12.6). This notion upsets Clement since Peter, unlike himself, is the herald of God who saves souls (12.7). This prompts Peter to point out the example of Jesus, saying: ὁ κύριος ἡμῶν ὁ ἐπὶ σωτηρίᾳ παντὸς τοῦ κόσμου ἐληλυθώς, μόνος ὑπὲρ πάντας εὐγενὴς ὤν, δουλείαν ὑπέμεινεν, ἵνα ἡμᾶς πείσῃ μὴ αἰδεῖσθαι τοῖς ἀδελθοῖς ἡμῶν τὰς δούλων ποιεῖν ὑπηρεσίας (12.7.5 [177,16–19]).

Biblia Patristica, following Rehm, suggests that there is a reception of the ransom logion in line 18, which states: ἵνα ἡμᾶς πείσῃ μὴ αἰδεῖσθαι τοῖς ἀδελθοῖς ἡμῶν τὰς δούλων ποιεῖν ὑπηρεσίας. This is surely incorrect since the statement has nothing to do with Jesus' service, but with the disciples' service. If there is a reception of the ransom logion in the above statement, then it comes from the previous line (17), which states about Jesus: δουλείαν ὑπέμεινεν. However, even here the similarity with the Mark 10.45/Matthew 20.28[a–b] is slim. The only parallel is the idea that Jesus serves.[68]

It is very difficult to see any substantive similarity between *Homilies* 12.7.5 and Mark 10.45/Matthew 20.28[a–b]. *Homilies* 12.7.5 appears to be much more reflective of John 13.4–17, which is also mentioned by Rehm as a possible allusion. The back-and-forth between Peter and Clement, and the distress of Clement that Peter would serve him, easily parallels the same exchange between Jesus and Peter (John 13.6–10). Therefore, if there is a reception, then it is most likely that Peter's recollection of Jesus' service is meant to focus on John 13.4–17, and not the ransom logion[a–b].

---

ence on one another is debated. The majority of scholars support the mutual independence of *Homilies* and *Recognitions*; however Jones notes that a few believe *Recognitions* is dependent on both the *Grundschrift* and *Homilies* ("The Pseudo-Clementines: A History of Research," in *Literature of the Early Church* [vol. 2 of *Studies in Early Christianity: A Collection of Scholarly Essays*; ed. E. Ferguson; New York and London: Garland, 1993], 208).

[67] The modern translation of *Homilies* and *Recognitions* was done by T. Smith in the *Ante-Nicene Fathers* 8.73–346 (Jones, "The Pseudo-Clementines: A History of Research," 201). A comparison between Smith's translations of *Homilies* 12.7 and *Recognitions* 7.7 demonstrates that they are the same, and so we are justified to depend on the Greek text of *Homilies* 12.7 in order to be as close as possible to the original Greek text of the *Grundschrift*. The only way to get closer would be to discern the common Greek text behind Rehm's critical Greek edition of *Homilies*, and the Syriac version of *Homilies* (The Syriac version represents an older stage of the Greek text [ibid., 197–98]).

[68] The vocabulary for service in *Homilies* 12.7.5 is δουλεία, but is διακονέω in Mark 10.45/Matthew 20.28[a–b].

In conclusion, the possibility of *Homilies* 12.7.5 being a reception of the ransom logion[a–b] is speculative at best. However, if I am missing something, and there is good evidence for the presence of the ransom logion[a–b], then I would suggest that the reception occurs alongside John 13.4–17. Also, there is a strong correspondence between the idea that Jesus was μόνος ὑπὲρ πάντας εὐγενὴς ὤν, δουλείαν ὑπέμεινεν (*Homilies* 12.7.5) and Philippians 2.6–7.

Source	Supposed Tradition	Exemplar	Simi-larity	Further Comments
Pseudo Clement of Rome, *Homilies* 12.7.5	Ransom Logion[a–b]	Mark 10.45[a–b]	S5	
	John 13.4–17	John 13.4–17	S4	Greater context in *Homilies* 12.5–7
	Philippians 2.6–7	Philippians 2.6–7	S4	

4.6 Didascalia Apostolorum 16[69]

Mark 10.45

ὁ υἱὸς τοῦ ἀνθρώπου οὐκ ἦλθεν διακονηθῆναι ἀλλὰ
διακονῆσαι καὶ δοῦναι τὴν ψυχὴν αὐτοῦ λύτρον ἀντὶ πολλῶν

Constitutiones
3.19.3 (215, 7–9)

ὡς καὶ ὁ κύριος ἡμῶν Ἰησοῦς[70] οὐκ ἦλθεν διακονηθῆναι, ἀλλὰ
διακονῆσαι καὶ δοῦναι τὴν ψυχὴν αὐτοῦ λύτρον ἀντὶ πολλῶν

Didascalia Apostolorum was originally a Greek work written in third-century Syria or Palestine.[71] The entire text is preserved in a Syriac translation from the early fourth century.[72] The major English translations by Connolly and Vööbus are from the Syriac.[73] Unfortunately, besides a few small fragments, the original Greek text is no longer extant. However, the author of Constitutiones Apostolorum used the original Greek text of Didascalia as a base for the first six books of Constitutiones.[74] Funk's Greek edition of Constitutiones

---

[69] F. Funk is the primary text for the original Greek of Didascalia (*Didascalia et Constitutiones Apostolorum* [2 vols.; Paderbornae, 1905. Repr. 2 vols. in 1; Torino: Bottega D'Erasmo, 1964]). A. Vööbus is the primary text for the English translation of Didascalia from the Syriac version (*The Didascalia Apostolorum* [CSCO. SS; Louvain: Peeters, 1979] Tome 180).

[70] The Syriac version of Didascalia includes "Son of Man."

[71] Scholars agree that Didascalia comes from the third century, though there is no consensus on a more approximate date.

[72] R. Connolly, *Didascalia Apostolorum: The Syriac Version Translated and Accompanied by the Verona Latin Fragments with Introduction and Notes* (Oxford: The Clarendon Press, 1929), xi, xviii. About two-fifths is preserved in a Latin translation.

[73] Connolly, *Didascalia Apostolorum*; Vööbus, *The Didascalia Apostolorum*, Tomes 176 and 180.

[74] Constitutiones dates to around 375 CE (Connolly, *Didascalia Apostolorum*, xx; Vööbus, *The Didascalia Apostolorum*, Tome 176: 30).

underlines everything that is not paralleled in his reconstructed Latin text of Didascalia.[75] The result is that much of the original Greek text of Didascalia is perceptible. However, the author of Constitutions was very free with Didascalia, and so using Constitutions to get to the Greek text of Didascalia must always accompany a heavy degree of uncertainty.[76]

Didascalia 16 contains instruction for deacons and deaconesses. Within this instruction is a very clear appeal to the ransom logion, along with several other scriptures. Vööbus's translation of the relevant material, along with Greek insertions from Funk, is as follows:

And know what the ministry is, according as our Lord and Savior said in the Gospel: "Whoso among you wishes to be chief, let him be to you a servant, even as the Son of Man came not to be ministered unto, but to minister, and to give His life a ransom for many" (ἦλθεν δι- ακονηθῆναι, ἀλλὰ διακονῆσαι καὶ δοῦναι τὴν ψυχὴν αὐτοῦ λύτρον ἀντὶ πολλῶν). Thus it is required of you also to do, deacons, if you have to lay down your life for your brethren in the ministry which is required for them. Indeed, also our Lord and Savior did not despise ministering unto us, as it is written in Isaiah: "To justify the righteous, who has wrought well a service for many" (δικαιῶσαι δίκαιον εὖ δουλεύοντα πολλοῖς). If then the Lord of heaven and earth "wrought a service" for us, and bore and endured everything on our account, how much more is it required of us that we likewise do for our brethren, that we may imitate Him. For we are imitators of Him, and we hold the place of Christ.

And again in the Gospel you find it written how our Lord "girded a linen cloth about His loins and cast water into a washing-basin" (λαβὼν γὰρ λέντιον διεζώσατο, εἶτα βάλλει ὕδωρ εἰς τὸν νιπτῆρα), while we reclined (at supper), and drew nigh "and washed the feet of us all and wiped them with the cloth" (ἔνιψεν τοὺς πόδας καὶ τῷ λεντίῳ ἐξέμαξεν). But this He did that He might show us the love and affection of brothers, that we also should do likewise one to another.[77]

Following what "our Lord and Savior said in his Gospel" is a clear appeal to the ransom logion, though this is not necessarily due to direct dependence on Mark 10.45/Matthew 20.28. J. J. C. Cox has insightfully noted that of the 134 appeals to the "Gospel" in Didascalia, 124 are citations of dominical sayings. Given this high dependence on sayings, Cox hypothesizes that the author of Didascalia is not directly dependent on the literary texts of the canonical or non-canonical gospels, but rather the author possesses sayings sources similar

---

[75] Funk, *Didascalia et Constitutiones Apostolorum*.

[76] It is important to note that according to Vööbus, we can be relatively sure that the Greek text of Didascalia incorporated into Constitutions was the same as the Greek text behind the Syriac translation. Vööbus states: "...the Didascalia was at the disposal of the Syriac translator, the Latin translator and the compiler of the Apostolic Constitutions in the same form representing substantially the same text...The kind of revision and editorial manipulation which appears with the work of the compiler of the Apostolic Constitutiones did not have its beginnings before his own time" (*The Didascalia Apostolorum*, Tome 176: 32).

[77] Vööbus, *The Didascalia Apostolorum*, Tome 180: 158 (line 23) through 159 (line 17). The Greek insertions come from Funk (*Didascalia et Constitutiones Apostolorum*, 1: 215).

to Q or Thomas. This would make sense if the origins of Didascalia are in Syria.[78]

Following the ransom logion is a citation of Isaiah 53.11. The author of Didascalia believes that Jesus' service described in the ransom logion is in fulfillment of the service described in Isaiah 53.11. Both the appeal to the ransom logion and the citation of Isaiah 53.11 are meant to exhort deacons to imitate the selfless ministry of Jesus. It is intriguing that the author does not limit the deacon's ability to imitate Jesus' service, neither in relation to the ransom logion, nor Isaiah 53.11. Concerning the ransom logion, the author expects the deacons similarly to lay down their lives for their brethren [also as a ransom?]. Concerning Isaiah 53.11, it initially appears that the author only focuses on the small part of Isaiah 53.11 to which the deacons can best relate: "To justify the righteous, who has wrought well a service for many."[79] However, the author explains the meaning of "wrought a service" by inserting the comment: "and bore and endured everything on our account." This comment is likely the author's summation of Isaiah 53.2–5, 12, which he quotes in Didascalia 8 in order to emphasize the sin-bearing task of Jesus, and to extend that task to the bishops.[80] After the comment, the author states: "how much more is it required of us that we likewise do for our brethren, that we may imitate Him."[81]

---

[78] Cox, "Some Prolegomena and Addenda to a Study of the Dominical *Logoi* as cited in the *Didascalia Apostolorum*" in *Studia Patristica* (vol. 16/2; Berlin: Akademie Verlag, 1985), 82–87.

[79] The LXX translation of Isaiah 53.11 is very different than the Hebrew. See 2.3 n. 36.

[80] Didascalia 8 contains the author's only other use of Isaiah 53. The relevant text reads as follows: "For it is required of you, o bishop, as a faithful steward, to care for everyone. For as you bear the sins of all those under your hands, more than every man you shall receive the abundant glory of God. For you are an imitator of Christ. And as He has taken upon Himself the sins of us all, so it is required of you also to bear the sins of all those under your hand. For it is written in Isaiah concerning our Savior thus: 'We have seen him that he had no brightness and no beauty, but his appearance was marred and humiliated beyond that of men; and as a man who suffers, and knows to bear infirmities. For his face was changed: he was despised, and was nothing accounted in our eyes. But he endured our sins, and for our sake did groan. But we accounted him as one smitten and afflicted and humiliated. But for our sins was he smitten, and was made sick for our iniquities, and through his blows all we are healed'. And again He says: 'He bore the sins of many, and for their iniquity was delivered up'. And in David and in all the prophets, and also in the Gospel, our Savior entreats for the sake of our sins, whereas He is without sin. Therefore, as you have Christ for an example, in this way be also an example to the people that are under your hands. And as He has taken (our) sins, so you also take the sins of the people. For you shall not think that the burden of the episcopacy is light or easy" (Vööbus, *The Didascalia Apostolorum,* Tome 176: 92 [line 20] – 93 [line 14]).

[81] The author's use of Isaiah 53 is a blend of what C. Markschies calls the "exemplary" and the "Christological" uses of Isaiah 53 ("Jesus Christ as a Man before God: Two Interpretive Models for Isaiah 53 in the Patristic Literature and Their Development," in *The Suffering*

After the ransom logion and Isaiah 53.11, the author makes a second appeal to the "gospel," which matches John 13.4–5. By appealing to Jesus' foot washing, the author showcases an aspect of Jesus' service, other than dying, that can be applied on a day-to-day basis. The last sentence appeals to the Johannine love motif, which is typically evoked when the Johannine writings occur alongside the ransom logion.

In conclusion, the author of Didascalia 16 makes two appeals to the "gospel." The first appeal is to the ransom logion, followed by a citation of Isaiah 53.11. Both the ransom logion and Isaiah 53 are interwoven in the author's mind because they both expresses Jesus' general service, as well as the benefits of his redemptive death. The author wishes the deacons to imitate Jesus in both of these respects. The second appeal draws on John's foot washing story as another example of Jesus' service, which his disciples should imitate out of their love for one another.

Source	Supposed Tradition	Exemplar	Similarity	Further Comments
Didascalia	Ransom Logion	Mark 10.45	S1	
Apostolorum	Isaiah 53.11	Isaiah 53.11	S1	
16	John 13.4–5	John 13.4–5	S2	
	Love Motif	N/A	N/A	Johannine love motif

4.7 The Teachings of Silvanus VII,4 104.12–13[82]

Mark 10.45ᶜ	καὶ δοῦναι τὴν ψυχὴν αὐτοῦ	λύτρον	ἀντὶ πολλῶν
Silvanus 104.12–13	ⲛ̄ϥⲙⲟⲩ ϩⲁⲣⲟⲕ	ⲛ̄ⲥⲱⲧⲉ	ⲙ̄ⲡⲉⲕⲛⲟⲃⲉ

The Teachings of Silvanus is a work originally written in Greek, but now exists only in a Coptic translation. Its contents indicate that it flourished on the outer edges of what became orthodox Christianity.[83] The thought of Silvanus is typically compared with the great figures of the Alexandrian school, spe-

---

Servant: Isaiah 53 in Jewish and Christian Sources [ed. B. Janowski and P. Stuhlmacher; trans. D. Bailey; Grand Rapids: Eerdmans, 2004], 231).

[82] The primary text comes from M. Peel, "The Teachings of Silvanus: Text and Notes," in *Nag Hammadi Codex VII* (ed. B. A. Pearson; NHMS 30; Leiden: Brill, 1996b), 278–368.

[83] While Silvanus has some conceptual similarities to Gnostic thought, both its cosmology and christology are in clear distinction to those consistently developed in Gnostic texts (M. Peel, "The Teachings of Silvanus: Introduction," in *Nag Hammadi Codex VII* [ed. B. Pearson; NHMS 30; Leiden: Brill, 1996a], 267–70; M. Peel and J. Zandee, "'The Teachings of Silvanus' from the Library of Nag Hammadi," *NovT* 14 [1972]: 307–09; J. Zandee, "Die 'Lehren des Silvanus' als Teil der Schriften von Nag Hammadi und der Gnostizismus," in *Essays on The Nag Hammadi Texts: In Honour of Pahor Labib* [ed. M. Krause; NHS 6; Leiden: Brill, 1975], 239–52).

cifically Clement and Origen.[84] These figures serve as the primary guides for dating Silvanus. If the comparison with Clement is emphasized, then a date is proposed in the latter half of the second century.[85] However, more recent studies have shown that Silvanus is not only dependent on Clement, but also on Origen.[86] Thus, the compilation of Silvanus can be dated just after the time of Origen, but no later than the council of Nicaea.[87]

The author of Silvanus is familiar with many writings of the New Testament, including the Gospel of Matthew.[88] There is a scholarly assumption that Silvanus 104.12–13 is a reception of the ransom logion[c].[89] There are, however, two noticeable differences between Silvanus 104.12–13 and Mark 10.45/Matthew 20.28[c]. First, in Mark 10.45/Matthew 20.28[c] Jesus' volitional self-sacrifice is very explicit. Silvanus 104.12–13 lacks such explicitness, though Jesus' volition could still be implied by his death being the goal of a purpose clause.[90]

Second, Mark 10.45/Matthew 20.28[c]'s language of ἀντὶ πολλῶν is different from ⲘⲠⲈⲔⲚⲞⲂⲈ. It is not common in the reception of the ransom logion to specify the ransom as "for your sin." There are a few New Testament texts that could be influencing Silvanus for this concept – 1Corinthians 15.3; Galatians 1.4; Romans 4.25; Matthew 26.28. Among these, the most interesting is Galatians 1.4, since there also Jesus' death for sin occurs alongside the ransom logion[c]. In my examination of Galatians 1.4, I concluded that it was best to understand the phrase, ὑπὲρ τῶν ἁμαρτιῶν ἡμῶν, as an allusion to Isaiah

---

[84] Peel, "The Teachings of Silvanus: Introduction," 263–67; Peel and Zandee, "The Teachings of Silvanus," 305–07. Parallels can also be made with the Sentences of Sextus, which like Silvanus, is in the genre of gentile-Christian wisdom literature.

[85] Zandee emphasizes the parallel with Clement and consistently wishes to date Silvanus towards the end of the second century (Peel and Zandee, "The Teachings of Silvanus," 310; J. Zandee, *'The Teachings of Silvanus' and Clement of Alexandria: A New Document of Alexandrian Theology* [MV 19; Leiden: Ex Oriente Lux, 1977], 1–2; "'The Teachings of Silvanus' (NHC VII, 4) and Jewish Christianity," in *Studies in Gnosticism and Hellenistic Religions* [ed. R. van den Broek and M. Vermaseren; Leiden: Brill, 1981], 498).

[86] R. Van den Broek, "The Theology of the Teachings of Silvanus," *VC* 40 [1986]: 2–5; Peel, "The Teachings of Silvanus: Introduction," 267.

[87] Peel, "The Teachings of Silvanus: Introduction," 273–74. Van den Broek dates the compilation of Silvanus to the 2nd/3rd decade of the fourth century. However, he acknowledges that the material in Silvanus is much older than this date, which makes sense given that Silvanus is wisdom literature ("The Theology of the Teachings of Silvanus," 17).

[88] C. Tuckett provides evidence for Silvanus' singular dependence on Matthew (*Nag Hammadi and the Gospel Tradition* [Edinburgh: T & T Clark, 1986], 42–47).

[89] Peel and Zandee, "The Teachings of Silvanus," 302; Tuckett, *Nag Hammadi and the Gospel Tradition*, 43; *et al.* In [Horner's] Coptic New Testament, Matthew 20.28 reads ⲚⲤⲰⲦⲈ (*The Coptic Version of the New Testament in the Southern Dialect Otherwise Called Sahidic and Thebaic* [5 vols; Oxford: The Clarendon Press, 1911], 1.220).

[90] The purpose element leads into the ransom logion[c] (ⲬⲈⲔⲀⲀⲤ...ⲚϤⲘⲞⲨ ⲀⲢⲞⲔ).

53.4, 5, 6, 10, 11, 12 LXX.[91] I believe the identical conclusion can be drawn regarding the parallel phrase: ⲙ̄ⲡⲉⲕⲛⲟⲃⲉ.

Outside of Silvanus 104.13, ⲛⲟⲃⲉ occurs nine times in Silvanus. Of these nine, only the occurrence in Silvanus 103.28 is in the same context as the occurrence in Silvanus 104.13, that is, the narrative of Jesus' incarnational descent into the underworld (Silvanus 103.23–104.14; cf. 110.14–111.4).[92] The occurrence of ⲛⲟⲃⲉ in Silvanus 103.28 is also the only one that shares with the occurrence in Silvanus 104.13 the idea that Jesus' suffering/death is *for your sin* (ⲉⲧⲃⲉ ⲡⲉⲕ ⲛⲟⲃⲉ [103.27–28]/ⲙ̄ⲡⲉⲕⲛⲟⲃⲉ [104.13]). Given the parallel wording and overall context, it is justifiable to read Silvanus 104.13 in light of Silvanus 103.27–28, and vice versa. This is significant because Silvanus 103.26–28 appears to be an allusion to Isaiah 53.

The author of Silvanus is familiar with Isaiah.[93] In Silvanus 103.26–28 the author states about Christ: ⳅⲣⲑⲗⲓⲃⲉ ⲅⲁⲣ ⲁⲩⲱ ⳅϥⲓ ⲙⲟⲕⲍ̄ⲥ ⲉⲧⲃⲉ ⲡⲉⲕ ⲛⲟⲃⲉ (For he is oppressed and bears affliction for your sin). On a conceptual level, this sounds like several statements made about the Isaianic servant in Isaiah 53.4, 5, 12 LXX.[94] On a verbal level, the fourth-century Coptic version of Isaiah 53.4, found in the Bodmer Papyrus XXIII, states in Isaiah 53.4: ⲛ̄ⲧⲟϥ ⲡⲉⲧⲛⲁϥⲓ ⳃⲁ ⲛⲉ̄-ⲛ̄ⲟⲃⲉ ⲁⲩⲱ ϥⲙⲟⲕⲍ̄ ⲉⲧⲃⲏⲏ-ⲧⲛ̄ (He bears our sin and is afflicted because of us).[95] This is very close to Silvanus 103.26–28.[96] Therefore, given the strong conceptual and verbal parallels it is reasonable to state that Silvanus 103.26–28 is influenced by Isaiah 53.

The only potential objection to the influence of Isaiah 53 on Silvanus 103.26–28 is that the Greek word θλίβω (θλῖψις), which lies behind ⳅⲣⲑⲗⲓⲃⲉ, does not occur in Isaiah 53. On the other hand, neither do other words such as πάθος and πάσχω, which in the earliest Christian literature are frequently as-

---

[91] See 2.3 above.

[92] Jesus' decent into the underworld is Silvanus' way of expressing the incarnation. For a discussion of this motif in Silvanus and in parallel literature, see M. Peel, "The 'Decensus ad Inferos' in 'The Teachings of Silvanus' (CG VII, 4)," *NVMEN* 26 (1979): 23–49; Zandee, "'The Teachings of Silvanus' (NHC VII, 4) and Jewish Christianity," 543–46.

[93] Peel, "The Teachings of Silvanus: Introduction," 259.

[94] Isaiah 53.4, 5, 12: "He bears our sins, and is pained for us; yet we accounted him to be in trouble, and in suffering, and in affliction. (5) But he was wounded on account of our sins, and was bruised because of our iniquities: the chastisement of our peace was upon him; and by his bruises we were healed…(12) He bore the sins of many, and was delivered because of their iniquities."

[95] R. Kasser, *Papyrus Bodmer XXIII: Esaïe XLVII, 1 – LXVI, 24 en sahidique* (Cologny-Genève: Bibliothèque Bodmer, 1965), 86. For the date in the fourth century, see A. Pietersma, "Bodmer Papyri," *ABD* 1:766.

[96] Of course, since Greek is the original language of Silvanus, it is not conclusive to draw parallels with Coptic texts. However, the presence of such parallels does show that whoever translated Silvanus into Coptic likely interpreted the Greek text in such a way that parallels with the Coptic translation tradition of Isaiah 53 were maintained.

sociated with the suffering of Jesus, and sometimes in explicit connection with Isaiah 53.[97] However, the problem with θλίβω is that it is not used with reference to Jesus' suffering in early Christian literature, much less with Isaiah 53.[98] This trend continues in the major Alexandrian contemporaries of Silvanus: Clement and Origen. Having examined their writings, I can locate only one possible instance where θλίβω/θλῖψις is used in reference to Christ, and where there may be a reference to Isaiah 53. In *Paedagogus* 2.19.3, Clement refers to Jesus as the great cluster, the word, which was bruised for us (ὁ μέγας βότρυς, ὁ λόγος ὁ ὑπὲρ ἡμῶν θλιβείς). The idea that Jesus suffered for us is reminiscent of Isaiah 53.4, 5. In the writings of Pachomius, there is an application of θλίβω to Jesus along with language that may allude to Isaiah 53. Pachomius states: "The Lord of life was in the midst of those who tormented him because of our sins" (ⲛ̄ⲛⲉⲧⲑⲗⲓⲃⲉ ⲙ̄ⲙⲟϥ ⲉⲧⲃⲉⲛⲉⲛ ⲛⲟⲃⲉ).[99] So it appears that what we have in Clement, Pachomius, and Silvanus is a special use of θλίβω, in the sense that it is applied to Jesus and is part of a reference to Isaiah 53. Overall, one can confidently say that part, if not all, of Silvanus 103.26–28 is dependent on Isaiah 53, especially Isaiah 53.4. If Silvanus 103.26–28 is dependent on Isaiah 53, then so also is the parallel phrase in Silvanus 104.13 (ⲙ̄ⲡⲉⲕⲛⲟⲃⲉ). It occurs in the same context and is the only other place in Silvanus that says Jesus' suffering is for our sin.

In conclusion, there are two points about the appearance of the ransom logion[c] in Silvanus 104.12–13. First, Silvanus interprets the ransom logion alongside influence from Isaiah 53.4, 5, 6, 10, 11, 12 LXX.[100] Given the results of the examination of Galatians 1.4, I suspect that the phrase ⲙ̄ⲡⲉⲕⲛⲟⲃⲉ may be an allusion to Isaiah 53. These suspicions are confirmed when Silvanus 104.12–13 is read in light of the parallel phrase in Silvanus 103.26–28, which has clearer ties with Isaiah 53. Second, Silvanus reads the ransom logion[c] within the greater context of the incarnation, which Silvanus describes as Jesus descent into the underworld.

---

[97] 1Peter 2.21–25; Barnabas 5.2–5.

[98] Of the 105 times that θλίβω/θλῖψις occurs in the New Testament and Apostolic Fathers the only place it refers to Jesus is in Colossians 1.24, and there it mostly refers to Paul (Elsewhere in 2Corinthians 1.4–5 Paul appears intentionally to avoid applying θλίβω/θλῖψις to Jesus). The vast majority of other instances describe the troubles of Christians.

[99] Pachomius, *Instruction on the Six Days of the Passover*, 4 (L. Lefort, *Œuvres de S. Pachôme et de Ses Disciples* [CSCO 160; Louvain: Peeters, 1956], 26; A. Veilleux, *Pachomian Koinonia: Instructions, Letters, and Other Writings of Saint Pachomius and His Disciples* [CSS 47; Kalamazoo, MI: Cistercian Publications Inc, 1982], 48).

[100] These are the verses in Isaiah that speak of the servant's work to remove sin.

Source	Supposed Tradition	Exemplar	Similarity	Further Comments
The	Ransom Logion[c]	Mark 10.45[c]	S3	
Teachings	Isaiah 53.4, 5, 6,	Isaiah 53.4, 5, 6,	S3	Confirmed by
of	10, 11, 12 LXX	10, 11, 12 LXX		parallel in Silvanus
Silvanus				103.26–28
104.12–13	Incarnation	N/A	N/A	Jesus' descent to the underworld

4.8 The Gospel of Philip II,3 52.35–53.3[101]

Mark 10.45[a, c]   ὁ υἱὸς τοῦ ἀνθρώπου οὐκ ἦλθεν... λύτρον...

Gospel of Philip 52.35–53.3   ⲁⲡⲉⲭⲣⲥ̄ⲉⲓ...   ⲉⲧⲣⲉϥⲥⲟⲧⲟⲩ

The Gospel of Philip (GPh) dates to the second or third century CE.[102] It contains a collection of excerpts that have been united together by an editor.[103] Within the text as it now exists, there are observable dependencies on New Testament writings, among which Matthew and John appear most frequently.[104] Evans, Webb, and Wiebe suggest that GPh 52.35–53.3 may be a reception of the ransom logion.[105] This text states that Christ came (ⲁⲡ

---

[101] The primary text comes from B. Layton, "The Gospel According to Philip," in *Nag Hammadi Codex II,2–7* (vol. 1; ed. B. Layton; NHS 20; Leiden: Brill, 1989), 143–214.

[102] The secondary literature is very inconsistent concerning the date of GPh. W. Isenberg proposes a date in the second half of the third century ("The Gospel According to Philip: Introduction," in *Nag Hammadi Codex II,2–7* [vol. 1; ed. B. Layton; NHS 20; Leiden: Brill, 1989], 134–35). P. Foster says there is a "scholarly consensus" for the first half of the third century ("The Gospel of Philip," *ExpTim* 118/9 [2007b]: 418). H. -M. Schenke dates GPh in the second century and claims this is "Die ältere und viel geäußerte Ansicht" (*Das Philippus-Evangelium (Nag-Hammadi-Codex II, 3)* [TU 143; Berlin: Akademie-Verlag, 1997], 5).

[103] Despite the document's composite nature, most believe that it is consistently Valentinian. E. Thomassen states that there is an "internal consistency and homogeneity of the theological notions it [GPh] contains" ("How Valentinian is the *Gospel of Philip*?," in *The Nag Hammadi Library after Fifty Years: Proceedings of the 1995 Society of Biblical Literature Commemoration* [ed. J. Turnier and A. McGuire; NHMS 44; Leiden: Brill, 1997], 252). The collective nature of GPh may have led to its placement after The Gospel of Thomas in NHC II (Isenberg, "The Gospel According to Philip," 138).

[104] E. Segelberg, "The Gospel of Philip and the New Testament," in *The New Testament and Gnosis* (ed. A. Logan and A. Wedderburn; Edinburgh: T & T Clark Limited, 1983), 205–12; W. J. Stroud, "New Testament Quotations in the Nag Hammadi Gospel of Philip," in *Society of Biblical Literature 1990 Seminar Papers* (ed. D. Lull; Atlanta: Scholars Press, 1990), 68–81; C. Tuckett, *Nag Hammadi and the Gospel Tradition* (Edinburgh: T & T Clark, 1986), 72–81; R. McL. Wilson, "The New Testament in the Nag Hammadi Gospel of Philip," *NTS* 9 (1963): 291.

[105] Evans, Webb, and Wiebe, *Nag Hammadi Texts and the Bible*, 146. GPh 52.35–53.3 is not listed in *Biblia Patristica*.

exp̄cei) to purchase (τοογ) some, to save (ναзм) others, to ransom/redeem others (coτ [=cωτε]).

The evidence for the presence of the ransom logion in GPh 52.35–53.3 is slim. Concerning Christ's coming (απεxp̄cei), Horner's Coptic text of Mark 10.45/Matthew 20.28[a] uses the verb ei.[106] However, this does not explain the absence of the "Son of Man" identification, especially since Jesus is identified as such elsewhere in GPh (76.1–2; 81.14–19).[107] Concerning the "ransom," most commentators translate τοογ as "ransom." However, if a parallel is drawn with Mark 10.45/Matthew 20.28[c], then the focus must instead be on coτ, which is the word used in Horner's Coptic text of Mark 10.45/Matthew 20.28[c], and also in Silvanus 104.12–13 (See 4.7 above).[108] Unfortunately, coτ does not stand out from the preceding two verbs: τοογ and ναзм.[109] Also, the separation of coτ from απεxp̄cei means that an overt reception of the ransom logion is certainly absent.[110]

What continues to make an echo of the ransom logion audible, however, is the allusion to John 10.17–18 in GPh 53.6–10.[111] There is a tradition that reads the ransom logion with parallel Johannine texts.[112] Therefore, the allusion to John 10.17–18 increases the possibility that GPh 52.35–53.3 is a reception of the ransom logion. However, beyond the presence of John 10.17–18, the evidence for the presence of the ransom logion in GPh 52.35–53.3 remains extremely slim.

---

[106] [Horner], *The Coptic Version of the New Testament*, 1.220, 524.

[107] Of course, all points of this nature assume that the composite nature of GPh does not negate the possibility of reading passages in light of one another.

[108] [Horner], *The Coptic Version of the New Testament*, 1.220, 524. According to W. Crum, τοογ, when used transitively, normally translates concepts related to purchase (i.e. ἀγοράζω; πρίαμαι) ("τοογ," *CD*, 441). However, Crum makes no mention of translating τοογ with -λυτ.

[109] coτ (cωτε) is used in GPh 53.13–14 to sum up what was said in 52.35–53.3. See Schenke on the chiastic structure of 52.35–53.14 (*Das Philippus-Evangelium*, 170).

[110] It is very difficult to determine the meaning of coτ in our passage. Elsewhere in GPh coτ refers to a certain sacrament (62.14; 67.29; 69.23; 71.2–3; 85.28). Irenaeus expresses knowledge of a coτ sacrament used in sectarian groups. In the preserved Greek text of Irenaeus, he refers to groups who believe they have experienced something called the redemption (ἀπολύτρωσις), as well as the experience of being redeemed (λυτρόω) (*Adversus Haereses* 1.13.6; 1.21.1–5). For helpful discussions on the complexities and interrelatedness of the sacraments in GPh, see A. DeConick, "The True Mysteries: Sacramentalism in the *Gospel of Philip*," *VC* 55 (2001): 225–61; E. Thomassen, *The Spiritual Seed: The Church of the 'Valentinians'* (NHMS 60; Leiden: Brill, 2006), 93–101.

[111] GPh 53.6–10: "It was not only when he appeared that he voluntarily laid down his life, but he voluntarily laid down his life from the very day the world came into being. Then he came first in order to take it, since it had been given as a pledge" (Translation is from Isenberg [1989: 145]).

[112] Clement of Alexandria, *Paedagogus* 1.9.85.1–2; *Quis Dives Salvetur* 37.1–4; The Acts of Thomas 39.

Source	Supposed Tradition	Exemplar	Similarity	Further Comments
Gospel of Philip 52.35–53.3	Ransom Logion John 10.17–18	Mark 10.45[a, c] John 10.17–18	S4 S3	

4.9 The Tripartite Tractate I,5 120.13[113]

Mark 10.45[a–b]   ὁ υἱὸς τοῦ ἀνθρώπου οὐκ ἦλθεν διακονηθῆναι
                     ἀλλὰ διακονῆσαι

Tripartite Tractate 120.13   ⲉⲁⲩⲧⲛ̄ⲛⲟⲟⲩϥ ⲁⲡⲱ̄ⲙ̄ⲱⲉ ⲛ̄ⲛⲁⲉⲓ

The Tripartite Tractate is a Valentinian work written sometime in the third century.[114] The suggested reception of the ransom logion[a–b] is in 120.13, where the text states that the Savior was sent as a service (ⲉⲁⲩⲧⲛ̄ⲛⲟⲟⲩϥ ⲁⲡⲱ̄ⲙ̄ⲱⲉ). This sending refers to the incarnation of the Savior's preexistent being (113.5–115.34).[115]

Unfortunately, the only evidence for the reception of the ransom logion[a–b] in The Tripartite Tractate 120.13 is the parallel idea of "service." The actual language of "service" (ⲱ̄ⲙ̄ⲱⲉ) is not the same as διακονέω from Mark 10.45/Matthew 20.28[a–b].[116] There is also no mention of the Son of Man.[117] Given the absence of these key terms, it remains highly uncertain if this should be considered to be a reception of the ransom logion[a–b].

Source	Supposed Tradition	Exemplar	Simi-larity	Further Comments
The Tripartite Tractate I,5 120.13	Ransom Logion[a–b] Incarnation	Mark 10.45[a–b] Incarnation	S4 N/A	See 113.5–115.34

---

[113] The primary text is from H. Attridge and E. Pagels, "NCH 1, 5: The Tripartite Trac-tate," in *Nag Hammadi Codex I (The Jung Codex): Introductions, Texts, Translations, Indices* (ed. H. Attridge; NHS 22; Leiden: Brill, 1985), 159–337. I am also dependent on their Eng-lish translation.

[114] E. Thomassen dates the work in the second half of the third century ("The Tripartite Tractate From Nag Hammadi: A New Translation with Introduction and Commentary" [Ph.D. diss., University of St Andrews, 1982], 31–36). Attridge and Pagels prefer the first half of the third century ("NCH 1, 5: The Tripartite Tractate," 178).

[115] Thomassen, *The Spiritual Seed*, 47–50.

[116] In The Tripartite Tractate 117.16, the author demonstrates familiarity with διακονέω as a Greek loan-word.

[117] The Son of Man is mentioned nowhere in The Tripartite Tractate (Attridge and Pagels, "NCH 1, 5: The Tripartite Tractate," 358).

4.10 Eusebius of Caesarea

The life of Eusebius is evenly divided between the third and fourth centuries. However, all of Eusebius' extant writings come from the early fourth century. According to *Biblia Patristica*, Eusebius receives the ransom logion[c] in *Demonstratio Evangelica*, *Commentary on Isaiah*, and *Commentary on Psalms*.[118] In addition, there is another pertinent reception in the Greek fragments of *De Theophania*.[119]

4.10.1 Demonstratio Evangelica 10.8.33–35[120] (Cf. De Theophania 9)[121]

Mark 10.45[c]	καὶ δοῦναι τὴν ψυχὴν αὐτοῦ λύτρον ἀντὶ πολλῶν
Demonstratio 10.8.33 (477, 6)	τοῦ κόσμου παντὸς λύτρον καὶ ἀντίψυχον ἀποδειχθῆναι
De Theophania 9 (24, 5–6)	λύτρον ἑαυτὸν ἐπιδοὺς καὶ ἀντίψυχον τῶν μελλόντων δι᾽ αὐτοῦ σωθήσεσθαι

Eusebius wrote *Demonstratio Evangelica* as a follow-up to *Praeparatio Evangelica*. Together these works are intended to convince the pagan of Christian truth, as well as strengthen the faithful in that same truth.[122] The reception of the ransom logion[c] in *Demonstratio* occurs in the second half of Eusebius' discussion of Jesus' call from the cross: ἠλὶ ἠλὶ λεμᾶ σαβαχθανί (Psalm 21:2 LXX). The relevant text is as follows:

His strong one forsook him then, because he wished him to go unto death, even the death of the cross (μέχρι θανάτου καὶ θανάτου σταυροῦ [Philippians 2.8]), and to be set forth as the ransom and sacrifice for the whole world (καὶ τοῦ κόσμου παντὸς λύτρον καὶ ἀν-

---

[118] *Biblia Patristica* 4.229. *Demonstratio Evangelica* dates to 314–18 (W. Ferrar, *The Proof of the Gospel Being the Demonstratio Evangelica of Eusebius of Caesarea* [2 vols.; TCLS 1; London: The Macmillan Company, 1920], xii–xiii). The *Commentary on Isaiah* dates around, or just after, the Council of Nicaea (M. Hollerich, *Eusebius of Caesarea's Commentary on Isaiah* [OECS; Oxford: Clarendon Press, 1999], 19–26). The *Commentary on Psalms* dates shortly after the Council of Nicaea (M. -J. Rondeau, *Les commentaires patristiques du psautier (IIIe–Ve siècles)* [vol. 1; OCA 219; Rome: Pont. Institutum orientalium studiorum, 1982], 66–69).

[119] I made this discovery through a *Thesaurus Linguae Graecae* search of λύτρον (Accessed on 29 July 2008).

[120] The primary text comes from I. Heikel, *Eusebius Werke VI. Die Demonstratio Evangelica* (GCS; Leipzig: J. C. Hinrichs'sche Buchhandlung, 1913). The English translation comes from Ferrar, *The Proof of the Gospel*, 1920.

[121] The primary text comes from H. Gressmann, *Eusebius Werke III. 2. Die Theophanie* (GCS; Leipzig: J. C. Hinrichs'sche Buchhandlung, 1904).

[122] Ferrar, *The Proof of the Gospel*, 1.ix–xii.

τίψυχον ἀποδειχθῆναι [ransom logion]), and to be the purification (καθάρσιον)[123] of the life of them that believe in him (τῶν εἰς αὐτὸν πιστευσάντων).[124] And he, since he understood at once his father's divine counsel, and because he discerned better than any other why he was forsaken by the father, humbled himself even more, and embraced death for us with all willingness, and became a curse for us (ὑπὲρ ἡμῶν κατάρα [Galatians 3.13]), holy and all-blessed though he was, and he that knew no sin, became sin, that we might become the righteousness of God in him (ἵνα ἡμεῖς γενώμεθα δικαιοσύνη θεοῦ ἐν αὐτῷ [2Corinthians 5.21]). Even more – to wash away our sins he was crucified, suffering what we who were sinful should have suffered, as our sacrifice and ransom (ἀντίψυχον ἡμῶν καὶ ἀντίλυτρον γεγενημένος), so that we may well say with the prophet, he bears our sins, and is pained for us, and he was wounded for our sins, and bruised for our iniquities, so that by his stripes we might be healed, for the Lord hath given him for our sins (αὐτὸς τὰς ἁμαρτίας ἡμῶν φέρει καὶ περὶ ἡμῶν ὀδυνᾶται καὶ αὐτὸς ἐτραυματίσθη διὰ τὰς ἁμαρτίας ἡμῶν, καὶ μεμαλάκισται διὰ τὰς ἀνομίας ἡμῶν, ἵνα τῷ μώλωπι αὐτοῦ ἡμεῖς ἰαθῶμεν [Isaiah 53.4, 5]). So, as delivered up by the Father, as bruised, as bearing our sins, he was led as a sheep to the slaughter (ὡς πρόβατον ἐπὶ σφαγὴν ἤχθη [Isaiah 53.7]). With this the apostle agrees when he says: Who spared not his own son, but delivered him for us all (ὅς γε τοῦ ἰδίου υἱοῦ οὐκ ἐφείσατο ἀλλ' ὑπὲρ ἡμῶν πάντων παρέδωκεν αὐτόν [Romans 8.32]). And it is to impel us to ask why the Father forsook him, that he says: Why have you forsaken me? The answer is, to ransom the whole human race, buying them with his precious blood (ἡ τοῦ παντὸς ἀνθρώπων γένους ἀπολύτρωσις, τῷ τιμίῳ αἵματι ἐξαγοραζομένη [1Peter 1.19]) from their former slavery to their invisible tyrants, the unclean demons, and the rulers and spirits of evil. And the Father forsook him for another reason, namely, that the love of Christ himself for men might be set forth. For no one had power over his life, but he gave it willingly for men, as he teaches us himself in the words, No one takes my life from me: I have power to lay it down, and I have power to take it again (οὐδεὶς αἴρει τὴν ψυχήν μου ἀπ ἐμοῦ· ἐξουσίαν ἔχω θεῖναι αὐτήν, καὶ ἐξουσίαν ἔχω πάλιν λαβεῖν αὐτήν [John 10.18]).[125]

This section is filled with references to scripture.[126] Some of these are given an introductory formula, and others are not. The potential reception of the ransom logion[c] occurs in the clause: καὶ τοῦ κόσμου παντὸς λύτρον καὶ ἀντίψυχον ἀποδειχθῆναι. The particular phrase, λύτρον καὶ ἀντίψυχον, is idiomatic for Eusebius. The phrase occurs again a few lines down as ἀντίψυχον ἡμῶν καὶ ἀντίλυτρον γεγενημένος.[127] This phrase also occurs in the

---

[123] The combination of ἀντίψυχον and καθάρσιον sounds like 4Maccabees 6.29. However, *Biblia Patristica* does not list any instances where Eusebius demonstrates dependence on 4Maccabees, nor the relevant verses in 2Maccabees 7.

[124] The same phrase, τῶν εἰς αὐτὸν πιστευσάντων, is used by Origen in his *Commentary on Matthew* 20.28 (Klostermann, *Origenes Werke X. 1*, 498, 10–14).

[125] Heikel, *Eusebius Werke VII*, 477, 4–34; Ferrar, *The Proof of the Gospel*, 2.220–221.

[126] Markschies states about Eusebius' quotation method: "he quotes so freely from other biblical texts that it is difficult to avoid the impression of an interpretation purely by means of a mosaic of quotations" ("Jesus Christ as a Man before God," 295). This is true in this case, but this does not mean that there is no method for preserving interpretive traditions amidst the quotation madness.

[127] Here it functions as an introduction to the citation of Isaiah 53.4, 5, 7. In fact, the only other place where ἀντίλυτρον occurs in Eusebius' extant writings is in his *Commentary on*

fragment from *De Theophania* 9 as λύτρον ἑαυτὸν ἐπιδοὺς καὶ ἀντίψυχον. Eusebius' insertion of the words ἑαυτὸν ἐπιδοὺς in between λύτρον and ἀντίψυχον means that there is sufficient similarity to consider this as a reception of the ransom logion[c]. Therefore, likewise in *Demonstratio* 10.8.33, the words λύτρον or ἀντίλυτρον in the phrase λύτρον/ἀντίλυτρον καὶ ἀντίψυχον can also be understood as reception of the ransom logion[c].

In sum, there is reason to believe that Eusebius receives the ransom logion[c] in *Demonstratio* 10.8.33. The extracted text above shows many of the co-traditions that have previously been observed alongside the ransom logion (Isaiah 53.4, 5, 7; John 10.18; Romans 8.32; Philippians 2.8; 1Peter 1.19). Therefore, this particular reception of the ransom logion[c] represents a capstone on all the previous examinations. Eusebius' position as an historian and his interaction with earlier traditions make him an appropriate person to bring together the previous traditions observed alongside the ransom logion.

4.10.2 Commentary on Isaiah 43.1–2; 60.5–7[128]

4.10.2.1 Commentary on Isaiah 43.1–2

Mark 10.45[c]		καὶ δοῦναι τὴν ψυχὴν αὐτοῦ λύτρον ἀντὶ πολλῶν

Isaiah 43.1–2		λύτρον ὑπὲρ τῆς σῆς σωτηρίας τὸ ἐμαυτοῦ παραδοὺς αἷμα
(277,11–12)		ἐλυτρωσάμην σε

What is most interesting about this reception of the ransom logion[c] is that it is the blood of Jesus, and not the soul, that is given as a ransom.[129] The substitution of blood for soul is due to influence from 1Peter 1.19. What confirms this is that several lines down, the wording of the reception is repeated, though without the word λύτρον. Here the text reads: ἐλυτρωσάμην τὸ τίμιον μου αἷμα ὑπὲρ τῆς σῆς σωτηρίας παραδοὺς, οὕτω καὶ σὺ ἐκείνων ἔσῃ ἄλλαγμα (277, 19–21). By using the phrase τὸ τίμιον μου αἷμα, Eusebius demonstrates his dependence on the same phrase in 1Peter 1.19, which is the only place in the Christian scriptures that uses the adjective "precious" (τίμιος) to describe Jesus blood.

Isaiah 53.5–6, and there it is also in the same phrase: γένηται ἀντίψυχον καὶ ἀντίλυτρον (J. Ziegler, *Eusebius Werke IX. Der Jesajakommentar* [GCS; Berlin: Akademie-Verlag, 1975], 2.42). This suggests that this phrase was very closely tied to Isaiah 53 in Eusebius' mind. Elsewhere in *Demonstratio*, Eusebius uses λύτρον, and more often ἀντίψυχος, in close connection to references to Isaiah 53 (Heikel, *Eusebius Werke VII*, 46, 4–9 and 28–30; 449, 31–35; 450, 24–26).

[128] The primary text comes from Ziegler, *Eusebius Werke IX*.

[129] It is too difficult to tell if Eusebius uses the ransom logion[c] because of influence from ἐλυτρωσάμην in Isaiah 43.1 or ἄλλαγμα in Isaiah 43.3.

4.10.2.2 Commentary on Isaiah 60.5–7

Mark 10.45ᶜ   καὶ δοῦναι τὴν ψυχὴν αὐτοῦ λύτρον ἀντὶ πολλῶν
Isaiah 60.5–7 (372, 18)   τὰ λύτρα τῆς αὐτῶν ψυχῆς

Isaiah 60.5–7 concerns the nations who bring their gifts to Jerusalem. Eusebius describes it as follows: δῶρα δὲ τῷ θεῷ προσφέρουσαι εἰκότως τὰ λύτρα τῆς αὐτῶν ψυχῆς. This does not appear to be a reception of the ransom logionᶜ. Neither λύτρα nor ψυχῆς apply to Jesus.

4.10.3 Commentary on Psalm 54.20; 71.12–14; 131.1[130]

4.10.3.1 Commentary on Psalm 54.20

Mark 10.45ᶜ   καὶ δοῦναι τὴν ψυχὴν αὐτοῦ λύτρον ἀντὶ πολλῶν

Psalm 54.20   Ἅπαξ γὰρ ὁ Υἱος τοῦ Θεοῦ λύτρον ἑαυτὸν διδοὺς καὶ ἀντάλλαγμα
(485, 52–54)   ὑπὲρ τῶν ἁμαρτωλῶν

The reception of the ransom logionᶜ occurs in a discussion of Psalm 54.20 LXX, which states οὐ γάρ ἐστιν αὐτοῖς ἀντάλλαγμα καὶ οὐκ ἐφοβήθησαν τὸν θεόν. The fuller context of the reception is as follows:

For there is no one who will give an exchange in behalf of them. For the Son of God gave himself once as a ransom and exchange in behalf of sinners, he purchases those who believe in him (ἐπεὶ μηδεὶς ἔσται ὁ ὑπὲρ αὐτῶν διδοὺς ἀντάλλαγμα. Ἅπαξ γὰρ ὁ Υἱος τοῦ Θεοῦ λύτρον ἑαυτὸν διδοὺς καὶ ἀντάλλαγμα ὑπὲρ τῶν ἁμαρτωλῶν, τοὺς μὲν εἰς αὐτὸν πεπιστευκότας ἐξηγόρασε); and he frees them from all of their former sins; and he heals the humble, because they did not belong to the precious thing that was given in behalf of them, nor did they believe in the precious blood of the redeemer and savior of all humanity (μηδὲ ἐπίστευσαν εἰς τὸ τίμιον αἷμα τοῦ πάντων ἀνθρώπων Λυτρωτοῦ καὶ Σωτῆρος).

There are three points of interest. First, the ransom logionᶜ is linked with ἀντάλλαγμα, even though λυτρόω was available to Eusebius in the previous verse (Psalm 54.19). Second, the idea that purchase is only of "those who believe in him [Jesus]" is a theme that occurred earlier in *Demonstratio* 10.8.33, and also in Origen's *Commentary on Matthew* 20.28. Third, we again see the τίμιον αἷμα motif, which ultimately comes from 1Peter 1.19.

---

[130] I use B. Montfaucon as the primary text for Psalm 54.20 and 71.12–14 (*Eusebii Pamphili: Commentaria in Psalmos* [ed. J. -P. Migne; PG 23; Paris, 1857]). I use A. Mai as the primary text for Psalm 131.1 (*Didymi Alexandrini: Expositio in Psalmos* [ed. J. -P. Migne; PG 39; Paris, 1863], 1156–1616). None of these Psalms are listed in *Biblia Patristica* as questionable regarding authenticity. Rondeau and Kirchmeyer confirm that the receptions in Psalm 54.20 and 71.12–14 are authentic ("*Les pasumes* L–XCV v. 3 (PG 23, 441c–1221c): leur authenticité est certaine" ["Eusèbe de Césarée," 1689]). I could not locate an independent confirmation for Psalm 131.1, which occurs in an edition of *Patrologia Graeca* (vol. 39) originally accredited to Didymus.

4.10.3.2 Commentary on Psalm 71.12–14

Mark 10.45ᶜ   καὶ δοῦναι τὴν ψυχὴν αὐτοῦ λύτρον ἀντὶ πολλῶν
Psalm 71.12–14 (812, 8–9)   τὸ αἷμα τὸ τίμιον λύτρον ὑπὲρ αὐτῶν δούς

The greater context of this reception is as follows: ἀλλ᾿ αὐτός, τὸ αἷμα τὸ τίμιον λύτρον ὑπὲρ αὐτῶν δούς, ἐλυτρώσατο τὰς ψυχὰς αὐτῶν· ὅθεν ὁ θεῖος Ἀπόστολος ἐδίδασκε λέγων· Χριστὸς ἡμᾶς ἐξηγόρασεν ἐκ τῆς κατάρας τοῦ νόμου, γενόμενος ὑπὲρ ἡμῶν κατάρα (812, 8–12).

The "precious blood" from 1Peter 1.19 is the ransom price.[131] The ransom logionᶜ itself occurs in a participial clause that modifies the verb ἐλυτρώσατο (λυτρώσεται in Psalm 71.14). The next sentence is a quote from Galatians 3.13.

4.10.3.2 Commentary on Psalm 113.1

Mark 10.45ᶜ   καὶ δοῦναι τὴν ψυχὴν αὐτοῦ λύτρον ἀντὶ πολλῶν
Psalm 131.1 (1588, 3)   λύτρον σαυτὸν ὑπὲρ πάντων τῶν ἁμαρτωλῶν

The greater context of this statement is as follows: μνήσθητι, Κύριε, κατὰ τὸν τῆς εἰς ἀνθρώπους σου παρουσίας καιρόν, ἐν ᾧ λύτρον σαυτὸν ὑπὲρ πάντων τῶν ἁμαρτωλῶν παρέξεις, ἄφεσιν ἁμαρτιῶν προξενῶν ἅπασιν ἀνθρώποις. The ransom logion is not further elaborated upon and is not used in any way that contributes to the overall discussion.

In conclusion, Eusebius' reception of the ransom logion is limited to the ransom logionᶜ. Judging by the frequency of occurrences, 1Peter 1.19 has the largest impact on Eusebius' reading of the ransom logionᶜ. Besides 1Peter 1.19, the only other tradition with multiple occurrences alongside the ransom logionᶜ is Galatians 3.13. The remaining co-traditions only occur within *Demonstratio* 10.8.33. Out of those, the receptions of Philippians 2.8, John 10.18, and Isaiah 53.4, 5, 7 have been seen regularly throughout the overall reception.

---

[131] The "precious blood" motif may be influenced by the Hebrew text, which reads דמם instead of ὄνομα αὐτῶν in Psalm 71.14 (72.14 Hebrew). Eusebius is aware of this (812, 36f).

Source	Supposed Tradition	Exemplar	Simi-larity	Further Comments
Eusebius *De-monstratio Evangelica* 10.8.33 (Cf. *De Theophania* 9)	Ransom Logion[c]	Mark 10.45[c]	S3	λύτρον is the only connection
	Philippians 2.8	Philippians 2.8	S1	Immediately before the ransom logion[c]
	Galatians 3.13	Galatians 3.13	S1	
	2Corinthians 5.21	2Corinthians 5.21	S1	
	Isaiah 53.4, 5, 7	Isaiah 53.4, 5, 7	S1	
	Romans 8.32	Romans 8.32	S1	
	1Peter 1.19	1Peter 1.19	S3	
	John 10.18	John 10.18	S1	
Eusebius, *Commentary on Isaiah* 43.1–2	Ransom Logion[c]	Mark 10.45[c]	S3	
	1Peter 1.19	1Peter 1.19	S3	Blood replaces soul as ransom price
Eusebius, *Commentary on Isaiah* 60.5–7	Ransom Logion[c]	Mark 10.45[c]	S5	
Eusebius, *Commentary on Psalm* 54.20	Ransom Logion[c]	Mark 10.45[c]	S3	
	1Peter 1.19	1Peter 1.19	S3	Blood replaces soul as ransom price
Eusebius, *Commentary on Psalm* 71.12–14	Ransom Logion[c]	Mark 10.45[c]	S3	
	1Peter 1.19	1Peter 1.19	S3	Blood replaces soul as ransom price
	Galatians 3.13	Galatians 3.13	S1	
Eusebius, *Commentary on Psalm* 113.1	Ransom Logion[c]	Mark 10.45[c]	S3	

4.11 Conclusion

The period between 200 and 300 CE is packed with receptions of the ransom logion.[132] Alongside these receptions, are four observable patterns. The first is Isaiah 53. It occurs in Hippolytus, *On Proverbs* 75; Origen, *Commentary on Psalm* 129.3–5; The Teachings of Silvanus 104.12–13; Didascalia Apostolo-rum 16; Eusebius, *Demonstratio Evangelica* 10.8.33. All of the uses of Isaiah 53 draw on the servant's death for sin, though this is only implicit in Didas-

---

[132] The number of receptions continues to increase in the fourth century.

calia Apostolorum 16.[133] The second is incarnation. This motif is typically used to interpret Mark 10.45/Matthew 20.28[a–b] and is sometimes evoked through an allusion to part of the poetic material in Philippians 2.6–8. It occurs in Origen, *Commentary on Matthew* 20.28; *Fragment on Luke* 14.6; The Acts of Thomas 39, 72; Pseudo Clement of Rome, *Homilies* 12.7.5; The Teachings of Silvanus 104.12–13; The Tripartite Tractate 120.13. It is likely that patristic writers perceive Mark 10.45/Matthew 20.28 and Philippians 2.6–8 to be saying the exact same thing, namely that Jesus was incarnated from preexistence in order to serve and die. Therefore, it naturally became part of the collective memory to read them together. The third is 1Peter 1.18–19. This tradition typically influences the replacement of Jesus' soul with his precious blood as the ransom payment. It occurs in Origen, *Commentary on Matthew* 20.28; *Commentary on Psalm* 29.10; 129.3–5; Eusebius, *Demonstratio Evangelica* 10.8.33; *Commentary on Isaiah* 43.1–2; *Commentary on Psalm* 50.20; 71.12–14.[134] Eusebius is likely indebted to Origen for this replacement. The fourth is ransom to Satan. It occurs in Origen's *Commentary on Matthew* 20.28; *Fragment on Ephesians* 1.7; *Fragment on* 1Corinthians 6.19–20; The Acts of Thomas 39. This motif appears to be a later development, although it makes sense of the emphasis on possession in the first part of Jesus ministry (especially in Mark 1–8).

Isaiah 53 and the incarnation motif continue from the previous periods. The Isaiah 53 tradition occurred in Galatians 1.4 and Diognetus 9.2–5. The incarnation motif occurred in Clement of Alexandria, *Paedagogus* 1.9.85.1–2 and *Quis Dives Salvetur* 37.1–4. The love motif, which was such a prominent part of the collective memory in the New Testament, drastically diminishes in the third century; it occurs only marginally in Didascalia 16.

Concerning where receptions of the ransom logion are obtained in this period, Origen is the only person who appears to be directly dependent on Mark 10.45/Matthew 20.28. The author of Didascalia Apostolorum uses a version of the ransom logion that almost exactly matches Mark 10.45/Matthew 20.28, but the source is probably a collection of dominical sayings rather than Mark 10.45/Matthew 20.28 itself. Several authors present a version of the ransom logion that may result from blending influences from Mark 10.45/Matthew 20.28 with other New Testament uses of the ransom logion. Foremost among these is The Teachings of Silvanus, which may blend influences from Mark 10.45/Matthew 20.28 and Galatians 1.4. Also, The Acts of Thomas may blend influences from Mark 10.45/Matthew 20.28 with John 10.11, 15. A more re-

---

[133] Isaiah 53 is used similarly with the ransom logion in the previous periods.

[134] The 1Peter 1.18–19 motif sometimes produces an additional allusion to John 1.29 (Origen's *Commentary on Psalm* 29.10; 129.3–5). John 1.29 shares the language of ἀμνὸς with 1Peter 1.19.

mote possibility is the Gospel of Philip (Mark 10.45/Matthew 20.28 with John 10.17–18).

Finally, there are some contributions that the reception of the ransom logion in this period makes to the three debatable issues surrounding Mark 10.45/Matthew 20.28 (See 1.2 above). First, concerning the (dis)association of the ransom logion with the Eucharist, Origen and Eusebius continually use blood as a replacement for soul as the ransom price. Origen also uses blood as an additional ransom payment. These uses of blood come primarily from the influence of 1Peter 1.18–19, and not from the Pauline or synoptic Last Supper traditions.

Second, concerning a preexistent coming in Mark 10.45/Matthew 20.28, Origen's *Commentary on Matthew* 20.28 interprets Jesus' coming in the ransom logion[a–b] as a "visitor among the generation of humans." In *Fragment on Luke* 14.16, Origen groups the ransom logion[a–b] with Philippians 2.7, presumably because he believes they share the same story of Jesus' incarnation from a preexistent state. In The Acts of Thomas 72, the author places an allusion from Philippians 2.7 before the ransom logion[c]. It may be that the author of The Acts of Thomas uses this allusion to an incarnational text as a replacement for the ransom logion[a–b].

Third, concerning the scriptural background of Mark 10.45/Matthew 20.28, as noted above, five separate authors receive the ransom logion with Isaiah 53 – Hippolytus, Origen, The Teachings of Silvanus, Didascalia Apostolorum, and Eusebius. There are no receptions with Daniel 7, 9. Although there are clear uses of the ransom logion[a] in the writings of Origen and Didascalia Apostolorum, none of these retain the Son of Man, which is a necessary element for a Danielic allusion.[135] There is one use of the ransom logion with Isaiah 43 in Eusebius' *Commentary on Isaiah* 43.1–2.

---

[135] Didascalia Apostolorum 16 retains the Son of Man in the Syriac version, but the absence of Son of Man in the parallel text from Constitutiones Apostolorum means that it was probably absent from the original Greek text of Didascalia Apostolorum. Of course, the title: "Son of Man" generally disappears early in the Christian tradition (See 5.5.1.2).

Chapter 5

The Significance for the Study of
Mark 10.45/Matthew 20.28

5.1 Introduction

Chapters Two through Four of this study examine the receptions of the ransom logion from the New Testament through the third century. Many of these receptions are part of interpretive patterns that have been perpetuated in the social memory of the earliest Christian communities. These patterns can be observed in the tradition-focused chart below in 5.2. The primary purpose of Chapter Five is to explore the possibility that some of these patterns reflect the meaning of Mark 10.45/Matthew 20.28, or the possibility that Mark 10.45/Matthew 20.28 itself is participating in some of these patterns (See 1.5.2). The specific issues surrounding Mark 10.45/Matthew 20.28 that are addressed in relation to the interpretive patterns are development in a Eucharistic setting (5.3), preexistent coming (5.4), and scriptural background (5.5). These three issues are introduced above in 1.2.1 through 1.2.3, and it may be helpful for the reader to review those sections. This chapter focuses on these three issues because they are the ones for which the interpretive patterns in the reception history of the ransom logion are relevant. Some interpretive patterns in the reception history are not fully integrated into this chapter because they are not relevant for specifically addressing the issues in the study of Mark 10.45/Matthew 20.28. For example, love is the most dominant motif associated with the ransom logion through 200 CE. However, it is not directly relevant for addressing the issues that are typically discussed in relation to Mark 10.45/Matthew 20.28.[1]

---

[1] Both Matthew and Mark identify obedience as the primary rationale for Jesus' self-sacrifice, rather than love. While love is a minor theme in Mark and Matthew (love between God and his Son [Mark 1.11; 9.7; 12.6; Matthew 3.17; 12.18; 17.5]; love for God and neighbor [Mark 12.30–33; Matthew 19.19; 22.37–39]), it is almost never used to describe Jesus' feelings or his motivation for ministry. The single exception is Mark 10.21, which states that Jesus loves the rich man seeking eternal life – Matthew omits this statement. In Mark 10.45/Matthew 20.28, the absence of love as Jesus' motivation for his self-sacrifice coheres with a similar absence throughout Mark and Matthew, but it is entirely opposite from the pattern in the reception history of the ransom logion where love is explicitly affirmed as the mo-

The guiding principle of this chapter is sensitivity to historical-critical discussions while exploring the potential significance of the reception history. The possibility for error lies in the temptation to construe the reception history so that it bears more weight than it should for contributing to historical-critical discussions. This error is opposite from the error that this study seeks to correct, which asserts that the reception history has little to no potential relevance for contributing to historical-critical discussions. Giving appropriate weight to the reception history means that the findings of this chapter will be modest and somewhat inconclusive. Despite the limited findings and the inevitable inconclusiveness, the potential for the reception history of the ransom logion to shed any additional light on the meaning of Mark 10.45/Matthew 20.28 should grant it status as a valuable tool for the study of Mark 10.45/Matthew 20.28. It should also serve as a stimulus for including early reception history as a contextual tool in the historical-critical approach to discerning the meaning of the New Testament.

5.2 Tradition-Focused Chart

Chapters Two through Four contain charts at the end of each section that summarize the findings for the source under examination. These charts are source-focused, in that the source is the organizing principle for the traditions. The purpose of the below chart is to introduce a tradition-focused chart, where the traditions are the organizing principle for the sources. The importance of a tradition-focused chart is that, unlike the source-focused charts, it allows for the observation of the big picture, wherein patterns are easily visible. These patterns possess the greatest potential relevance for the study of Mark 10.45/Matthew 20.28.

---

tivation for Jesus' self-sacrificial actions (e.g. Galatians 2.20; Ephesians 5.2, 25; John 15.13; 1John 3.16; Clement of Alexandria, *Paedagogus* 1.9.85.1–2; *Quis Dives Salvetur* 37.4).

Supposed Tradition	Sources
Incarnation or Philippians 2.6–8	Clement of Alexandria, *Paedagogus* 1.9.85.1–2; *Quis Dives Salvetur* 37.4; The Tripartite Tractate 120.13; Origen, *Commentary on Matthew* 20.28; *Fragment on Luke* 14.16; The Acts of Thomas 39; 72; Pseudo Clement of Rome, *Homilies* 12.7.5; The Teachings of Silvanus 104.12–13; Eusebius, *Demonstratio Evangelica*, 10.8.33
Isaiah 53 (various verses)	Galatians 1.4; 1Peter 1.18–19; Diognetus 9.2; Hippolytus, *On Proverbs* 75; Origen, *Commentary on Psalm* 129.3–5; Didascalia Apostolorum 16; The Teachings of Silvanus 104.12–13; Eusebius, *Demonstratio Evangelica*, 10.8.33
1Peter 1.18–19	Origen, *Commentary on Matthew* 20.28; *Commentary on Psalm* 29.10; *Commentary on Psalm* 129.3–5; Eusebius, *Demonstratio Evangelica* 10.8.33; *Commentary on Isaiah* 43.1–2; *Commentary on Psalm* 54.20; *Commentary on Psalm* 71.12–14
Love Motif	Galatians 2.20; Ephesians 5.2, 25; John 10.11, 15; 15.13; 1John 3.16; Diognetus 9.2; Clement of Alexandria, *Paedagogus* 1.9.85.1–2; *Quis Dives Salvetur* 37.4; Didascalia Apostolorum 16
John 10.11, 15, 17–18	Clement of Alexandria, *Paedagogus* 1.9.85.1–2; *Quis Dives Salvetur* 37.4; The Acts of Thomas 39; Gospel of Philip 52.35–53.3; Eusebius, *Demonstratio Evangelica*, 10.8.33
Ransom to Satan	Origen, *Commentary on Matthew* 20.28; *Fragment on Ephesians* 1.7; *Fragment on 1Corinthians* 6.19–20; The Acts of Thomas 39
John 13–14	Clement of Alexandria, *Quis Dives Salvetur* 37.4; Pseudo Clement of Rome, *Homilies* 12.7.5; Didascalia Apostolorum 16
Isaiah 43.1–4	Clement of Alexandria, *Paedagogus* 1.9.85.1–2; Eusebius, *Commentary on Isaiah* 43.1–2
Romans 8.32	Diognetus 9.2; Eusebius, *Demonstratio Evangelica*, 10.8.33
John 1.29	Origen, *Commentary on Psalm* 29.10; *Commentary on Psalm* 129.3–5
Revelation 5.9	The Gospel of Truth 20.13–14; The Acts of Thomas 72

Ephesians 1.7	Irenaeus, *Against Heresies* 5.1.1; Origen, *Fragment on Ephesians* 1.7
Galatians 3.13	Eusebius, *Demonstratio Evangelica*, 10.8.33; *Commentary on Psalm* 71.12–14
1Timothy 2.6	Irenaeus, *Against Heresies* 5.1.1
Isaiah 42.6–7; 49.6–8	Titus 2.14; 1Timothy 2.5–6
Passover Lamb	1Peter 1.18–19
1Peter 3.18	Diognetus 9.2
Romans 5.18–19	Diognetus 9.2
Matthew 26.28	The Gospel of Truth 20.13–14
Hebrews 2.17; 12.2	The Gospel of Truth 20.13–14
Yom Kippur	Hippolytus, *On Proverbs* 75
Proverbs 30.31	Hippolytus, *On Proverbs* 75
Colossians 1.15–16	Origen, *Commentary on Matthew* 20.28
1Corinthians 7.23	Origen, *Commentary on Matthew* 20.28
Luke 23.46	Origen, *Commentary on Matthew* 20.28
Psalm 15.10	Origen, *Commentary on Matthew* 20.28
Luke 22.27	Origen, *Fragment on Luke* 14.16

Supposed Tradition	Sources
1 Corinthians 6.18, 20	Origen, *Fragment on 1 Corinthians* 6.19–20
2 Corinthians 5.21	Eusebius, *Demonstratio Evangelica*, 10.8.33

5.3 Significance for the Disassociation of the Ransom Logion with the Eucharist

There is an assumption in New Testament studies that the ransom logion developed in a Eucharistic setting (See 1.2.1). Supporting this assumption are the perceived connections between Mark 10.45/Matthew 20.28 and Mark 14.24/Matthew 26.28, which include the statement that Jesus' death is "for many" (preposition plus πολλῶν) and the supposed background of Isaiah 53. However, there are also important differences between Mark 10.45/Matthew 20.28 and Mark 14.24/Matthew 26.28, which include mention of the Son of Man, service, and λύτρον. These differences may betray the fact that there is no significant connection between Mark 10.45/Matthew 20.28 and Mark 14.24/Matthew 26.28, and consequently no evidence from Mark or Matthew that the ransom logion developed in a Eucharistic setting.

Chapters Two through Four reveal that there is no association between the ransom logion and the Eucharist, or Last Supper traditions, in the reception history. The purpose of this section is to review this pattern of disassociation in the reception history (5.3.1), and then consider the possibility that the reception history reflects a similar disassociation in Mark and Matthew (5.3.2). If there is no significant connection between Mark 10.45/Matthew 20.28 and Mark 14.24/Matthew 26.28, then there is no remaining reason to suggest the ransom logion developed in a Eucharistic setting.

5.3.1 The Reception of the Ransom Logion

There are no patterns in the reception history that associate the ransom logion with the Eucharist or Last Supper traditions that are similar to the ones from the synoptics and Paul (Matthew 26.26–29; Mark 14.22–25; Luke 22.15–20; 1Corinthians 11.23–25). It appears that for most early Christians the ransom logion and the Eucharist, or Last Supper traditions, have little to do with each other. Below are two further notes concerning this disassociation in the reception history.

First, several receptions of the ransom logion clearly affirm that Jesus' blood, rather than his soul, is the primary ransom payment (Irenaeus, *Against Heresies* 5.1.1; Origen, *Commentary on Matthew* 20.28; *Commentary on Psalm* 29.10; *Commentary on Psalm* 129.3–5; *Fragment on Ephesians* 1.7; Eusebius, *Commentary on Isaiah* 43.1–2; *Commentary on Psalm* 54.20; *Commentary on Psalm* 71.12–14).[2] One would assume that the substitution of blood for soul results from the influence of the Eucharist, or Last Supper traditions from the synoptics or Paul. However, the substitution of blood for soul

---

[2] Cf. Origen, *Commentary on Romans* 3.7; 3.8 (1.3.2 n. 52 above).

is always due to the influence of 1Peter 1.18–19 or Ephesians 1.7, and there is never mention of the Eucharist or Last Supper traditions.

Second, there are two receptions from the survey in Chapters Two through Four that could be suggested to combine the ransom logion with Last Supper traditions, but neither is likely. The first reception is The Gospel of Truth 20.13–14. This text reminisces upon Jesus' knowledge that his death is life for many (ⲡⲓⲙⲟⲩ ⲛ̄ⲧⲟⲟⲧϥ̄ ⲟⲩⲱⲛⲍ̄ ⲛ̄ⲟⲁⲍ ⲡⲉ). The lack of a self-giving motif and the absence of "ransom" (ⲥⲱⲧⲉ) language means that this text is not sufficiently similar to Mark 10.45/Matthew 20.28ᶜ. Instead, it is probably a reception of Mark 14.24/Matthew 26.28, as supported by the language of "covenant" (ⲇⲓⲁⲑⲏⲕⲏ) in the following line (GTr 20.15). Thus, while a combination may be present, the evidence suggests that GTr 20.13–14 is only a reception of Mark 14.24/Matthew 26.28. The second reception is Luke 22.24–27. This text is Luke's version of Mark 10.41–45ᵇ. It is possible that Luke situates his version of Mark 10.41–45ᵇ later in his Gospel because of influence from non-Markan sources that also place the account there.[3] If this is the case, then the suggestion could be made that the non-Markan sources have the account there because the Mark 10.41–45 material originated in the context of the Eucharist. However, the problem with this rationale, other than the hypothetical non-Markan sources, is that Luke's placement of his version of Mark 10.41–45ᵇ is not next to the relevant statements about the bread and the wine at the Last Supper (Luke 22.15–20). Rather, it is next to Jesus' condemnation of the one who would betray him (Luke 22.21–23). Luke's motive for this placement is that he wants the reader to observe the disciples' transition from questioning who would betray Jesus (Luke 22.23) to questioning who among them is the greatest (22.24). This transition allows the reader to see that all the disciples have betrayed Jesus and his message.[4] Therefore, Luke's placement of his version of Mark 10.41–45ᵇ in Luke 22.24–27 is demonstrably tied to Jesus' condemnation of the one who would betray him (Luke 22.21–23), and not to the relevant statements about the bread and the wine (Luke 22.15–20).

In sum, there is no evidence from the reception history that the ransom logion is ever associated with the Eucharist, or Last Supper traditions from the synoptics or Paul. This is true even when Jesus' blood is substituted for his soul as the ransom payment.[5] The disassociation of the ransom logion and

---

[3] The natural placement of Mark 10.41–45 is in Luke 18.15–43, which uses the material from Mark 10.13–52, except Mark 10.35–45.

[4] J. Green, *The Gospel of Luke* (NICNT; Grand Rapids: Eerdmans, 1997), 766.

[5] It may be worth noting that the motifs displayed in the reception history of the ransom logion are largely foreign to those displayed in the reception history of the Last Supper traditions, and vice versa. So not only are the ransom logion and the Last Supper tradition never clearly received together, but their interpretive patterns are also different. For example, a prominent theme in the reception of the Last Supper traditions is to speak of Jesus as the "vine of David" (*Didache* 9.2; Ignatius, *Epistle to the Ephesians* 20.2; Clement of Alexan-

Last Supper traditions in the social memory of early Christians may reflect a similar disassociation in Mark and Matthew.

5.3.2 Exegetical Considerations

Mark 14.24	*Matthew 26.28*	*Mark 10.45/Matthew 20.28*
		ὁ υἱὸς τοῦ ἀνθρώπου οὐκ ἦλθεν διακονηθῆναι ἀλλὰ διακονῆσαι καὶ δοῦναι τὴν ψυχὴν αὐτοῦ λύτρον
τοῦτό ἐστιν	τοῦτο γάρ ἐστιν	
τὸ αἷμά μου	τὸ αἷμά μου	
τῆς διαθήκης τὸ	τῆς διαθήκης τὸ	
ἐκχυννόμενον ὑπὲρ πολλῶν	περὶ πολλῶν ἐκχυννόμενον εἰς ἄφεσιν ἁμαρτιῶν.	ἀντὶ πολλῶν.

Mark 10.45 and 14.24 are the only two passages in Mark where Jesus describes the effectiveness of his death. Mark's position as the earliest gospel, combined with scholarship's interest in the earliest interpretations of Jesus' death, means that a connection is often drawn between these two passages. Almost all commentators mention the one when they are commenting on the other. However, the only verbal similarity between the Mark 10.45/Matthew 20.28 and Mark 14.24/Matthew 26.28 is the preposition plus πολλῶν. This verbal similarity, more than the shared subject matter of Jesus' beneficial death, is typically the catalyst for connecting the passages together.[6]

Those who connect Mark 10.45/Matthew 20.28 with Mark 14.24/Matthew 26.28 based on the shared preposition plus πολλῶν often make a further claim that in both passages the preposition plus πολλῶν is part of an allusion to Isaiah 53, which justifies connecting them together.[7] In Mark 10.45/Matthew 20.28, it is possible that the preposition plus πολλῶν is part of an allusion to Isaiah 53 (See 5.5.2). Mark 10.45/Matthew 20.28 shares with Isaiah 53, not

---

dria, *Quis Dives Salvetur* 29). Another prominent theme is the mixing of wine with water in the cup (Justin, *Apology* 1.66; Irenaeus, *Against Heresies* 4.33.2; 5.36.3; Clement of Alexandria, *Paedagogus* 2.2). A final prominent theme is Jeremiah 11.19 LXX (Melito of Sardis, *Peri Pascha* 63–64; 67; Justin, *Dialogue with Trypho* 72; Tertullian, *An Answer to the Jews* 10; *Against Marcion* 3.19; 4.40). These three themes – the vine of David, the mingled cup, Jeremiah 11.19 LXX – are not paralleled in the reception of the ransom logion.

[6] For example, M. Hengel states: "The saying over the cup and the saying about the ransom are connected by the universal service 'for the many'..." (*The Atonement: The Origins of the Doctrine in the New Testament* [trans. J. Bowden; Philadelphia: Fortress Press, 1981], 73).

[7] For example, R. France states about Matthew 26.28: "'Poured out for many' recalls the 'many' who are repeatedly referred to in Isa 53:11–12...an allusion already familiar to us from 20:28, where again it was specifically linked to the purpose of Jesus' death" (*The Gospel of Matthew* [NICNT; Grand Rapids: Eerdmans, 2007], 994).

only the preposition plus πολλῶν, but also the concepts of service and soul, which are missing in Mark 14.24/Matthew 26.28.[8] In Mark 14.24/Matthew 26.28, the preposition plus πολλῶν is likely part of a larger allusion, not to Isaiah 53, but to Exodus 24.6–8.

The first clause in Mark 14.24/Matthew 26.28 is almost identical. It records Jesus saying: τοῦτο [γάρ – Matthew] ἐστιν τὸ αἷμά μου τῆς διαθήκης. There is widespread agreement that this first clause is an allusion to Exodus 24.8, the wider context of which is the covenant ratification on Sinai. Exodus 24.8 records the moment when Moses sprinkles the "blood of the covenant" on the people – λαβὼν δὲ Μωυσῆς τὸ αἷμα κατεσκέδασεν τοῦ λαοῦ καὶ εἶπεν ἰδοὺ τὸ αἷμα τῆς διαθήκης (דם־הברית) ἧς διέθετο κύριος πρὸς ὑμᾶς περὶ πάντων τῶν λόγων τούτων. Other relevant texts for the first clause include Zechariah 9.11, which itself may be drawing on Exodus 24.8, and Jeremiah 31.31–34 (38.31 LXX).[9]

The second clause in Mark 14.24/Matthew 26.28 is not the same. Mark's second clause states: τὸ ἐκχυννόμενον ὑπὲρ πολλῶν, whereas Matthew's states: τὸ περὶ πολλῶν ἐκχυννόμενον εἰς ἄφεσιν ἁμαρτιῶν. In both Mark and Matthew, the description of Jesus' blood as poured out (ἐκχυννόμενον) is often interpreted as an allusion to Isaiah 53 with the rationale that ἐκχυννόμενον matches הערה from Isaiah 53.12. The *Hebrew and Aramaic Lexicon of the Old Testament* states that ערה can be rendered as "tip out" in the Hiphil, though Isaiah 53.12 is the only example given.[10] There are, however, two problems with connecting ἐκχυννόμενον to הערה. First, the LXX translates הערה in Isaiah 53.12 with παρεδόθη. Second, the LXX never translates ערה with ἐκχέω; ἐκχύννω does not occur in the LXX. In light of these difficulties, ἐκχυννόμενον should probably not be considered an allusion to הערה in Isaiah 53.12, but to ἐνέχεεν or προσέχεεν in Exodus 24.6 – λαβὼν δὲ Μωυσῆς τὸ ἥμισυ τοῦ αἵματος ἐνέχεεν εἰς κρατῆρας τὸ δὲ ἥμισυ τοῦ αἵματος προσέχεεν πρὸς τὸ θυσιαστήριον. This makes sense given that the first clause in Mark 14.24/Matthew 26.28 is an allusion to Exodus 24.8.

Matthew adds the phrase, εἰς ἄφεσιν ἁμαρτιῶν, to the second clause. Matthew has likely moved the phrase from Mark 1.4 where it is connected with John's baptism.[11] The phrase indicates that Matthew understands the blood poured out for the many as atoning. Its addition may be part of the continued influence of Exodus 24.6–8. There is a Jewish tradition in the first cen-

---

[8] It is possible that Mark 10.45/Matthew 20.28 also shares with Isaiah 53 the notion of atonement (λύτρον) (See 5.5.2–5.5.3).

[9] For a discussion of the relevant texts, see McKnight, *Jesus and His Death* (Waco: Baylor University Press, 2005), 284–92.

[10] L. Koehler and W. Baumgartner, "ערה," *HALOT* 1.882.

[11] D. Gurtner, *The Torn Veil: Matthew's Exposition of the Death of Jesus* (SNTSMS 139; Cambridge: Cambridge University Press, 2007), 134.

tury that interprets the Sinai offering in Exodus 24.6–8 as atoning. This tradition is present in Hebrews 9.19–22, which narrates the Sinai event and then
cites a version of Exodus 24.8. Next, the author states: καὶ χωρὶς αἱματεκ-
χυσίας οὐ γίνεται ἄφεσις. Similarly, *Targums Onkelos* and *Pseudo-
Jonathan* interpret Moses' actions in Exodus 24.6–8 as making atonement for
the people.[12] Besides Exodus 24.6–8, it is also possible that Jeremiah 31.34
has influenced Matthew's addition of the phrase. Matthew probably understands the covenant that Jesus inaugurates as the new covenant from Jeremiah
31.31, though he does not use the crucial adjective "new," which is used in
the Lucan and Pauline Last Supper. Jeremiah 31.34 includes the forgiveness
of sins as part of this new covenant: "For I will forgive their sin and will no
longer call to mind the wrong they have done" (Jeremiah 31.34).[13] Whether
Matthew's addition of the phrase, εἰς ἄφεσιν ἁμαρτιῶν, is influenced by
atoning interpretations of Exodus 24.6–8 or Jeremiah 31.34, the point is that it
is likely not due to influence from Isaiah 53.[14]

To sum up the discussion so far, the preposition plus πολλῶν is the only
verbal connection between Mark 10.45/Matthew 20.28 and Mark 14.24/Mat-
thew 26.28. While it is possible that the preposition plus πολλῶν in Mark
10.45/Matthew 20.28 is part of a larger allusion to Isaiah 53, this is unlikely
in Mark 14.24/Matthew 26.28 where the preposition plus πολλῶν is part of a
larger allusion to Exodus 24.6–8 and perhaps also Jeremiah 31.31–34. There
are two other interrelated points that further damage the already weak verbal
connection and further disassociate Mark 10.45/Matthew 20.28 and Mark
14.24/Matthew 26.28.

First, "many" (πολύς) is a word that Mark often uses substantively to describe those with whom Jesus interacts.[15] The word is similarly used in Mat-

---

[12] J. Kugel, *Traditions of the Bible: A Guide to the Bible as It Was at the Start of the
Common Era* (Cambridge: Harvard University Press, 1998), 667. Originally, Exodus 24.6–8
had nothing to do with atonement, as A. Collins states: "In and of itself, this type of sacrifice
has nothing to do with sin" ("Finding Meaning in the Death of Jesus," *JR* 78 [1998]: 176).
Atonement interpretations were added later, and were present in the first century.

[13] It should be noted that A. Collins believes the phrase, εἰς ἄφεσιν ἁμαρτιῶν may be influenced by Leviticus 4.7, 18, 20, 25, which use ἐκχέω to describe the priest pouring out
blood with the result that sin is atoned ("Mark's Interpretation of the Death of Jesus," *JBL*
128/3 [2009]: 549–50).

[14] Strictly speaking, Isaiah 53 does not use the vocabulary of "forgiveness."

[15] Mark 1.34: So he healed many (πολλοὺς) who were sick with various diseases and
drove out many demons. But he would not permit the demons to speak, because they knew
him. Mark 2.2: So many (πολλοί) gathered that there was no longer any room, not even by
the door, and he preached the word to them. Mark 2.15: As Jesus was having a meal in Levi's
home, many tax collectors and sinners were eating with Jesus and his disciples, for there were
many (πολλοί) who followed him. Mark 3.10: For he had healed many (πολλοὺς), so that all
who were afflicted with diseases pressed toward him in order to touch him. Mark 6.2: When
the Sabbath came, he began to teach in the synagogue. Many (πολλοί) who heard him were

thew, though it is less common and has a more negative tone.[16] If Mark 10.45/Matthew 20.28 and Mark 14.24/Matthew 26.28 were the only places in Mark and Matthew where πολύς occurred then it might be justified to suggest that there is a special connection between the passages. However, πολύς is a common word in Mark and Matthew, which dampens the possibility of a special connection between its use in Mark 10.45/Matthew 20.28 and Mark 14.24/Matthew 26.28.

Second, Mark 10.45/Matthew 20.28 and Mark 14.24/Matthew 26.28 are separated from each other by a large distance. This point is obvious, but very important. If Mark 10.45/Matthew 20.28 occurred in the pericope immediately proceeding Mark 14.24/Matthew 26.28, then these two texts could be seen as significantly connected. However, as it is, they are very far apart, and since the gospels are written to be heard, it is hard to imaging Mark or Matthew intending hearers to connect Mark 10.45/Matthew 20.28 and Mark 14.24/Matthew 26.28 on the basis of a single word (πολύς) that already occurs often in their gospels.

---

astonished, saying, "Where did he get these ideas? And what is this wisdom that has been given to him? What are these miracles that are done through his hands?" Mark 6.13: They cast out many demons and anointed many (πολλούς) sick people with oil and healed them. Mark 6.31: He said to them, "Come with me privately to an isolated place and rest a while" (for many (πολλοί) were coming and going, and there was no time to eat). Mark 6.33: But many (πολλοί) saw them leaving and recognized them, and they hurried on foot from all the towns and arrived there ahead of them. Mark 9.26: It shrieked, threw him into terrible convulsions, and came out. The boy looked so much like a corpse that many (πολλούς) said, "He is dead!" Mark 10.31: But many (πολλοί) who are first will be last, and the last first. Mark 10.45: For even the Son of Man did not come to be served but to serve, and to give his life as a ransom for many (πολλῶν). Mark 10.48: Many (πολλοί) scolded him to get him to be quiet, but he shouted all the more, "Son of David, have mercy on me!" Mark 11.8: Many (πολλοί) spread their cloaks on the road and others spread branches they had cut in the fields. Mark 15.41: When he was in Galilee, they had followed him and given him support. Many (πολλαί) other women who had come up with him to Jerusalem were there too.

[16] Matthew 7.22: On that day, many (πολλοί) will say to me, "Lord, Lord, didn't we prophesy in your name, and in your name cast out demons and do many powerful deeds?" Matthew 8.11: I tell you, many (πολλοί) will come from the east and west to share the banquet with Abraham, Isaac, and Jacob in the kingdom of heaven. Matthew 8.16: When it was evening, many (πολλούς) demon-possessed people were brought to him. He drove out the spirits with a word, and healed all who were sick. Matthew 12.15: Now when Jesus learned of this, he went away from there. Many (πολλοί) [crowds] followed him, and he healed them all. Matthew 19.30: But many (πολλοί) who are first will be last, and the last first. Matthew 20.28: just as the Son of Man did not come to be served but to serve, and to give his life as a ransom for many (πολλῶν). Matthew 22.14: For many (πολλοί) are called, but few are chosen. Matthew 24.10–12: Then many (πολλοί) will be led into sin, and they will betray one another and hate one another. And many (πολλοί) false prophets will appear and deceive many (πολλούς), and because lawlessness will increase so much, the love of many (πολλῶν) will grow cold. Matthew 27.53: They came out of the tombs after his resurrection and went into the holy city and appeared to many people (πολλοῖς).

Given the weakness of the verbal connection between Mark 10.45/Matthew 20.28 and Mark 14.24/Matthew 26.28, the lack of a similar contextual allusion, the frequency of the substantive use of πολύς (especially in Mark), and the distance between Mark 10.45/Matthew 20.28 and Mark 14.24/Matthew 26.28, it is justified to conclude that Mark 10.45/Matthew 20.28 and Mark 14.24/Matthew 26.28 are largely disassociated in the Gospels of Mark and Matthew. This means that they cannot function as evidence to support the assumption that the ransom logion originated in a Eucharistic setting. It is important to note that this conclusion does not mean that Mark 10.45/Matthew 20.28 and Mark 14.24/Matthew 26.28 are incompatible in the mind of Mark or Matthew, but only that they are sufficiently disassociated in Mark and Matthew so that they do not support the assumption of the ransom logion originating in a Eucharistic setting.[17]

5.3.3 Conclusion

The reception history demonstrates that for early Christians the ransom logion and the Eucharist, or Last Supper traditions, have almost nothing to do with each other.[18] Even where we might expect mention of the Eucharist or Last Supper traditions – where Jesus' blood is substituted for his soul as the ransom payment – we only see influence from 1Peter 1.18–19 or Ephesians 1.7.

The disassociation between the ransom logion and the Last Supper traditions in the reception history reflects a similar disassociation in Mark and Matthew. Mark 10.45/Matthew 20.28 and Mark 14.24/Matthew 26.28 have a weak verbal connection (preposition plus πολλῶν), and different contextual allusions. Mark and Matthew use πολύς as a substantive throughout their gospels, which removes the possibility of a unique verbal connection. Finally, Mark 10.45/Matthew 20.28 and Mark 14.24/Matthew 26.28 are distant from one another within the narratives. For these reasons, it is not valid to see in Mark 10.45/Matthew 20.28 and Mark 14.24/Matthew 26.28 a connection that could support the assumption that the ransom logion developed in a Eucharistic setting. Rather, the disassociation between the ransom logion and the Eucharist, or Last Supper traditions, in the reception history through 300 CE reflects the disassociation between Mark 10.45/Matthew 20.28 and Mark 14.24/Matthew 26.28. While it could be true that the ransom logion developed in a Eucharistic setting, the contribution of this section has been to show that those Eucharistic origins were quickly forgotten, and that there are no extant

---

[17] Below in 5.5.2, we note Pitre's argument that understanding λύτρον in Mark 10.45/Matthew 20.28 to mean "redemption from exile" results in a strong compatibility with the theme of Passover and New Exodus that are associated with the Last Supper traditions.

[18] We might suspect that early Christians would connect Mark 10.45/Matthew 20.28 and Mark 14.24/Mathew 26.28 based on their conceptual and verbal similarities. The fact that they do not is striking.

connections between the ransom logion and the Eucharist, or Last Supper traditions, that might serve as evidence to support those origins.

5.4 Significance for a Preexistent Coming
in Mark 10.45/Matthew 20.28

Simon Gathercole's monograph, *The Preexistent Son*, argues that the "coming" in Mark 10.45/Matthew 20.28 is from a state of preexistence (See 1.2.2).[19] Gathercole grounds his argument in the parallels with angelic figures, who use a 'I have come' formula to describe their mission to earth from their preexistent life in heaven. The purpose of this section is to investigate the proposal of a preexistent coming in Mark 10.45/Matthew 20.28, not based on parallels with angelic figures, but based on the reception history. The reception history, though limited in scope, assumes an incarnational coming from preexistence. This assumption appears to be grounded in the connection between the ransom logion and Philippians 2.6–8, which patristic writers likely consider to be telling the same story of Jesus' incarnation from preexistence in order to serve and to die.[20] The patristic connection between the ransom logion and Philippians 2.6–8 should prompt the historical-critical investigation into possibility that Mark 10.45/Matthew 20.28 represents the appropriation of an incarnational narrative that is similar to the one found in the Philippians hymn.

5.4.1 The Reception of the Ransom Logion

5.4.1.1 Pattern Applicable to the Ransom Logion[a–b]

There are only seven receptions of the ransom logion[a–b] that are examined in Chapters Two through Four. Only three of these are relevant for discussions about a preexistent coming.[21]

---

[19] Early in his monograph, Gathercole points out that it is the voluntary coming, and not the Son of Man title, which indicates preexistence. He states: "The Son of Man offers little evidence of preexistence independent of the 'coming' motif…" (*The Preexistent Son: Recovering the Christologies of Matthew, Mark, and* Luke [Grand Rapids: Eerdmans, 2006], 19). This observation matches the reception of the ransom logion[a–b], where the impetus for invoking an incarnational motif is never motivated by the title, Son of Man. In fact, the Son of Man title appears to be completely unimportant to those who receive the ransom logion[a–b] (See 5.5.1.2).

[20] Once the ransom logion and Philippians 2.6–8 were recognized as reinforcing the same narrative sequence, it was natural for them to continue to be connected in the collective memory.

[21] The other four are Luke 22.27; The Tripartite Tractate 120.13; Pseudo Clement of Rome, *Homilies* 12.7.5; Didascalia Apostolorum 16.

(1) Clement of Alexandria, *Paedagogus* 1.9.85.1–2. Within a chiasm, Clement mirrors the ransom logion[a–b] (Οὐκ ἦλθον, φησί, διακονηθῆναι, ἀλλὰ διακονῆσαι) with a reference to Jesus' voluntary incarnation as a human from his preexistent status as Lord (ἐξὸν εἶναι κύριον, ἀδελφὸς εἶναι βεβούληται).[22]

(2) Origen, *Commentary on Matthew* 20.28. Origen's comments on the ransom logion[a–b] are brief. However, he does note that Jesus stayed as a "visitor in the generation of humans" (ἐπεδήμησε γὰρ τῷ γένει τῶν ἀνθρώπων). This statement appears to be motivated by the "coming" from the ransom logion[a–b].

(3) Origen, *Fragment on Luke* 14.16. Origen states that Christ was sent (ἀποστελλόμενος ὁ Χριστὸς) to call everyone to serve the Father. Origen supports this statement with a combination the ransom logion[a–b], Luke 22.27, and Philippians 2.7. These can be understood to affirm Jesus' preexistent coming, especially with the inclusion of the phrase μορφὴν δούλου λαβὼν from Philippians 2.7, which Origen understands as a reference to the incarnation.[23] For Origen, the same story of Jesus coming as a servant is being told in the ransom logion[a–b], Luke 22.27, and Philippians 2.7, and together these explain what it means for Christ to be sent.

5.4.1.2 Pattern Applicable to the Ransom Logion[c]

Most receptions of the ransom logion in Chapters Two through Four only contain the ransom logion[c]. There are two cases in which the ransom logion[c] is preceded by an incarnational motif that implies preexistence.[24] It is possible

---

[22] It is interesting that Clement does not give an incarnational interpretation to the other "Son of Man has come" statement from Luke 19.10 (ἦλθεν γὰρ ὁ υἱὸς τοῦ ἀνθρώπου ζητῆσαι καὶ σῶσαι τὸ ἀπολωλός). *Biblia Patristica* (1.367) lists two receptions of Luke 19.10 in the writings of Clement of Alexandria. The first, from *Stromata* 3.94.2, is not a clear use of the Luke 19.10 tradition. It says: "But the Lord assuredly came for those things which had been deceived" (ἀλλὰ καὶ ὁ κύριος ἐπὶ τὰ πεπλανημένα ὁμολογουμένως ἦλθε). The second, from *Stromata* 4.35.3, is a clear reception of the Luke 19.10 tradition. Clement quotes Jesus' words as follows: "The Son of Man, coming today, has found what was lost" (ὁ υἱὸς τοῦ ἀνθρώπου ἐλθὼν σήμερον τὸ ἀπολωλὸς εὗρεν). Clement picks up the "today" language from Luke 19.9 – "Today salvation has come to this [Zacchaeus'] house." Clement's qualification of the Son of Man's coming with "today" represents a local (not preexistent) coming.

[23] G. Bostock, "Origen's Exegesis of the Kenosis Hymn (Philippians 2:5–11)," in *Origeniana Sexta: Origène et la Bible / Origen and the Bible* (ed. G. Dorival and A. le Boulluec; BETL 118; Leuven: Peeters/Leuven University Press, 1995), 531–47. Clement of Alexandria has a same understanding of the phrase (See discussion of *Paedagogus* 3.2.2 below in 5.4.1.3).

[24] Additionally, Eusebius uses Philippians 2.8 before the ransom logion[c] in *Demonstratio Evangelica* 10.8.33.

that this incarnational motif is used to overshadow or replace the ransom logion[a-b].

(1) Clement of Alexandria, *Quis Dives Salvetur* 37.1–4. Clement uses the ransom logion[c] in *Quis Dives Salvetur* 37.4 (λύτρον ἑαυτὸν ἐπιδιδούς). Preceding this is a narrative in which God's preexistent begotten-self (αὐτὸς ἐγέννησεν ἐξ αὐτοῦ) comes down to earth (κατῆλθε), clothes himself as a man (ἄνθρωπον ἐνέδυ), and voluntarily suffers human conditions (τὰ ἀνθρώπων ἑκὼν ἔπαθεν). In *Paedagogus* 1.9.85.1–2, Clement demonstrates his tendency to interchange the ransom logion[a-b] with an incarnational motif. It is possible that the same interchange occurs in *Quis Dives Salvetur* 37.1–4.

(2) The Acts of Thomas 72. The author uses the ransom logion[c] (σὺ εἶ κύριε ὁ ἑαυτὸν δοὺς ὑπὲρ ἡμῶν...τῆς σῆς ψυχῆς ἧς ἔδωκας [ἀντικατάλλαγμα] ὑπὲρ ἡμῶν). Preceding this material the author states: Ἰησοῦ ὁ τύπον λαβὼν καὶ γενόμενος ὡς ἄνθρωπος. This incarnational statement is very likely influenced by Philippians 2.7 (...μορφὴν δούλου λαβών, ἐν ὁμοιώματι ἀνθρώπων γενόμενος).

5.4.1.3 The Importance of Philippians 2.6–8

The narrative from Philippians 2.6–8 assists some interpretations of the "coming" from the ransom logion[a-b] as a reference to Jesus' incarnation from a preexistent state. Origen, *Fragment on Luke* 14.16, is the clearest example of combining the ransom logion[a-b] with a phrase from Philippians 2.6–8 (μορφὴν δούλου λαβών). Another example is The Acts of Thomas 72, where the author uses a phrase that is influenced by Philippians 2.7 (Ἰησοῦ ὁ τύπον λαβὼν καὶ γενόμενος ὡς ἄνθρωπος) as a lead in to the ransom logion[c].

The influence of Philippians 2.6–8 is not as overt in Clement of Alexandria, but it is likely still present. In *Paedagogus* 1.9.85.1–2, Clement interprets the ransom logion[a-b] as the voluntary incarnation of the Lord as a human (ἐξὸν εἶναι κύριον, ἀδελφὸς εἶναι βεβούληται). This is very similar to the thought of Philippians 2.6–7.

Paedagogus 1.9.85.2[a]	ἐξὸν εἶναι κύριον,
Philippians 2.6	ὃς ἐν μορφῇ θεοῦ ὑπάρχων...
Paedagogus 1.9.85.2[b]	ἀδελφὸς εἶναι βεβούληται
Philippians 2.7	ἀλλὰ ἑαυτὸν ἐκένωσεν...ἐν ὁμοιώματι ἀνθρώπων γενόμενος· καὶ σχήματι εὑρεθεὶς ὡς ἄνθρωπος

Both *Paedagogus* 1.9.85.2 and Philippians 2.6–7 share the unique story that contrasts Jesus' pre-incarnate status and his subsequent voluntary incarnation as a man. In the second part of the contrast, both texts express Jesus' choice (βεβούληται/ἑαυτὸν ἐκένωσεν) to be human (ἀδελφὸς/ἀνθρώπων... ἄνθρωπος). In the first part of the contrast, there is a shared assumption of Jesus' pre-incarnate existence, either as Lord (κύριον) or in the form of God (ἐν μορφῇ θεοῦ). It is important to note that later in *Paedagogus* 3.2.2, Clement calls Jesus "Lord" (κύριον) with reference to his pre-incarnate status, from which he humbles himself in Philippians 2.7. Clement states: "For that which is of flesh has the form of a servant. The apostle says, speaking of the Lord, 'Because He emptied Himself, taking the form of a servant,' calling the outward man servant, *previous to the Lord becoming a servant and wearing flesh* (πρὶν ἢ δουλεῦσαι καὶ σαρκοφρῆσαι τὸν κύριον)."

In *Quis Dives Salvetur* 37.1–4, just before the ransom logion[c] (λύτρον ἑαυτὸν ἐπιδιδούς), Clement describes how God's preexistent begotten self (αὐτὸς ἐγέννησεν ἐξ αὐτοῦ) comes down (κατῆλθε), clothes himself as a man (ἄνθρωπον ἐνέδυ), and voluntarily suffers human conditions (τὰ ἀνθρώπων ἑκὼν ἔπαθεν). It is possible that the narrative in Philippians 2.6–8 influences this description.

Quis Dives 37.2	αὐτὸς ἐγέννησεν ἐξ αὐτοῦ...
Philippians 2.6	ὃς ἐν μορφῇ θεοῦ ὑπάρχων...
Quis Dives 37.3	κατῆλθε...ἄνθρωπον ἐνέδυ...
Philippians 2.7	ἀλλὰ ἑαυτὸν ἐκένωσεν...ἐν ὁμοιώματι ἀνθρώπων
Quis Dives 37.3–4	τὰ ἀνθρώπων ἑκὼν ἔπαθεν...λύτρον ἑαυτὸν ἐπιδιδούς...
Philippians 2.8	ἐταπείνωσεν ἑαυτὸν γενόμενος ὑπήκοος μέχρι θανάτου

In sum, Philippians 2.7 is connected with the ransom logion[a–b] in Origen's *Fragment on Luke* 14.16. Philippians 2.7 also appears before a use of the ransom logion[c] in The Acts of Thomas 72. As for Clement of Alexandria, *Paedagogus* 1.9.85.1–2 offers good evidence that Clement interprets the ransom logion[a–b] as the incarnational coming of the preexistent Lord. It is not completely clear if this interpretation is guided by the narrative in Philippians 2.6–8. However, *Paedagogus* 1.9.85.2 and Philippians 2.6–7 share the unique contrastive story of Jesus' pre-incarnate status and his subsequent voluntary incarnation as a man. In my opinion, given the precedent set in Origen, *Fragment on Luke* 14.16, and The Acts of Thomas 72, there is a strong possibility that there is a real influence from Philippians 2.6–7, at least in *Paedagogus* 1.9.85.2, and maybe also in *Quis Dives Salvetur* 37.2–4.

5.4.1.4 Conclusion

There are two interrelated patterns from the reception of the ransom logion that are applicable to a preexistent coming in Mark 10.45/Matthew 20.28. The earliest witness for both patterns is Clement of Alexandria, who is also the earliest possible witness since he is the first person outside of Mark 10.45/Matthew 20.28 clearly to use the ransom logion[a–b]. Clement's interpretation of the ransom logion[a–b] may be the first extant occurrence of an earlier phenomenon.

(1) The ransom logion[a–b] is interpreted as a reference to Jesus' incarnation as a human.[25] Within this interpretation, the preexistence of Jesus is certainly assumed, but is not overly emphasized. This under-emphasis is not surprising since the important point for early Christians was not the nature of Jesus' preexistence, but the reality of his incarnation. The texts that support the incarnational interpretation of the ransom logion[a–b] are Clement of Alexandria, *Paedagogus* 1.9.85.1–2; Origen, *Commentary on Matthew* 20.28; *Fragment on Luke* 14.16. Other texts that may support this interpretation of the ransom logion[a–b] are Clement of Alexandria, *Quis Dives Salvetur* 37.1–4 and The Acts of Thomas 72.[26]

(2) Philippians 2.6–8 assists some preexistent interpretations the ransom logion. The texts that clearly demonstrate influence from Philippians 2.7 are Origen, *Fragment on Luke* 14.16 and The Acts of Thomas 72. There is a good possibility that Philippians 2.6–7 influences Clement of Alexandria, *Paedagogus* 1.9.85.2. *Quis Dives Salvetur* 37.2–3 may also draw influence from Philippians 2.6–8.

5.4.2 Significance for a Preexistent Coming in Mark 10.45/Matthew 20.28

This section explores the significance of the two interrelated patterns from the reception history for a preexistent coming in Mark 10.45/Matthew 20.28. First, it explores the historical and exegetical possibilities that the coming in Mark 10.45/Matthew 20.28 can be understood as an incarnational coming from preexistence (5.4.2.1). Second, it explores the possibility that the connection between the ransom logion and Philippians 2.6–8 in the reception history reflects Mark 10.45/Matthew 20.28's appropriation of a narrative sequence that is similar to Philippians 2.6–8 (5.4.2.2).

5.4.2.1 Historical and Exegetical Considerations

The discussion of preexistence in Mark 10.45/Matthew 20.28 must begin with the historical context of the synoptic gospels between the Pauline Epistles and the Gospel of John.

The Gospel of John was likely written at the end of the first century or the beginning of the second century.[27] John's Gospel makes explicit statements about Jesus' preexistence, which John uses to explain Jesus' unique heavenly

---

[25] All the texts discussed in this section emphasize Jesus' incarnation as a human (ἄνθρωπος/ἀδελφός), except for Origen's *Fragment on Luke* 14.16, which uses δοῦλος.

[26] *Quis Dives Salvetur* 37.1–4 and The Acts of Thomas 72 may have completely replaced the ransom logion[a–b] with an incarnational motif.

[27] On the date of John's Gospel, see R. Brown, *The Gospel According to John (i–xii)* (AB 29; New York: Doubleday, 1966), lxxx–lxxxvi.

knowledge.[28] The prologue asserts that the logos was with God in the beginning (John 1.1–3). In John 8.58, Jesus asserts his existence prior to that of Abraham. In John 12.41, Jesus is assumed to be the figure that Isaiah sees in Isaiah 6.10. In John 17.5, Jesus asks the Father to glorify him with the glory they shared before the existence of the world (i.e. as expressed in John 1.1–2). The most relevant statements in John for this study are those that depict Jesus saying that he has come "down from heaven" (John 6.38, 42), "into this world" (John 9.39; 12.46; 16.28; 18.37; cf. 1John 4.2; 2John 7). These statements demonstrate an early preexistent interpretation of the "I have come" sayings.[29]

J. Dunn proposes that the Christian belief in Christ's preexistence begins with John's Gospel. Dunn suggests that the last decades of the first century witness a "rather sudden" "cultural evolution" wherein "the *real* pre-existence of heavenly beings came to the surface of religious thought."[30] This cultural evolution manifests itself in Christian literature for the first time in the Gospel of John. According to Dunn, "as the first century of the Christian era drew to a close we find a concept of Christ's real pre-existence beginning to emerge, but only with the Fourth Gospel can we speak of a full blown conception of Christ's personal pre-existence."[31] Dunn's claim that the belief in Christ's personal preexistence is not demonstrable in pre-Johannine Christian literature has proved very controversial. This is because several Pauline texts are normally thought plainly to assert Christ's personal preexistence.

Before discussing Pauline literature, it should be briefly noted that there are other first-century texts that may affirm Jesus' preexistence. Hebrews 1.2 places Jesus (the Son) at the creation of the world (υἱῷ...δι᾽ οὗ καὶ

---

[28] J. McGrath states that John's Jesus "was not merely a human being who had ascended to receive revelation, but the incarnation of one who had pre-existed in heaven, and who on this basis could reveal what he saw there in a way that no other could (*John's Apologetic Christology: Legitimation and Development in Johannine Christology* (SNTSMS 111; Cambridge: Cambridge University Press, 2001), 195. C.f. L. Hurtado for a discussion of Christology and Conflict in the Johannine community (*Lord Jesus Christ: Devotion to Jesus in Earliest Christianity* [Grand Rapids: Eerdmans, 2003], 349–426).

[29] Gathercole notes the "overwhelming *scholarly* consensus that these Johannine sayings – because of the references to 'heaven' and 'the world' and the setting with John's logos Christology more broadly – imply preexistence" (*The Preexistent Son*, 83 – italics original). John's Gospel also clearly presents the Son of Man as preexistent. There are similar conceptions of the Son of Man in the *Similitudes of Enoch* and *4 Ezra*; for a discussion of these texts, see J. Dunn, *Christology in the Making: A New Testament Inquiry into the Origins of the Doctrine of the Incarnation* [London: SCM Press, 1980], 75–81; 259–60.

[30] Ibid., 259–60 – italics original. Specifically Dunn states that there was "a rather sudden appearance...at the end of the first century and beginning of the second century on several fronts of ideas of divine redeemer figures who can be said to have pre-existed in heaven prior to their appearance on earth" (Ibid., 259).

[31] Ibid., 258.

ἐποίησεν τοὺς αἰῶνας).[32] Jude 5 states that Jesus saved the people out of Egypt (Ἰησοῦς [κύριος] ἅπαξ λαὸν ἐκ γῆς Αἰγύπτου σώσας).[33] Colossians 1.16–17 says that all things were created by him...All things were created through him and for him...He is before all things and all things hold together in him (ἐν αὐτῷ ἐκτίσθη τὰ πάντα...τὰ πάντα δι᾽ αὐτοῦ καὶ εἰς αὐτὸν ἔκτισται...αὐτός ἐστιν πρὸ πάντων καὶ τὰ πάντα ἐν αὐτῷ συνέστηκεν). The dating of Hebrews, Jude, and Colossians are uncertain.[34]

Several Pauline texts are normally thought to imply a belief in Christ's preexistence. 1Corinthians 15.47: Jesus is the man from heaven (ἄνθρωπος ἐξ οὐρανοῦ). Galatians 4.4: God sent his son to be born of a woman (ἐξαπέστειλεν ὁ θεὸς τὸν υἱὸν αὐτοῦ, γενόμενον ἐκ γυναικός). Romans 8.3: God sent his son in the likeness of sinful flesh (ὁ θεὸς τὸν ἑαυτοῦ υἱὸν πέμψας ἐν ὁμοιώματι σαρκὸς ἁμαρτίας). 1Corinthians 10.4: Christ was the rock that followed the Israelites in the wilderness (ἡ πέτρα δὲ ἦν ὁ Χριστός). 1Corinthians 8.6: One Lord Jesus Christ, through whom are all things (εἷς κύριος Ἰησοῦς Χριστὸς δι᾽ οὗ τὰ πάντα). Philippians 2.6–7: Jesus existed in the form of God...but he emptied himself...coming in the likeness of humans (ὃς ἐν μορφῇ θεοῦ ὑπάρχων...ἀλλὰ ἑαυτὸν ἐκένωσεν... ἐν ὁμοιώματι ἀνθρώπων γενόμενος). 2Corinthians 8.9: Jesus, though rich, became poor so that through his poverty you might become rich (ἐπτώχευσεν πλούσιος ὤν, ἵνα ὑμεῖς τῇ ἐκείνου πτωχείᾳ πλουτήσητε).[35]

Dunn has been, and continues to be, the most prominent dissenting voice to the notion of preexistence in these texts.[36] Dunn understands the texts that describe God sending his son (Galatians 4.4; Romans 8.3) to affirm a divine commissioning as God's agent rather than an actual sending from preexis-

---

[32] Hebrews also appears to have an incarnational christology. Hebrews 2.14, 17 states: Επεὶ οὖν τὰ παιδία κεκοινώνηκεν αἵματος καὶ σαρκός, καὶ αὐτὸς παραπλησίως μετέσχεν τῶν αὐτῶν...ὅθεν ὤφειλεν κατὰ πάντα τοῖς ἀδελφοῖς ὁμοιωθῆναι. Even Dunn says that Hebrews has "some concept of pre-existence" (Ibid., 258).

[33] There is a text-critical problem in Jude 5 concerning the originality of Ἰησοῦς or κύριος. The external evidence favors Ἰησοῦς, and internally it is much easier to envision a change from Ἰησοῦς to κύριος (P. Bartholomä, "Did Jesus Save the People Out of Egypt? A Re-examination of a Textual Problem in Jude 5," NovT 50/2 [2008]: 143–58). However, even if κύριος is original, it probably still refers to Jesus since Jude 4 describes Jesus as "our only master and Lord" (τὸν μόνον δεσπότην καὶ κύριον ἡμῶν Ἰησοῦν Χριστὸν) (Gathercole, The Preexistent Son, 40).

[34] For introductory discussions of the relevant issues, see B. Ehrman, The New Testament: A Historical Introduction to the Early Christian Writings (New York: Oxford University Press, 1997), 320–29; W. Lane, "Hebrews," DLNTD 443–58; R. Webb, "Jude," DLNTD 611–20.

[35] All of these texts are discussed by Gathercole (The Preexistent Son, 23–31).

[36] Dunn discusses these texts elsewhere in The Theology of Paul the Apostle (Grand Rapids: Eerdmans, 1998), and most recently in Beginning from Jerusalem: Christianity in the Making, vol. 2 (Grand Rapids: Eerdmans, 2009).

tence in heaven.[37] Dunn believes that Paul's identification of Christ with the rock in the wilderness (1Corinthians 10.4) should not be taken literally, but typologically so that the rock is a type of Christ.[38] Dunn's perspectives on Galatians 4.4, Romans 8.3, and 1Corinthians 10.4 are less controversial than his view of 1Corinthians 8.6. In 1Corinthians 8.6 according to Dunn, "Christ is being identified here not with a pre-existent being but with the creative power and action of God. And the thought is not of Christ as pre-existent but of the creative act and power of God now embodied in a final and complete way in Christ."[39] The problem with Dunn's view is that 1Corinthians 8.6 rather clearly seems to say that all things originally came from the Father and through Jesus Christ, and not through the creative power of God that is subsequently identified with Jesus Christ (εἷς θεὸς ὁ πατὴρ ἐξ οὗ τὰ πάντα...καὶ εἷς κύριος Ἰησοῦς Χριστὸς δι' οὗ τὰ πάντα).[40] Certainly Jewish traditions that place Wisdom at the creation are being drawn upon,[41] but in 1Corinthians 8.6, it is ultimately Jesus, and not Wisdom, that Paul asserts is the mediator of God's creative activity.[42]

Dunn's view of Philippians 2.6–8 is his most controversial. Dunn is convinced that Philippians 2.6–8 should be understood through the lens of Adam christology. Dunn thinks that μορφὴ θεοῦ compares with Adam being made in the image (εἰκών) of God in Genesis 1.27.[43] Further, Dunn thinks that the notion of "equality with God" (τὸ εἶναι ἴσα θεῷ) is comparable to Adam's temptation to be "as gods" (ὡς θεοὶ) (Genesis 3.5).[44] The result, according to Dunn, is that Philippians 2.6–8 refers to the humility of the *earthly* Jesus in contrast to the arrogance of Adam. Both Jesus and Adam were in the image/form of God. Adam tried to become equal with God, but Jesus denied

---

[37] Dunn, *Christology*, 40. Dunn draws a parallel with the parable of the tenants (Matthew 21.33–41), where the landowner sends (ἀποστέλλω) his son, just as he previously sends (ἀποστέλλω) his slaves. For both the son and the slaves, the sending is simply a commissioning, and does not imply preexistence.

[38] Ibid., 183–84. Although, S. McDonough has noted how Christ's actual mediation between God and Israel through the rock coheres with Christ's position as mediator between God and the creation in 1Corinthians 8.6 (*Christ as Creator: Origins of a New Testament Doctrine* [Oxford: Oxford University Press, 2009], 152).

[39] Dunn, *Christology*, 182.

[40] Hurtado, *Lord Jesus Christ*, 126. Hurtado goes on to exhort: "we should understand these attributions of preexistence to Jesus as the expression of profound theological/christological convictions that we risk making banal if we attempt to fit them into what may seem to us more reasonable categories."

[41] Proverbs 8.22–31; Wisdom of Solomon 9.9; cf. 1Corinthians 1.24, 30.

[42] The inclusion of Jesus into the *Shema*-like statement in 1Corinthians 8.6 is an important adaptation of a similar statement in Romans 11.36 (R. Bauckham, *God Crucified: Monotheism and Christology in the New Testament* [Grand Rapids: Eerdmans, 1998], 37–40).

[43] Dunn, *Christology*, 115.

[44] Ibid., 115–16.

such equality. Adam fell into a corrupted state, whereas Jesus freely chose to empty himself of Adam's glory and accept humanity's slavery (μορφὴν δούλου λαβών) (Philippians 2.7).[45] Thus, Jesus' actions serve to reverse Adam's.

Dunn's thesis may be partially correct. It is, after all, undeniable that Adam is an important person for Paul to compare with Jesus (Romans 5.18–19; 1Corinthians 15.45–47). However, there are two problems with the Adam comparison. First, μορφή θεοῦ does not occur in the Genesis account, and it is never used in any pre-Pauline literature as an allusion to Adam.[46] Additionally, Paul uses εἰκών θεοῦ in 1Corinthians 11.7 to allude to the Genesis account, which then raises the question of why he would not use it in Philippians 2.6 if he intends a comparison with Adam. Second, the phrase "equality with God" (τὸ εἶναι ἴσα θεῷ) is never used in other literature in reference to Adam.[47] Therefore, if there is comparison between Jesus and Adam in Philippians 2.6–8, then it is being made on conceptual, rather than verbal, grounds.[48]

Concerning preexistence, the main problem with Dunn's thesis is not his conceptual comparison between Jesus and Adam but his assumption that a comparison with Adam necessitates an earthly Jesus. Certainly a heavenly figure who denies his equality with God could also serve as a comparison with Adam.[49] Adam was in the image of God on earth and Jesus was in the form of God in heaven. Adam tried to become equal with God, whereas Jesus already possessed equality with God, but did not take advantage of it.[50] Adam fell into a corrupted state, whereas Jesus willingly left his preexistent life in heaven and humbled himself by coming in the likeness as a human. Therefore, even if Paul is drawing on the Genesis account in order to make a comparison between Jesus and Adam, this does not prevent the passage from asserting Jesus' preexistence.

The ultimate attractiveness for seeing Jesus' preexistence asserted in Philippians 2.6 is that it forms a neat narrative sequence that flows from Jesus' preexistent life in heaven (2.6), to his choice (ἑαυτὸν ἐκένωσεν) to be incar-

---

[45] Ibid., 117.

[46] Hurtado, *Lord Jesus Christ*, 122.

[47] Ibid., 122–23.

[48] There is also a potential comparison with Roman rulers (J. Reumann, *Philippians: A New Translation with Introduction and Commentary* [AYB 33B; New Haven: Yale University Press, 2008], 368–69).

[49] L. Hurst, "Re-enter the Pre-existent Christ in Philippians 2:5–11?" *NTS* 32 (1986): 449–57.

[50] It is best to understand ἁρπαγμός as communicating Christ's unwillingness to take advantage of the equality with God that he already possessed. On the translation of οὐχ ἁρπαγμὸν ἡγήσατο τὸ εἶναι ἴσα θεῷ, see R. Hoover, "The Harpagmos Enigma: A Philological Solution," *HTR* 64 (1971): 95–119.

nated as a human (2.7), to his death on the cross (2.8).[51] Significantly, Jesus' descent from his preexistent life in heaven is mirrored in Philippians 2.9–11 with his return (exaltation) back to his life in heaven. The parabolic structure of Philippians 2.6–11, along with the other Pauline passages that seem to assume Jesus' preexistence (especially 1Corinthians 8.6), has convinced the majority of scholars that Philippians 2.6 affirms Jesus' preexistence.[52]

Turning back to Mark and Matthew, these Gospels lie (historically) between the Pauline Epistles and the Gospel of John. The expression of Jesus' preexistence is overt in John, but is more implicit and less widespread in Paul, as well as the other non-Pauline texts mentioned above (Hebrews 1.2, etc.). Because of its implicit nature, it is difficult to discern how influential the belief in Jesus' preexistence was in the pre-70 CE Christian communities.[53] One important consideration is the probability that Mark operates within the Pauline sphere of influence.[54] If Mark is influenced by Paul, then his Gospel

---

[51] 2Corinthians 8.9 asserts something similar to the descent described in Philippians 2.6–7.

[52] E.g., M. Bockmuehl, *The Epistle to the Philippians* (BNTC 11; Peabody, MA: Hendrickson, 1998), 131–33; G. Fee, *Paul's Letter to the Philippians* (NICNT; Grand Rapids: Eerdmans, 1995), 191–214; Gathercole, *The Preexistent Son*, 24–26; Hurtado, *Lord Jesus Christ*, 118–26; *et al.* Dunn's stratification of preexistence to John's Gospel and a sudden cultural evolution at the end of the first century is ultimately too artificial and fails to adequately account for several Pauline texts.

[53] This is much more cautious than Gathercole, who says that Jesus' preexistence is so widespread in early Christian circles that "one would actually *expect* to find such a christology in Matthew, Mark, and Luke" (*The Preexistent Son*, 23 – italics original).

[54] On the whole, the Gospel of Mark (also Matthew) offers no sure evidence of a direct knowledge of the Pauline Epistles (neither does Acts). However, there is a growing consensus that Mark writes in a Pauline sphere of influence with the result that Pauline thoughts are present in Mark's Gospel (J. Fenton, "Paul and Mark," in *Studies in the Gospels: Essays in Memory of R. H. Lightfoot* [ed. D. Nineham; Oxford: Blackwell, 1955], 89–112; J. Marcus, *Mark 1–8* [ABC 27; New York: Doubleday, 1999], 73–75; "Mark – Interpreter of Paul," *NTS* 46 [2000]: 473–87; W. Telford, *The Theology of the Gospel of Mark* (NTT; Cambridge: Cambridge University Press, 1999), 164–69; *Writing on the Gospel of Mark* [GABR; London: DEO Publishing, 2009], 147–49, 467–69). Among the similarities between Mark and Paul listed by Marcus are the following: "Both [Mark and Paul]…make the term εὐαγγέλιον a central aspect of their theology (e.g. Mark 1.1; Gal 1.6–9; Rom 1.16–17)…Both Mark and Paul have negative things to say about Peter and about members of Jesus' family (e.g. Mark 3.20–1, 31–5; 8.31–3; Gal 2)…Both assert that Jesus came…for the Jews first (πρῶτον) but also for the Gentiles (Mark 7.27–9; Rom 1.16; 2.9–10; cf. Rom 11). And both think that the widening of God's purposes to incorporate the Gentiles was accomplished by an apocalyptic change in the Law that had previously separated Jews from Gentiles, a change that included an abrogation of the OT food laws (Mark 7.19 [καθαρίζων πάντα τὰ βρώματα]; Rom 14.20 [πάντα μὲν καθαρά])" ("Mark – Interpreter of Paul," 475–76). On the Gentiles in Mark, see K. Iverson, *Gentiles in the Gospel of Mark: 'Even the Dogs Under the Table Eat the Children's Crumbs'* (LNTS 339; London: T&T Clark International, 2007). Of course, there are also some differences between Mark and Paul. The most prominent of these is Mark's lack of concern for the Pauline issue of circumcision (though, perhaps Mark's silence on the issue is

may share Paul's belief in Jesus' preexistence. However, it is important to avoid the simplistic conclusion that because an idea is in Paul, it must also be in Mark; Mark may disagree with Paul about Jesus' preexistence. Therefore, it is necessary to take Mark and Matthew on their own terms. If we are to believe that Mark and Matthew, like Paul, believe in Jesus' preexistence, then it must be demonstrated from their writings.

The christology of the synoptic gospels is largely implicit, which makes it difficult to determine if a belief in Jesus' preexistence lies beneath the surface of the narratives.[55] However, Gathercole argues that the synoptic assumption of Jesus' preexistence can be demonstrated. One of his supporting arguments for preexistence concerns the transcendence of Jesus in the synoptic gospels.[56] According to Gathercole, the synoptic Jesus transcends the heaven/earth divide as well as the God/creation divide.[57] Gathercole also notes that Matthew's picture of Jesus is more transcendent than Mark's.[58] Gathercole is aware that the transcendence of Jesus in the synoptic gospels does not neces-

---

an indirect way of agreeing with Paul). The current consensus on Mark and Paul is in contrast to M. Werner's influential work that argued for the complete lack of connection between Mark and Paul (*Der Einfluss paulinischer Theologie im Markusevangelium* [BZNW 1; Giessen: Alfred Töpelmann, 1923]). For a recent challenge to the consensus, see J. Crossley, "Mark, Paul and the Question of Influences," in *Paul and the Gospels: Christologies, Conflicts and Convergences* (LNTS 411; ed. M. Bird and J. Willitts; London: T&T Clark International, 2011), 10–29.

[55] For a thorough overview of scholarly opinion on Mark's christology, see D. Johansson, "The Identity of Jesus in the Gospel of Mark: Past and Present Proposals," *CBR* 9 (2011): 364–93. According to Johansson, recent Markan scholarship (since 1970) has viewed Jesus as a divinely empowered human being, lacking preexistence. For another good discussion of Jesus in Mark and Matthew, see Hurtado, *Lord Jesus Christ*, 283–340. Telford's invaluable volume has an extensive list of works on Mark's christology (*Writing on the Gospel of Mark*, 328–40).

[56] His other supporting argument is the pre-synoptic belief in Jesus' pre-existence (*The Preexistent Son*, 23–43). We have already discussed this topic above.

[57] Ibid., 47–77. Examples of the heaven/earth divide include the Transfiguration and Jesus' recognition by other heavenly figures, like demons. The section on the God/creation divide focuses on Jesus' unique authority – commanding the elements, forgiving sins, etc.

[58] Matthew's Jesus is able to transcend space, is reverenced (προσκυνέω), sends the prophets, and encourages his followers to meet in his name. Matthew has the *Emmanuel* motif, and the famous "bolt from the Johannine blue" (11.27). Matthew's Jesus also has a miraculous birth (ibid., 77–79; 284–85). Mark lacks a birth narrative, but he may hint at his knowledge of Jesus' miraculous birth in Mark 6.3 where those in Jesus' hometown, who are offended by him, refer to him as the "son of Mary" (ὁ υἱὸς τῆς Μαρίας). It may be that those mocking Jesus are actually claiming what the readers know to be true about him – he was miraculously born of Mary (Hurtado, *Lord Jesus Christ*, 321). For other instances of similar irony in Mark see 14.65; 15.32, 39. If Mark is aware of Jesus' miraculous birth, then he probably does not include it in his gospel because he is concerned to present Jesus' life in a way that is parallel to the believer's life, which begins with baptism and ends with death (ibid., 311).

sitate that Jesus is considered to be preexistent. However, Gathercole believes that it would be strange if the synoptic gospels did not regard Jesus as preexistent. He states that Jesus "would then be a divine, heavenly, space-transcending figure who was somehow not preexistent."[59] Gathercole uses his discussion of Jesus' transcendence to support his main evidence for preexistence, which are the "I have come" sayings. According to Gathercole, the best parallel for the "I have come" sayings are the sayings of angelic figures who use a similar formula to describe their mission to earth from their preexistent life in heaven.[60] If Gathercole's parallel is meaningful, then the "I have come" sayings represent places where the synoptic evangelists' assumptions about Jesus' preexistence are working their way to the surface of the narratives.[61]

The purpose of this study is to further address one of Gathercole's "I have come" sayings, namely, Mark 10.45/Matthew 20.28.[62] According to Gathercole, Jesus' coming to serve in Mark 10.45/Matthew 20.28[b] does not describe his ministry, but his entire human life. Thus, Jesus came *from heaven* not to be served, but to serve.[63] I would add that if "many" in Mark 10.45/Matthew 20.28[c] is understood as humanity, as the tradition in 1Timothy 2.6 seems to assert, then the "coming" in Mark 10.45/Matthew 20.28[b] is also incarnational (cf. Hebrews 2.14, 17); the voluntary nature of the coming would then imply preexistence. There is not much beyond these points that can be said about the potential for preexistence specifically in Mark 10.45/Matthew 20.28. The purpose of the next section is to reintroduce the reception history and to explore how it might add further support to a preexistent coming in Mark 10.45/Matthew 20.28.

---

[59] *The Preexistent Son*, 79. Gathercole also discusses the titles of Jesus in the synoptics (ibid., 231–83), but these are likewise not determinative for preexistence. I disagree with Gathercole that the transcendence of the synoptic Jesus should lead us to *expect* that the synoptic writers considered him to be preexistent.

[60] Ibid., 113–47.

[61] It is important to note that the validity of Gathercole's thesis ultimately rests on his argument that the "I have come" sayings imply preexistence.

[62] Some of the other "I have come" sayings discussed by Gathercole include Mark 1.24; 1.38; Matthew 5.17; 8.29; 10.34–35; Mark 2.17/Matthew 9.13. Gathercole also discusses the sending sayings (*The Preexistent Son*, 83–189).

[63] Gathercole thinks that if the coming in Mark 10.45/Matthew 20.28[a–b] only referred to Jesus' ministry, then it would be hard to reconcile Mark 10.45/Matthew 20.28[a] (ὁ υἱὸς τοῦ ἀνθρώπου οὐκ ἦλθεν διακονηθῆναι) with Mark 10.45/Matthew 20.28[b] (ἀλλὰ διακονῆσαι) since there would be no expectation for someone beginning his ministry to be served. There would, however, be such an expectation for a figure from heaven (Ibid., 167–68).

5.4.2.2 The Importance of Philippians 2.6–8

Origen is the earliest extant writer who certainly connects the ransom logion with the Philippians' hymn. It is highly probable that Clement of Alexandria's incarnational interpretation of the ransom logion is also influenced by the Philippians' hymn.[64] Because Clement of Alexandria is the first person outside of Mark 10.45/Matthew 20.28 to clearly receive the ransom logion[a–b], it is difficult to determine the antiquity of his interpretation. The purpose of this section is to explore the possibility that the patristic connection between the ransom logion and the Philippians hymn reflects Mark 10.45/Matthew 20.28's appropriation of a narrative sequence that is similar to Philippians 2.6–8

Philippians 2.6–8	Mark 10.45/Matthew 20.28
V.6 ὃς ἐν μορφῇ θεοῦ ὑπάρχων οὐχ ἁρπαγμὸν ἡγήσατο τὸ εἶναι ἴσα θεῷ,	ὁ υἱὸς τοῦ ἀνθρώπου οὐκ ἦλθεν διακονηθῆναι
V.7 ἀλλὰ ἑαυτὸν ἐκένωσεν μορφὴν δούλου λαβών, ἐν ὁμοιώματι ἀνθρώπων γενόμενος· καὶ σχήματι εὑρεθεὶς ὡς ἄνθρωπος	ἀλλὰ [ἦλθεν] διακονῆσαι
V.8 ἐταπείνωσεν ἑαυτὸν γενόμενος ὑπήκοος μέχρι θανάτου, θανάτου δὲ σταυροῦ	καὶ δοῦναι τὴν ψυχὴν αὐτοῦ λύτρον ἀντὶ πολλῶν

There is not much shared vocabulary between Philippians 2.6–8 and Mark 10.45/Matthew 20.28. This is expected since Mark and Matthew probably have no direct contact with Pauline texts. However, if we assume a preexistent coming in Mark 10.45/Matthew 20.28, then Philippians 2.6–8 and Mark 10.45/Matthew 20.28 do share the same narrative sequence of Jesus' preexistence, followed by his service, and his voluntary death. Significantly, both narrative sequences are similarly divided by ἀλλά, which serves to contrast the loftiness of Jesus and his worthiness to be served with his self-abasement as a servant, who serves unto death. What follows is a brief discussion of the main elements in the shared narrative sequence: (1) Preexistence, (2) Service, and (3) Voluntary Death, and then some conclusions about the potential connection between Mark 10.45/Matthew 20.28 and the Philippians' hymn.

(1) *Preexistence*: As discussed above, Philippians 2.6–8 is most naturally read as a narrative sequence that flows from Jesus' preexistent life in heaven (2.6), to his incarnation as a human (2.7), to his death on the cross (2.8). The return to heaven in Philippians 2.9–11 reinforces this reading, as do the other Pauline texts that assume Jesus' preexistence. In Mark 10.45/Matthew 20.28, the preexistence of Jesus is implicit in his coming to serve, where the service is understood to describe the purpose of his earthly life. There are two further parallels between the Philippians' hymn and Mark 10.45/Matthew 20.28 concerning preexistence. First, Philippians 2.7 may share with Mark

---

[64] It may be significant that both Clement and Origen are in Alexandria.

10.45/Matthew 20.28 the expression of Jesus' incarnation from preexistence as a "coming" (ἐν ὁμοιώματι ἀνθρώπων γενόμενος). Second, the nature of the coming in Mark 10.45/Matthew 20.28 and Philippians 2.7 is voluntary.

(2) *Service*: Philippians 2.7 and Mark 10.45/Matthew 20.28[b] assert that Jesus' position in this world is one of service. Philippians 2.7 uses δοῦλος, and Mark 10.45/Matthew 20.28[b] uses διακονέω.[65] In both cases, Jesus' service is presented in contrast (ἀλλά) to what precedes. In Philippians 2.7, service is used to describe the purpose of Jesus' entire human life (μορφὴν δούλου λαβών, ἐν ὁμοιώματι ἀνθρώπων γενόμενος). If the service in Mark 10.45/Matthew 20.28[b] also describes the purpose of Jesus' entire life, then its meaning is extremely close to Philippians 2.7.

(3) *Voluntary Death*: In Philippians 2.8, Jesus humbles himself by becoming obedient to the point of death (ἐταπείνωσεν ἑαυτὸν γενόμενος ὑπήκοος μέχρι θανάτου). In Mark 10.45/Matthew 20.28[c], Jesus gives his life (δοῦναι τὴν ψυχὴν αὐτοῦ). Mark 10.45/Matthew 20.28[c] further describes the benefit of Jesus' sacrifice (λύτρον ἀντὶ πολλῶν). The beneficial nature of Jesus' death is noticeably absent from Philippians 2.6–11, which makes it the major difference in the comparison.

In conclusion, the above comparison between Mark 10.45/Matthew 20.28 and Philippians 2.6–8 shows that the two texts do not share much vocabulary. This is not surprising since Mark and Matthew probably have no direct contact with Pauline texts. However, if we assume a preexistent coming in Mark 10.45/Matthew 20.28[a–b], then Philippians 2.6–8 and Mark 10.45/Matthew 20.28 do share a unique narrative sequence of Jesus' preexistence, service, and voluntary death. Within this narrative sequence are significant parallels, such as the volitional "coming" from preexistence, the contrastive ἀλλά and its similar placement in the division, and the vocation of service used to describe the entirety of Jesus' life. Contemporary scholars have typically overlooked the potential for a shared tradition between Mark 10.45 and Philippians 2.6–8, at least in the English-speaking world.[66] This oversight is probably

---

[65] There are a limited number of places in the New Testament that speak of Jesus' service. Romans 15.8 and Luke 22.27 are the only other places in the New Testament where διακον- or δουλ- are connected with Jesus' service (the New Testament never describes Jesus with ὑπηρετ-). Acts 3.13, 26; 4.27, 30 refer to Jesus as God's servant (παῖς), which is very likely due to influence from Isaiah 52.13 (cf. 53.11). John 13 also presents Jesus as a servant, though without using servant vocabulary.

[66] None of the works comparing Mark and Paul, which are listed above in n. 54, compare Mark 10.45 with Philippians 2.6–8. Marcus discusses Philippians 2.6–8 in his commentary on Mark 10.45, but only as it relates to the mutual use of Isaiah 53 (*Mark 8–16*, 756–57). Marcus does not mention Mark 10.45 and Philippians 2.6–8 in his other works that are specifically focused on Mark and Paul. The vast majority of English commentaries on Mark and Philippians also do not mention the connection. There have been, however, a few German writers who have noted similarities between Mark 10.45 and Philippians 2.6–8. The first of these I

due to the widespread assumption that the "coming" in Mark 10.45/Matthew 20.28 is not from preexistence. However, Gathercole's work has reinvigorated the discussion of preexistence in the synoptics. If Gathercole is correct, and Jesus' preexistence is implied in the "coming" from Mark 10.45/Matthew 20.28, then Mark 10.45/Matthew 20.28 and Philippians 2.6–8 do share a similar narrative sequence of Jesus' preexistence, service, and voluntary death. This shared narrative sequence may not be coincidental, but may be due to Mark's location in a Pauline sphere of influence where such a (pre-Pauline) narrative sequence circulated. If so, then the general narrative sequence of Jesus' preexistence, service, and voluntary death may be the points of more direct contact between Mark 10.45/Matthew 20.28 and Philippians 2.6–8, that is, direct contact through a shared narrative sequence.[67]

5.4.3 Conclusion

Mark and Matthew are historically situated between an implicit confession of Jesus' preexistence in Paul and an overt assertion of Jesus' preexistence in the

---

found is H. Riesenfeld, who states: "Das Jesuswort vom Menschensohn, Mk 10,45 par, und das christologische 'Kompendium' in Phil 2,6–11 stimmen in ihrer Struktur dermassen überein, dass ich davon überzeugt bin, dass der paulinische Text eine im Wissen um das Christusereignis durchreflektierte Auslegung des Menschensohnwortes ist" ("Unpoetische Hymnen im Neuen Testament? Zu Phil 2,1–11," in *Glaube und Gerechtigkeit: In Memoriam Rafael Gyllenberg* [ed. J. Kiilunen, V. Riekkinen, and H. Räisänen; SESJ 38; Helsinki: Vammalan Kirjapaino Oy, 1983], 167). A more recent German scholar is D. Häusser. Häusser lists others who have noted the connection between all or parts of Mark 10.35–45 and Philippians 2.1–11, though Häusser states that this notation has only happened sporadically (vereinzelt) (*Christusbekenntnis und Jesusüberlieferung bei Paulus* [WUNT 2/210; Tübingen: Mohr Siebeck, 2006], 254 n. 170). Included in Häusser's list is Riesenfeld, as well as Häusser's doctoral supervisor, R. Riesner, who follows Häusser by comparing Mark 10.45 and Philippians 2.7 ("Back to the Historical Jesus through Paul and His School (The Ransom Logion–Mark 10.45; Matthew 20.28)" *JSHJ* [2003]: 171–99). In my investigations, only Riesenfeld and Häusser (followed by Riesner) give substantive attention to the parallels between Mark 10.45 and Philippians 2.6–8. The other writers listed by Häusser – Bockmuehl, Hawthorne, Hurtado, Thompson, and Wenham – do not make any extended comments about the parallel between Mark 10.45 and Philippians 2.6–8, but only note it in passing. For example, M. Thompson, on the page listed by Häusser, states: "Paul's frequent use of δοῦλος...most likely found its primary inspiration in the teaching and example of Jesus (cf. Mk 10.44; 13.34; Mk 10.24–25; 18.23–32...)" (*Clothed with Christ: The Example and Teaching of Jesus in Romans 12.1–15.13* [JSNTSup 59; Sheffield: JSOT Press, 1991], 220). Additionally, R. France mentions Philippians 2.6–8 in his commentary on Matthew 20.28 (*The Gospel of Matthew* [NICNT; Grand Rapids: Eerdmans], 761). Also, see John Calvin (*Commentary on a Harmony of the Evangelists, Matthew, Mark, and Luke* [vol. 2; trans. W. Pringle; Grand Rapids: Eerdmans, 1965], 426–27).

[67] I imagine that the connection between Mark 10.45/Matthew 20.28 and Philippians 2.6–8, if present, is an evolutionary connection, where they both share an ancestral narrative sequence, but have appropriated that tradition in different ways.

Gospel of John. While Mark may be in a Pauline sphere of influence, this is no proof that Mark or Matthew share Paul's confession of a preexistent Jesus. Mark and Matthew do portray Jesus as a transcendent figure through whom God is working in an unprecedented manner, but this portrayal does not necessitate that Jesus be preexistent. In fact, there is very little in Mark or Matthew that might prove Jesus' preexistence. This is why Gathercole's "I have come" sayings are important, because they may be the single piece of demonstrable evidence for Jesus' preexistence in the synoptic gospels.[68]

The reception history of the ransom logion may corroborate Gathercole's case for Jesus' preexistence specifically in Mark 10.45/Matthew 20.28. The key pattern from the reception history is the connection between the ransom logion and Philippians 2.6–8. This connection, which typically goes unnoticed in modern scholarship, may reflect Mark 10.45/Matthew 20.28's appropriation of a narrative sequence that is similar to Philippians 2.6–8.[69] If we assume a preexistent coming in Mark 10.45/Matthew 20.28, then Philippians 2.6–8 and Mark 10.45/Matthew 20.28 share the same narrative sequence of Jesus' preexistence, service, and voluntary death. Other important parallels also emerge, such as the volitional "coming," the contrastive ἀλλά, and the vocation of service used to describe the entirety of Jesus' life. The shared narrative sequence between Philippians 2.6–8 and Mark 10.45/Matthew 20.28, and the other parallels that result from seeing preexistence in Mark 10.45/Matthew 20.28, suggest that the preexistent perspective of Mark 10.45/Matthew 20.28 is correct, and the subsequent patristic writers are correct to connect the two traditions together.

Finally, it is possible that a shared narrative sequence between Philippians 2.6–8 and Mark 10.45/Matthew 20.28 results from Mark's participation in a Pauline sphere of influence where such a narrative sequence circulated. This possibility, as well as the possibility that the reception history reflects Mark 10.45/Matthew 20.28's appropriation of a narrative sequence that is similar to Philippians 2.6–8, is diagrammed below.

---

[68] P. Foster states about Gathercole's work: "In fact it is fair to say that the success or otherwise of the thesis being advanced in this book will largely stand or fall depending on whether the christological significance that Gathercole attributes to the 'I have come' sayings is found to be persuasive" (Review of S. Gathercole, *The Preexistent Son: Recovering the Christologies of Matthew, Mark, and Luke, ExpTim* 118/7 [2007], 357).

[69] L. Hardwick observes the ability of reception history to "focus critical attention back towards the ancient source and sometimes frame new questions or retrieve aspects of the source which have been marginalized or forgotten" (*Reception Studies* [NSC 33; Oxford: Oxford University Press, 2003], 4).

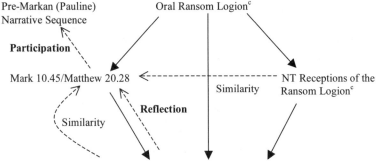

Clement of Alexandria, *Paedagogus* 1.9.85.1–2; *Quis Dives Salvetur* 37.1–4; The Acts of
Thomas 72; Origen, *Commentary on Matthew* 20.28; *Fragment on Luke* 14.16

5.5 Significance for the Scriptural Background
of Mark 10.45/Matthew 20.28

After authenticity, scriptural background is the most debated issue in the
modern study of Mark 10.45/Matthew 20.28.[70] Isaiah 53, Daniel 7; 9, and
Isaiah 43 are the three texts typically put forward as the scriptural background. Significantly, all three texts claim linguistic and conceptual connections with different parts of Mark 10.45/Matthew 20.28, and none of these
connections are mutually exclusive (See 1.2.3). The purpose of this section is
to review the patterns from the reception history that are relevant to the scriptural background discussion (5.5.1), to offer some exegetical considerations
(5.5.2), and then to explore what contribution, if any, the patterns in the reception history might make to the scriptural background discussion (5.5.3).

5.5.1 The Reception of the Ransom Logion

5.5.1.1 Pattern Applicable to Isaiah 53

1Clement 16.3–14 and 1Peter 2.21–25 demonstrate that Isaiah 53 was read as
a unit very early. Influence from various verses in Isaiah 53, most of which
emphasize atonement, occurs seven times alongside the reception of the ransom logion.[71] These are listed below in reverse order of their appearance in
Chapters Two through Four.[72]

---

[70] This thesis does not address authenticity. See 1.2 n. 5 above.

[71] The ambiguous reception from 1Peter 1.18–19 is not included amongst the seven.

[72] In addition to these seven, Titus 2.14 and 1Timothy 2.6 receive the ransom logion[c] with
Isaiah 42.6–7; 49.6–8. This appears to be a unique reading. However, it may be congruent
with the larger pattern to interpret the ransom logion through the lens of the Isaianic servant.

(1) Eusebius, *Demonstratio Evangelica* 10.8.33. Eusebius' reception of the ransom logion[c] is as follows: λύτρον καὶ ἀντίψυχον...ἀντίψυχον ἡμῶν καὶ ἀντίλυτρον γεγενημένος.[73] This is directly followed by a citation of Isaiah 53.4, 5, 7.[74]

(2) The Teachings of Silvanus 104.12–13. The author of Silvanus incorporates the phrase ⲘⲡⲉⲕⲚⲟⲂⲉ into the ransom logion[c], thus: ⲚϥⲘⲟⲨ ⲰⲀⲢⲟⲔ ⲚⲤⲰⲧⲉ ⲘⲡⲉⲕⲚⲟⲂⲉ. The phrase, ⲘⲡⲉⲕⲚⲟⲂⲉ, derives from the influence of Isaiah 53. We know this because the parallel use of the phrase occurs a few lines earlier in Silvanus 103.26–28, which states: ϥⲐⲟⲗⲓⲂⲉ ⲄⲀⲢ ⲀⲨⲰ ϥϥⲓ ⲘⲟⲔϩⲤ ⲉⲧⲂⲉ ⲡⲉⲕ ⲚⲟⲂⲉ.[75] This parallel has demonstrable ties to the verses from Isaiah 53 that speak of the servant's work to remove sin (53. 4, 5, 6, 10, 11, 12 LXX). If Silvanus 103.26–28 is dependent on Isaiah 53, then so also is ⲘⲡⲉⲕⲚⲟⲂⲉ in Silvanus 104.13.

(3) Didascalia Apostolorum 16. The author of Didascalia has a clear reception of the ransom logion[a–c]. Following the ransom logion, the author quotes from the service part of Isaiah 53.11 (δικαιῶσαι δίκαιον εὖ δουλεύοντα πολλοῖς). The author believes that the ransom logion describes the same service as is described in Isaiah 53.11. The author expands on the meaning of this service by inserting the comment "and bore and endured everything on our account." This comment is likely the author's summation of Isaiah 53.2–5, 12, which the author quotes in *Didascalia* 8. Didascalia 8 and 16 are the author's only uses of Isaiah 53.

(4) Origen, *Commentary on Psalm* 129.3–5. Origen's reception of the ransom logion[c] is followed by an allusion to John 1.29 and Isaiah 53.4. It reads as follows, Τὸ γὰρ τίμιον αὐτοῦ λύτρον ὑπὲρ ἡμῶν δέδωκεν αἷμα, γενόμενος ἀμνὸς τοῦ Θεοῦ· οὗτος γὰρ τὰς ἁμαρτίας ἡμῶν φέρει, καὶ περὶ ἡμῶν ὀδυνᾶται. It is difficult to determine whether the author understood οὗτος to be linked with the immediately preceding ἀμνός, or with the subject of δέδωκεν, or both.

(5) Hippolytus, *On Proverbs* 75. Hippolytus writes six participial clauses that give a scriptural interpretation of *Proverbs* 30.31. Clause five is a reception of the ransom logion[c] (καὶ ἀνθρώπων λύτρον γεννηθείς). Clauses one

---

[73] This was determined to be a potential use of the ransom logion because of the similar phrase in *De Theophania* 9 – λύτρον ἑαυτὸν ἐπιδοὺς καὶ ἀντίψυχον. Eusebius inserts the words ἑαυτὸν ἐπιδοὺς in between λύτρον and ἀντίψυχον.

[74] The only other place where ἀντίλυτρον occurs in Eusebius' extant writings is in his *Commentary on Isaiah* 53.5–6, and there it is also in the same phrase: γένηται ἀντίψυχον καὶ ἀντίλυτρον. This suggests that this phrase was very closely tied to Isaiah 53 in Eusebius' mind.

[75] Silvanus 103.26–28 is in the same context as Silvanus 104.12–13. The word ⲚⲟⲂⲉ in Silvanus 103.28 and 104.13 is similarly used to communicate the idea that Jesus' suffering/death is *for your sin* (ⲉⲧⲂⲉ ⲡⲉⲕ ⲚⲟⲂⲉ [103.27–28]//ⲘⲡⲉⲕⲚⲟⲂⲉ [104.13]).

and two are probably influenced by Isaiah 53.6–7 (Οὗτος γάρ, φησίν, ἐστὶν ὁ ὑπὲρ ἁμαρτίας κόσμου σφαγεὶς καὶ ὡς θῦμα προσαχθείς).

(6) Epistle to Diognetus 9.2–5. Diognetus 9.2 contains a reception of the ransom logion[c] – αὐτὸς τὸν ἴδιον υἱὸν ἀπέδοτο λύτρον ὑπὲρ ἡμῶν. Immediately preceding the ransom logion[c] is a statement that is dependent on Isaiah 53.4, 11 – ἐλεῶν αὐτὸς [θεὸς] τὰς ἡμετέρας ἁμαρτίας ἀνεδέξατο. The proximity of this statement to the ransom logion[c], as well as the verbal similarities, means that the author of Diognetus likely assumes that Isaiah 53.4, 11 is mutually interpretive with the ransom logion[c]. This conclusion is reinforced by the other two statements in Diognetus 9.2–5 that maintain a more vague influence from Isaiah 53.11 and/or from other early Christian interpretations of Isaiah 53.11 (1Peter 3.18; Romans 5.18[b]–19).

(7) Galatians 1.4. Galatians 1.4 states: [Ἰησοῦ Χριστοῦ] τοῦ δόντος ἑαυτὸν ὑπὲρ τῶν ἁμαρτιῶν ἡμῶν. This is the only primary New Testament text that is suspected of receiving the ransom logion[c] with Isaiah 53. Specific to the ransom logion[c] is the concept of Jesus' self-sacrifice, as well as the structural similarities between Galatians 1.4 and Mark 10.45/Matthew 20.28[c].[76] Specific to Isaiah 53 is the phrase ὑπὲρ τῶν ἁμαρτιῶν ἡμῶν, which Paul draws from Isaiah 53.4, 5, 6, 10, 11, 12 LXX.[77]

To summarize, influence from various verses in Isaiah 53 occurs alongside seven receptions of the ransom logion. These receptions are limited to the ransom logion[c], with the exception of Didascalia 16, which includes the ransom logion[a–c]. The influence from Isaiah 53 always draws on the servant's death for sin, though this is implicit in Didascalia Apostolorum 16. It can be concluded that there is a pattern for receiving the ransom logion[c] alongside

---

[76] The only missing element is –λυτ. However, pseudo-Paul does interpret the forgiveness of sins with ἀπολύτρωσιν (Colossians 1.14; Ephesians 1.7).

[77] Proving this point starts with 1Corinthians 15.3, which contains a pre-Pauline tradition that Christ died for our sins (ὑπὲρ τῶν ἁμαρτιῶν ἡμῶν), and this is according to the scriptures (κατὰ τὰς γραφάς). Since the phrase ὑπὲρ τῶν ἁμαρτιῶν ἡμῶν only occurs in the Pauline corpus in Galatians 1.4 and 1Corinthians 15.3, we can assume that Paul would have thought its use in Galatians 1.4 was similarly according to the scriptures. It is almost sure that one of the main scriptures Paul had in mind was Isaiah 53. Paul exhibits dependence on Isaiah 53 in Romans 4.25 (There is a rare unanimity of scholarly opinion that Isaiah 53 is the background to Romans 4.25). Romans 4.25 is almost identical to Galatians 1.4/1Corinthians 15.3. Thus, if the phrase, παρεδόθη διὰ τὰ παραπτώματα ἡμῶν, in Romans 4.25 is from Isaiah 53, then we have no reason to doubt a similar dependence in Galatians 1.4. Other evidence for the influence of Isaiah 53 on Galatians 1.4 is Clement's citation of Isaiah 53.6 in 1Clement 16. 1Clement 16.3–14 quotes from a literary text of Isaiah 53.1–12, and it quotes Isaiah 53.6 as reading: καὶ κύριος παρέδωκεν αὐτὸν ὑπὲρ τῶν ἁμαρτιῶν ἡμῶν. Although Clement is writing later than Paul, this is hard evidence that the precise phrase, ὑπὲρ τῶν ἁμαρτιῶν ἡμῶν, could be extracted directly from a text of Isaiah 53.6.

influence from the atonement ideas in Isaiah 53.[78] However, it is important to note that this pattern does not necessitate that Isaiah 53 is similarly influencing Mark 10.45/Matthew 20.28.

5.5.1.2 Pattern Applicable to Daniel 7; 9

There are no references to Daniel 7; 9 in the reception history of the ransom logion. This is odd since Daniel 7.13–14 is almost certainly behind the Son of Man in Mark 10.45/Matthew 20.28[a]. However, both the Son of Man and ransom logion[a] are largely absent from the reception history. Since a reference to Daniel 7 requires a primary connection with the Son of Man from the ransom logion[a], and since these elements are largely absent from the reception history, it is not surprising that references to Daniel 7 are also absent.

In the New Testament there are no receptions of the ransom logion[a] outside of Mark 10.45/Matthew 20.28[a].[79] In the Early Christian periods there are only four occurrences of the ransom logion[a], and all of these either omit or ignore the Son of Man. Clement of Alexandria, *Paedagogus* 1.9.85.1–2, omits the Son of Man (Οὐκ ἦλθον...διακονηθῆναι, ἀλλὰ διακονῆσαι...δοῦναι τὴν ψυχὴν τὴν ἑαυτοῦ λύτρον ἀντὶ πολλῶν). Likewise Origen, *Fragment on Luke* 14.16, only omits the Son of Man (οὐ γὰρ ἦλθεν διακονηθῆναι ἀλλὰ διακονῆσαι). In Origen's *Commentary on Matthew* 20.28, the Son of Man is retained, but is then reinterpreted as the Son of God, or is substituted with Colossians 1.15–16 (δέδοται δὲ λύτρον ὑπὲρ ἡμῶν ἡ ψυχὴ τοῦ υἱοῦ τοῦ θεοῦ...ἡ θειότης τῆς εἰκόνος τοῦ θεοῦ τοῦ ἀοράτου...λύτρον ἐδόθη ἀντὶ πολλῶν). Didascalia Apostolorum 16 retains the Son of Man in the Syriac version, but the absence of Son of Man in the parallel text from Constitutiones Apostolorum means that it was probably absent from the original Greek text of Didascalia Apostolorum.

The omission of the Son of Man from the Early Christian receptions of the ransom logion[a] reflects the general move away from the title very early in Christian history. The New Testament is largely silent about the Son of Man outside of the canonical gospels.[80] The Apostolic Fathers are similarly silent about the Son of Man, with one of the two occurrences stating: Ἰησοῦς, οὐχὶ υἱὸς ἀνθρώπου ἀλλὰ υἱὸς τοῦ Θεοῦ (Barnabas 12.10). It is difficult to de-

---

[78] When surveying the use of Isaiah 53 in Christian literature, Markschies observes that "Isaiah 53 is not a central text," but more of an "upper middle class" text ("Jesus Christ as a Man before God: Two Interpretive Models for Isaiah 53 in the Patristic Literature and Their Development," in *The Suffering Servant: Isaiah 53 in Jewish and Christian Sources* [ed. B. Janowski and P. Stuhlmacher; trans. D. Bailey; Grand Rapids: Eerdmans, 2004], 228). This observation might be true in general, but for the ransom logion[c], Isaiah 53 appears to be more of a central text.

[79] It is possible that the ransom logion[a–b] originated in the mind of Mark (See 1.5.1).

[80] The primary exception is Acts 7.56.

termine what factors contribute to the omission of the Son of Man from much of the earliest Christian literature. However, one likely factor is the change of setting from a Palestinian Jewish mission to an Hellenistic mission, wherein the esoteric notion of an exalted Danielic Son of Man was probably viewed as confusing and unhelpful for gentiles, who were not as well versed in the Hebrew scriptures, but who needed to understand the significance of Jesus' person. Another interrelated factor is the eventual association of the Son of Man title, not with the exalted figure from Daniel 7, but with Jesus' coming in the flesh (Ἰησοῦ Χριστῷ, τῷ κατὰ σάρκα ἐκ γένους Δαυείδ, τῷ υἱῷ ἀνθρώπου καὶ υἱῷ Θεοῦ, [Ignatius of Antioch, *Ephesians* 20.2]). After the resurrection the focus shifts towards Jesus' exalted place at God's right hand and his coming again, not as the earthly Son of Man, but as vindicated Messiah, God's Son, or Lord.[81] These two interrelated factors – the Hellenistic mission and the association with Jesus' earthly status – make the Son of Man title ineffective and undesirable. In the natural process of memory distortion, which ensures that only the most effective titles for Jesus continue in the mnemonic socialization process, the Son of Man title is omitted. This omission is exemplified in the few Early Christian receptions of the ransom logion[a], and it may explain why references to Daniel 7 never occur in the reception history of the ransom logion, even though such a reference is surely behind Mark 10.45/Matthew 20.28[a].

5.5.1.3 Pattern Applicable to Isaiah 43

References to Isaiah 43 occur twice alongside the reception of the ransom logion. First, Eusebius receives the ransom logion[c] in his *Commentary on Isaiah* 43.1–2. It is difficult to determine if Eusebius uses the ransom logion[c] because of influence from ἐλυτρωσάμην in Isaiah 43.1, ἄλλαγμα in Isaiah 43.3, or both. This may be significant for Grimm's thesis, which is grounded in the connection between λύτρον (Mark 10.45/Matthew 20.28[c]) and כפר/ἄλλαγμα (Isaiah 43.3). Second, Clement of Alexandria, *Paedagogus* 1.9.85.1–2, alludes to Isaiah 43.2 before a chiasm containing the ransom logion. The placement of Isaiah 43.2 outside the boundaries of the chiasm makes it difficult to determine what connection Clement might perceive between Isaiah 43.2 and the ransom logion. Aside from Eusebius and Clement, there is no further evidence that Isaiah 43 influences the early reception history of the ransom logion.[82]

---

[81] R. Bultmann, *Theology of the New Testament* [trans. K. Grobel; New York: Charles Schribner's Sons, 1951], 80, 124; Dunn, *Beginning from Jerusalem*, 224–25.

[82] There could have been a reliance on the Hebrew text in order to initially connect λύτρον ἀντί (Mark 10.45/Matthew 20.28[c]) with כפר...תחת (Isaiah 43.3–4). Of course, reliance on the Hebrew text disappears early in Christian history in preference to the LXX, which translates כפר...תחת with ἄλλαγμα...ὑπέρ.

5.5.2 Exegetical Considerations

Before discussing the potential contribution of the reception history, it is necessary to frame the scriptural backgrounds with some broader exegetical considerations. These considerations begin with Isaiah 53, followed by Daniel 7; 9, and Isaiah 43. The purpose of these considerations is to survey the broader rationale for each position, as well as the problems, so that it becomes clearer where the reception history might contribute to the discussion.

Isaiah 53: The Isaiah 53 background is the traditional background. It focuses on the linguistic and conceptual connections between Jesus' service unto death as a benefit to the many in Mark 10.45/Matthew 20.28, and the death of the servant as a benefit to the many in Isaiah 53 (See 1.2.3.1). What follows is an attempt to show how the greater contexts of both Mark and Matthew might be construed to support the Isaiah 53 background to Mark 10.45/Matthew 20.28, as well as noting the difficulties with such a construal.

The Gospel of Mark begins with the author's assertion that his gospel of Jesus Christ is according to Isaiah – Ἀρχὴ τοῦ εὐαγγελίου Ἰησοῦ Χριστοῦ [υἱοῦ θεοῦ]. Καθὼς γέγραπται ἐν τῷ Ἡσαΐᾳ τῷ προφήτῃ.[83] The word, εὐαγγέλιον, features throughout deutero-Isaiah (Isaiah 40.9; 52.7; 60.6; 61.1). Mark's initial appeal to Isaiah is probably meant to cast an Isaianic shadow across his gospel. This shadow is observable in Mark 8.22–10.52, which is marked by the use of ὁδός (8.27; 9.33–34; 10.17, 32, 46, 52). Mark uses ὁδός as an allusion to Isaiah 40.3, as it is quoted in the first few lines of his gospel: ἡ ὁδός κύριος. Mark 8.22–10.52 also contains the passion predictions, which show that Jesus' Isaianic way (ὁδός) will not lead to triumph, as the disciples expect, but to death (Mark 8.31; 9.31; 10.32–34).[84] In the second and third passion predictions, the Son of Man is predicted to be "handed-over" (παραδίδωμι) (Mark 9.31; 10.33). In an Isaianic framework, these could be seen as allusions to Isaiah 53.6, 12 (κύριος παρέδωκεν αὐτὸν ταῖς ἁμαρτίαις ἡμῶν...παρεδόθη εἰς θάνατον ἡ ψυχὴ αὐτοῦ...καὶ διὰ τὰς ἁμαρτίας αὐτῶν παρεδόθη).[85] Mark 9.12 is the most important contextual

---

[83] This assertion is followed by a conflation of texts from Exodus 23.20, Malachi 3.1, and Isaiah 40.3 (ἰδοὺ ἀποστέλλω τὸν ἄγγελόν μου πρὸ προσώπου σου, ὃς κατασκευάσει τὴν ὁδόν σου· φωνὴ βοῶντος ἐν τῇ ἐρήμῳ· ἑτοιμάσατε τὴν ὁδὸν κυρίου, εὐθείας ποιεῖτε τὰς τρίβους αὐτοῦ.). However, Mark only lists Isaiah. For a discussion, see J. Marcus, *The Way of the Lord* (Louisville, KY: Westminster John Knox, 1992), 12–47; R. Watts, *Isaiah's New Exodus and Mark* (WUNT 2/88; Tübingen: Mohr Siebeck, 1997), 53–90.

[84] Mark 8.22–10.52 is bracketed by two miracle stories where Jesus heals the blind. This blindness is likely meant to parallel the blindness of the disciples, who repeatedly fail to understand that Jesus' way leads to death. See Isaiah 42.16, which states: καὶ ἄξω τυφλοὺς ἐν ὁδῷ ᾗ οὐκ ἔγνωσαν.

[85] However, παραδίδωμι is used frequently in Mark and Matthew without a possible reference to the Isaianic servant (e.g. Mark 1.14; 4.29; 7.13; 13.9, 11–12; Matthew 4.12; 5.25; 10.17, 19, 21; 18.34; 24.9).

factor for seeing Isaiah 53 behind Mark 10.45. Mark 9.12 describes the suffering and rejection of the Son of Man as according to the scriptures – πῶς
γέγραπται ἐπὶ τὸν υἱὸν τοῦ ἀνθρώπου ἵνα πολλὰ πάθῃ καὶ ἐξου-
δενηθῇ.[86] The vocabulary of πάσχω and ἐξουδενέω may demonstrate influence from Isaiah 53. 1Peter 2.23 explicitly associates πάσχω with the sufferings described in Isaiah 53. Symmachus, Aquilla, and Theodotion all use
ἐξουδενώμενος in Isaiah 53.3.[87] If Isaiah 53 is the scriptural influence behind
the suffering Son of Man in Mark 9.12, then it would naturally be the influence for the suffering Son of Man in Mark 10.45, and so the argument goes,
this would all fit nicely in a section marked by influence from Isaiah (Mark
8.22–10.52).

Unlike the Gospel of Mark, the Gospel of Matthew does not open with a
statement that sets Isaiah apart as the preeminent proclamation of the gospel.
Matthew also does not have a parallel to Mark 9.12.[88] Matthew does, however, use Isaiah extensively throughout his gospel (Matthew 1.22–23; 4.14–
16; 8.17; 12.17–21; 13.14–15; 15.7–9; 21.13).[89] He even cites Isaiah 53.4 in
Matthew 8.17 – ὅπως πληρωθῇ τὸ ῥηθὲν διὰ Ἡσαΐου τοῦ προφήτου
λέγοντος· αὐτὸς τὰς ἀσθενείας ἡμῶν ἔλαβεν καὶ τὰς νόσους ἐβάστασεν.
While this citation does not explicitly affirm atonement for sin, it does explicitly demonstrate Matthew's willingness to connect Isaiah 53 with Jesus, and

---

[86] The Son of Man's suffering is similarly predicted in Mark 8.31, where the author uses
δεῖ instead of γέγραπται; δεῖ likely has the same meaning as γέγραπται (H. Tödt, *The Son of
Man in the Synoptic Tradition* [trans. D. Barton; Philadelphia: Westminster Press, 1965],
167–68). Mark 8.31 and 9.12 may parallel 1Corinthians 15.3, where Jesus' death for sin is
described as according to the scriptures (κατὰ τὰς γραφάς), and Isaiah 53 is the most likely
scripture in Paul's mind (See 2.3 above).

[87] Watts, *Isaiah's New Exodus*, 259–65; "Jesus' Death, Isaiah 53, and Mark 10:45: A Crux
Revisited," in *Jesus and the Suffering Servant* (ed. W. Bellinger, Jr. and W. Farmer; Harrisburg: Trinity Press International, 1998), 131–34. Also see McKnight, *Jesus and His Death*,
210–15.

[88] Matthew 16.21 does maintain δεῖ from Mark 8.31.

[89] See R. Beaton, "Isaiah in Matthew's Gospel," in *Isaiah in the New Testament* (ed. S.
Moyise and M. Menken; London: T & T Clark International, 2005), 63–78. J. Patrick argues
that Matthew's citations of Isaiah function as kernels around which the narrative about Jesus
is structured ("Matthew's *Pesher* Gospel Structured around Ten Messianic Citations of
Isaiah," *JTS* 61/1 [2010]: 43–81). On Matthew's reference to Jesus as ὁ παῖς μου in Matthew
12.18, see R. Beaton's monograph, *Isaiah's Christ in Matthew's Gospel* (SNTSMS 123;
Cambridge: Cambridge University Press, 2002). L. Huizenga argues that there is no coherent
Isaianic servant concept in the gospel of Matthew ("The Incarnation of the Servant: The 'Suffering Servant' and Matthean Christology," *HBT* 27 [2005]: 25–58; *The New Isaac: Tradition
and Intertextuality in the Gospel of Matthew* [NovTSup 131; Leiden: Brill, 2009], 189–97).
Huizenga's argument is based on the lack of a coherent understanding of an Isaianic servant
in Second Temple Judaism. There is also a lack of coherence amongst the few early Christian
references to Jesus as the servant (J. Jeremias, "παῖς θεοῦ in Later Judaism in the Period
after the LXX," *TDNT* 5:700–09).

Jesus' work to remove the effects of evil. Matthew does make a few statements that reveal his belief in Jesus' atoning death. He opens his gospel by
stating that Jesus' purpose is to "save his people from their sins" (1.21), and
he closes his gospel by stating that Jesus' death is "for the forgiveness of sin"
(26.28).[90] Given Matthew's concern for atonement through Jesus' death and
his connection of Jesus with the servant in Isaiah 53, it is plausible that he accepts Mark 10.45 into his gospel as another allusion to Isaiah 53.

One of the objections typically brought against an Isaiah 53 background to
Mark 10.45/Matthew 20.28 is that it speaks of the Son of Man, not the
Isaianic servant. This objection could be countered with the point that Mark
often combines texts from the Hebrew Scriptures (Mark 1.2–3 [Exodus 23.20;
Malachi 3.1; and Isaiah 40.3]; Mark 1.11 [Psalm 2.7; Isaiah 42.1]; Mark 11.17
[Isaiah 56.7; Jeremiah 7.11]; Mark 13.24 [Isaiah 13.10; 34.4; Joel 2.10; Daniel 7.13–14]; Mark 14.62 [Daniel 7.13; Psalm 110.1]).[91] Further, the contrastive ἀλλά in Mark 10.45/Matthew 20.28 encourages the reader to see that a
move is being made away from Daniel 7.13–14 where the Son of Man is
served, rather than serving. However, this explanation, though satisfying for
Mark 10.45/Matthew 20.28 where there is a contrast, may be more difficult in
Mark 9.12, where the Son of Man is still the subject, but there is no contrastive element that encourages a move away from Daniel.

A second objection is that λύτρον is absent from Isaiah 53. Most of this
criticism centers on the supposed inability of λύτρον to translate אשם, which
is rendered as περὶ ἁμαρτίας in the LXX of Isaiah 53.10.[92] However, it is
possible that Mark and Matthew use λύτρον, not as the translation of a word

---

[90] It is unlikely that Matthew considers this phrase as an allusion to Isaiah 53 (See 5.3.2).

[91] This method of combining texts is typical of Second Temple Judaism, especially
amongst the Dead Sea Scrolls (H. Kee, "The Function of Scriptural Quotations and Allusions
in Mark 11–16," in *Jesus und Paulus: Festschrift für Werner Georg Kümmel zum 70. Geburtstag* [ed. E. Ellis and E. Gräßer; Göttingen: Vandenhoeck & Ruprecht, 1975], 175–88).

[92] C. Barrett, "The Background of Mark 10:45," in *New Testament Essays: Studies in
Memory of T. W. Manson* (ed. A. Higgins; Manchester: Manchester University Press, 1959),
5–6; M. Hooker, *Jesus and the Servant: The Influence of the Servant Concept of Deutero-
Isaiah in the New Testament* (London: S.P.C.K. 1959), 77. The insistence that λύτρον cannot
translate אשם comes from a reaction against J. Jeremias' famous claim that Mark 10.45
matches Isaiah 53.10 "word for word" (*New Testament Theology: Part 1, The Proclamation
of Jesus* [trans. J. Bowden; New York: Charles Scribner's Sons, 1971], 292). Such a match is
conceivable on two conditions. First, the initial dependence must be on the Hebrew text of
Isaiah 53.10 (אם־תשים אשם נפשו), and (תשים) must be understood as a 2ms, not a 3ms. The
LXX of Isaiah 53.10 understands soul as a subject, rather than an object (ἡ ψυχὴ ὑμῶν
ὄψεται...). Second, there would need to be evidence that אשם could be rendered as λύτρον,
but the LXX renders it as περὶ ἁμαρτίας. However, Watts has pointed out that Aquila translates אשם in Leviticus 5.18 and 25 with λύτρωσις ("Jesus' Death," 139–40). Thus, there is
some evidence that Mark and Matthew could have understood λύτρον as an equivalent to
אשם in Isaiah 53.10, which then supports Jeremias' claim.

in Isaiah 53, but as a description of the salvation that directly results from the servant's work in Isaiah 53. It is certainly true that -λυτ vocabulary plays an important role in describing salvation, or New Exodus, in Isaiah (35.9; 41.14; 43.1, 14; 44.22–24; 52.3; 62.12; 63.9). It would be very easy for Mark and Matthew, who are familiar with Isaiah, to use the word λύτρον as a way to describe this salvation, which ultimately results from the servant's work in Isaiah 53.[93] This is Watts's position on λύτρον in Mark 10.45.[94] According to Watts, Mark 9.12 and the mention of "service," "life," and "for many" in Mark 10.45/Matthew 20.28[b-c] strongly tie Mark 10.45/Matthew 20.28 to Isaiah 53. It is not necessary that λύτρον also be a specific allusion to Isaiah 53 in order to maintain an Isaiah 53 background to Mark 10.45/Matthew 20.28. Rather, λύτρον is an appeal to the larger Isaianic New Exodus. Watts views the service and death of the servant for the many in Isaiah 53 as the key mechanism for the Isaianic New Exodus. Watts thinks that Mark 10.45/Matthew 20.28 is alluding to Isaiah 53 by presenting Jesus as the servant whose death for the many is the mechanism for the Isaianic New Exodus, that is, λύτρον. Therefore, from Watts's perspective, λύτρον in Mark 10.45/Matthew 20.28 is best rendered as "redemption" or "New Exodus," which is prophesied throughout Isaiah and is the result of the service and death of the servant for the many, as described in Isaiah 53 and in Mark 10.45/Matthew 20.28.[95]

Another possibility is that Mark and Matthew use λύτρον, not as the translation of a word in Isaiah 53, nor as a description of the salvation that results from the servant's work in Isaiah 53, but specifically to mean "atonement" as generally described in Isaiah 53.4, 5, 6, 10, 11, 12.[96] A. Collins's research into the meaning of Mark 10.45 among Gentile Christians reveals that language such as λύτρον "has cultic and expiatory connotations," and that it "served to speak of transactions between human beings and gods in which sins were forgiven and offenses expiated."[97] Collins reaches similar conclusions concern-

---

[93] Important is Isaiah 52.3, because of its proximity to Isaiah 53. Also important is Isaiah 44.22, which connects -λυτ with the forgiveness of sin – ἰδοὺ γὰρ ἀπήλειψα ὡς νεφέλην τὰς ἀνομίας σου καὶ ὡς γνόφον τὰς ἁμαρτίας σου ἐπιστράφητι πρός με καὶ λυτρώσομαί σε.

[94] Watts, *Isaiah's New Exodus*, 270–84.

[95] However, it should be noted that Watts is not completely opposed to translating λύτρον as "atonement" (ibid., 282).

[96] So W. Davies and D. Allison state: "We do not claim that Mt 20.28 par. is a *translation* of any portion of Isaiah 53, LXX, MT, or targum. Rather, it is a summary which describes the *'ebed* who gives his life as a sin offering for many" (*Matthew* [vol. 3; ICC; Edinburgh: T &T Clark, 1997], 96 – Italics original).

[97] A. Collins, "The Signification of Mark 10:45 among Gentile Christians," *HTR* 90/4 (1997): 371 n. 1, 382.

ing the use of -λυτ in the LXX,[98] and in early Christian literature.[99] Not surprisingly, Collins concludes concerning λύτρον in Mark 10:45: "The evidence thus suggests that the term λύτρον ('ransom') in Mark 10:45 is a synonym of ἱλαστήριον ('expiation' or 'propitiation'). Jesus' death is interpreted here as a metaphorical ritual act of expiation for the offenses of many."[100] If Collins is correct to understand λύτρον in Mark 10.45 as atonement for the sins of the many, then the chances of a specific connection with the servant in Isaiah 53, who also atones for the sins of the many, is strengthened.[101] Collins's understanding of λύτρον in Mark 10.45 has been challenged by S. Dowd and E. Struthers Malbon, who argue that Mark never connects Jesus' death with atonement elsewhere in his narrative.[102] They point out that when Mark introduces the forgiveness of sins, he connects it with John's baptism, repentance and confession, and not the death of Jesus (Mark 1.4–5). Mark portrays the forgiveness of sins as being part of Jesus' ministry, and without any mention of his forthcoming suffering (Mark 2.5–10). Similarly, Mark connects prayer with forgiveness of sins, and again not Jesus' death (Mark 11.25).[103] Because Mark appears to believe in the forgiveness of sin without direct recourse to Jesus' death, there is seemingly no real reason to read the idea of atonement into λύτρον in Mark 10.45.[104]

It is important to point out an overstatement by Dowd and Struthers Malbon when they assert: "As all parties to the discussion admit, the word group

---

[98] A. Collins, *Mark* (Hermeneia; Minneapolis: Fortress Press, 2007), 500–02. Collins focuses on Exodus 21.29–30, where -λυτ is used as a payment, which substitutes for the execution of a guilty person. Also helpful for Collins is Exodus 30.11–16, where in the course of a census, the Israelites are to make a -λυτ for their souls (λύτρα τῆς ψυχῆς [30.12]), which is later conveyed as an atonement for their souls (ἐξιλάσασθαι περὶ τῶν ψυχῶν ὑμῶν [30.15, 16]). J. Marcus discusses other Jewish texts that similarly equate -λυτ with atonement (*Mark 8–16* [AYB 27A; New Haven: Yale University Press, 2009], 749–50).

[99] Ephesians 1.7; Colossians 1.14; Didache 4.6; Barnabas 19.10.

[100] A. Collins, "Mark's Interpretation," 549. Collins believes that Isaiah 53 is an important background to Mark 10.45. However, while arguing forcefully that λύτρον in Mark 10.45 concerns sin, Collins curiously does not return to suggest that λύτρον could be Mark's summation of the servant's bearing the sin of the many in Isaiah 53.

[101] It could be that Mark and Matthew are using λύτρον specifically to describe the idea that they perceive is already in Isaiah 53.6, 12 (κύριος παρέδωκεν αὐτὸν [λύτρον] ταῖς ἁμαρτίαις ἡμῶν//αὐτὸς ἁμαρτίας πολλῶν ἀνήνεγκεν καὶ διὰ τὰς ἁμαρτίας αὐτῶν [λύτρον] παρεδόθη) – The servant bears the sins of the many, and God hands him over *as a lutron [i.e. an atonement]* because of their sins.

[102] S. Dowd and E. Struthers Malbon "The Significance of Jesus' Death in Mark: Narrative Context and Authorial Audience," *JBL* 125/2 (2006).

[103] Ibid., 275–76, 88.

[104] Dowd and Struthers Malbon state: "Interpreters have often read the statement [in Mark 10.45] as if it meant Jesus' death ransomed all people from sin. Wherever the connection between Jesus' death and the forgiveness of sin is coming from…it is not coming from the Markan narrative context of this ransom statement." (Ibid., 280–81).

λυτρόω, λύτρον, λύτρα relates to the necessity of setting free those being held captive or enslaved by another."[105] In a response article, Collins counters: "All would agree that the word group concerns 'loosing' or 'setting free,' but the question of 'from what' or 'from whom' depends on the context and shared cultural assumptions."[106] This is an important question for interpreting λύτρον in Mark 10.45: "From what or whom are the many set free?" If the freedom is from an offense or from sin, then it is clear that λύτρον can be used as a synonym for atonement. However, it is difficult to see this in Mark's narrative. Despite Mark's Isaianic overlay, he does not seem concerned to connect the forgiveness of sin with Jesus' death anywhere else in his narrative; in fact, it is quite the opposite (Mark 1.4–5; 2.10; 11.25). In sum, understanding λύτρον to mean "atonement," as Collins suggests, is a legitimate translation of the word, but only if that is what the context demands. Dowd and Struthers Malbon show that this translation does not fit easily in Mark's narrative. It may do better in Matthew, where the author connects Jesus' ministry with Isaiah 53, and Jesus' death with atonement.

Daniel 7; 9: The Daniel 7; 9 background has received its strongest support from the work of B. Pitre.[107] Pitre emphasizes that Mark 10.45 is the end of a unified section that begins at Mark 10.35.[108] He argues that this section is guided by allusions to Daniel, primarily chapters seven and nine.[109] Pitre sees the request of James and John to sit to the right and left of Jesus in his glory (Mark 10.35–37) as presupposing the eschatological kingdom that is pictured in Daniel 7.11–27, where the Son of Man is exalted along with the saints.[110] Jesus' response to the request of James and John is that the suffering of the saints and of the Son of Man must take place *before* their exaltation (Mark 10.38–39, 45).[111] This partially coheres with the picture in Daniel 7 where the saints are handed over (παραδίδωμι [7.25]) and made to suffer in the eschato-

---

[105] Ibid., 283.

[106] Collins, "Mark's Interpretation," 546.

[107] B. Pitre, *Jesus*, 384–417; "The 'Ransom for Many,' the New Exodus, and the End of the Exile: Redemption as the Restoration of All Israel (Mark 10:35–45)," *LetSp* 1 (2005): 41–68. Also see McKnight, *Jesus and His Death*, 235–39. Both Pitre and McKnight are interested in authenticity, which I am not.

[108] On the unity of Mark 10.35–45, see Pitre, *Jesus*, 386–90. I agree that the author intends for Mark 10.45 to be understood as the end of a longer literary unit that starts in 10.35. However, I do not think that the ransom logion (especially the ransom logion[c]) was unified with the traditions present in Mark 10.35–44 in the pre-Markan history (See 1.5.1 above).

[109] The mention of resurrection is the most obvious allusion to Daniel in the three passion predictions that lead up to Mark 10.35–45 (Mark 8.31; 9.31; 10.34//Daniel 12.1–3).

[110] Pitre, *Jesus*, 390–94; "The 'Ransom for Many,'" 43–47.

[111] "Cup" and "baptism" are used as metaphors for suffering (cf. Mark 14.36//Matthew 26.39) (H. Bayer, *Jesus' Predictions of Vindication and Resurrection: The Provenance, Meaning and Correlation of the Synoptic Predictions* [WUNT 2/20; Tübingen: Mohr Siebeck, 1986], 70–85).

logical tribulation *before* taking possession of the kingdom (Daniel 7.21–22, 25–27). However, while Daniel 7 describes the suffering of the saints, it says nothing specifically about a suffering Son of Man. According to Daniel 7.14, the Son of Man does not suffer, but inherits an eternal kingdom and is served by all people.[112] This explains the first part of the contrast in Mark 10.45. Jesus says that "the Son of Man did not come to be served," that is, as you expected from reading Daniel 7.14.

The second part of the contrast in Mark 10.45, which states that the Son of Man came to serve and to give his life as a ransom for many, is the point where supporters of an Isaiah 53 background see a transition being made from Daniel 7.14 to the Isaianic servant. However, Pitre believes that it is not absolutely necessary for Isaiah 53 to complete the thought in the second part of Mark 10.45. Rather, Mark 10.45's notion of the beneficial death of the Son of Man is understood to come from Daniel 9.24–27.

[24]Seventy weeks of years are decreed concerning you people and your holy city, to finish the transgression, to put an end to sin, and to atone for iniquity, to bring in everlasting righteousness, to seal both vision and prophet, and to anoint a most holy one. [25]Know therefore and understand that from the going forth of the word to restore and build Jerusalem to the coming of a Messiah, a prince, there shall be seven weeks. Then for sixty-two weeks it shall be built again with squares and moat, but in a troubled time. [26]And after sixty-two weeks, a Messiah shall be cut off, and shall have nothing; and the people of the prince who is to come shall destroy the city and the sanctuary. His end shall come with a flood, and to the end there shall be war; desolations are decreed. [27]And he shall make a strong covenant with many for one

---

[112] It is possible to infer from the observation that the eternal kingdom in Daniel 7 is given to both the Son of Man and to the saints (Daniel 7.14, 18, 22, 27) that the author of Daniel 7 understands the Son of Man as representing the saints. It could be further inferred that because the Son of Man represents the saints, he also suffers with them in Daniel 7. However, these inferences are far from clear and are lacking any scholarly consensus (For a discussion of the Son of Man, the saints, and their relation to one another in Daniel 7, see J. Collins, *Daniel: A Commentary on the Book of Daniel* [Hermeneia; Minneapolis: Fortress Press, 1993], 304–18). What is clear is that the earliest Jewish and Christian interpretations of the Son of Man have an individual interpretation of the title, and not a collective interpretation (ibid. 306–308). This is certainly true of Mark and Matthew, who view the Danielic Son of Man as an individual, Jesus. So D. Burkett concludes about the potential for a corporate interpretation of the Son of Man sayings in the gospels: "none of the Son of Man sayings require it, while most demand a reference to Jesus alone" (*The Son of Man Debate: A History and Evaluation* [SNTSMS 107; Cambridge: Cambridge University Press, 2000], 37). Mark's and Matthew's individualizing view of the Danielic Son of Man means that when reading Daniel 7, they very likely understand the saints to be suffering, and not the Son of Man. Therefore, while it is conceivable that for the author of Daniel 7 the Son of Man/saints suffer (this is Pitre's view [*Jesus*, 445], as well as McKnight's [*Jesus and His Death*, 234]), it is highly unlikely that Mark and Matthew have a corporate understanding of the Son of Man. More importantly for Pitre's argument (see below), if Mark equates the Son of Man from Daniel 7 with the individual messiah from Daniel 9 then Mark must have an individual perspective of the Son of Man in Daniel 7, where the saints, not the Son of Man, suffer.

week; and for half of the week he shall cause sacrifice and offering to cease; and upon the wing an abomination that makes desolate, until the decreed end is poured out on the desolator.[113]

In Daniel 9.24–27 we have a messiah, who dies in the eschatological tribulation, and his death is connected with the end of sin and atonement. The result of the messiah's death in the great tribulation is redemption from exile. It is clear from the greater context of Daniel's prayer in chapter 9 that the problem is Israel's exile, as prophesied by Jeremiah (Daniel 9.2, 7). The tribulation and the death of the messiah described by Gabriel in Daniel 9.24–27 bring about the end of sin, which naturally gives way to the end of Israel's exile.[114] Those going through the tribulation are described as the "many" (πολύς) in Daniel 9.27 (cf. Daniel 11.33, 34, 39). These "many" also experience the resurrection (Daniel 12.1–3, 10).

Pitre demonstrates that -λυτ language, while absent from Daniel 7; 9, is most often used in the Hebrew Bible to describe a release from exile, especially in the prophetic literature.[115] He notes that writers use -λυτ to recall the first release from exile that occurred in the Exodus (e.g. Exodus 6.6–8; Psalm 78.42–55; Micah 6.4). Writers also use -λυτ to anticipate a new release from exile, or a New Exodus for the scattered elect of Israel (e.g. Isaiah 43.1–2; 52.2–3; Jeremiah 31.10–12; Micah 4.1–2, 8, 10; Zechariah 10.8–10). Pitre also argues that the language of "many" in Second Temple Judaism is used to evoke hope for a release from exile, and among his examples is Daniel 9.27 as well as Isaiah 53.11-12.[116] However, "many" is a more common and less technical word in Mark and Matthew.[117]

Turning back to Mark 10.45, Pitre understands Jesus to be saying that the Son of Man did not come to be served, as you were expecting from Daniel 7.14, but to serve and give his life for the redemption of the many from exile, as it is written in Daniel 9.24–27. This view of Mark 10.45 connects the Son of Man from Daniel 7.13–14 with the dying messiah in Daniel 9.24–27. In other words, Mark (or someone before him) recognizes that the tribulation for the saints in Daniel 7 is the same tribulation of the messiah in Daniel 9.24–27. Therefore, the messiah from Daniel 9 and the Son of Man from Daniel 7 must be the same individual.[118] As Pitre states about the explanatory power of this connection for Mark 10.45: "It explains why Jesus would even suggest that

---

[113] Pitre's "modified" version of the RSV (*Jesus*, 401; "The 'Ransom for Many,'" 50).

[114] Pitre, *Jesus*, 401–03; "The 'Ransom for Many,'" 51.

[115] Pitre, *Jesus*, 404–14; "The 'Ransom for Many,'" 52–60.

[116] Pitre, *Jesus*, 414–15; "The 'Ransom for Many,'" 60–64.

[117] See 5.3.2 n. 15, 16 above.

[118] This is congruent with Jewish literature roughly contemporary with the synoptic gospels, which also recognized the Son of Man from Daniel 7 as the messiah (T. Slater, "One Like a Son of Man in First-Century CE Judaism," *NTS* 41 [1995]: 183–98).

'the Son of Man' would die in the tribulation, when no such death is de-scribed in Daniel 7."[119] The result is that there is no absolute need to turn to Isaiah 53 to explain the contrast in the last half of Mark 10.45. The Son of Man/messiah who dies to redeem (λύτρον) the many from exile can be ex-plained as dependent on Daniel 7; 9. If Pitre is correct about Mark 10.45, then the same conclusion could be offered for Matthew 20.28. The greater context of Matthew 20.28 (20.20–28) matches the greater context of Mark 10.45 (10.35–45), and thus has the same allusions to Daniel.[120] One point of concern for a Daniel 7; 9 background to Mark 10.45/Matthew 20.28 is the verbal ab-sence of the Son of Man/messiah's "service" in Daniel 7; 9, which is present in Isaiah 53.[121]

Two points can be made about the potential benefits of Pitre's view. First, it allows for a consistent influence from Daniel across the statement in Mark 9.12 about the suffering and rejection of the Son of Man. Pitre argues that in Mark 9.12 the author uses the suffering Son of Man/messiah from Daniel to draw an analogy with Elijah, both of whom suffer in the eschatological tribu-lation – the Son of Man in Daniel 7; 9 and Elijah in Malachi 4.5–6 (cf. Sirach 48.10).[122] Using Daniel 7; 9 to explain the suffering and rejection of the Son of Man in Mark 9.12 could remove the need for Isaiah 53 to explain the suf-fering. However, it remains that the language of πάσχω and ἐξουδενώμενος has verbal parallels with Isaiah 53, which are lacking in Daniel.[123]

Second, Pitre's view may provide theological coherence with Mark's and Matthew's Last Supper accounts.[124] Pitre makes three points about this theo-

---

[119] Pitre, *Jesus*, 403; "The 'Ransom for Many,'" 52.

[120] Matthew has more explicit allusions to Danielic eschatology elsewhere, especially Matthew 24.15 (cf. Matthew 13.43; 19.28; 24.10; 24.21; 24.30; 25.46; 28.18).

[121] It is important to note that Pitre does not completely discount an influence from Isaiah 53 on Mark 10.45. He states: "Jesus' words about the 'ransom for many' in the end appear to be a *combination* of figures from Daniel and Isaiah that draws on their common hope for a new exodus and the restoration of Israel" (*Jesus*, 417; "The 'Ransom for Many,'" 65 – italics original). However, this concession only comes after a fervent argument for the primacy of Daniel 7; 9.

[122] Pitre, *Jesus*, 180–88. Pitre believes that the suffering of Elijah is "*implied* in Mal 4:5–6, insofar as he is prophesied to return during a period of eschatological tribulation" (ibid., 186 – italics original).

[123] McKnight sees the rationale for Daniel in Mark 9.12, but he finds Isaiah 53 to be the more convincing background due to the verbal parallels (*Jesus and His Death*, 210–15). It should be noted that Psalm 21 LXX is frequently suggested as a possible background to Mark 9.12. Psalm 21, verses eighteen and one are used later in Mark at 15.24 and 15.34 (S. Ahearne-Kroll, *The Psalms of Lament in Mark's Passion* [SNTSMS 142; Cambridge: Cam-bridge University Press, 2007]). Psalm 21.7 uses the language of ἐξουδένημα. However, the ideas in Psalm 21 do not carry over into the atonement ideas present in Mark 10.45, and in my view, it is necessary that the background to Mark 9.12 should also function as the back-ground to Mark 10.45.

[124] Of course, coherence is very different than connectedness. See 5.3 above.

logical coherence. First, Pitre suggests that both Mark 10.45 and the Last Supper accounts "tie the death of Jesus to the eschatological tribulation."[125] As discussed above, Pitre thinks that Daniel 7; 9 tie Mark 10.45 to Daniel's eschatological tribulation. Pitre also thinks that the Last Supper accounts make a connection with Daniel's eschatological tribulation, as indicated by the reference to the Son of Man being handed-over (παραδίδωμι) in Mark 14.21 (Matthew 26.24). Pitre sees this as a reference to παραδίδωμι in Daniel 7.25, though here it is applied to the saints, not the Son of Man.[126] Second, Pitre suggests that both Mark 10.45 and the Last Supper accounts "tie the death of Jesus to the forgiveness of sins."[127] Pitre says that the forgiveness of sins is "implicit" in Mark 10.45 insofar as it is tied to Daniel 9.24. Pitre states that the forgiveness of sins is also implied by the phrase "for many" from Mark 14.24; the phrase "for the forgiveness of sins" is added in Matthew 26.28. In my view, the implicit nature of this second point makes it negligible.[128] Third, Pitre suggests that both Mark 10.45 and the Last Supper accounts "tie the death of Jesus to the End of the Exile."[129] As discussed above, Pitre sees λύτρον in Mark 10.45 being used to describe the redemption of the many from exile. Pitre sees the "paschal character" of the Last Supper accounts, as well as the phrase "blood of the covenant" (Mark 14.24; Matthew 26.28) as alluding to the first redemption from exile (the Exodus), and thus also pointing to the new redemption from exile for "the many" – a description that occurs in both Mark 10.45 and 14.24. The theme of redemption from exile that is potentially present in both Mark 10.45/Matthew 20.28 and the Last Supper accounts is Pitre's strongest point of coherence. However, the same point of coherence can be maintained with an Isaiah 53 background to Mark 10.45/Matthew 20.28 as long as λύτρον is understood as a reference to the Isaianic New Exodus rather than a synonym for "atonement."[130]

One final point of concern: Pitre's interest in the historical Jesus and Jewish backgrounds guides his understanding of λύτρον as a specific reference to the redemption from exile for the tribes of Israel, which are scattered among the nations as a result of the Assyrian conquest.[131] While this may have been Jesus' concern, and thus a potential breakthrough in historical Jesus research, I am not sure that the return of the exiled tribes is Mark's and Matthew's concern. I agree that the tradition in Mark 10.35–45[a]/Matthew 20.20–28[a] likely follows Daniel, and that Daniel 7:14; 9.24–27 has some small potential for

---

[125] Pitre, *Jesus*, 444.
[126] See n. 112 above.
[127] Ibid., 446–47.
[128] Forgiveness of sins is not explicit in either Mark 10.45 or 14.24.
[129] Ibid., 446–50.
[130] See discussion of λύτρον in Isaiah 53 above.
[131] Ibid., 31–40.

explaining the force of Mark 10.45/Matthew 20.28[b-c], but I remain skeptical that Mark and Matthew understand λύτρον as a release from exile, specifically for the tribes that are scattered amongst the nations. If λύτρον is understood to mean redemption from exile/enslavement, or a New Exodus, then Mark and Matthew may be better understood as asserting redemption from enslavement to Satan or demons. This idea may not cohere well with the redemption from exile (-λυτ) promised in the Hebrew Bible, but humanity's slavery to demonic forces is not a prominent theme in the Hebrew Bible as it is in Mark and Matthew. Satan is an important figure within Mark and Matthew (Mark 1.12–13/Matthew 4.1–11; Mark 3.22–27/Matthew 12.22–30; Mark 4.13–20/Matthew 13.18–23/Matthew 13.36–43; Mark 8.31–33/Matthew 16.21–23). Further, the story of the strong man from Mark 3.27/Matthew 12.29 appears to convey the idea that humanity is in some sort of bondage to Satan, even Peter appears to be possessed (Mark 8.33/Matthew 16.23). Paul also appears to believe that humanity is bound by demonic forces (Galatians 4.8; cf. Romans 6.6, 16–20). Additionally, Mark and Matthew present exorcisms as a major part of Jesus' ministry (Mark 1.23–27; 1.34, 39; 3.15, 22–27; 5.1–13; 6.7, 13; 7.24–30; 9.25, 38; Matthew 4.24; 7.22; 8.16, 28–34; 9.32–34; 10.1, 8; 12.24–29; 17.18). This must indicate their belief that an important part of the redemption Jesus brings to the many is from bondage to Satan and/or demonic powers. So while I am generally sympathetic to Pitre's presentation of Daniel 7.14; 9.24–27 as the background to Mark 10.35–45/Matthew 20.20–28, as well as understanding λύτρον to mean redemption from exile, I am not convinced that Mark or Matthew has in mind the victims of the Assyrian conquest. It seems that Mark and Matthew are more concerned about enslavement to the power of demons/Satan, from which the many need redemption in order to enter the kingdom of God.[132] Watts supports this perspective. He states: "in Mark it is the unclean spirits/demons who are to be understood as the oppressors who hold God's people captive…Jesus' exorcisms, it appears, are the Markan equivalent of the release of the Isaian captive."[133]

---

[132] Willitts has argued that Matthew focuses on the release from exile for the "lost sheep of the house of Israel" (Matthew 10.5–6; 15.24) (J. Willitts, *Matthew's Messianic Shepherd-King: In Search of "the Lost Sheep of the House of Israel"* [BZNW 147; Berlin: de Gruyter, 2007]). However, it is difficult to see this as a thoroughgoing focus of Matthew's gospel, which appears to be more universal in its mission (Matthew 28.16-20).

[133] Watts, *Isaiah's New Exodus*, 168–69. Dowd and Struthers Malbon also support this perspective, although in addition to demonic forces, they see human tyrants as enslaving Mark's audience. They state: "what 'the many' need – and, in fact, what the Markan Jesus urges his followers to provide – is ransoming from 'their great ones who are tyrants over them' and 'those whom they recognize as their rulers [who] lord it over them (10:42)" ("The Significance of Jesus' Death," 281). Collins counters: "the theme of liberation from human tyrants is a minor and subtle one in Mark. The liberation from demonic powers, in contrast, is

Isaiah 43: The Isaiah 43 background is certainly the weakest of the suggested backgrounds. There are five issues that, when considered together,
prevent this study from giving Isaiah 43 consideration as the primary scriptural background to Mark 10.45/Matthew 20.28. First, Isaiah 43.1–4 is not
well supported in the reception history. Second, Mark and Matthew never
quote or allude to Isaiah 43.1–4.[134] On a related point, there is nothing about
Mark 9.12 that alludes to Isaiah 43.1–4. Third, Isaiah 43.1–4 contains no motifs of service or death, which are important in Mark 10.45/Matthew 20.28.
Fourth, the LXX of Isaiah 43.3–4 does not maintain the most essential correspondence between Isaiah 43.3–4 and Mark 10.45/Matthew 20.28, which is
λύτρον ἀντί (Mark 10.45/Matthew 20.28) and כפר...תחת (Isaiah 43.3–4). The
LXX translates כפר with ἄλλαγμα and תחת with ὑπέρ.[135] Fifth, and most importantly, the Isaiah 43 background requires that Mark and Matthew understand Jesus to take the place of the nations as a ransom price for Israel. This
concept cannot be related to Mark or Matthew.[136]

Summary Isaiah 53, Daniel 7; 9, and Isaiah 43 are the suggested scriptural
background texts for Mark 10.45/Matthew 20.28. For various reasons, the
Isaiah 43 background is untenable, and it is difficult to find a recent supporter,
especially in the English-speaking world where this background has not
gained a foothold. As for the Isaiah 53 and Daniel 7; 9 backgrounds, there are
various reasons to support each of them, which is probably why the supporters of one are hesitant to completely discount the other.[137]

---

a major theme, especially in the first part of Mark (1:1–8:26)" ("Mark's Interpretation," 550).
I agree with Collins. Jesus' example of gentile rulers in Mark 10.42 is simply the use of a
negative example to teach his disciples about service (ibid., 546). The abusive relationship
between gentile rulers and their subjects is not the relational paradigm from which the Markan Jesus offers liberation.

[134] This statement is dependent on the quotation and allusion lists at the back of the UBS[4].

[135] However, λυτρόω does occur in Isaiah 43.1. Also Symmachus, as noted by Eusebius,
does read ἀντί for תחת (J. Ziegler, *Eusebius Werke IX. Der Jesajakommentar* [GCS; Berlin:
Akademie-Verlag, 1975], 277, 23–24).

[136] Pitre states: "It is precisely this element of Jesus' taking the place of the nations which,
while certainly possible, is difficult to square with the text of Mark 10:35–45 itself, which (as
far as I can tell) nowhere suggests this" (Pitre, *Jesus*, 397 n. 50). Even W. Grimm, who is the
main proponent of the Isaiah 43 background, sees this problem. Grimm states: "Es bleibt die
Frage, warum in Mk. 10,45 der 'Menschensohn' als Lösegeld hingegeben wird und nicht wie
in Jes. 43,3f die Heidenvölker" (*Weil ich dich liebe: Die Verkündigung Jesu und Deuterojesaja* [Frankfurt/M.: Peter Lang, 1976], 253).

[137] After arguing fervently for a Daniel 7; 9 background, Pitre opts for a "combination" of
influences from Isaiah 53 and Daniel 7; 9 (*Jesus*, 417). Similarly, Watts, who makes an extended argument for Isaiah 53, concludes: "the argument for the primary influence of Isaiah
53 on Jesus' predictions of his suffering and death ought not be taken as excluding a role for
Daniel 7 or other passages" (*Isaiah's New Exodus*, 285).

An important point in the discussion concerns how to understand λύτ-ρον.[138] Watts and Pitre similarly understand λύτρον to mean "redemption from exile" or "New Exodus."[139] For Watts, Mark 10.45/Matthew 20.28 transitions (ἀλλά) from the Danielic Son of Man, who is served (Daniel 7.14), to the Isaianic servant who "serves" and gives his "life" "for the many" (Isaiah 53), in order to guarantee a New Exodus (λύτρον). Watts's position is supported by the broader context of Mark's gospel, which consists of the opening words (καθὼς γέγραπται ἐν τῷ Ἠσαΐᾳ) and the "way" section (Mark 8.22–10.52). The verbal connections between Mark 9.12 and Isaiah 53 also favor Watts's position.

For Pitre, Mark 10.45/Matthew 20.28 transitions (ἀλλά) from the Son of Man in Daniel 7 to the messiah in Daniel 9.24–27, whose death brings about the end of the exile (λύτρον) for the "many." Pitre's position enjoys the close contextual support in Mark and Matthew. The Son of Man from Daniel 7.13 and the resurrection from Daniel 12.1–3 appear in the three passion predictions that lead up to Mark 10.45/Matthew 20.28. Allusions to Daniel, especially chapter 7, guide the entire section of which Mark 10.45/Matthew 20.28 is specifically a part (Mark 10.35–45/Matthew 20.20–28).

Collins has a different understanding of λύτρον. For Collins λύτρον can be rendered as "atonement." This rendering more specifically matches the servant's work in Isaiah 53. Collins supports this rendering with various texts from the LXX, early Christian writings, and contemporary pagan literature. While Collins's rendering is tenable, it does not easily cohere with Mark's disassociation between Jesus' death and the forgiveness of sins. It may fit better in Matthew where Jesus' ministry is linked with Isaiah 53, and Jesus' death with atonement.

5.5.3 Conclusion: The Contribution of the Reception History

The reception history makes two small and interrelated contributions to the scriptural background discussion. First, there are no references to Daniel 9.24–27 in the reception history of the ransom logion[c]. Above in 5.5.1.2, we

---

[138] It should be noted that there are other texts, which are not discussed above, that could impact use of λύτρον in Mark 10.45/Matthew 20.28. The first is Proverbs 13.8, which states: λύτρον ἀνδρὸς ψυχῆς ὁ ἴδιος πλοῦτος πτωχὸς δὲ οὐχ ὑφίσταται ἀπειλήν. The second is Psalm 48.8–9, which states: ἀδελφὸς οὐ λυτροῦται λυτρώσεται ἄνθρωπος οὐ δώσει τῷ θεῷ ἐξίλασμα αὐτοῦ καὶ τὴν τιμὴν τῆς λυτρώσεως τῆς ψυχῆς αὐτοῦ. Neither Proverbs 13.8 nor Psalm 48.8–9 is influential in the reception history of the ransom logion. Also, since the suggested scriptural backgrounds can satisfactorily account for the whole of Mark 10.45/Matthew 20.28, there is no need to further multiply backgrounds.

[139] Watts and Pitre differ concerning what the many are redeemed from: the continuing effects of the Assyrian conquest or demonic oppression. The reception history offers some support for redemption from demonic oppression (Origen, *Commentary on Matthew* 20.28, *Fragment on Ephesians* 1.7, *Fragment on 1 Corinthians* 6.19–20; *The Acts of Thomas* 39).

discuss how the absence of Daniel 7 from the reception history could be explained by the general absence of the Son of Man and the ransom logion[a]. To repeat: Since a reference to Daniel 7 requires a primary connection with the Son of Man from the ransom logion[a], and since these elements are largely absent from the reception history, it is not surprising that references to Daniel 7 are also absent. However, there is no such explanation for the absence of influence from Daniel 9.24–27 on the ransom logion[c]. There are many occurrences of the ransom logion[c] in the reception history, yet none of these demonstrate any influence from Daniel 9.24–27. This includes those who receive ransom logion[c] from Mark 10.45/Matthew 20.28, where the close context supposedly encourages a Danielic background across Mark 10.45/Matthew 20.28.[140] Therefore, it appears that there is no inclination among early Christians who receive the ransom logion[c] to interpret it through the lens of Daniel 9.24–27. If Daniel 9.24–27 is influencing Mark 10.45/Matthew 20.28[c], then the early Christians who receive the ransom logion[c], even from Mark 10.45/Matthew 20.28, have failed to notice this influence.

Second, influence from Isaiah 53 occurs seven times alongside seven receptions of the ransom logion[c]. Six of the seven emphasize atonement for sin. So there appears to be a small pattern among early Christians who receive the ransom logion[c] to interpret it through the lens of Isaiah 53, and specifically the verses that emphasize the servant's death for sin. Even λύτρον is interpreted as atonement for sin, which aligns with Collins's interpretation of the word.

The reception history boasts many receptions of the ransom logion[c]. None of these demonstrate any influence from Daniel 9.24–27, whereas seven of them demonstrate influence from Isaiah 53. The main question concerns whether this reflects Mark 10.45/Matthew 20.28[c]. I think it may, at least partially. The Daniel 9.24–27 background to Mark 10.45/Matthew 20.28[c], while conceivable, ultimately lacks the connections with Mark 10.45/Matthew 20.28 that Isaiah 53 possesses. While it is true that the tradition in Mark 10.35–45[a]/Matthew 20.20–28[a] likely follows Daniel 7, the contrastive ἀλλά in Mark 10.45/Matthew 20.28 encourages a move away from Daniel 7.14. The question is: where – to the messiah in Daniel 9.24–27…to the servant in Isaiah 53? The parallels shared between Mark 10.45/Matthew 20.28[b–c] and Daniel 9.24–27 (dying figure, and "many") are also shared between Mark 10.45/Matthew 20.28[b–c] and Isaiah 53.[141] However, Isaiah 53 has additional

---

[140] However, as noted above in 5.5.1.2, the few receptions of the ransom logion[a] typically omit the Danielic Son of Man, which means that they may not be expected to then read Daniel throughout the rest of the logion.

[141] In Daniel 9.24–27, the "many" are mentioned in same context as the dying messiah, whereas in Isaiah 53 the servant's death is specifically portrayed as beneficial to the "many" (Isaiah 53.12).

parallels with Mark 10.45/Matthew 20.28[b–c] that Daniel 9.24–27 does not possess. These include the vocabulary of ψυχή (Isaiah 53.12), and most importantly, the notion that Jesus "serves" for the benefit of the many (δικαιῶσαι δίκαιον εὖ δουλεύοντα πολλοῖς [Isaiah 53.11]). So while Daniel 9.24–27 has parallels with Mark 10.45/Matthew 20.28[b–c] that could be meaningful, Isaiah 53 has those same parallels and additional ones, which make it seem the more likely influence on Mark 10.45/Matthew 20.28[b–c].[142] Therefore, the absence of influence from Daniel 9.24–27, and the presence of influence from Isaiah 53, in the reception history of the ransom logion[c] likely reflects a similar absence and presence in Mark 10.45/Matthew 20.28[b–c].

However, it is important to state that the influence of Isaiah 53 in the reception history of the ransom logion[c] particularly emphasizes the atoning value of Jesus' death – it is for sin. This is difficult to harmonize with Mark, though less so with Matthew. Mark appears to connect the forgiveness of sins with everything but Jesus' death, and it may be that this is the point where the reception history is out of step with Mark, or better, Mark is out of step with the trends for receiving the ransom logion[c]. However, we should not completely discount Collins's argument that in Mark 10.45 λύτρον means "atonement." This appears to be a natural understanding for Mark's contemporaries (Ephesians 1.7 [Ἐν ᾧ ἔχομεν τὴν ἀπολύτρωσιν διὰ τοῦ αἵματος αὐτοῦ, τὴν ἄφεσιν τῶν παραπτωμάτων]; Colossians 1.14 [ἐν ᾧ ἔχομεν τὴν ἀπολύτρωσιν, τὴν ἄφεσιν τῶν ἁμαρτιῶν]; Didache 4.6 [δώσεις λύτρωσιν ἁμαρτιῶν σου]; Barnabas 19.10 [εἰς λύτρον ἁμαρτιῶν σου]). It is also natural in the reception history of the ransom logion[c] (The Teachings of Silvanus 104.12–13 [ⲚⲤⲰⲦⲈ Ⲙ̄ⲠⲈⲔⲚⲞⲂⲈ]; Epistle to Diognetus 9.2 [ἐλεῶν αὐτὸς [θεὸς] τὰς ἡμετέρας ἁμαρτίας ἀνεδέξατο. αὐτὸς [θεὸς] τὸν ἴδιον υἱὸν ἀπέδοτο λύτρον ὑπὲρ ἡμῶν]). If we accept that the transition in Mark 10.45/Matthew 20.28[b–c] is specifically towards the image of the servant in Isaiah 53, who serves and dies for the benefit of the many, then it should be considered a strong possibility that λύτρον does not just mean "redemption" or "New Exodus," but has something to do with atonement for sin since that is the thrust of Isaiah 53.4, 5, 6, 10, 11, 12. However, while understanding λύτρον to mean "atonement" would bring Mark 10.45/Matthew 20.28 into a closer reflection of the reception history, and even a potential participation with a pre-Markan tendency (see the diagram below), the greater context of Mark, which disassociates Jesus' death with the forgiveness of sins and em-

---

[142] It is possible that Daniel 9.24–27 was excluded from the mnemonic socialization process for interpreting the ransom logion[c], just as Daniel 7.13 was excluded for the ransom logion[a]. However, there is nothing in Mark 10.45/Matthew 20.28[c] that demands a particular allusion to Daniel 9.24–27 in the same way that the Son of Man in Mark 10.45/Matthew 20.28[a] demands a particular allusion to Daniel 7.13–14.

phasizes freedom from demonic oppression, will always remain in tension with this understanding.

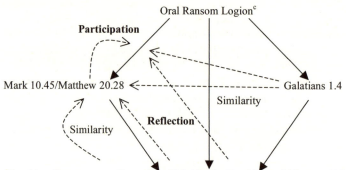

Eusebius, *Demonstratio Evangelica* 10.8.33; The Teachings of Silvanus 104.12–13; Didascalia Apostolorum 16; Origen, *Commentary on Psalm* 129.3–5; Hippolytus, *On Proverbs* 75; Epistle to Diognetus 9.2–5.

Chapter 6

Conclusion

This thesis examines the reception of the ransom logion and explores the significance of that examination for the critical study of Mark 10.45/Matthew 20.28. Chapters Two through Four examine the reception of the ransom logion from the New Testament through the third century. This examination uncovers several interpretive patterns, which are perpetuated in the social memory of early Christian communities. Chapter Five explores the significance of relevant interpretive patterns for the critical study of Mark 10.45/Matthew 20.28. The following paragraphs offer brief summaries of the main findings from Chapters Two through Five. Chapter Six concludes with some thoughts on the potential for early reception history to be a useful contextual tool for the historical approach to the New Testament.

Chapters Two through Four examine the reception of the ransom logion from the New Testament through the third century. Chapter Two examines the reception of the ransom logion in the New Testament. All the primary occurrences of the ransom logion in the New Testament are limited to the ransom logion[c], and none of these are exactly alike. This suggests that the ransom logion[c] has an independent oral existence apart from its incorporation into Mark 10.45/Matthew 20.28. The two motifs that accompany the ransom logion[c] in the New Testament are the love motif (Galatians 2.20, Ephesians 5.2, 25, and the Johannine literature), and Isaianic servant texts (Isaiah 42.6–7; 49.6–8 in 1Timothy 2.6; Titus 2.14, and Isaiah 53 in Galatians 1.4).

Chapter Three examines the reception of the ransom logion from the New Testament through 200 CE. The reception of the ransom logion with a love motif continues in the writings of Clement of Alexandria, though Clement is the last person to receive the ransom logion with a love motif. The reception of the ransom logion with Isaiah 53 continues in Diognetus 9.2–5. This period also witnesses a new phenomenon, which is the interpretation of the ransom logion[a–b] as an incarnational narrative. This occurs in the writings of Clement of Alexandria, who is also the first person outside of Mark 10.45/Matthew 20.28 clearly to receive the ransom logion[a–b]. The interpretation of the ransom logion[a–b] as an incarnational narrative is likely due to the perception that Mark 10.45/Matthew 20.28 and Philippians 2.6–8 say the same thing, namely that Jesus was incarnated from preexistence in order to serve and die. Therefore, it naturally becomes part of the collective memory to read these texts together.

Chapter Four examines the reception of the ransom logion from 200 through 300 CE. Receptions of the ransom logion with Isaiah 53 are prominent in this period (Hippolytus, *On Proverbs* 75; Origen, *Commentary on Psalm* 129.3–5; The Teachings of Silvanus 104.12–13; Didascalia Apostolorum 16; Eusebius, *Demonstratio Evangelica* 10.8.33). Receptions with an incarnational motif are also prominent (Origen, *Commentary on Matthew* 20.28; *Fragment on Luke* 14.6; The Acts of Thomas 39; 72; Pseudo Clement of Rome, *Homilies* 12.7.5; The Teachings of Silvanus 104.12–13; The Tripartite Tractate 120.13). 1Peter 1.18–19 emerges in this period as the primary influence for the replacement of Jesus' soul with his precious blood as the ransom payment (Origen, *Commentary on Matthew* 20.28; *Commentary on Psalm* 29.10; 129.3–5; Eusebius, *Demonstratio Evangelica* 10.8.33; *Commentary on Isaiah* 43.1–2; *Commentary on Psalm* 54.20; 71.12–14).

Chapter Five explores the significance of several interpretive patterns for the critical study of Mark 10.45/Matthew 20.28. The specific issues surrounding Mark 10.45/Matthew 20.28, for which the interpretive patterns are relevant, are the development of the ransom logion in a Eucharistic setting, a preexistent coming, and scriptural background.

Concerning the development of the ransom logion in a Eucharistic setting, there are no patterns in the reception history that associate the ransom logion with the Eucharist or with Last Supper traditions from the synoptics or Paul. Even when Jesus' blood is substituted for his soul as the ransom payment, there is still no indication of influence from the Eucharist or Last Supper traditions. The disassociation in the reception history reflects a similar disassociation in Mark and Matthew. Mark 10.45/Matthew 20.28 and Mark 14.24/ Matthew 26.28 have a weak verbal connection (preposition plus πολλῶν), lack a similar contextual allusion, and are separated by a great distance. The disassociation between Mark 10.45/Matthew 20.28 and Mark 14.24/Matthew 26.28 means that there are no extant connections between the ransom logion and the Eucharist, or Last Supper traditions, through 300 CE, which might serve as evidence to support the hypothesis that the ransom logion developed in a Eucharistic setting. Therefore, while it could be true that the ransom logion originated in a Eucharistic setting there are no extant connections between the ransom logion and the Eucharist, or Lord's Supper traditions, that might serve as evidence to support those origins.

Concerning a preexistent coming, the Gospels of Mark and Matthew are historically situated between an implicit confession of Jesus' preexistence in Paul and an overt assertion of Jesus' preexistence in the Gospel of John. However, Mark's and Matthew's historical placement, as well as their portrayal of Jesus as a transcendent figure, does not mean they think Jesus is preexistent. Gathercole's "I have come" sayings are perhaps the single piece of demonstrable evidence to support Jesus' preexistence in Mark and Matthew.

Mark 10.45/Matthew 20.28 represents one of Gathercole's "I have come" sayings. The association between the ransom logion and Philippians 2.6–8 in the reception history may reflect Mark 10.45/Matthew 20.28's appropriation of a narrative sequence similar to the one found in Philippians 2.6–8, thus corroborating Gathercole's case for Jesus' preexistence specifically in Mark 10.45/Matthew 20.28. If we assume a preexistent coming in Mark 10.45/Matthew 20.28, then Philippians 2.6–8 and Mark 10.45/Matthew 20.28 share the same narrative sequence of Jesus' preexistence, service, and voluntary death. Other important parallels also emerge, such as the volitional "coming," the contrastive ἀλλά, and the vocation of service used to describe the entirety of Jesus' life. All these parallels, which result from seeing preexistence in Mark 10.45/Matthew 20.28, suggest that the preexistent perspective of Mark 10.45/Matthew 20.28 is correct and that patristic writers were correct to connect Mark 10.45/Matthew 20.28 with Philippians 2.6–8.

Concerning scriptural background, Daniel 7.13–14 is the background for the service to the Son of Man, which is assumed in Mark 10.45/Matthew 20.28[a]. The options for the background to Mark 10.45/Matthew 20.28[b–c] are Isaiah 53 and Daniel 9.24–27; the Isaiah 43 background is ultimately untenable. Daniel 9.24–27 occurs nowhere in the reception history of the ransom logion[c], whereas Isaiah 53 occurs seven times alongside receptions of the ransom logion[c]. This likely reflects a similar absence and presence in Mark 10.45/Matthew 20.28. The transition away from the Son of Man being served in Mark 10.45/Matthew 20.28[a] to the Son of Man serving and giving his life as a λύτρον for the many in Mark 10.45/Matthew 20.28[b–c] is most likely influenced by Isaiah 53, which possesses the same parallels with Mark 10.45/Matthew 20.28[b–c] that Daniel 9.24–27 possesses (dying figure and "many"), but has the additional parallels of ψυχή and "service," specifically for the many. However, the influence of Isaiah 53 in the reception history of the ransom logion[c] emphasizes the atoning value of Jesus' death. While it is possible to understand λύτρον to mean "atonement," and many of Mark's and Matthew's contemporaries use λύτρον this way, this understanding may not fit easily in Mark where the forgiveness of sins is connected with everything but Jesus' death.

In conclusion, I hope that both the examination of the ransom logion and the exploration of its significance for the critical study of Mark 10.45/Matthew 20.28 might contribute towards the establishment of the principle that early reception history can be a valuable contextual tool for the historical-critical approach to the New Testament. While it is certainly true that early Christian writings can demonstrate a lack of continuity with what precedes, this thesis has shown that early Christian writings can also demonstrate continuity with what precedes, especially when there are interpretive patterns. Extending the context of historical-critical inquiry into the first few centuries CE can only enhance historical investigation of the New Testament. The notion that interpretive patterns from the early reception history can reflect the way a tradition is used in the New Testament opens avenues of inquiry whereby reception history becomes a valuable conversation partner, and framer of questions, for those doing critical work in the New Testament. I hope that the greater impact of this study might be to inspire others to examine the reception history of traditions that flow through the New Testament into the Early Christian periods, and then to explore what significance that examination has for historical-critical questions about the meaning of those traditions as they exist in the New Testament. If this approach is judged to be promising, it will be because it actually produces results, that is, it will turn up early patterned receptions that are relevant for New Testament exegesis.

Bibliography

A. Primary Sources

Achelis, H. *Hippolytus Werke I. 2. Kleinere exegetische und homiletische Schriften.* Griechischen Christlichen Schriftsteller. Leipzig: J. C. Hinrichs, 1897.

Attridge, H. W. and E. H. Pagels. "NCH 1, 5: The Tripartite Tractate." Pages 159–337 in *Nag Hammadi Codex I (The Jung Codex): Introductions, Texts, Translations, Indices.* Edited by H. W. Attridge. Nag Hammadi Studies 22. Leiden: Brill, 1985.

Attridge, H. W. and G. W. MacRae. "NCH 1, 3: The Gospel of Truth." Pages 55–117 in *Nag Hammadi Codex I (The Jung Codex): Introductions, Texts, Translations, Indices.* Edited by H. W. Attridge. Nag Hammadi Studies 22. Leiden: Brill, 1985a.

Connolly, R. H. *Didascalia Apostolorum: The Syriac Version Translated and Accompanied by the Verona Latin Fragments with Introduction and Notes.* Oxford: The Clarendon Press, 1929.

De La Rue, C. V. *Origenes II.* Patrologia Graeca 12. Edited by J. -P. Migne. Paris, 1862.

Edwards, R. A. and R. A. Wild. *The Sentences of Sextus.* Texts and Translations 22. Chico, CA: Scholars Press, 1981.

Ehrman, B. D. *The Apostolic Fathers*, 2 Vols. The Loeb Classical Library 24, 25. Cambridge: Harvard University Press, 2003.

Ferrar, W. J. *The Proof of the Gospel Being the Demonstratio Evangelica of Eusebius of Caesarea.* 2 vols. Translations of Christian Literature Series 1. London: The Macmillan Company, 1920.

Funk, F. X. *Didascalia et Constitutiones Apostolorum.* 2 vols. Paderbornae, 1905. Repr. 2 vols. in 1, Torino: Bottega D'Erasmo, 1964.

Gregg, J. A. F. "The Commentary of Origen upon the Epistle to the Ephesians." *The Journal of Theological Studies* 10 (1902): 233–44.

Gressmann, H. *Eusebius Werke III. 2. Die Theophanie.* Griechischen Christlichen Schriftsteller. Leipzig: J. C. Hinrichs'sche Buchhandlung, 1904.

Heikel, I. *Eusebius Werke VI. Die Demonstratio Evangelica.* Griechischen Christlichen Schriftsteller. Leipzig: J. C. Hinrichs'sche Buchhandlung, 1913.

[Horner, G.]. *The Coptic Version of the New Testament in the Southern Dialect Otherwise Called Sahidic and Thebaic.* 5 vols. Oxford: The Clarendon Press, 1911–24.

Jenkins, C. "Origen on I Corinthians." *The Journal of Theological Studies* 35 (1908): 353–72.

Kasser, R. *Papyrus Bodmer XXIII: Esaïe XLVII, 1 – LXVI, 24 en sahidique.* Cologny-Genève: Bibliothèque Bodmer, 1965.

Klostermann, E. *Origenes Werke X. 1. Matthäuserklärung.* Griechischen Christlichen Schriftsteller. Leipzig: J. C. Hinrichs'sche Buchhandlung, 1935.

—. *Origenes Werke XII. 3. Matthäuserklärung.* Griechischen Christlichen Schriftsteller. Leipzig: J. C. Hinrichs Verlag, 1941.

Layton, B. "The Gospel According to Philip." Pages 143–214 in *Nag Hammadi Codex II,2–7*, vol. 1. Edited by B. Layton. Nag Hammadi Studies 20. Leiden: Brill, 1989.

Lefort, L. Th. *Œuvres de S. Pachôme et de Ses Disciples*. Corpus Scriptorum Christianorum Orientalium 160. Louvain: Peeters, 1956.

Lipsius, R. A. and M. Bonnet. *Acta Apostolorum Apocrypha*. Lipsiae: Apud Hermannum Mendelssohn, 1891–1903.

Mai, A. *"Eusebii Pamphili: Commentaria in Psalmos."* Pages 9–76 in Patrologia Graeca 24. Edited by J. -P. Migne. Paris, 1857.

—. *"Didymi Alexandrini: Expositio in Psalmos."* Pages 1156–1616 in Patrologia Graeca 39. Edited by J. -P. Migne. Paris, 1863.

Marcovich, M. *Clementis Alexandrini Paedagogus*. Supplements to Vigiliae Christianae 61. Leiden: Brill, 2002.

Montfaucon, B. *Eusebii Pamphili: Commentaria in Psalmos*. Patrologia Graeca 23. Edited by J. -P. Migne. Paris, 1857.

Nautin, P. *Homélies Pascales*. vol. 2. Sources Chrétiennes 36. Paris: Éditions du Cerf, 1953.

Peel, M. L. "The Teachings of Silvanus: Text and Notes." Pages 278–368 in *Nag Hammadi Codex VII*. Edited by B. A. Pearson. Nag Hammadi and Manichaean Studies 30. Leiden: Brill, 1996b.

Perler, O. *Méliton de Sardes, Sur la Pâque et Fragments: Introduction, Texte Critique, Traduction et Notes*. Sources Chrétiennes 123. Paris: Éditions du Cerf, 1966.

Pitra, J. B. *Analecta Sacra Spicilegio Solesmensi Parata*, vol. 3. Parisiis: Jonby et Roger, 1883.

Rauer, M. *Origenes Werke IX. Die Homilien zu Lukas*. Griechischen Christlichen Schriftsteller. Berlin: Akademie-Verlag, 1959.

Rehm, B. *Die Pseudoklementinen I. Homilien*. Griechischen Christlichen Schriftsteller. Berlin: Akademie-Verlag, 1953.

—. *Die Pseudoklementinen II. Rekognitionen in Rufins Übersetzung*. Griechischen Christlichen Schriftsteller. Berlin: Akademie-Verlag, 1965.

Richard, M. "Les fragments du commentaire de S. Hippolyte sur les Proverbes de Salomon." *Le Muséon* 79 (1966): 75–94.

Rondeau, M. -J. "A propos d'une édition de Didyme l'Aveugle." *Revue des études Grecques* 81 (1968): 385–400.

Rousseau, A. *Irénée de Lyon, Contre les Hérésie Livre V*. vol. 2. Sources Chrétiennes 153. Paris: Éditions du Cerf, 1969.

Scheck, T. P., trans. *Origen, Commentary on the Epistle to the Romans: Books 1–5*. The Fathers of the Church 103. Washington: The Catholic University of America Press, 2001.

Schmidt, C. and W. Schubart. *ΠΡΑΞΕΙΣ ΠΑΥΛΟΥ: Acta Pauli: Nach dem Papyrus der Hamburger Staats- und Universitäts-Bibliothek*. Glückstadt and Hamburg: J. J. Augustin, 1936.

Stählin, O. *Clemens Alexandrinus III. Stromata Buch VII und VIII, Excerpta Ex Theodoto – Eclogae Propheticae, Quis Dives Salvetur – Fragmente*. Griechischen Christlichen Schriftsteller. Berlin: Akademie-Verlag, 1970.

Veilleux, A. *Pachomian Koinonia: Instructions, Letters, and Other Writings of Saint Pachomius and His Disciples*. Cistercian Studies Series 47. Kalamazoo, MI: Cistercian Publications Inc, 1982.

Vööbus, A. *The Didascalia Apostolorum*. Corpus Scriptorum Christianorum Orientalium. Scriptores Syri 175–176, 179–180. Louvain: Peeters, 1979.

Wisse, F. "NHC XII, *I*: The Sentences of Sextus." Pages 295–321 in *Nag Hammadi Codices XI, XII, XIII*. Edited by C. W. Hedrick. Nag Hammadi Studies 28. Leiden: Brill, 1990.

Wright, W. *Apocryphal Acts of the Apostles*. London: Williams & Norgate, 1871.

Ziegler, J. *Eusebius Werke IX. Der Jesajakommentar*. Griechischen Christlichen Schriftsteller. Berlin: Akademie-Verlag, 1975.

B. Secondary Literature

Achtemeier, P. J. *1 Peter*. Hermeneia. Philadelphia: Fortress Press, 1996.

Ahearne-Kroll, S. P. *The Psalms of Lament in Mark's Passion: Jesus' Davidic Suffering*. Society for New Testament Studies Monograph Series 142. Cambridge: Cambridge University Press, 2007.

Arai, S. *Die Christologie des Evangelium Veritatis: Eine Religionsgeschichtliche Untersuchung*. Leiden: Brill, 1964.

Attridge, H. W. "The Gospel of Truth as an Exoteric Text." Pages 239–55 in *Nag Hammadi, Gnosticism, & Early Christianity*. Edited by C. W. Hedrick and R. Hodgson, Jr. Peabody, MA: Hendrickson Publishers, 1986.

Attridge, H. W. and G. W. MacRae. "NCH 1, 3: The Gospel of Truth." Pages 39–135 in *Nag Hammadi Codex I (The Jung Codex): Notes*. Edited by H. W. Attridge. Nag Hammadi Studies 23. Leiden: Brill, 1985b.

Bailey, D. P. "Appendix: Isaiah 53 in the Codex A Text of 1 Clement 16:3–14." Pages 321–23 in *The Suffering Servant: Isaiah 53 in Jewish and Christian Sources*. Edited by B. Janowski and P. Stuhlmacher. Translated by D. P. Bailey. Grand Rapids: Eerdmans, 2004.

Baltzer, K. *Deutero–Isaiah: A Commentary on Isaiah 40–55*. Translated by Margaret Kohl. Hermeneia. Minneapolis: Fortress Press, 2001.

Barnard, L. W. "The Epistle ad Diognetum. Two Units from One Author?" *Zeitschrift für die Neutestamentliche Wissenschaft* 56 (1965): 130–37.

Barrett, C. K. "The Background of Mark 10:45." Pages 1–18 in *New Testament Essays: Studies in Memory of T. W. Manson*. Edited by A. J. B. Higgins. Manchester: Manchester University Press, 1959.

Bartholomä, P. F. "Did Jesus Save the People out of Egypt? A Re–examination of a Textual Problem in Jude 5." *Novum Testamentum* 50/2 (2008): 143–58.

Barton, J. "Historical-Critical Approaches." Pages 9–20 in *The Cambridge Companion to Biblical Interpretation*. Edited by J. Barton. Cambridge: Cambridge University Press, 1998.

Bauckham, R. "John for Readers of Mark." Pages 147–71 in *The Gospels for All Christians*. Edited by R. Bauckham. Grand Rapids: Eerdmans, 1998.

—. *God Crucified: Monotheism and Christology in the New Testament*. Grand Rapids: Eerdmans, 1998.

Bauer, W. F. W. Danker, W. F. Arndt, and F. W. Gingrich. *A Greek-English Lexicon of the New Testament and Other Early Christian Literature*. 3rd ed. Chicago: The University of Chicago Press, 2000.

Bayer, H. F. *Jesus' Predictions of Vindication and Resurrection: The Provenance, Meaning and Correlation of the Synoptic Predictions*. Wissenschaftliche Untersuchungen zum Neuen Testament 2/20. Tübingen: Mohr Siebeck, 1986.

Beale, G. K. *The Book of Revelation*. The New International Greek Testament Commentary. Grand Rapids: Eerdmans, 1999.

Beare, F. W. *The First Epistle of Peter*. Oxford: The Alden Press, 1947.

Beaton, R. *Isaiah's Christ in Matthew's Gospel*. Society for New Testament Studies Monograph Series 123. Cambridge: Cambridge University Press, 2002.

—. "Isaiah in Matthew's Gospel." Pages 63–78 in *Isaiah in the New Testament*. Edited by S. Moyise and M. J. J. Menken. London: T & T Clark International, 2005.

Berényi, G. "Gal 2:20: a pre-Pauline or a Pauline text?" *Biblica* 65/4 (1984): 490–537.

Best, E. *1 Peter*. New Century Bible. London: Oliphants, 1971.

Betz, H. D. *Galatians*. Hermeneia. Philadelphia: Fortress Press, 1979.

Biblia Patristica: Index des citations et allusions bibliques dans la littérature patristique. Vol. 1, *Des origines à Clément d'Alexandrie et Tertullian.* Vol. 2, *Le troisième siècle (Origène excepté).* Vol. 3, *Origène.* Vol. 4, *Eusèbe de Césarée, Cyrille de Jérusalem, Épiphane de Salamine.* Edited by J. Allenbach, *et al.* Paris: Éditions du Centre National de la Recherche Scientifique, 1975, 1977, 1980, 1987.

Bockmuehl, M. "A Commentator's Approach to the 'Effective History' of Philippians." *Journal for the Study of the New Testament* 18 (1996): 57–88.

—. *The Epistle to the Philippians.* Black's New Testament Commentary 11. Peabody, MA: Hendrickson, 1998.

—. *Seeing the Word: Refocusing New Testament Study.* Studies in Theological Interpretation. Grand Rapids: Baker Academic, 2006.

—. "New Testament Wirkungsgeschichte and the Early Christian Appeal to Living Memory." Pages 341–61 in *Memory in the Bible and Antiquity: The Fifth Durham-Tübingen Research Symposium (Durham, September 2004).* Edited by S. C. Barton, L. T. Stuckenbruck, and B. G. Wold. Wissenschaftliche Untersuchungen zum Neuen Testament 212. Tübingen: Mohr Siebeck, 2007.

Bostock, G. "Origen's Exegesis of the Kenosis Hymn (Philippians 2:5–11)." Pages 531–47 in *Origeniana Sexta: Origène et la Bible / Origen and the Bible.* Edited by G. Dorival and A. le Boulluec. Bibliotheca Ephemeridum Theologicarum Lovaniensium 118. Leuven: Peeters/Leuven University Press, 1995.

Bovon, F. "Une Formule Prepaulinienne dans L'Epitre aux Galates (Ga 1,4–5)." Pages 91–107 in *Paganisme, Judaïsme, Christianisme: Influences et affrontements dans le monde antique: Mélanges offert à Marcel Simon.* Edited by A. Benoit. Paris: Boccard, 1978.

—. *L'Évangile Selon Saint Luc 19,28–24,53.* Commentaire du Nouveau Testament IIId. Genève: Labor et Fides, 2009.

Branscomb, H. B. *The Gospel of Mark.* The Moffatt New Testament Commentary. London: Hodder and Stoughton Limited, 1937.

Bremmer, J. N. *The Rise of Christianity through the Eyes of Gibbon, Harnack and Rondey Stark.* Groningen: Barkhuis, 2010.

Brown, R. E. *The Gospel According to John (i–xii).* The Anchor Bible 29. New York: Doubleday, 1966.

—. *The Epistles of John.* The Anchor Bible 30. New York: Doubleday, 1982.

Büchsel, F. "λύτρον, ἀντίλυτρον, λυτρόω, λύτρωσις, λυτρωτής, ἀπολύτρωσις." Pages 340–56 in vol. 4 of *Theological Dictionary of the New Testament.* Edited by G. Kittel and G. Friedrich. Translated by G. Bromiley. Grand Rapids: Eerdmans, 1967.

Bultmann, R. *Theology of the New Testament.* Translated by K. Grobel. New York: Charles Schribner's Sons, 1951.

—. *The History of the Synoptic Tradition.* Translated by J. Marsh. New York: Harper and Row, 1963.

Burkett, D. *The Son of Man Debate: A History and Evaluation.* Society for New Testament Studies Monograph Series 107. Cambridge: Cambridge University Press, 2000.

—. *Rethinking the Gospel Sources: From Proto-Mark to Mark.* New York: T & T Clark International, 2004.

Byrsog, S. "A New Quest for the *Sitz im Leben*: Social Memory, the Jesus Tradition and the Gospel of Matthew." *New Testament Studies* 52 (2006): 319–36.

Calvin, J. *Commentary on a Harmony of the Evangelists, Matthew, Mark, and Luke.* Vol. 2. Translated by W. Pringle. Grand Rapids: Eerdmans, 1965.

Cerrato, J. A. *Hippolytus between East and West.* Oxford Theological Monographs. Oxford: Oxford University Press, 2002.

Chadwick, H. *The Sentences of Sextus: A Contribution to the History of Early Christian Ethics*. Texts and Studies 5. Cambridge: Cambridge University Press, 1959.

Collins, A. Y. "The Suffering Servant: Isaiah Chapter 53 as a Christian Text." Pages 201–06 in *Hebrew Bible or Old Testament?* Edited by R. Brooks and J. J. Collins. Notre Dame: University of Notre Dame Press, 1990.

—. "The Signification of Mark 10:45 among Gentile Christians." *Harvard Theological Review* 90/4 (1997): 371–82.

—. "Finding Meaning in the Death of Jesus." *The Journal of Religion* 78 (1998): 175–96.

—. *Mark*. Hermeneia. Minneapolis: Fortress Press, 2007.

—. "Mark's Interpretation of the Death of Jesus." *Journal of Biblical Literature* 128/3 (2009): 545–54.

Collins, J. J. *Daniel: A Commentary on the Book of Daniel*. Hermeneia. Minneapolis: Fortress Press, 1993.

A Committee of the Oxford Society of Historical Theology. *The New Testament in the Apostolic Fathers*. Oxford: Clarendon Press, 1905.

Cosaert, C. P. *The Text of the Gospels in Clement of Alexandria*. The New Testament in the Greek Fathers 9. Atlanta: Society of Biblical Literature, 2008.

Cox, J. J. C. "Some Prolegomena and Addenda to a Study of the Dominical *Logoi* as cited in the *Didascalia Apostolorum*." Pages 82–87 in *Studia Patristica* vol. 16/2. Berlin: Akademie Verlag, 1985.

Cranfield, C. E. B. *A Critical and Exegetical Commentary on the Epistle to the Romans*. 2 Vols. The International Critical Commentary. Edinburgh: T & T Clark, 1975, 1979.

Crossley, J. G. *The Date of Mark's Gospel: Insight from the Law in Earliest Christianity*. Journal for the Study of the New Testament Supplement Series 266. London: T & T Clark, 2004.

—. "Mark, Paul and the Question of Influences." Pages 10–29 in *Paul and the Gospels: Christologies, Conflicts and Convergences*. Library of New Testament Studies 411. Edited by M. Bird and J. Willitts. London: T&T Clark International, 2011.

Crouzel, H. *Origen*. Translated by A. S. Worrall. Edinburgh: T & T Clark, 1989.

Crum, W. E. *A Coptic Dictionary*. Cairo: Institut Français d'archéologie orientale, 1939. Repr. Oxford: The Clarendon Press, 1972.

Cummins, S. A. *Paul and the Crucified Christ in Antioch: Maccabean Martyrdom and Galatians 1 and 2*. Society for New Testament Studies Monograph Series 114. Cambridge: Cambridge University Press, 2001.

Davids, P. *The First Epistle of Peter*. New International Commentary on the New Testament. Grand Rapids: Eerdmans, 1990.

Davies, W. D. and D. C. Allison. *Matthew*. Vol 3. The International Critical Commentary. Edinburgh: T&T Clark, 1997.

DeConick, A. D. "The True Mysteries: Sacramentalism in the *Gospel of Philip*." *Vigiliae Christianae* 55 (2001): 225–61.

Deichgräber, R. *Gotteshymnus und Christushymnus in der frühen Christenheit: Untersuchungen zu Form, Sprache und Stil der frühchristlichen Hymnen*. Studien zur Umwelt des Neuen Testaments 5. Göttingen: Vandenhoeck & Ruprecht, 1967.

Delling, G. "Zur Hellenisierung des Christentums in den 'Sprüchen des Sextus'." Pages 208–41 in *Studien zum Neuen Testament und zur Patristik. Festschrift für Erich Klostermann*. Texte und Untersuchungen 77. Berlin: Akademie-Verlag, 1961.

De Saeger, L. "'Für unsere Sünden': 1 Kor 15,3b und Gal 1,4a im exegetischen Vergleich." *Ephemerides Theologicae Lovanienses* 1 (2001): 169–191.

Dibelius, M. and H. Conzelmann. *The Pastoral Epistles*. Translated by P. Buttolph and A. Yarbro. Hermeneia. Philadelphia: Fortress Press, 1972.

Dowd, S. and E. Struthers Malbon. "The Significance of Jesus' Death in Mark: Narrative Context and Authorial Audience." *Journal of Biblical Literature* 125/2 (2006): 271–97.

Duling, D. C. "Social Memory and Biblical Studies: Theory, Method, and Application," *Biblical Theology Bulletin* 36 (2006): 2–4.

Dunn, J. D. G. *Christology in the Making: A New Testament Inquiry into the Origins of the Doctrine of the Incarnation.* London: SCM Press, 1980.

—. *Romans.* 2 Vols. Word Biblical Commentary 38A, 38B. Dallas: Word Books, 1988.

—. *The Theology of Paul the Apostle.* Grand Rapids: Eerdmans, 1998.

—. *The Epistle to the Galatians.* Black's New Testament Commentary 9. Peabody, MA: Hendrickson, 1993.

—. *The Acts of the Apostles.* Epworth Commentary. Peterborough, UK: Epworth Press, 1996.

—. "Social Memory and the Oral Jesus Tradition." Pages 179–94 in *Memory in the Bible and Antiquity: The Fifth Durham-Tübingen Research Symposium (Durham, September 2004).* Edited by S. C. Barton, L. T. Stuckenbruck, and B. G. Wold. Wissenschaftliche Untersuchungen zum Neuen Testament 212. Tübingen: Mohr Siebeck, 2007.

—. *Beginning from Jerusalem: Christianity in the Making, vol. 2.* Grand Rapids: Eerdmans, 2009.

Edwards, J. C. "The Christology of Titus 2.13 and 1 Tim 2.5." *Tyndale Bulletin* 62/1 (2011): 141–47.

Ehrman, B. D. *The New Testament: A Historical Introduction to the Early Christian Writings.* New York: Oxford University Press, 1997.

Elliott, J. H. *1 Peter: A New Translation with Introduction and Commentary.* The Anchor Bible Commentary 37B. New York: Doubleday, 2000.

Elliott, J. K. *The Apocryphal New Testament: A Collection of Apocryphal Christian Literature in an English Translation based on M. R. James.* Oxford: Oxford University Press, 1993.

Eriksson, A. *Traditions as Rhetorical Proof: Pauline Argumentation in 1 Corinthians.* Coniectanea Biblica – New Testament Series. Stockholm: Almqvist & Wiksell International, 1998.

Evans, C. A. *Mark 8:27–16:20.* Word Biblical Commentary 34B. Nashville: Thomas Nelson Publishers, 2001.

Evans, C. A., R. L. Webb, and R. A. Wiebe. *Nag Hammadi Texts and the Bible: A Synopsis and Index.* New Testament Tools and Studies 18. Leiden: Brill, 1993.

Fee, G. D. *Paul's Letter to the Philippians.* The New International Commentary on the New Testament. Grand Rapids: Eerdmans, 1995.

Fenton, J. C. "Paul and Mark." Pages 89–112 in *Studies in the Gospels: Essays in Memory of R. H. Lightfoot.* Edited by D. E. Nineham. Oxford: Blackwell, 1955.

Fitzmyer, J. A. *The Gospel According to Luke (I–IX), (X–XXIV).* 2 Vols. Anchor Bible Commentary 28, 28A. Garden City: Doubleday, 1981, 1985.

—. *Romans.* Anchor Bible Commentary 33. Garden City: Doubleday, 1993.

—. *The Interpretation of Scripture: In Defense of the Historical-Critical Method.* New York: Paulist Press, 2008.

Foster, P. "The Epistle to Diognetus." *The Expository Times* 118/4 (2007): 162–68.

—. Review of S. J. Gathercole, *The Preexistent Son: Recovering the Christologies of Matthew, Mark, and Luke. Expository Times* 118/7 (2007): 357–58.

—. "The Gospel of Philip." *The Expository Times* 118/9 (2007): 417–27.

—. *The Gospel of Peter: Introduction, Critical Edition and Commentary.* Texts and Editions for New Testament Study 4. Leiden: Brill, 2010.

—. "Paul and Matthew: Two Strands of the Early Jesus Movement with Little Sign of Connection." Pages 86–115 in *Paul and the Gospels: Christologies, Conflicts and Conver-*

gences. Library of New Testament Studies 411. Edited by M. Bird and J. Willitts. London: T&T Clark International, 2011.

France, R. T. *The Gospel of Matthew*. The New International Commentary on the New Testament. Grand Rapids: Eerdmans, 2007.

Furnish, V. *The Love Command in the New Testament*. London: SCM Press, 1972.

—. "'He Gave Himself (Was Given) Up...': Paul's Use of a Christological Assertion." Pages 109–121 in *The Future of Christology: Essays in Honor of Leander E. Keck*. Edited by A. J. Malherbe and W. A. Meeks. Minneapolis: Fortress Press, 1993.

Gadamer, H. G. *Truth and Method*. 2d rev. ed. Translated by J. Weinsheimer and D. G. Marshall. London: Continuum, 2004.

Gathercole, S. J. The Son of Man in Mark's Gospel. *The Expository Times* 115 (2004): 366–72.

—. *The Preexistent Son: Recovering the Christologies of Matthew, Mark, and Luke*. Grand Rapids: Eerdmans, 2006.

Gese, M. *Das Vermächtnis des Apostels: Die Rezeption der paulinischen Theologie im Epheserbrief*. Wissenschaftliche Untersuchungen zum Neuen Testament 2/99. Tübingen: Mohr Siebeck, 1997.

Gibson, J. "Paul's 'Dying Formula': Prolegomena to an Understanding of Its Import and Significance." Pages 20–41 in *Celebrating Romans: Template for Pauline Theology*. Edited by S. E. McGinn. Grand Rapids: Eerdmans, 2004.

Goodacre, M. S. *The Case Against Q: Studies in Markan Priority and the Synoptic Problem*. Harrisburg, PA: Trinity Press International, 2002.

Green, J. B. *The Death of Jesus: Tradition and Interpretation in the Passion Narrative*. Wissenschaftliche Untersuchungen zum Neuen Testament 2/33. Tübingen: Mohr Siebeck, 1988.

—. *The Gospel of Luke*. The New International Commentary on the New Testament. Grand Rapids: Eerdmans, 1997.

Gregory, A. F. *The Reception of Luke and Acts in the Period before Irenaeus*. Wissenschaftliche Untersuchungen zum Neuen Testament 2/169. Tübingen: Mohr Siebeck, 2003.

Gregory, A. F. and C. M. Tuckett. "Reflections on Method: What Constitutes the Use of the Writings that Later Formed the New Testament in the Apostolic Fathers." Pages 61–82 in *The Reception of the New Testament in the Apostolic Fathers*. Edited by A. F. Gregory and C. M. Tuckett. Oxford: Oxford University Press, 2005.

Grimm, W. *Weil ich dich liebe: Die Verkündigung Jesu und Deuterojesaja*. Frankfurt/M.: Peter Lang, 1976.

Grobel, K. *The Gospel of Truth: A Valentinian Meditation on the Gospel*. London: Adam & Charles Black, 1960.

Gundry, R. H. *Mark: A Commentary on His Apology for the Cross*. Grand Rapids: Eerdmans, 1993.

Gurtner, D. M. *The Torn Veil: Matthew's Exposition of the Death of Jesus*. Society for New Testament Studies Monograph Series 139. Cambridge: Cambridge University Press, 2007.

Hagner, D. A. *The Use of the Old and New Testaments in Clement of Rome*. Supplements to Novum Testamentum 34. Leiden: Brill, 1973.

Halbwachs, M. *Les Cadres sociaux de la mémoire*. Paris: F. Alcan, 1925.

Hardwick, L. *Reception Studies*. Greece & Rome. New Survey in the Classics 33. Oxford: Oxford University Press, 2003.

Hare, D. R. A. *The Son of Man Tradition*. Minneapolis: Fortress Press, 1990.

Harrington, J. M. *The Lukan Passion Narrative: The Markan Material in Luke 22,54–23,25: A Historical Survey: 1891–1997*. New Testament Tools and Studies 30. Leiden: Brill, 2000.

Häusser, D. *Christusbekenntnis und Jesusüberlieferung bei Paulus.* Wissenschaftliche Untersuchungen zum Neuen Testament 2/210. Tübingen: Mohr Siebeck, 2006.

Hays, R. B. "'Who Has Believed Our Message?' Paul's Reading of Isaiah." Pages 25–49 in *The Conversion of the Imagination: Paul as Interpreter of Israel's Scripture.* Grand Rapids: Eerdmans, 2005.

Hengel, M. *The Atonement: The Origins of the Doctrine in the New Testament.* Translated by J. Bowden. Philadelphia: Fortress Press, 1981.

—. *Studies in the Gospel of Mark.* Translated by J. Bowden. London: SCM Press, 1985.

Hentschel, A. *Diakonia im Neuen Testament.* Wissenschaftliche Untersuchungen zum Neuen Testament 2/226. Tübingen: Mohr Siebeck, 2007.

Herzer, J. "Rearranging the 'House of God': A New Perspective on the Pastoral Epistles." Pages 547–66 in *Empsychoi Logoi – Religious Innovations in Antiquity: Studies in Honour of Pieter Willem van der Horst.* Edited by A. Houtman, A. de Jong, and M. Misset-van de Weg. Ancient Judaism and Early Christianity 73. Leiden: Brill, 2008.

Hill, C. E. "Hades of Hippolytus or Tartarus of Tertullian? The Authorship of the Fragment *De Universo.*" *Vigiliae Christianae* 43 (1989): 105–26.

—. *From the Lost Teaching of Polycarp: Identifying Irenaeus' Apostolic Presbyter and the Author of Ad Diognetum.* Wissenschaftliche Untersuchungen zum Neuen Testament 186. Tübingen: Mohr Siebeck, 2006.

Hofius, O. "The Fourth Servant Song in the New Testament Letters." Pages 163–88 in *The Suffering Servant: Isaiah 53 in Jewish and Christian Sources.* Edited by B. Janowski and P. Stuhlmacher. Grand Rapids: Eerdmans, 2004.

Hollerich, M. J. *Eusebius of Caesarea's Commentary on Isaiah.* Oxford Early Christian Studies. Oxford: Clarendon Press, 1999.

Hooker, M. D. *Jesus and the Servant: The Influence of the Servant Concept of Deutero-Isaiah in the New Testament.* London: S.P.C.K, 1959.

—. "Did the Use of Isaiah 53 to Interpret His Mission Begin with Jesus?" Pages 88–103 in *Jesus and the Suffering Servant.* Edited by W. H. Bellinger, Jr. and W. R. Farmer. Harrisburg: Trinity Press International, 1998.

Hoover, R. W. "The Harpagmos Enigma: A Philological Solution." *Harvard Theological Review* 64 (1971): 95–119.

Hübner, H. *Vestus Testamentum in Novo.* Vol 2. Göttingen: Vandenhoeck & Ruprecht, 1997.

Huizenga, L. A. "The Incarnation of the Servant: The 'Suffering Servant' and Matthean Christology." *Horizons in Biblical Theology* 27 (2005): 25–58.

—. *The New Isaac: Tradition and Intertextuality in the Gospel of Matthew* Supplements to Novum Testamentum 131. Leiden: Brill, 2009.

Hurst, L. D. "Re-enter the Pre-existent Christ in Philippians 2:5–11?" *New Testament Studies* 32 (1986): 449–57.

Hurtado, L. W. *Lord Jesus Christ: Devotion to Jesus in Earliest Christianity.* Grand Rapids: Eerdmans, 2003.

Isenberg, W. W. "The Gospel According to Philip: Introduction." Pages 131–39 in *Nag Hammadi Codex II,2–7*, vol. 1. Edited by B. Layton. Nag Hammadi Studies 20. Leiden: Brill, 1989.

Iverson, K. R. *Gentiles in the Gospel of Mark: 'Even the Dogs Under the Table Eat the Children's Crumbs'.* Library of New Testament Studies 339. London: T&T Clark International, 2007.

Jeremias, J. "παῖς θεοῦ in Later Judaism in the Period after the LXX." Pages 677–717 in vol. 5 of *Theological Dictionary of the New Testament.* Edited by G. Kittel and G. Friedrich. Translated by G. Bromiley. Grand Rapids: Eerdmans, 1967.

—. *New Testament Theology: Part 1, The Proclamation of Jesus*. Translated by J. Bowden. New York: Charles Scribner's Sons, 1971.

Jewett, R. *Romans*. Hermeneia. Philadelphia: Fortress Press, 2007.

Johansson, D. "The Identity of Jesus in the Gospel of Mark: Past and Present Proposals." *Currents in Biblical Research* 9 (2011): 364–93.

Johnson, L. T. *The First and Second Letters to Timothy*. Anchor Bible Commentary 35A. New York: Doubleday, 2001.

Johnson, L. T. and W. S. Kurz. *The Future of Catholic Biblical Scholarship: A Constuctive Conversation*. Grand Rapids: Eerdmans, 2002.

Jones, F. S. "The Pseudo-Clementines: A History of Research." Pages 195–262 in *Literature of the Early Church*. Vol. 2 of *Studies in Early Christianity: A Collection of Scholarly Essays*. Edited by E. Ferguson. New York and London: Garland, 1993.

—. "The Pseudo-Clementines." Pages 285–304 in *Jewish Christianity Reconsidered*. Edited by M. Jackson-McCabe. Minneapolis: Fortress Press, 2007.

Kannengiesser, C. *Handbook of Patristic Exegesis*. Edited by D. J. Bingham. The Bible in Ancient Christianity 1. Leiden: Brill, 2004.

Katter, C. K. "Luke 22:14–38: A Farewell Address." Ph.D. diss., University of Chicago, 1993.

Kee, H. C. "The Function of Scriptural Quotations and Allusions in Mark 11–16." Pages 165–88 in *Jesus und Paulus: Festschrift für Werner Georg Kümmel zum 70. Geburtstag*. Edited by E. Earle Ellis and Erich Gräßer. Göttingen: Vandenhoeck & Ruprecht, 1975.

Kelly, J. N. D. *A Commentary on the Pastoral Epistles*. Black's New Testament Commentaries. London: Adam & Charles Black, 1963.

Kirk, A. and T. Thatcher, eds. *Memory, Tradition, and Text: Uses of the Past in Early Christianity*. Semeia 52. Leiden: Brill, 2005.

Klijn, A. F. J. *The Acts of Thomas: Introduction, Text, and Commentary*. Supplements to Novum Testamentum 108. Leiden: Brill, 2003.

Knöppler, T. *Sühne im Neuen Testament: Studien zum urchristlichen Verständnis der Heilsbedeutung des Todes Jesu*. Wissenschaftliche Monographien zum Alten und Neuen Testament 88. Neukirchen-Vluyn: Neukirchener Verlag, 2001.

Koehler, L., and W. Baumgartner. *The Hebrew and Aramaic Lexicon of the Old Testament*, 2 vols. Translated by M. E. J. Richardson. Leiden: Brill, 2002.

Köhler, W. D. *Die Rezeption des Matthäusevangeliums in der Zeit vor Irenäus*. Wissenschaftliche Untersuchungen zum Neuen Testament 2/24. Tübingen: Mohr Siebeck, 1987.

Kramer, W. *Christ, Lord, Son of God*. Translated by B. Hardy. Studies in Biblical Theology 50. London: S. C. M. Press, 1966.

Kugel, J. L. *Traditions of the Bible: A Guide to the Bible as It Was at the Start of the Common Era*. Cambridge: Harvard University Press, 1998.

Lane, W. L. "Hebrews." Pages 443–58 in *Dictionary of the Later New Testament and Its Developments*. Edited by R. Martin and P. Davids. Downers Grove, IL: Inter-Varsity Press, 1997.

Lau, A. Y. *Manifest in Flesh: The Epiphany Christology of the Pastoral Epistles*. Wissenschaftliche Untersuchungen zum Neuen Testament 2/86. Tübingen: Mohr Siebeck, 1996.

Le Donne, A. *The Historiographical Jesus: Memory, Typology, and the Son of David*. Waco, TX: Baylor University Press, 2009.

Lee, A. *From Messiah to Preexistent Son: Jesus' Self-Consciousness and Early Christian Exegesus of Messianic Psalms*. Wissenschaftliche Untersuchungen zum Neuen Testament 2/192. Tübingen: Mohr Siebeck, 2005.

Lindemann, A. *Die Clemensbriefe*. Handbuch zum Neuen Testament 17. Tübingen: Mohr Siebeck, 1992.

Lona, H. E. *Der erste Clemensbrief.* Kommentar zu den Apostolischen Vätern 2. Göttingen: Vandenhoeck & Ruprecht, 1998.

—. *An Diognet: Übersetzt und erklärt.* Kommentar zu frühchristlichen Apologeten 8. Freiburg: Herder, 2001.

Luz, U. *Matthew 1–7.* Translated by W. C. Linss. Hermeneia. Minneapolis: Augsburg Fortress, 1990.

—. *Matthew in History: Interpretation, Influence, and Effects.* Minneapolis: Fortress Press, 1994.

—. *Matthew 8–20.* Hermeneia. Minneapolis: Fortress Press, 2001.

Lyons, W. J. "Hope for a Troubled Discipline? Contributions to New Testament Studies from Reception History." *Journal for the Study of the New Testament* 33 (2010): 207–20.

Marcus, J. *The Way of the Lord.* Louisville, KY: Westminster John Knox, 1992.

—. *Mark 1–8.* Anchor Bible Commentary 27. New York: Doubleday, 1999.

—. "Mark – Interpreter of Paul." *New Testament Studies* 46 (2000): 473–87.

—. *Mark 8–16.* The Anchor Yale Bible 27A. New Haven: Yale University Press, 2009.

Markschies, C. "Jesus Christ as a Man before God: Two Interpretive Models for Isaiah 53 in the Patristic Literature and Their Development." Pages 225–320 in *The Suffering Servant: Isaiah 53 in Jewish and Christian Sources.* Edited by B. Janowski and P. Stuhlmacher. Translated by D. P. Bailey. Grand Rapids: Eerdmans, 2004.

Marrou, H. I. *A Diognète: Introduction, édition critique, traduction et commentaire.* Sources Chrétiennes 29. Paris: Éditions du Cerf, 1951.

Marshall, I. H. *The Gospel of Luke: A Commentary on the Greek Text.* The New International Greek Testament Commentary. Exeter: The Paternoster Press, 1978.

—. *The Pastoral Epistles.* The International Critical Commentary. Edinburgh: T & T Clark, 1999.

Martyn, J. L. *Galatians: A New Translation with Introduction and Commentary.* Anchor Bible Commentary 33A. New York: Doubleday, 1997.

Massaux, E. *The Influence of the Gospel of Saint Matthew on Christian Literature before Saint Irenaeus.* Macon, GA: Mercer University Press, 1990, 1992, 1993.

McDonough, S. *Christ as Creator: Origins of a New Testament Doctrine.* Oxford: Oxford University Press, 2009.

McGrath, J. *John's Apologetic Christology: Legitimation and Development in Johannine Christology.* Society for New Testament Studies Monograph Series 111. Cambridge: Cambridge University Press, 2001.

McKnight, S. *Jesus and His Death.* Waco: Baylor University Press, 2005.

Meecham, H. G. *The Epistle to Diognetus: The Greek Text with Introduction, Translation, and Notes.* Manchester: Manchester University Press, 1949.

Meeks, W. A. *The First Urban Christians: The Social World of the Apostle Paul.* New Haven: Yale University Press, 1983.

Ménard, J.-É. *L'Évangile de Vérité.* Nag Hammadi Studies 2. Leiden: Brill, 1972.

Metzger, B. M. *A Textual Commentary on the Greek New Testament.* 2d ed. Stuttgart: Deutsche Bibelgesellschaft, 2002.

Michaels, J. R. *1 Peter.* Word Biblical Commentary 49. Waco: Word Books, 1988.

Moo, D. *The Epistle to the Romans.* New International Commentary on the New Testament. Grand Rapids: Eerdmans, 1996.

Mühlenberg, E. "Zur Überlieferung des Psalmenkommentars von Origenes." Pages 441–51 in *Texte und Textkritik: Eine Aufsatzsammlung.* Edited by J. Dummer. Texte und Untersuchungen 133. Berlin: Akademie-Verlag, 1987.

Nicholls, R. *Walking on the Water: Reading Mt. 14:22–33 in the Light of Its Wirkungsgeschichte.* Biblical Interpretation Series 90. Leiden: Brill, 2008.

Nineham, D. E. *The Gospel of Saint Mark*. New York: Penguin, 1963.

North, W. S. "John for Readers of Mark? A Response to Richard Bauckham's Proposal." *Journal for the Study of the New Testament* 25/4 (2003): 449–68.

Oberlinner, L. *Die Pastoralbriefe. Dritte Folge, Kommentar zum Titusbrief*. Herders theologischer Kommentar zum Neuen Testament 11/2. Freiburg: Herder, 1996.

Olick, J. K. and J. Robbins. "Social Memory Studies: From 'Collective Memory' to the Historical Sociology of Mnemonic Practices." *Annual Review of Sociology* 24 (1998): 105–40.

Orbe, A. *Teología de San Ireneo I: Comentario al Libro V del «Adversus haereses»*. Biblioteca de Autores Cristianos 25. Madrid: La Editorial Catolica, 1985.

Page, S. "The Authenticity of the Ransom Logion (Mark 10:45b)." Pages 137-61 in *Gospel Perspectives: Studies of History and Tradition in the Four Gospels*. Volume 1. Edited by R. France and D. Wenham. Sheffield: JSOT Press, 1980.

Patrick, J. E. "Matthew's *Pesher* Gospel Structured around Ten Messianic Citations of Isaiah." *Journal of Theological Studies* 61/1 (2010): 43–81.

Peel, M. L. "The 'Decensus ad Inferos' in 'The Teachings of Silvanus' (CG VII, 4)." *NVMEN* 26 (1979): 23–49.

—. "The Teachings of Silvanus: Introduction." Pages 249–76 in *Nag Hammadi Codex VII*. Edited by B. A. Pearson. Nag Hammadi and Manichaean Studies 30. Leiden: Brill, 1996a.

Peel, M. L. and J. Zandee. "'The Teachings of Silvanus' from the Library of Nag Hammadi." *Novum Testamentum* 14 (1972): 294–311.

Perrin, N. "The Use of (para)didonai in Connection with the Passion of Jesus in the New Testament." Pages 204–12 in *Der Ruf Jesu und die Antwort der Gemeinde*. Göttingen: Vandenhoeck and Ruprecht, 1970.

Pesch, R. *Das Markusevangelium II. Teil: Kommentar zu Kap. 8,27–16,20*. Herders Theologischer Kommentar zum Neuen Testament. Freiburg: Herder, 1977.

Petzer, K. "Style and Text in the Lucan Narrative of the Institution of the Lord's Supper." *New Testament Studies* 37 (1991): 113–29.

Pietersma, A. "Bodmer Papyri." Pages 766–67 in vol. 1 of *The Anchor Bible Dictionary*. Edited by D. N. Freedman. 6 vols. New York: Doubleday, 1992.

Pitre, B. *Jesus, the Tribulation, and the End of the Exile*. Wissenschaftliche Untersuchungen zum Neuen Testament 2/204. Tübingen: Mohr Siebeck, 2005.

—. "The 'Ransom for Many,' the New Exodus, and the End of the Exile: Redemption as the Restoration of All Israel (Mark 10:35–45)." *Letter and Spirit* 1 (2005): 41–68.

Popkes, W. *Christus Traditus: Eine Untersuchung zum Begriff der Dahingabe im Neuen Testament*. Zurich: Zwingli Verlag, 1967.

Popović, M., ed. *Authoritative Scriptures in Ancient Judaism*. Supplements to the Journal for the Study of Judaism 141. Leiden: Brill, 2010.

Quinn, J. D. "The Last Volume of Luke: The Relation of Luke–Acts to the Pastoral Epistles." Pages 62–75 in *Perspectives on Luke–Acts*. Edited by C. H. Talbert. Edinburgh, 1978.

Reumann, J. *Philippians: A New Translation with Introduction and Commentary*. The Anchor Yale Bible 33B. New Haven: Yale University Press, 2008.

Richard, M. "Hippolyte de Rome (saint)." Pages 531–71 in vol. 7 of *Dictionnaire de Spiritualité*. Edited by M. Viller, F. Cavallera, and J. DeGuibert. Paris: Beauchesne, 1969.

Riesenfeld, H. "Unpoetische Hymnen im Neuen Testament? Zu Phil 2,1–11." Pages 155–68 in *Glaube und Gerechtigkeit: In Memoriam Rafael Gyllenberg*. Edited by J. Kiilunen, V. Riekkinen, and H. Räisänen. Suomen Eksegeettisen Seuran Julkaisuja 38. Helsinki: Vammalan Kirjapaino Oy, 1983.

Riesner, R. "Back to the Historical Jesus through Paul and His School (The Ransom Logion–Mark 10.45; Matthew 20.28)" *Journal for the Study of the Historical Jesus* (2003): 171–99.

Rodriguez, R. *Structuring Early Christian Memory: Jesus in Tradition, Performance and Text*. Library of New Testament Studies 407. London: T&T Clark International, 2010.

Roloff, J. "Anfänge der soteriologischen Deutung des Todes Jesu (Mk. X. 45 und Lk. XXII. 27)." *New Testament Studies* 19 (1972–73): 38–64.

—. *Der erste Brief an Timotheus*. Evangelisch-Katholischer Kommentar zum Neuen Testament 15. Zürich: Benziger Verlag, 1988.

Romaniuk, K. "L'origine des formules pauliniennes 'Le Christ s'est livré pour nous', 'Le Christ nous a aimés et s'est livré pour nous.'" *Novum Testamentum* 5/1 (1962): 55–76.

Rondeau, M. -J. *Les commentaires patristiques du psautier (IIIe–Ve siècles)*, vol. 1: *Les travaux des pères grecs et latins sur le psautier: Recherches et bilans*. Orientalia Christiana Analecta 219. Rome: Pont. Institutum orientalium studiorum, 1982.

Rondeau, M. -J. and J. Kirchmeyer. "Eusèbe de Césarée." Pages 1687–90 in vol. 4 of *Dictionnaire de Spiritualité*. Edited by M. Viller, F. Cavallera, and J. DeGuibert. Paris: Beauchesne, 1960.

Schenke, H. -M. *Das Philippus-Evangelium (Nag-Hammadi-Codex II, 3)*. Texte und Untersuchungen 143. Berlin: Akademie-Verlag, 1997.

Schimanowski, G. *Die himmlische Liturgie in der Apokalypse des Johannes: Die frühjüdischen Traditionen in Offenbarung 4–5 unter Einschluß der Hekhalotliteratur*. Wissenschaftliche Untersuchungen zum Neuen Testament 2/154. Tübingen: Mohr Siebeck, 2002.

Schmidt, C. *Studien zu den Pseudo-Clementinen*. Texte und Untersuchungen 46.1. Leipzig: J.C. Hinrichs, 1929.

Schürmann, H. *Jesu Abschiedsrede, Lk 22, 21–38. III Teil, Einer quellenkritischen Untersuchung des lukanischen Abendmahlsberichtes Lk 22, 7–38*. Neutestamentliche Abhandlungen 20/5. Münster: Aschendorff, 1957.

Segelberg, E. "The Gospel of Philip and the New Testament." Pages 204–12 in *The New Testament and Gnosis*. Edited by A. H. B. Logan and A. J. M. Wedderburn. Edinburgh: T. & T. Clark, 1983.

Shauf, S. "Galatians 2.20 in Context." *New Testament Studies* 52 (2006): 86–101.

Shum, S. -L. *Paul's Use of Isaiah in Romans: A Comparative Study of Paul's Letter to the Romans and the Sibyline and Qumran Sectarian Texts*. Wissenschaftliche Untersuchungen zum Neuen Testament 2/156. Tübingen: Mohr Siebeck, 2002.

Sim, D. C. "Matthew and the Pauline Corpus: A Preliminary Intertextual Study." *Journal for the Study of the New Testament* 31/4 (2009): 401–22.

Slater, T. B. "One Like a Son of Man in First-Century CE Judaism." *New Testament Studies* 41 (1995): 183–98.

Smith, M. S. "Bĕrît 'am/Bĕrît 'ôlām: A New Proposal for the Crux of Isa 42:6." *Journal of Biblical Literature* 100/2 (1981): 241–43.

Soards, M. L. *The Passion According to Luke: The Special Material of Luke 22*. Journal for the Study of the New Testament Supplement Series 14. Sheffield: Sheffield Academic Press, 1987.

Stettler, H. *Die Christologie der Pastoralbriefe*. Wissenschaftliche Untersuchungen zum Neuen Testament 2/103. Tübingen: Mohr Siebeck, 1998.

Stökl Ben Ezra, D. *The Impact of Yom Kippur on Early Christianity: The Day of Atonement from Second Temple Judaism to the Fifth Century*. Wissenschaftliche Untersuchungen zum Neuen Testament 163. Tübingen: Mohr Siebeck, 2003.

Story, C. I. K. *The Nature of Truth in "The Gospel of Truth" and in the Writings of Justin Martyr: A Study of the Pattern of Orthodoxy in the Middle of the Second Christian Cen-*

tury. Supplements to Novum Testamentum 25. Leiden: Brill, 1970.

Stroud, W. J. "New Testament Quotations in the Nag Hammadi Gospel of Philip." Pages 68–81 in *Society of Biblical Literature 1990 Seminar Papers*. Edited by D. J. Lull. Atlanta: Scholars Press, 1990.

Stuhlmacher, P. *Reconciliation, Law, & Righteousness*. Translated by E. Kalin. Philadelphia: Fortress, 1986.

Tanner, R. G. "The Epistle to Diognetus and Contemporary Greek Thought." Pages 1.495–508 in *Studia Patristica* 15. Edited by E. Livingstone, 1984.

Taylor, V. *The Passion Narrative of St Luke: A Critical and Historical Investigation*. Society for New Testament Studies Monograph Series 19. Cambridge: Cambridge University Press, 1972.

Telford, W. R. *The Theology of the Gospel of Mark*. New Testament Theology. Cambridge: Cambridge University Press, 1999.

—. *Writing on the Gospel of Mark*. Guides to Advanced Biblical Research. London: DEO Publishing, 2009.

Thesaurus Linguae Graecae: A Digital Library of Greek Literature. Search for "λύτρον" on 29 July 2008. Online: http://www.tlg.uci.edu/.

Thomassen, E. "The Tripartite Tractate From Nag Hammadi: A New Translation with Introduction and Commentary." Ph.D. diss., University of St Andrews, 1982.

—. "How Valentinian is the *Gospel of Philip*?" Pages 251–79 in *The Nag Hammadi Library after Fifty Years: Proceedings of the 1995 Society of Biblical Literature Commemoration*. Edited by J. D. Turnier and A. McGuire. Nag Hammadi and Manichaean Studies 44. Leiden: Brill, 1997.

—. *The Spiritual Seed: The Church of the "Valentinians."* Nag Hammadi and Manichaean Studies 60. Leiden: Brill, 2006.

Thompson, M. *Clothed with Christ: The Example and Teaching of Jesus in Romans 12.1–15.13*. Journal for the Study of the New Testament Supplement Series 59. Sheffield: JSOT Press, 1991.

Tödt, H. E. *The Son of Man in the Synoptic Tradition*. Translated by D. M. Barton. Philadelphia: Westminster Press, 1965.

Towner, P. H. *The Goal of Our Instruction: The Structure of Theology and Ethics in the Pastoral Epistles*. Journal for the Study of the New Testament Supplement Series 34. Sheffield: JSOT Press, 1989.

—. *The Letters to Timothy and Titus*. The New International Commentary on the New Testament. Grand Rapids: Eerdmans, 2006.

Trolmie, F. D. *Persuading the Galatians: A Text-Centered Rhetorical Analysis of a Pauline Letter*. Wissenschaftliche Untersuchungen zum Neuen Testament 2/190. Tübingen: Mohr Siebeck, 2005.

Trummer, P. *Die Paulustradition Der Pastoralbriefe*. Beiträge zur biblischen Exegese und Theologie 8. Frankfurt am Main: Peter Lang, 1978.

Tuckett, C. M. *Nag Hammadi and the Gospel Tradition*. Edinburgh: T & T Clark, 1986.

Tzamalikos, P. *Origen: Philosopy of History & Eschatology*. Supplements to Vigiliae Christianae 85. Leiden: Brill, 2007.

Van den Broek, R. "The Theology of the Teachings of Silvanus." *Vigiliae Christianae* 40 (1986): 1–23.

Van den Hoek, A. "Techniques of Quotation in Clement of Alexandria: A View of Ancient Literary Wording Methods." *Vigiliae Christianae* 50 (1996): 223–43.

Van Henten, J. W. *The Maccabean Martyrs as Saviours of the Jewish People: A Study of 2 and 4 Maccabees*. Supplements to the Journal for the Study of Judaism 57. Leiden: Brill, 1997.

Vansina, J. *Oral Tradition as History*. Madison: University of Wisconsin Press, 1985.

Van Unnik, W. C. "The 'Gospel of Truth' and the New Testament." Pages 79–129 in *The Jung Codex: A Newly Recovered Gnostic Papyrus*. Translated and Edited by F. L. Cross. London: A. R. Mowbray & Co. Limited, 1955.

—. "The Redemption in 1Peter 1:18–19 and the Problem of the First Epistle of Peter." Pages 3–82 in *Sparsa Collecta: The Collected Essays of W. C. van Unnik. Novum Testamentum Supplements* 30. Leiden: Brill, 1980.

Versnel, H. S. "Making Sense of Jesus' Death: The Pagan Contribution." Pages 215–94 in *Deutungen des Todes Jesu im Neuen Testament*. Edited by J. Frey and J. Schröter. Wissenschaftliche Untersuchungen zum Neuen Testament 181. Tübingen: Mohr Siebeck, 2005.

Vogt, H. J. "Origen of Alexandria." Pages 536–74 in *Handbook of Patristic Exegesis*. Edited by D. J. Bingham. The Bible in Ancient Christianity 1. Leiden: Brill, 2004.

Vos, J. S. "Die Argumentation des Paulus in Galater 1,1–2,10." Pages 11–43 in *The Truth of the Gospel: Galatians 1:1–4:11*. Edited by J. Lambrecht. Monographic Series of Benedictina. Biblical-Ecumenical Section 12. Rome: Benedictina Publishing, 1993.

Wagner, J. R. *Heralds of the Good News: Isaiah and Paul "In Concert" in the Letter to the Romans*. Supplements to Novum Testamentum 101. Leiden: Brill, 2003.

Warnke, G. *Gadamer: Hermeneutics, Tradition and Reason*. Stanford: Stanford University Press, 1987.

Watts, R. E. *Isaiah's New Exodus and Mark*. Wissenschaftliche Untersuchungen zum Neuen Testament 2/88. Tübingen: Mohr Siebeck, 1997.

—. "Jesus' Death, Isaiah 53, and Mark 10:45: A Crux Revisited." Pages 125–51 in *Jesus and the Suffering Servant*. Edited by W. H. Bellinger, Jr. and W. R. Farmer. Harrisburg: Trinity Press International, 1998.

Webb, R. L. "Jude." Pages 611–20 in *Dictionary of the Later New Testament and Its Developments*. Edited by R. Martin and P. Davids. Downers Grove, IL: Inter-Varsity Press, 1997.

Wengst, K. "Christologische Formeln und Lieder des Urchristentums." Ph.D. diss., Universität Bonn, 1967.

Werner, M. *Der Einfluss paulinischer Theologie im Markusevangelium*. Beihefte zur Zeitschrift für die neutestamentliche Wissenschaft 1. Giessen: Alfred Töpelmann, 1923.

Wilcox, M. "On the Ransom-Saying in Mark 10:45c, Matt 20:28c." Pages 173–86 in *Geschichte–Tradition–Reflexion: Festschrift für Martin Hengel zum 70. Geburtstag*, vol 3: *Frühes Christentum*. Edited by H. Cancik, H. Lichtenberger, and P. Schäfer. Tübingen: Mohr Siebeck, 1996.

Wilken, R. L. "Wisdom and Philosophy in Early Christianity." Pages 143–68 in *Aspects of Wisdom in Judaism and Early Christianity*. Edited by R. L. Wilken. Notre Dame: University of Notre Dame Press, 1975.

Williams, J. A. *Biblical Interpretation in the Gnostic Gospel of Truth from Nag Hammadi*. Society of Biblical Literature Dissertation Series 79. Atlanta: Scholars Press, 1988.

Williams, S. K. *Jesus' Death as Saving Event: The Background and Origin of a Concept*. Harvard Dissertations in Religion 2. Missoula, MT: Scholars Press, 1975.

Willitts, J. *Matthew's Messianic Shepherd-King: In Search of "the Lost Sheep of the House of Israel."* Beihefte zur Zeitschrift für die neutestamentliche Wissenschaft und die Kunde der älteren Kirche 147. Berlin: de Gruyter, 2007.

Wilson, R. McL. "The New Testament in the Nag Hammadi Gospel of Philip." *New Testament Studies* 9 (1963): 291–94.

—. "Valentinianism and the *Gospel of Truth*." Pages 133–41 in *The Rediscovery of Gnosticism*. Vol. 1. Edited by B. Layton. Leiden: Brill, 1980.

Zandee, J. "Die 'Lehren des Silvanus' als Teil der Schriften von Nag Hammadi und der Gnostizismus." Pages 239–52 in *Essays on The Nag Hammadi Texts: In Honour of Pahor Labib*. Edited by M. Krause. Nag Hammadi Studies 6. Leiden: Brill, 1975.

—. *'The Teachings of Silvanus' and Clement of Alexandria: A New Document of Alexandrian Theology*. Mededelingen en Verhandelingen 19. Leiden: Ex Oriente Lux, 1977.

—. "'The Teachings of Silvanus' (NHC VII, 4) and Jewish Christianity." Pages 498–584 in *Studies in Gnosticism and Hellenistic Religions*. Edited by R. van den Broek and M. J. Vermaseren. Leiden: Brill, 1981.

Zerubavel, E. "Social Memories: Steps to a Sociology of the Past." *Qualitative Sociology* 19 (1996): 283–99.

Index of Ancient Sources

A. Old Testament (with Deuterocanonicals)

C. Old Testament Pseudepigrapha

D. Early Christian Literature

Index of Modern Authors

Index of Subjects

Wissenschaftliche Untersuchungen zum Neuen Testament

Alphabetical Index of the First and Second Series

Becker, Eve-Marie: Das Markus-Evangelium im Rahmen antiker Historiographie. 2006. *Vol. 194.*

Becker, Eve-Marie and *Peter Pilhofer* (Ed.): Biographie und Persönlichkeit des Paulus. 2005. *Vol. 187.*

– and *Anders Runesson* (Ed.): Mark and Matthew I. 2011. *Vol. 271.*

Becker, Michael: Wunder und Wundertäter im frührabbinischen Judentum. 2002. *Vol. II/144.*

Becker, Michael and *Markus Öhler* (Ed.): Apokalyptik als Herausforderung neutestamentlicher Theologie. 2006. *Vol. II/214.*

Bell, Richard H.: Deliver Us from Evil. 2007. *Vol. 216.*

– The Irrevocable Call of God. 2005. *Vol. 184.*

– No One Seeks for God. 1998. *Vol. 106.*

– Provoked to Jealousy. 1994. *Vol. II/63.*

Bennema, Cornelis: The Power of Saving Wisdom. 2002. *Vol. II/148.*

Bergman, Jan: see *Kieffer, René*

Bergmeier, Roland: Das Gesetz im Römerbrief und andere Studien zum Neuen Testament. 2000. *Vol. 121.*

Bernett, Monika: Der Kaiserkult in Judäa unter den Herodiern und Römern. 2007. *Vol. 203.*

Betho, Benjamin: see *Clivaz, Claire.*

Betz, Otto: Jesus, der Messias Israels. 1987. *Vol. 42.*

– Jesus, der Herr der Kirche. 1990. *Vol. 52.*

Beyschlag, Karlmann: Simon Magus und die christliche Gnosis. 1974. *Vol. 16.*

Bieringer, Reimund: see *Koester, Craig.*

Bird, Michael F. and *Jason Maston* (Ed.): Earliest Christian History. 2012. *Vol. II/320.*

Bittner, Wolfgang J.: Jesu Zeichen im Johannesevangelium. 1987. *Vol. II/26.*

Bjerkelund, Carl J.: Tauta Egeneto. 1987. *Vol. 40.*

Blackburn, Barry Lee: Theios Aner and the Markan Miracle Traditions. 1991. *Vol. II/40.*

Blackwell, Ben C.: Christosis. 2011. *Vol. II/314.*

Blanton IV, Thomas R.: Constructing a New Covenant. 2007. *Vol. II/233.*

Bock, Darrell L.: Blasphemy and Exaltation in Judaism and the Final Examination of Jesus. 1998. *Vol. II/106.*

– and *Robert L. Webb* (Ed.): Key Events in the Life of the Historical Jesus. 2009. *Vol. 247.*

Bockmuehl, Markus: The Remembered Peter. 2010. *Vol. 262.*

– Revelation and Mystery in Ancient Judaism and Pauline Christianity. 1990. *Vol. II/36.*

Bøe, Sverre: Cross-Bearing in Luke. 2010. *Vol. II/278.*

– Gog and Magog. 2001. *Vol. II/135.*

Böhlig, Alexander: Gnosis und Synkretismus. Vol. 1 1989. *Vol. 47* – Vol. 2 1989. *Vol. 48.*

Böhm, Martina: Samarien und die Samaritai bei Lukas. 1999. *Vol. II/111.*

Börstinghaus, Jens: Sturmfahrt und Schiffbruch. 2010. *Vol. II/274.*

Böttrich, Christfried: Weltweisheit – Menschheitsethik – Urkult. 1992. *Vol. II/50.*

– and *Herzer, Jens* (Ed.): Josephus und das Neue Testament. 2007. *Vol. 209.*

Bolyki, János: Jesu Tischgemeinschaften. 1997. *Vol. II/96.*

Bosman, Philip: Conscience in Philo and Paul. 2003. *Vol. II/166.*

Bovon, François: New Testament and Christian Apocrypha. 2009. *Vol. 237.*

– Studies in Early Christianity. 2003. *Vol. 161.*

Brändl, Martin: Der Agon bei Paulus. 2006. *Vol. II/222.*

Braun, Heike: Geschichte des Gottesvolkes und christliche Identität. 2010. *Vol. II/279.*

Breytenbach, Cilliers: see *Frey, Jörg.*

Broadhead, Edwin K.: Jewish Ways of Following Jesus Redrawing the Religious Map of Antiquity. 2010. *Vol. 266.*

Brocke, Christoph vom: Thessaloniki – Stadt des Kassander und Gemeinde des Paulus. 2001. *Vol. II/125.*

Brunson, Andrew: Psalm 118 in the Gospel of John. 2003. *Vol. II/158.*

Büchli, Jörg: Der Poimandres – ein paganisiertes Evangelium. 1987. *Vol. II/27.*

Bühner, Jan A.: Der Gesandte und sein Weg im 4. Evangelium. 1977. *Vol. II/2.*

Burchard, Christoph: Untersuchungen zu Joseph und Aseneth. 1965. *Vol. 8.*

– Studien zur Theologie, Sprache und Umwelt des Neuen Testaments. Ed. by D. Sänger. 1998. *Vol. 107.*

Burnett, Richard: Karl Barth's Theological Exegesis. 2001. *Vol. II/145.*

Byron, John: Slavery Metaphors in Early Judaism and Pauline Christianity. 2003. *Vol. II/162.*

Byrskog, Samuel: Story as History – History as Story. 2000. *Vol. 123.*

Calhoun, Robert M.: Paul's Definitions of the Gospel in Romans 1. 2011. *Vol. II/316.*

Cancik, Hubert (Ed.): Markus-Philologie. 1984. *Vol. 33.*

Capes, David B.: Old Testament Yaweh Texts in Paul's Christology. 1992. *Vol. II/47.*

Caragounis, Chrys C.: The Development
of Greek and the New Testament. 2004.
Vol. 167.
– The Son of Man. 1986. *Vol. 38.*
– see *Fridrichsen, Anton.*
Carleton Paget, James: The Epistle of Barna-
bas. 1994. *Vol. II/64.*
– Jews, Christians and Jewish Christians in
Antiquity. 2010. *Vol. 251.*
Carson, D.A., O'Brien, Peter T. and *Mark
Seifrid* (Ed.): Justification and Variegated
Nomism.
Vol. 1: The Complexities of Second Temple
Judaism. 2001. *Vol. II/140.*
Vol. 2: The Paradoxes of Paul. 2004.
Vol. II/181.
Caulley, Thomas Scott and *Hermann Lichten-
berger* (Ed.): Die Septuaginta und das frühe
Christentum – The Septuagint and Christian
Origins. 2011. *Vol. 277.*
– see *Lichtenberger, Hermann.*
Chae, Young Sam: Jesus as the Eschatological
Davidic Shepherd. 2006. *Vol. II/216.*
Chapman, David W.: Ancient Jewish and
Christian Perceptions of Crucifixion. 2008.
Vol. II/244.
Chester, Andrew: Messiah and Exaltation. 2007.
Vol. 207.
Chibici-Revneanu, Nicole: Die Herrlichkeit des
Verherrlichten. 2007. *Vol. II/231.*
Ciampa, Roy E.: The Presence and Function
of Scripture in Galatians 1 and 2. 1998.
Vol. II/102.
Classen, Carl Joachim: Rhetorical Criticsm of
the New Testament. 2000. *Vol. 128.*
Claußen, Carsten (Ed.): see *Frey, Jörg.*
*Clivaz, Claire, Andreas Dettwiler, Luc Devil-
lers, Enrico Norelli* with *Benjamin Bertho*
(Ed.): Infancy Gospels. 2011. *Vol. 281.*
Colpe, Carsten: Griechen – Byzantiner – Se-
miten – Muslime. 2008. *Vol. 221.*
– Iranier – Aramäer – Hebräer – Hellenen.
2003. *Vol. 154.*
Cook, John G.: Roman Attitudes Towards the
Christians. 2010. *Vol. 261.*
Coote, Robert B. (Ed.): see *Weissenrieder,
Annette.*
Coppins, Wayne: The Interpretation of Freedom
in the Letters of Paul. 2009. *Vol. II/261.*
Crump, David: Jesus the Intercessor. 1992.
Vol. II/49.
Dahl, Nils Alstrup: Studies in Ephesians. 2000.
Vol. 131.
Daise, Michael A.: Feasts in John. 2007.
Vol. II/229.

Deines, Roland: Die Gerechtigkeit der Tora im
Reich des Messias. 2004. *Vol. 177.*
– Jüdische Steingefäße und pharisäische
Frömmigkeit. 1993. *Vol. II/52.*
– Die Pharisäer. 1997. *Vol. 101.*
Deines, Roland, Jens Herzer and *Karl-Wilhelm
Niebuhr* (Ed.): Neues Testament und
hellenistisch-jüdische Alltagskultur. III.
Internationales Symposium zum Corpus
Judaeo-Hellenisticum Novi Testamenti.
21.–24. Mai 2009 in Leipzig. 2011. *Vol. 274.*
– and *Karl-Wilhelm Niebuhr* (Ed.): Philo und
das Neue Testament. 2004. *Vol. 172.*
Dennis, John A.: Jesus' Death and the Gathering
of True Israel. 2006. *Vol. 217.*
Dettwiler, Andreas and *Jean Zumstein* (Ed.):
Kreuzestheologie im Neuen Testament.
2002. *Vol. 151.*
– see *Clivaz, Claire.*
Devillers, Luc: see *Clivaz, Claire.*
Dickson, John P.: Mission-Commitment in
Ancient Judaism and in the Pauline Commu-
nities. 2003. *Vol. II/159.*
Dietzfelbinger, Christian: Der Abschied des
Kommenden. 1997. *Vol. 95.*
Dimitrov, Ivan Z., James D.G. Dunn, Ulrich Luz
and *Karl-Wilhelm Niebuhr* (Ed.): Das Alte
Testament als christliche Bibel in orthodoxer
und westlicher Sicht. 2004. *Vol. 174.*
Dobbeler, Axel von: Glaube als Teilhabe. 1987.
Vol. II/22.
Docherty, Susan E.: The Use of the Old Testa-
ment in Hebrews. 2009. *Vol. II/260.*
Dochhorn, Jan: Schriftgelehrte Prophetie.
2010. *Vol. 268.*
Downs, David J.: The Offering of the Gentiles.
2008. *Vol. II/248.*
Dryden, J. de Waal: Theology and Ethics in
1 Peter. 2006. *Vol. II/209.*
Dübbers, Michael: Christologie und Existenz
im Kolosserbrief. 2005. *Vol. II/191.*
Dunn, James D.G.: The New Perspective on
Paul. 2005. *Vol. 185.*
Dunn, James D.G. (Ed.): Jews and Christians.
1992. *Vol. 66.*
– Paul and the Mosaic Law. 1996. *Vol. 89.*
– see *Dimitrov, Ivan Z.*
–, *Hans Klein, Ulrich Luz,* and *Vasile Mihoc*
(Ed.): Auslegung der Bibel in orthodoxer
und westlicher Perspektive. 2000. *Vol. 130.*
Ebel, Eva: Die Attraktivität früher christlicher
Gemeinden. 2004. *Vol. II/178.*
Ebertz, Michael N.: Das Charisma des Gekreu-
zigten. 1987. *Vol. 45.*

Eckstein, Hans-Joachim: Der Begriff Syn-
eidesis bei Paulus. 1983. *Vol. II/10.*
– Verheißung und Gesetz. 1996. *Vol. 86.*
–, *Christoph Landmesser* and *Hermann Lichtenberger* (Ed.): Eschatologie – Eschato-
logy. The Sixth Durham-Tübingen Research
Symposium. 2011. *Vol. 272.*
Edwards, J. Christopher: The Ransom Logion
in Mark and Matthew. 2012. *Vol. II/327.*
Ego, Beate: Im Himmel wie auf Erden. 1989.
Vol. II/34.
Ego, Beate, Armin Lange and *Peter Pilhofer*
(Ed.): Gemeinde ohne Tempel – Community
without Temple. 1999. *Vol. 118.*
– and *Helmut Merkel* (Ed.): Religiöses Lernen
in der biblischen, frühjüdischen und früh-
christlichen Überlieferung. 2005. *Vol. 180.*
Eisele, Wilfried: Welcher Thomas? 2010.
Vol. 259.
Eisen, Ute E.: see *Paulsen, Henning.*
Elledge, C.D.: Life after Death in Early Juda-
ism. 2006. *Vol. II/208.*
Ellis, E. Earle: Prophecy and Hermeneutic in
Early Christianity. 1978. *Vol. 18.*
– The Old Testament in Early Christianity.
1991. *Vol. 54.*
Elmer, Ian J.: Paul, Jerusalem and the Judaisers.
2009. *Vol. II/258.*
Endo, Masanobu: Creation and Christology.
2002. *Vol. 149.*
Ennulat, Andreas: Die 'Minor Agreements'.
1994. *Vol. II/62.*
Ensor, Peter W.: Jesus and His 'Works'. 1996.
Vol. II/85.
Eskola, Timo: Messiah and the Throne. 2001.
Vol. II/142.
– Theodicy and Predestination in Pauline
Soteriology. 1998. *Vol. II/100.*
Farelly, Nicolas: The Disciples in the Fourth
Gospel. 2010. *Vol. II/290.*
Fatehi, Mehrdad: The Spirit's Relation to the
Risen Lord in Paul. 2000. *Vol. II/128.*
Feldmeier, Reinhard: Die Krisis des Gottes-
sohnes. 1987. *Vol. II/21.*
– Die Christen als Fremde. 1992. *Vol. 64.*
Feldmeier, Reinhard and *Ulrich Heckel* (Ed.):
Die Heiden. 1994. *Vol. 70.*
Felsch, Dorit: Die Feste im Johannesevange-
lium. 2011. *Vol. II/308.*
Finnern, Sönke: Narratologie und biblische Ex-
egese. 2010. *Vol. II/285.*
Fletcher-Louis, Crispin H.T.: Luke-Acts:
Angels, Christology and Soteriology. 1997.
Vol. II/94.
Förster, Niclas: Marcus Magus. 1999. *Vol. 114.*

Forbes, Christopher Brian: Prophecy and In-
spired Speech in Early Christianity and its
Hellenistic Environment. 1995. *Vol. II/75.*
Fornberg, Tord: see *Fridrichsen, Anton.*
Fossum, Jarl E.: The Name of God and the
Angel of the Lord. 1985. *Vol. 36.*
Foster, Paul: Community, Law and Mission in
Matthew's Gospel. *Vol. II/177.*
Fotopoulos, John: Food Offered to Idols in
Roman Corinth. 2003. *Vol. II/151.*
Frank, Nicole: Der Kolosserbrief im Kontext
des paulinischen Erbes. 2009. *Vol. II/271.*
Frenschkowski, Marco: Offenbarung und
Epiphanie. Vol. 1 1995. *Vol. II/79* – Vol. 2
1997. *Vol. II/80.*
Frey, Jörg: Eugen Drewermann und die bibli-
sche Exegese. 1995. *Vol. II/71.*
– Die johanneische Eschatologie. Vol. I. 1997.
Vol. 96. – Vol. II. 1998. *Vol. 110.* – Vol. III.
2000. *Vol. 117.*
Frey, Jörg, Carsten Claußen and *Nadine Kessler*
(Ed.): Qumran und die Archäologie. 2011.
Vol. 278.
– and *Cilliers Breytenbach* (Ed.): Aufgabe und
Durchführung einer Theologie des Neuen
Testaments. 2007. *Vol. 205.*
– *Jens Herzer, Martina Janßen* and *Clare K.
Rothschild* (Ed.): Pseudepigraphie und Ver-
fasserfiktion in frühchristlichen Briefen.
2009. *Vol. 246.*
– *James A. Kelhoffer* and *Franz Tóth* (Ed.): Die
Johannesapokalypse. 2012. *Vol. 287.*
– *Stefan Krauter* and *Hermann Lichtenberger*
(Ed.): Heil und Geschichte. 2009. *Vol. 248.*
– and *Udo Schnelle (Ed.):* Kontexte des Jo-
hannesevangeliums. 2004. *Vol. 175.*
– and *Jens Schröter* (Ed.): Deutungen des
Todes Jesu im Neuen Testament. 2005.
Vol. 181.
– Jesus in apokryphen Evangelienüberliefe-
rungen. 2010. *Vol. 254.*
–, *Jan G. van der Watt,* and *Ruben Zimmer-
mann* (Ed.): Imagery in the Gospel of John.
2006. *Vol. 200.*
Freyne, Sean: Galilee and Gospel. 2000.
Vol. 125.
Fridrichsen, Anton: Exegetical Writings. Edited
by C.C. Caragounis and T. Fornberg. 1994.
Vol. 76.
Gadenz, Pablo T.: Called from the Jews and
from the Gentiles. 2009. *Vol. II/267.*
Gäbel, Georg: Die Kulttheologie des Hebräer-
briefes. 2006. *Vol. II/212.*
Gäckle, Volker: Die Starken und die Schwachen
in Korinth und in Rom. 2005. *Vol. 200.*

Garlington, Don B.: 'The Obedience of Faith'. 1991. *Vol. II/38.*
– Faith, Obedience, and Perseverance. 1994. *Vol. 79.*
Garnet, Paul: Salvation and Atonement in the Qumran Scrolls. 1977. *Vol. II/3.*
Garský, Zbynek: Das Wirken Jesu in Galiläa bei Johannes. 2012. *Vol. II/325.*
Gemünden, Petra von (Ed.): see *Weissenrieder, Annette.*
Gese, Michael: Das Vermächtnis des Apostels. 1997. *Vol. II/99.*
Gheorghita, Radu: The Role of the Septuagint in Hebrews. 2003. *Vol. II/160.*
Gordley, Matthew E.: The Colossian Hymn in Context. 2007. *Vol. II/228.*
– Teaching through Song in Antiquity. 2011. *Vol. II/302.*
Gräbe, Petrus J.: The Power of God in Paul's Letters. 2000, ²2008. *Vol. II/123.*
Gräßer, Erich: Der Alte Bund im Neuen. 1985. *Vol. 35.*
– Forschungen zur Apostelgeschichte. 2001. *Vol. 137.*
Grappe, Christian (Ed.): Le Repas de Dieu / Das Mahl Gottes. 2004. *Vol. 169.*
Gray, Timothy C.: The Temple in the Gospel of Mark. 2008. *Vol. II/242.*
Green, Joel B.: The Death of Jesus. 1988. *Vol. II/33.*
Gregg, Brian Han: The Historical Jesus and the Final Judgment Sayings in Q. 2005. *Vol. II/207.*
Gregory, Andrew: The Reception of Luke and Acts in the Period before Irenaeus. 2003. *Vol. II/169.*
Grindheim, Sigurd: The Crux of Election. 2005. *Vol. II/202.*
Gundry, Robert H.: The Old is Better. 2005. *Vol. 178.*
Gundry Volf, Judith M.: Paul and Perseverance. 1990. *Vol. II/37.*
Häußer, Detlef: Christusbekenntnis und Jesus-überlieferung bei Paulus. 2006. *Vol. 210.*
Hafemann, Scott J.: Suffering and the Spirit. 1986. *Vol. II/19.*
– Paul, Moses, and the History of Israel. 1995. *Vol. 81.*
Hahn, Ferdinand: Studien zum Neuen Testament.
  Vol. I: Grundsatzfragen, Jesusforschung, Evangelien. 2006. *Vol. 191.*
  Vol. II: Bekenntnisbildung und Theologie in urchristlicher Zeit. 2006. *Vol. 192.*

Hahn, Johannes (Ed.): Zerstörungen des Jerusalemer Tempels. 2002. *Vol. 147.*
Hamid-Khani, Saeed: Relevation and Concealment of Christ. 2000. *Vol. II/120.*
Hannah, Darrel D.: Michael and Christ. 1999. *Vol. II/109.*
Hardin, Justin K.: Galatians and the Imperial Cult? 2007. *Vol. II /237.*
Harrison, James R.: Paul and the Imperial Authorities at Thessolanica and Rome. 2011. *Vol. 273.*
– Paul's Language of Grace in Its Graeco-Roman Context. 2003. *Vol. II/172.*
Hartman, Lars: Text-Centered New Testament Studies. Ed. von D. Hellholm. 1997. *Vol. 102.*
Hartog, Paul: Polycarp and the New Testament. 2001. *Vol. II/134.*
Hasselbrook, David S.: Studies in New Testament Lexicography. 2011. *Vol. II/303.*
Hays, Christopher M.: Luke's Wealth Ethics. 2010. *Vol. 275.*
Heckel, Theo K.: Der Innere Mensch. 1993. *Vol. II/53.*
– Vom Evangelium des Markus zum vier-gestaltigen Evangelium. 1999. *Vol. 120.*
Heckel, Ulrich: Kraft in Schwachheit. 1993. *Vol. II/56.*
– Der Segen im Neuen Testament. 2002. *Vol. 150.*
– see *Feldmeier, Reinhard.*
– see *Hengel, Martin.*
Heemstra, Marius: The Fiscus Judaicus and the Parting of the Ways. 2010. *Vol. II/277.*
Heiligenthal, Roman: Werke als Zeichen. 1983. *Vol. II/9.*
Heininger, Bernhard: Die Inkulturation des Christentums. 2010. *Vol. 255.*
Heliso, Desta: Pistis and the Righteous One. 2007. *Vol. II/235.*
Hellholm, D.: see *Hartman, Lars.*
Hemer, Colin J.: The Book of Acts in the Setting of Hellenistic History. 1989. *Vol. 49.*
Henderson, Timothy P.: The Gospel of Peter and Early Christian Apologetics. 2011. *Vol. II/301.*
Hengel, Martin: Jesus und die Evangelien. Kleine Schriften V. 2007. *Vol. 211.*
– Die johanneische Frage. 1993. *Vol. 67.*
– Judaica et Hellenistica. Kleine Schriften I. 1996. *Vol. 90.*
– Judaica, Hellenistica et Christiana. Kleine Schriften II. 1999. *Vol. 109.*
– Judentum und Hellenismus. 1969, ³1988. *Vol. 10.*

– Kreuz und Weisheit. 2003. *Vol. 159.*
– see *Hofius, Otfried.*
Karakolis, Christos, Karl-Wilhelm Niebuhr and *Sviatoslav Rogalsky* (Ed.): Gospel Images of Jesus Christ in Church Tradition and in Biblical Scholarship. Fifth International East-West Symposium of New Testament Scholars, Minsk, September 2 to 9, 2010. 2012. *Vol. 288.*
– see *Alexeev, Anatoly A.*
Karrer, Martin und *Wolfgang Kraus* (Ed.): Die Septuaginta – Texte, Kontexte, Lebenswelten. 2008. *Vol. 219.*
– see *Kraus, Wolfgang.*
Kelhoffer, James A.: The Diet of John the Baptist. 2005. *Vol. 176.*
– Miracle and Mission. 2000. *Vol. II/112.*
– Persecution, Persuasion and Power. 2010. *Vol. 270.*
– see *Ahearne-Kroll, Stephen P.*
– see *Frey, Jörg.*
Kelley, Nicole: Knowledge and Religious Authority in the Pseudo-Clementines. 2006. *Vol. II/213.*
Kennedy, Joel: The Recapitulation of Israel. 2008. *Vol. II/257.*
Kensky, Meira Z.: Trying Man, Trying God. 2010. *Vol. II/289.*
Kessler, Nadine (Ed.): see *Frey, Jörg.*
Kieffer, René and *Jan Bergman* (Ed.): La Main de Dieu / Die Hand Gottes. 1997. *Vol. 94.*
Kierspel, Lars: The Jews and the World in the Fourth Gospel. 2006. *Vol. 220.*
Kim, Seyoon: The Origin of Paul's Gospel. 1981, ²1984. *Vol. II/4.*
– Paul and the New Perspective. 2002. *Vol. 140.*
– "The 'Son of Man'" as the Son of God. 1983. *Vol. 30.*
Klauck, Hans-Josef: Religion und Gesellschaft im frühen Christentum. 2003. *Vol. 152.*
Klein, Hans, Vasile Mihoc und *Karl-Wilhelm Niebuhr* (Ed.): Das Gebet im Neuen Testament. Vierte, europäische orthodox-westliche Exegetenkonferenz in Sambata de Sus, 4.–8. August 2007. 2009. Vol. 249.
– see Dunn, James D.G.
Kleinknecht, Karl Th.: Der leidende Gerechtfertigte. 1984, ²1988. *Vol. II/13.*
Klinghardt, Matthias: Gesetz und Volk Gottes. 1988. *Vol. II/32.*
Kloppenborg, John S.: The Tenants in the Vineyard. 2006, student edition 2010. *Vol. 195.*
Koch, Michael: Drachenkampf und Sonnenfrau. 2004. *Vol. II/184.*

Koch, Stefan: Rechtliche Regelung von Konflikten im frühen Christentum. 2004. *Vol. II/174.*
Köhler, Wolf-Dietrich: Rezeption des Matthäusevangeliums in der Zeit vor Irenäus. 1987. *Vol. II/24.*
Köhn, Andreas: Der Neutestamentler Ernst Lohmeyer. 2004. *Vol. II/180.*
Koester, Craig and *Reimund Bieringer* (Ed.): The Resurrection of Jesus in the Gospel of John. 2008. *Vol. 222.*
Konradt, Matthias: Israel, Kirche und die Völker im Matthäusevangelium. 2007. *Vol. 215.*
Kooten, George H. van: Cosmic Christology in Paul and the Pauline School. 2003. *Vol. II/171.*
– Paul's Anthropology in Context. 2008. *Vol. 232.*
Korn, Manfred: Die Geschichte Jesu in veränderter Zeit. 1993. *Vol. II/51.*
Koskenniemi, Erkki: Apollonios von Tyana in der neutestamentlichen Exegese. 1994. *Vol. II/61.*
– The Old Testament Miracle-Workers in Early Judaism. 2005. *Vol. II/206.*
Kraus, Thomas J.: Sprache, Stil und historischer Ort des zweiten Petrusbriefes. 2001. *Vol. II/136.*
Kraus, Wolfgang: Das Volk Gottes. 1996. *Vol. 85.*
– see *Karrer, Martin.*
– see *Walter, Nikolaus.*
– and *Martin Karrer* (Hrsg.): Die Septuaginta – Texte, Theologien, Einflüsse. 2010. *Bd. 252.*
– and *Karl-Wilhelm Niebuhr* (Ed.): Frühjudentum und Neues Testament im Horizont Biblischer Theologie. 2003. *Vol. 162.*
Krauter, Stefan: Studien zu Röm 13,1-7. 2009. *Vol. 243.*
– see *Frey, Jörg.*
Kreplin, Matthias: Das Selbstverständnis Jesu. 2001. *Vol. II/141.*
Kreuzer, Siegfried, Martin Meiser and *Marcus Sigismund* (Ed.): Die Septuaginta – Entstehung, Sprache, Geschichte. 2012. *Vol. 286.*
Kuhn, Karl G.: Achtzehngebet und Vaterunser und der Reim. 1950. *Vol. 1.*
Kvalbein, Hans: see *Ådna, Jostein.*
Kwon, Yon-Gyong: Eschatology in Galatians. 2004. *Vol. II/183.*
Laansma, Jon: I Will Give You Rest. 1997. *Vol. II/98.*
Labahn, Michael: Offenbarung in Zeichen und Wort. 2000. *Vol. II/117.*

Lambers-Petry, Doris: see *Tomson, Peter J.*
Lampe, Peter: Die stadtrömischen Christen in den ersten beiden Jahrhunderten. 1987, ²1989. *Vol. II/18.*
Landmesser, Christof: Wahrheit als Grundbegriff neutestamentlicher Wissenschaft. 1999. *Vol. 113.*
– Jüngerberufung und Zuwendung zu Gott. 2000. *Vol. 133.*
– see *Eckstein, Hans-Joachim.*
Lange, Armin: see *Ego, Beate.*
Lau, Andrew: Manifest in Flesh. 1996. *Vol. II/86.*
Lawrence, Louise: An Ethnography of the Gospel of Matthew. 2003. *Vol. II/165.*
Lee, Aquila H.I.: From Messiah to Preexistent Son. 2005. *Vol. II/192.*
Lee, Pilchan: The New Jerusalem in the Book of Relevation. 2000. *Vol. II/129.*
Lee, Sang M.: The Cosmic Drama of Salvation. 2010. *Vol. II/276.*
Lee, Simon S.: Jesus' Transfiguration and the Believers' Transformation. 2009. *Vol. II/265.*
Lichtenberger, Hermann: Das Ich Adams und das Ich der Menschheit. 2004. *Vol. 164.*
– see *Avemarie, Friedrich.*
– see *Caulley, Thomas Scott.*
– see *Eckstein, Hans-Joachim.*
– see *Frey, Jörg.*
Lierman, John: The New Testament Moses. 2004. *Vol. II/173.*
– (Ed.): Challenging Perspectives on the Gospel of John. 2006. *Vol. II/219.*
Lieu, Samuel N.C.: Manichaeism in the Later Roman Empire and Medieval China. ²1992. *Vol. 63.*
Lindemann, Andreas: Die Evangelien und die Apostelgeschichte. 2009. *Vol. 241.*
– Glauben, Handeln, Verstehen. Studien zur Auslegung des Neuen Testaments. 2011. *Vol. II/282.*
Lincicum, David: Paul and the Early Jewish Encounter with Deuteronomy. 2010. *Vol. II/284.*
Lindgård, Fredrik: Paul's Line of Thought in 2 Corinthians 4:16–5:10. 2004. *Vol. II/189.*
Livesey, Nina E.: Circumcision as a Malleable Symbol. 2010. *Vol. II/295.*
Loader, William R.G.: Jesus' Attitude Towards the Law. 1997. *Vol. II/97.*
Löhr, Gebhard: Verherrlichung Gottes durch Philosophie. 1997. *Vol. 97.*
Löhr, Hermut: Studien zum frühchristlichen und frühjüdischen Gebet. 2003. *Vol. 160.*
– see *Hengel, Martin.*

Löhr, Winrich Alfried: Basilides und seine Schule. 1995. *Vol. 83.*
Lorenzen, Stefanie: Das paulinische Eikon-Konzept. 2008. *Vol. II/250.*
Luomanen, Petri: Entering the Kingdom of Heaven. 1998. *Vol. II/101.*
Luz, Ulrich: see *Alexeev, Anatoly A.*
– see *Dunn, James D.G.*
Lykke, Anne und *Friedrich T. Schipper* (Ed.): Kult und Macht. 2011. *Vol. II/319.*
Lyu, Eun-Geol: Sünde und Rechtfertigung bei Paulus. 2012. *Vol. II/318.*
Mackay, Ian D.: John's Relationship with Mark. 2004. *Vol. II/182.*
Mackie, Scott D.: Eschatology and Exhortation in the Epistle to the Hebrews. 2006. *Vol. II/223.*
Magda, Ksenija: Paul's Territoriality and Mission Strategy. 2009. *Vol. II/266.*
Maier, Gerhard: Mensch und freier Wille. 1971. *Vol. 12.*
– Die Johannesoffenbarung und die Kirche. 1981. *Vol. 25.*
Markschies, Christoph: Valentinus Gnosticus? 1992. *Vol. 65.*
Marshall, Jonathan: Jesus, Patrons, and Benefactors. 2009. *Vol. II/259.*
Marshall, Peter: Enmity in Corinth: Social Conventions in Paul's Relations with the Corinthians. 1987. *Vol. II/23.*
Martin, Dale B.: see *Zangenberg, Jürgen.*
Maston, Jason: Divine and Human Agency in Second Temple Judaism and Paul. 2010. *Vol. II/297.*
– see *Bird, Michael F.*
Mayer, Annemarie: Sprache der Einheit im Epheserbrief und in der Ökumene. 2002. *Vol. II/150.*
Mayordomo, Moisés: Argumentiert Paulus logisch? 2005. *Vol. 188.*
McDonough, Sean M.: YHWH at Patmos: Rev. 1:4 in its Hellenistic and Early Jewish Setting. 1999. *Vol. II/107.*
McDowell, Markus: Prayers of Jewish Women. 2006. *Vol. II/211.*
McGlynn, Moyna: Divine Judgement and Divine Benevolence in the Book of Wisdom. 2001. *Vol. II/139.*
McNamara, Martin: Targum and New Testament. 2011. *Vol. 279.*
Meade, David G.: Pseudonymity and Canon. 1986. *Vol. 39.*
Meadors, Edward P.: Jesus the Messianic Herald of Salvation. 1995. *Vol. II/72.*
Meiser, Martin: see *Kreuzer, Siegfried.*

Meißner, Stefan: Die Heimholung des Ketzers. 1996. *Vol. II/87.*

Mell, Ulrich: Die „anderen" Winzer. 1994. *Vol. 77.*

– see *Sänger, Dieter.*

Mengel, Berthold: Studien zum Philipperbrief. 1982. *Vol. II/8.*

Merkel, Helmut: Die Widersprüche zwischen den Evangelien. 1971. *Vol. 13.*

– see *Ego, Beate.*

Merklein, Helmut: Studien zu Jesus und Paulus. Vol. 1 1987. *Vol. 43.* – Vol. 2 1998. *Vol. 105.*

Merkt, Andreas: see *Nicklas, Tobias*

Metzdorf, Christina: Die Tempelaktion Jesu. 2003. *Vol. II/168.*

Metzler, Karin: Der griechische Begriff des Verzeihens. 1991. *Vol. II/44.*

Metzner, Rainer: Die Rezeption des Matthäusevangeliums im 1. Petrusbrief. 1995. *Vol. II/74.*

– Das Verständnis der Sünde im Johannesevangelium. 2000. *Vol. 122.*

Mihoc, Vasile: see *Dunn, James D.G.*

– see *Klein, Hans.*

Mineshige, Kiyoshi: Besitzverzicht und Almosen bei Lukas. 2003. *Vol. II/163.*

Mittmann, Siegfried: see *Hengel, Martin.*

Mittmann-Richert, Ulrike: Magnifikat und Benediktus. *1996. Vol. II/90.*

– Der Sühnetod des Gottesknechts. 2008. *Vol. 220.*

Miura, Yuzuru: David in Luke-Acts. 2007. *Vol. II/232.*

Moll, Sebastian: The Arch-Heretic Marcion. 2010. *Vol. 250.*

Morales, Rodrigo J.: The Spirit and the Restorat. 2010. *Vol. 282.*

Mournet, Terence C.: Oral Tradition and Literary Dependency. 2005. *Vol. II/195.*

Mußner, Franz: Jesus von Nazareth im Umfeld Israels und der Urkirche. Ed. von M. Theobald. 1998. *Vol. 111.*

Mutschler, Bernhard: Das Corpus Johanneum bei Irenäus von Lyon. 2005. *Vol. 189.*

– Glaube in den Pastoralbriefen. 2010. *Vol. 256.*

Myers, Susan E.: Spirit Epicleses in the Acts of Thomas. 2010. *Vol. 281.*

Myers, Susan E. (Ed.): Portraits of Jesus. 2012. *Vol. II/321.*

Nguyen, V. Henry T.: Christian Identity in Corinth. 2008. *Vol. II/243.*

Nicklas, Tobias, Andreas Merkt und *Joseph Verheyden* (Ed.): Gelitten – Gestorben – Auferstanden. 2010. *Vol. II/273.*

– see *Verheyden, Joseph*

Nicolet-Anderson, Valérie: Constructing the Self. 2012. *Vol. II/324.*

Niebuhr, Karl-Wilhelm: Gesetz and Paränese. 1987. *Vol. II/28.*

– Heidenapostel aus Israel. 1992. *Vol. 62.*

– see *Deines, Roland.*

– see *Dimitrov, Ivan Z.*

– see *Karakolis, Christos.*

– see *Klein, Hans.*

– see *Kraus, Wolfgang.*

Nielsen, Anders E.: "Until it is Fullfilled". 2000. *Vol. II/126.*

Nielsen, Jesper Tang: Die kognitive Dimension des Kreuzes. 2009. *Vol. II/263.*

Nissen, Andreas: Gott und der Nächste im antiken Judentum. 1974. *Vol. 15.*

Noack, Christian: Gottesbewußtsein. 2000. *Vol. II/116.*

Noormann, Rolf: Irenäus als Paulusinterpret. 1994. *Vol. II/66.*

Norelli, Enrico: see *Clivaz, Claire.*

Norin, Stig: see *Hultgård, Anders.*

Novakovic, Lidija: Messiah, the Healer of the Sick. 2003. *Vol. II/170.*

Obermann, Andreas: Die christologische Erfüllung der Schrift im Johannesevangelium. 1996. *Vol. II/83.*

Öhler, Markus: Barnabas. 2003. *Vol. 156.*

– see *Becker, Michael.*

– (Ed.): Aposteldekret und antikes Vereinswesen. 2011. *Vol. 280.*

Okure, Teresa: The Johannine Approach to Mission. 1988. *Vol. II/31.*

Onuki, Takashi: Heil und Erlösung. 2004. *Vol. 165.*

Oropeza, B. J.: Paul and Apostasy. 2000. *Vol. II/115.*

Ostmeyer, Karl-Heinrich: Kommunikation mit Gott und Christus. 2006. *Vol. 197.*

– Taufe und Typos. 2000. *Vol. II/118.*

Pao, David W.: Acts and the Isaianic New Exodus. 2000. *Vol. II/130.*

Park, Eung Chun: The Mission Discourse in Matthew's Interpretation. 1995. *Vol. II/81.*

Park, Joseph S.: Conceptions of Afterlife in Jewish Insriptions. 2000. *Vol. II/121.*

Parsenios, George L.: Rhetoric and Drama in the Johannine Lawsuit Motif. 2010. *Vol. 258.*

Pate, C. Marvin: The Reverse of the Curse. 2000. *Vol. II/114.*

Paulsen, Henning: Studien zur Literatur und Geschichte des frühen Christentums. Ed. von Ute E. Eisen. 1997. *Vol. 99.*

Pearce, Sarah J.K.: The Land of the Body. 2007. *Vol. 208.*

Peres, Imre: Griechische Grabinschriften und neutestamentliche Eschatologie. 2003. *Vol. 157.*

Perry, Peter S.: The Rhetoric of Digressions. 2009. *Vol. II/268.*

Pierce, Chad T.: Spirits and the Proclamation of Christ. 2011. *Vol. II/305.*

Philip, Finny: The Origins of Pauline Pneumatology. 2005. *Vol. II/194.*

Philonenko, Marc (Ed.): Le Trône de Dieu. 1993. *Vol. 69.*

Pilhofer, Peter: Presbyteron Kreitton. 1990. *Vol. II/39.*

– Philippi. Vol. 1 1995. *Vol. 87.* – Vol. 2 ²2009. *Vol. 119.*

– Die frühen Christen und ihre Welt. 2002. *Vol. 145.*

– see *Becker, Eve-Marie.*

– see *Ego, Beate.*

Pitre, Brant: Jesus, the Tribulation, and the End of the Exile. 2005. *Vol. II/204.*

Plümacher, Eckhard: Geschichte und Geschichten. 2004. *Vol. 170.*

Pöhlmann, Wolfgang: Der Verlorene Sohn und das Haus. 1993. *Vol. 68.*

Poirier, John C.: The Tongues of Angels. 2010. *Vol. II/287.*

Pokorný, Petr and *Josef B. Souček:* Bibelauslegung als Theologie. 1997. *Vol. 100.*

– and *Jan Roskovec* (Ed.): Philosophical Hermeneutics and Biblical Exegesis. 2002. *Vol. 153.*

Popkes, Enno Edzard: Das Menschenbild des Thomasevangeliums. 2007. *Vol. 206.*

– Die Theologie der Liebe Gottes in den johanneischen Schriften. 2005. *Vol. II/197.*

Porter, Stanley E.: The Paul of Acts. 1999. *Vol. 115.*

Prieur, Alexander: Die Verkündigung der Gottesherrschaft. 1996. *Vol. II/89.*

Probst, Hermann: Paulus und der Brief. 1991. *Vol. II/45.*

Puig i Tàrrech, Armand: Jesus: An Uncommon Journey. 2010. *Vol. II/288.*

Rabens, Volker: The Holy Spirit and Ethics in Paul. 2010. *Vol. II/283.*

Räisänen, Heikki: Paul and the Law. 1983, ²1987. *Vol. 29.*

Rehfeld, Emmanuel L.: Relationale Ontologie bei Paulus. 2012. *Vol. II/326.*

Rehkopf, Friedrich: Die lukanische Sonderquelle. 1959. *Vol. 5.*

Rein, Matthias: Die Heilung des Blindgeborenen (Joh 9). 1995. *Vol. II/73.*

Reinmuth, Eckart: Pseudo-Philo und Lukas. 1994. *Vol. 74.*

Reiser, Marius: Bibelkritik und Auslegung der Heiligen Schrift. 2007. *Vol. 217.*

– Syntax und Stil des Markusevangeliums. 1984. *Vol. II/11.*

Reynolds, Benjamin E.: The Apocalyptic Son of Man in the Gospel of John. 2008. *Vol. II/249.*

Rhodes, James N.: The Epistle of Barnabas and the Deuteronomic Tradition. 2004. *Vol. II/188.*

Richards, E. Randolph: The Secretary in the Letters of Paul. 1991. *Vol. II/42.*

Riesner, Rainer: Jesus als Lehrer. 1981, ³1988. *Vol. II/7.*

– Die Frühzeit des Apostels Paulus. 1994. *Vol. 71.*

Rissi, Mathias: Die Theologie des Hebräerbriefs. 1987. *Vol. 41.*

Röcker, Fritz W.: Belial und Katechon. 2009. *Vol. II/262.*

Röhser, Günter: Metaphorik und Personifikation der Sünde. 1987. *Vol. II/25.*

Rogalsky, Sviatoslav: see *Karakolis, Christos.*

Rose, Christian: Theologie als Erzählung im Markusevangelium. 2007. *Vol. II/236.*

– Die Wolke der Zeugen. 1994. *Vol. II/60.*

Roskovec, Jan: see *Pokorný, Petr.*

Rothschild, Clare K.: Baptist Traditions and Q. 2005. *Vol. 190.*

– Hebrews as Pseudepigraphon. 2009. *Vol. 235.*

– Luke Acts and the Rhetoric of History. 2004. *Vol. II/175.*

– see *Frey, Jörg.*

– and *Trevor W. Thompson* (Ed.): Christian Body, Christian Self. 2011. *Vol. 284.*

Rudolph, David J.: A Jew to the Jews. 2011. *Vol. II/304.*

Rüegger, Hans-Ulrich: Verstehen, was Markus erzählt. 2002. *Vol. II/155.*

Rüger, Hans Peter: Die Weisheitsschrift aus der Kairoer Geniza. 1991. *Vol. 53.*

Ruf, Martin G.: Die heiligen Propheten, eure Apostel und ich. 2011. *Vol. II/300.*

Runesson, Anders: see *Becker, Eve-Marie.*

Sänger, Dieter: Antikes Judentum und die Mysterien. 1980. *Vol. II/5.*

– Die Verkündigung des Gekreuzigten und Israel. 1994. *Vol. 75.*

– see *Burchard, Christoph*

– and *Ulrich Mell* (Ed.): Paulus und Johannes. 2006. *Vol. 198.*

Salier, Willis Hedley: The Rhetorical Impact of the Semeia in the Gospel of John. 2004. *Vol. II/186.*

Salzmann, Jörg Christian: Lehren und Ermahnen. 1994. *Vol. II/59.*

Samuelsson, Gunnar: Crucifixion in Antiquity. 2011. *Vol. II/310.*

Sandnes, Karl Olav: Paul – One of the Prophets? 1991. *Vol. II/43.*

Sato, Migaku: Q und Prophetie. 1988. *Vol. II/29.*

Schäfer, Ruth: Paulus bis zum Apostelkonzil. 2004. *Vol. II/179.*

Schaper, Joachim: Eschatology in the Greek Psalter. 1995. *Vol. II/76.*

Schimanowski, Gottfried: Die himmlische Liturgie in der Apokalypse des Johannes. 2002. *Vol. II/154.*

– Weisheit und Messias. 1985. *Vol. II/17.*

Schipper, Friedrich T.: see *Lykke, Anne.*

Schlichting, Günter: Ein jüdisches Leben Jesu. 1982. *Vol. 24.*

Schließer, Benjamin: Abraham's Faith in Romans 4. 2007. *Vol. II/224.*

Schnabel, Eckhard J.: Law and Wisdom from Ben Sira to Paul. 1985. *Vol. II/16.*

Schnelle, Udo: see *Frey, Jörg.*

Schröter, Jens: Von Jesus zum Neuen Testament. 2007. *Vol. 204.*

– see *Frey, Jörg.*

Schutter, William L.: Hermeneutic and Composition in I Peter. 1989. *Vol. II/30.*

Schwartz, Daniel R.: Studies in the Jewish Background of Christianity. 1992. *Vol. 60.*

Schwemer, Anna Maria: see *Hengel, Martin*

Scott, Ian W.: Implicit Epistemology in the Letters of Paul. 2005. *Vol. II/205.*

Scott, James M.: Adoption as Sons of God. 1992. *Vol. II/48.*

– Paul and the Nations. 1995. *Vol. 84.*

Shi, Wenhua: Paul's Message of the Cross as Body Language. 2008. *Vol. II/254.*

Shum, Shiu-Lun: Paul's Use of Isaiah in Romans. 2002. *Vol. II/156.*

Siegert, Folker: Drei hellenistisch-jüdische Predigten. Teil I 1980. *Vol. 20* – Teil II 1992. *Vol. 61.*

– Nag-Hammadi-Register. 1982. *Vol. 26.*

– Argumentation bei Paulus. 1985. *Vol. 34.*

– Philon von Alexandrien. 1988. *Vol. 46.*

Siggelkow-Berner, Birke: Die jüdischen Feste im Bellum Judaicum des Flavius Josephus. 2011. *Vol. II/306.*

Sigismund, Marcus: see *Kreuzer, Siegfried.*

Simon, Marcel: Le christianisme antique et son contexte religieux I/II. 1981. *Vol. 23.*

Smit, Peter-Ben: Fellowship and Food in the Kingdom. 2008. *Vol. II/234.*

Smith, Julien: Christ the Ideal King. 2011. *Vol. II/313.*

Snodgrass, Klyne: The Parable of the Wicked Tenants. 1983. *Vol. 27.*

Söding, Thomas: Das Wort vom Kreuz. 1997. *Vol. 93.*

– see *Thüsing, Wilhelm.*

Sommer, Urs: Die Passionsgeschichte des Markusevangeliums. 1993. *Vol. II/58.*

Sorensen, Eric: Possession and Exorcism in the New Testament and Early Christianity. 2002. *Vol: II/157.*

Souček, Josef B.: see *Pokorný, Petr.*

Southall, David J.: Rediscovering Righteousness in Romans. 2008. *Vol. 240.*

Spangenberg, Volker: Herrlichkeit des Neuen Bundes. 1993. *Vol. II/55.*

Spanje, T.E. van: Inconsistency in Paul? 1999. *Vol. II/110.*

Speyer, Wolfgang: Frühes Christentum im antiken Strahlungsfeld. Vol. I: 1989. *Vol. 50.*

– Vol. II: 1999. *Vol. 116.*

– Vol. III: 2007. *Vol. 213.*

Spittler, Janet E.: Animals in the Apocryphal Acts of the Apostles. 2008. *Vol. II/247.*

Sprinkle, Preston: Law and Life. 2008. *Vol. II/241.*

Stadelmann, Helge: Ben Sira als Schriftgelehrter. 1980. *Vol. II/6.*

Stein, Hans Joachim: Frühchristliche Mahlfeiern. 2008. *Vol. II/255.*

Stenschke, Christoph W.: Luke's Portrait of Gentiles Prior to Their Coming to Faith. *Vol. II/108.*

Stephens, Mark B.: Annihilation or Renewal? 2011. *Vol. II/307.*

Sterck-Degueldre, Jean-Pierre: Eine Frau namens Lydia. 2004. *Vol. II/176.*

Stettler, Christian: Der Kolosserhymnus. 2000. *Vol. II/131.*

– Das letzte Gericht. 2011. *Vol. II/299.*

Stettler, Hanna: Die Christologie der Pastoralbriefe. 1998. *Vol. II/105.*

Stökl Ben Ezra, Daniel: The Impact of Yom Kippur on Early Christianity. 2003. *Vol. 163.*

Strobel, August: Die Stunde der Wahrheit. 1980. *Vol. 21.*

Stroumsa, Guy G.: Barbarian Philosophy. 1999. *Vol. 112.*

Stuckenbruck, Loren T.: Angel Veneration and Christology. 1995. *Vol. II/70.*

–, *Stephen C. Barton* and *Benjamin G. Wold* (Ed.): Memory in the Bible and Antiquity. 2007. *Vol. 212.*

Stuhlmacher, Peter (Ed.): Das Evangelium und die Evangelien. 1983. *Vol. 28.*

– Biblische Theologie und Evangelium. 2002. *Vol. 146.*

Sung, Chong-Hyon: Vergebung der Sünden. 1993. *Vol. II/57.*

Svendsen, Stefan N.: Allegory Transformed. 2009. *Vol. II/269.*

Tajra, Harry W.: The Trial of St. Paul. 1989. *Vol. II/35.*

– The Martyrdom of St.Paul. 1994. *Vol. II/67.*

Tellbe, Mikael: Christ-Believers in Ephesus. 2009. *Vol. 242.*

Theißen, Gerd: Studien zur Soziologie des Urchristentums. 1979, ³1989. *Vol. 19.*

Theobald, Michael: Studien zum Corpus Iohanneum. 2010. *Vol. 267.*

– Studien zum Römerbrief. 2001. *Vol. 136.*

– see *Mußner, Franz.*

Thompson, Trevor W.: see *Rothschild, Clare K.*

Thornton, Claus-Jürgen: Der Zeuge des Zeugen. 1991. *Vol. 56.*

Thüsing, Wilhelm: Studien zur neutestamentlichen Theologie. Ed. von Thomas Söding. 1995. *Vol. 82.*

Thurén, Lauri: Derhethorizing Paul. 2000. *Vol. 124.*

Thyen, Hartwig: Studien zum Corpus Iohanneum. 2007. *Vol. 214.*

Tibbs, Clint: Religious Experience of the Pneuma. 2007. *Vol. II/230.*

Tilling, Chris: Paul's Divine Christology. 2012. *Vol. II/323.*

Toit, David S. du: Theios Anthropos. 1997. *Vol. II/91.*

Tolmie, D. Francois: Persuading the Galatians. 2005. *Vol. II/190.*

Tomson, Peter J. and *Doris Lambers-Petry* (Ed.): The Image of the Judaeo-Christians in Ancient Jewish and Christian Literature. 2003. *Vol. 158.*

Toney, Carl N.: Paul's Inclusive Ethic. 2008. *Vol. II/252.*

– siehe *Frey, Jörg.*

Tóth, Franz: see *Frey, Jörg.*

Trebilco, Paul: The Early Christians in Ephesus from Paul to Ignatius. 2004. *Vol. 166.*

Treloar, Geoffrey R.: Lightfoot the Historian. 1998. *Vol. II/103.*

Troftgruben, Troy M.: A Conclusion Unhindered. 2010. *Vol. II/280.*

Tso, Marcus K.M.: Ethics in the Qumran Community. 2010. *Vol. II/292.*

Tsuji, Manabu: Glaube zwischen Vollkommenheit und Verweltlichung. 1997. *Vol. II/93.*

Twelftree, Graham H.: Jesus the Exorcist. 1993. *Vol. II/54.*

Ulrichs, Karl Friedrich: Christusglaube. 2007. *Vol. II/227.*

Urban, Christina: Das Menschenbild nach dem Johannesevangelium. 2001. *Vol. II/137.*

Vahrenhorst, Martin: Kultische Sprache in den Paulusbriefen. 2008. *Vol. 230.*

Vegge, Ivar: 2 Corinthians – a Letter about Reconciliation. 2008. *Vol. II/239.*

Verheyden, Joseph, Korinna Zamfir and *Tobias Nicklas* (Ed.): Prophets and Prophecy in Jewish and Early Christian Literature. 2010. *Vol. II/286.*

– see *Nicklas, Tobias*

Visotzky, Burton L.: Fathers of the World. 1995. *Vol. 80.*

Vollenweider, Samuel: Horizonte neutestamentlicher Christologie. 2002. *Vol. 144.*

Vos, Johan S.: Die Kunst der Argumentation bei Paulus. 2002. *Vol. 149.*

Waaler, Erik: The Shema and The First Commandment in First Corinthians. 2008. *Vol. II/253.*

Wagener, Ulrike: Die Ordnung des „Hauses Gottes". 1994. *Vol. II/65.*

Wagner, J. Ross: see *Wilk, Florian.*

Wahlen, Clinton: Jesus and the Impurity of Spirits in the Synoptic Gospels. 2004. *Vol. II/185.*

Walker, Donald D.: Paul's Offer of Leniency (2 Cor 10:1). 2002. *Vol. II/152.*

Walter, Nikolaus: Praeparatio Evangelica. Ed. von Wolfgang Kraus und Florian Wilk. 1997. *Vol. 98.*

Wander, Bernd: Gottesfürchtige und Sympathisanten. 1998. *Vol. 104.*

Wardle, Timothy: The Jerusalem Temple and Early Christian Identity. 2010. *Vol. II/291.*

Wasserman, Emma: The Death of the Soul in Romans 7. 2008. *Vol. 256.*

Waters, Guy: The End of Deuteronomy in the Epistles of Paul. 2006. *Vol. 221.*

Watt, Jan G. van der (Ed.): Eschatology of the New Testament and Some Related Documents. 2011. *Vol. II/315.*

– see *Frey, Jörg*

– see *Zimmermann, Ruben*

Watts, Rikki: Isaiah's New Exodus and Mark. 1997. *Vol. II/88.*

Webb, Robert L.: see *Bock, Darrell L.*

Wedderburn, Alexander J.M.: Baptism and Resurrection. 1987. *Vol. 44.*
– Jesus and the Historians. 2010. *Vol. 269.*
Wegner, Uwe: Der Hauptmann von Kafarnaum. 1985. *Vol. II/14.*
Weiß, Hans-Friedrich: Frühes Christentum und Gnosis. 2008. *Vol. 225.*
Weissenrieder, Annette: Images of Illness in the Gospel of Luke. 2003. Vol. II/164.
–, and *David L. Balch* (Ed.): Contested Spaces. 2012. *Vol. 285.*
–, and *Robert B. Coote* (Ed.): The Interface of Orality and Writing. 2010. *Vol. 260.*
–, *Friederike Wendt* and *Petra von Gemünden* (Ed.): Picturing the New Testament. 2005. *Vol. II/193.*
Welck, Christian: Erzählte ‚Zeichen‘. 1994. *Vol. II/69.*
Wendt, Friederike (Ed.): see *Weissenrieder, Annette.*
Wiarda, Timothy: Peter in the Gospels. 2000. *Vol. II/127.*
Wifstrand, Albert: Epochs and Styles. 2005. *Vol. 179.*
Wilk, Florian and *J. Ross Wagner* (Ed.): Between Gospel and Election. 2010. *Vol. 257.*
– see *Walter, Nikolaus.*
Williams, Catrin H.: I am He. 2000. *Vol. II/113.*
Wilson, Todd A.: The Curse of the Law and the Crisis in Galatia. 2007. *Vol. II/225.*
Wilson, Walter T.: Love without Pretense. 1991. *Vol. II/46.*
Winn, Adam: The Purpose of Mark's Gospel. 2008. *Vol. II/245.*
Winninge, Mikael: see *Holmberg, Bengt.*
Wischmeyer, Oda: Von Ben Sira zu Paulus. 2004. *Vol. 173.*
Wisdom, Jeffrey: Blessing for the Nations and the Curse of the Law. 2001. *Vol. II/133.*
Witmer, Stephen E.: Divine Instruction in Early Christianity. 2008. *Vol. II/246.*
Wold, Benjamin G.: Women, Men, and Angels. 2005. *Vol. II/2001.*

Wolter, Michael: Theologie und Ethos im frühen Christentum. 2009. *Vol. 236.*
– see *Stuckenbruck, Loren T.*
Worthington, Jonathan: Creation in Paul and Philo. 2011. *Vol. II/317.*
Wright, Archie T.: The Origin of Evil Spirits. 2005. *Vol. II/198.*
Wucherpfennig, Ansgar: Heracleon Philologus. 2002. *Vol. 142.*
Yates, John W.: The Spirit and Creation in Paul. 2008. *Vol. II/251.*
Yeung, Maureen: Faith in Jesus and Paul. 2002. *Vol. II/147.*
Young, Stephen E.: Jesus Tradition in the Apostolic Fathers. 2011. *Vol. II/311.*
Zamfir, Corinna: see *Verheyden, Joseph*
Zangenberg, Jürgen, Harold W. Attridge and *Dale B. Martin* (Ed.): Religion, Ethnicity and Identity in Ancient Galilee. 2007. *Vol. 210.*
Zimmermann, Alfred E.: Die urchristlichen Lehrer. 1984, ²1988. *Vol. II/12.*
Zimmermann, Johannes: Messianische Texte aus Qumran. 1998. *Vol. II/104.*
Zimmermann, Ruben: Christologie der Bilder im Johannesevangelium. 2004. *Vol. 171.*
– Geschlechtermetaphorik und Gottesverhältnis. 2001. *Vol. II/122.*
– (Ed.): Hermeneutik der Gleichnisse Jesu. 2008. *Vol. 231.*
– and *Jan G. van der Watt* (Ed.): Moral Language in the New Testament. Vol. II. 2010. *Vol. II/296.*
– see *Frey, Jörg.*
– see *Horn, Friedrich Wilhelm.*
Zugmann, Michael: „Hellenisten" in der Apostelgeschichte. 2009. *Vol. II/264.*
Zumstein, Jean: see *Dettwiler, Andreas*
Zwiep, Arie W.: Christ, the Spirit and the Community of God. 2010. *Vol. II/293.*
– Judas and the Choice of Matthias. 2004. *Vol. II/187.*

For a complete catalogue please write to the publisher
Mohr Siebeck • P.O. Box 2030 • D–72010 Tübingen/Germany
Up-to-date information on the internet at www.mohr.de

Wissenschaftliche Untersuchungen
zum Neuen Testament · 2. Reihe

Herausgeber / Editor
Jörg Frey (Zürich)

Mitherausgeber / Associate Editors
Friedrich Avemarie (Marburg)
Markus Bockmuehl (Oxford)
James A. Kelhoffer (Uppsala)
Hans-Josef Klauck (Chicago, IL)

327